WILLIAM ALEXANDER PERCY

WILLIAM ALEXANDER PERCY

*The Curious Life of
a Mississippi Planter and
Sexual Freethinker*

BENJAMIN E. WISE

University of North Carolina Press
CHAPEL HILL

This book was published with the assistance of the Center for the Study of the American South at the University of North Carolina at Chapel Hill.

The University of North Carolina Press has been a member of the
Green Press Initiative since 2003.

Library of Congress Cataloging-in-Publication Data
Wise, Benjamin E.
William Alexander Percy : the curious life of a Mississippi planter
and sexual freethinker / Benjamin E. Wise.
p. cm.
Includes bibliographical references and index.
ISBN 978-0-8078-3535-7 (cloth : alk. paper)
1. Percy, William Alexander, 1885-1942. 2. Poets, American—
20th century—Biography. 3. Landowners—Mississippi—Greenville—
Biography. 4. Plantation life—Mississippi—Greenville. I. Title.
PS3531.E65Z98 2012
811'.52—dc23
[B]
2011036531

Much of chapter 9 appeared previously as "On Naïve and Sentimental Poetry:
Nostalgia, Sex, and the Souths of William Alexander Percy," *Southern Cultures*
14, no. 1 (Spring 2008): 54–79; and other portions of the book appeared in
Craig T. Friend, ed., *Southern Masculinity: Perspectives on Manhood in the South
since Reconstruction* (Athens: University of Georgia Press, 2009).

For Alston

CONTENTS

ILLUSTRATIONS

WILLIAM ALEXANDER PERCY

INTRODUCTION
Stories of Belonging
Greenville, Mississippi, 1910

On December 5, 1910, William Alexander Percy spent the better part of the day in his law office in Greenville, Mississippi. He was to argue a railroad case in court the next morning, but his mind was on other things.

The fifth of December that year was a rain-soaked Monday. In the mail Percy received a letter from Harold Bruff, his best friend and likely his lover from Harvard Law School. Bruff, recently diagnosed with tuberculosis, informed Percy that he was leaving the country; his doctor had advised him to take six months of vacation to rest his body. Bruff's job as a Manhattan attorney, his doctor said, was not conducive to recovery. Percy wrote in his diary that night that Bruff's letter "filled me with longing" and left him stuck "midway between exasperation and restlessness."[1]

Will Percy and Harold Bruff had met at Harvard in 1905. The two lived in a rooming house called Winthrop Hall, a recently built Gothic structure with a fireplace in each room, hardwood casing around the windows, and a long trough in the basement for bathing. The Charles River was just visible from their bedroom windows.[2] Percy—of slight build, with brown hair and blue eyes, his face bearing both his father's strong jawline and his mother's dimpled chin—was the more mild mannered of the two. Before law school, he had attended college at the University of the South in Sewanee, Tennessee, and after graduation he had lived in Paris for a year. He was a piano player and a poet. Those who knew him described him as soft-spoken and magnetic, a person in whom others confided. His poetic temperament and quiet humor offset Bruff's brusque, lawyerly style. Percy admired Bruff's frank New York sensibility, which enlivened their conversation and counterbalanced his own Mississippi reticence. When Percy wrote his autobiography near the end of his life, he described being with Harold Bruff as "ecstasy."[3]

Bruff was one of those whom Percy referred to as a "Mayflower princeling," so common among Harvard students at the time: Bruff could trace his ancestry on his father's side directly to a man who arrived on the Mayflower. Through the centuries, the Bruff family rose in prominence in New England life, and most of them were established and engaged in business in New York by the early 1700s. Harold Bruff's father, William Jenkins Bruff, grew wealthy in the gun and munitions business. Harold Bruff grew up on Pierrepont Street in Brooklyn Heights, a block off the promenade overlooking Manhattan. He went to Phillips-Andover Academy. At Yale, his peers voted him "Brightest Graduate," and he went directly to Harvard Law School, where he became an editor of the *Harvard Law Review*. Harold Bruff was in many ways an ideal counterpart to Will Percy: where Percy was romantic and temperamental, Bruff was ambitious and resolute; where Percy was small in stature, Bruff was stocky and thickset; where Percy's face was angular and melancholic, Bruff's was round and friendly. While at Harvard, Percy and Bruff were inseparable. They traveled to Europe together, to New York, to Chicago and New Hampshire and Maine. They bought season tickets to the Boston Opera and learned the scores on the piano. Percy wrote that "every concert was an adventure and usually we'd be plumed and dripping fire as we made for the Brattle Street trolley through the winter murk."[4]

After law school, Percy moved home to Mississippi to join his father's law practice, though he traveled regularly between Greenville and New York to see Bruff. Bruff loved Percy's visits and what the energy of the city did for their relationship. "You must stay here many days," Bruff wrote to Percy before one such visit. "There are so many distractions that seem to frighten away the desired mood but maybe—who knows?" Beyond this, New York was a place they could "see lots of each other and possibly even talk 'de profundis'—but that is very difficult." The difficulties, though, seemed at the time less pronounced in New York than in Mississippi. In Mississippi, Percy felt alone. He had not lived there for eight years, and he often second-guessed his decision to move south. He wrote in his diary: "The maelstrom of New York sucks in more and more of the people I love."[5]

On nights like December 5, 1910—the day he received Bruff's letter in the mail—Percy often went to the Greenville opera, to dances, to poetry and history readings to relax. Sometimes he would walk to his friend Carrie Stern's house, where they read and critiqued each other's poetry. "Poetry fascinated me," Percy wrote, "like a fearful sin." He and Stern would occasionally get out a Ouija board and demand messages from Matthew Arnold or from God. Most often, though, Percy took walks alone on the levee overlooking the Mississippi River, filled with what he called "sheer lonesomeness and confusion of soul."[6]

William Alexander Percy, ca. 1910 (Courtesy of the Mississippi Department of Archives and History, Jackson, Mississippi)

This particular December night, the Washington County Historical Society was to present a reading of the reminiscences of Samuel Worthington, a prominent local plantation owner. Worthington's memories of antebellum planter life, the Civil War, and Reconstruction provided intimate details of the local past. His story would have been one Percy had heard before—it was a story many white southerners loved to tell themselves, a story of belonging. Variations of this story were woven into the texture of Will Percy's life. The story, however, worked to deepen both his belonging and his restlessness. One can imagine Percy sitting in the audience, tired from the day's work, anxious to be elsewhere with Harold Bruff but pleased to be among friends hearing a familiar story of his place and his people.[7]

"In days of yore and in times long since gone by," Worthington's reminiscence began, "a feudal aristocracy reigned supreme in Washington County." Worthington recounted the settling of Washington County by white men in the 1820s, the backbreaking slave labor required to clear out the brush and the hardwood bottoms and the cane—work done always with guns nearby, since bears and panthers and wildcats then roamed the Delta. This work, while full of hardship and toil, was well worth it, for, in time, this founding generation of Deltans all "became millionaires." Worthington's story evoked the distinctly southern themes of plantation life, a planter aristocracy, and slavery. The balm of nostalgia soothed the inherent tensions within this history for his Greenville audience in 1910. These Mississippians wanted to find solace in history, not conflict.[8]

Worthington went on to describe magnificent plantation homes with libraries of 5,000 books and chandeliers that alone cost over $3,000. Planters regularly gave handsome dinner parties, he said, and the young gentry gathered two to three times a week for balls at which they danced to brass bands composed of slaves. Worthington told of planters' travels to New Orleans and Louisville to buy furniture and jewelry and English hunting guns; he told of steamboats with names like *Fanny Bullett* and *General Quitman*, which stopped at Greenville with plows for the planters, whiskey for the slaves, and ten-pound bags of candy for the children. He told of duels and Derringer pistols; he told of gold and silver money, with which Delta planters traded almost exclusively. When these men went to New Orleans to do their banking, he said, "'the pregnant hinges of the knee' were bent to them everywhere."[9]

"My father always said the negroes were the happiest race and freer from care than any other people on earth," Worthington continued. "My recollection is they were always fiddling and dancing every idle minute they got; every plantation could boast a fiddler or two and all negroes could pat and dance even when no fiddler was around." As a rule, Worthington said, slaves were "docile" and idolized their owners; and though they hated their overseers, they "bragged of their master's wealth and the number of 'niggers' he owned." Except for the plantation overseers, he claimed, "there were practically no poor white people in Washington County then."[10]

Poor white people and blacks, though, were not central to the story that

Worthington wanted to tell. As his reminiscences neared their end, he called his audience back to what he felt was their true heritage: "the old chivalrous slaveholding aristocracy, to whom my heart ever warms." Despite the tragedy of the Civil War with its death and destruction, despite the horrors inflicted on Mississippi by "Negro domination" during Reconstruction, Delta residents could forever look to those who preceded them, those who "embodied all those generous virtues which belong to chivalry, disinterestedness, contempt of danger, unblemished honor, knightly courtesy." They could look to the past, the rich history of the South with its glories untarnished by time. Worthington called on his audience to join him in doing so. One can imagine the sense of solidarity in that room in 1910, a moment when a common identity was being forged over a shared version of a virtuous history. "As I sit here now," Worthington remembered, "I can see it in all its beauty, as it once was. In my mind's eye, it is summer again, all gold and green. Avenues of magnolia trees in bloom rise up before me. In the leafy branches sit mockingbirds singing. In the borders are flowers dreamingly waving their fair heads." Though the world is now so "changed," so "desolate," Worthington concluded, the history of the South and the nobility of the Old Regime "echo through the centuries like spirit voices."[11]

The history of the South, Worthington believed, ought to deepen its hearers' roots. And it did. His story—the story of so many white southerners —was one in which everyone had a belonging. It was a story of a lost, harmonious world in which the hierarchies were stable and the rulers were magnanimous. It was primarily a story about powerful white men. The history of African Americans, the history of women, the history of the working class and Native Americans and immigrants—these were auxiliaries to the larger story of benevolent white supremacy and planter rule; the glory and bounty of the plantation; the tragedy of the Civil War; the disaster of Reconstruction. The story was about men and their accomplishments, their conquests, their many virtues.

Growing up in Mississippi, and surely on this night in 1910, Will Percy both accepted and did battle with this history of the South. He valued his home. He valued the stories of his place and his people. His local stories of belonging—the partisan, white, nostalgic history of the planter class—gave depth to his Mississippi attachments. They shaped his perspectives on class and race relations. They created in him a distinct feeling of belonging.

These stories also articulated a great deal about what it meant to be a *man* in his society—and as such marked the central conflict in Percy's relationship with the cultural values of his place and his time. Looking to history for solace, Percy often found displacement instead. He yearned to get out from beneath these stories peopled with men so unlike himself. He came to question the notion that to be a man was to be practical, moderate, Christian, and unemotional. He came to reject the notion that to be a man was to love women. Even as he accepted so many of the other norms and customs of the South, he came to believe that cultural values concerning gender were arbitrary, contingent, and subject to change. The stories he heard of men in Mississippi, their values and their priorities, were only partially his. "I like to hear about them," he wrote of these Delta planters, "but I doubt if I should have been at ease living among them."[12] Percy's own story of belonging, which he would revise throughout his life, needed a fuller cast of characters. His own story of belonging—which emerges in his poetry, his diaries, his correspondence, his memoir—had a distinctly more diverse cast. It included different kinds of men: sculptors, poets, travelers, gardeners, and drifters; men who married and men who did not; men with practical sensibilities and men who were lovers of peace and beauty. Percy's efforts to create his own stories of belonging make up much of his biography.

IN 1910 GREENVILLE, MISSISSIPPI, was a New South port town. Situated behind a levee on the Mississippi River, Greenville boasted its own opera house and a new four-story hotel with a telephone in every room and hot water in most. For a small southern town, it was bustling and diverse. Russian and Greek and Chinese immigrants ran many of the storefront businesses downtown. The Yazoo and Mississippi Valley Railroad's trains came and went fifteen times a day. Steamboats docked at the landing and off-loaded whiskey and burlap and dry goods from New Orleans and Memphis. Blacks outnumbered whites eight to one in the surrounding countryside, where their labor on cotton plantations created wealth for families like the Percys. Will Percy's ancestors were among the first white people to settle in the Mississippi Delta in the 1830s and 1840s, and the Percys remained among the South's foremost families. In 1910 Percy's father, LeRoy, was campaigning for reelection to the U.S. Senate. Will Percy lived with his parents in a mansion on a tree-lined avenue named Percy Street.[13]

That summer and fall of 1910, LeRoy Percy's senatorial campaign consumed the energies of the Percy family. Prominent men and women came regularly to Percy Street. One evening, a journalist from Jackson was in the parlor drinking whiskey highballs with LeRoy when Will Percy came home from work. "He was a shy, timid, slender, soft-spoken youth, a bit effeminate," the journalist later remembered. Will Percy offered a hasty greeting

The Percy family home, located at the corner of Percy Street and Broadway in Greenville, Mississippi, ca. 1910 (Courtesy of the Mississippi Department of Archives and History, Jackson, Mississippi)

to the visitor before going upstairs to his room. LeRoy Percy turned to his guest and said, "Fred, that's the queerest chicken ever hatched in a Percy brood." The journalist wrote that people in Greenville thought Will Percy was "somewhat of a sissy" and that they "could not understand him." He described Percy as "a poet, a dreamer, an idyllist, an aristocrat by heredity, high-strung, temperamental, a lover of peace." There were other queer folks in Mississippi, too, and this is how journalists and others tended to write about them: they called attention to their gender nonconformity but stopped short of categorizing them. Percy was "a bit effeminate," "a sissy," "a dreamer"—and people in Mississippi knew what this meant. By and large, though, they felt no need to speak more explicitly about sexuality in public. It remained an "open secret."[14]

Will Percy wrote in his diary on October 17, 1910—perhaps even the same night as this encounter with his father and the journalist—about the difficulty of living in Greenville. He had just returned from visiting Bruff in New York. Greenville, it seemed to Percy, was too much his father's world. Percy wrote that he was a poet above all; he was a lover of the sublime and the possibilities of art. Greenville was too busy for art, he felt, too concerned with daily living. It was a place with real problems that could and should be addressed by strong men with practical minds. "Poets are always needed but it takes an effort to realize it," he wrote, "while it takes no effort to see the good a practical man with a passion for righteousness could do here." As he would occasionally throughout his life, he concluded before going to sleep that night: "I'm the right man in the wrong place."[15]

Percy's unease in Mississippi, his sense that sometimes Greenville felt like "the wrong place," should not be understated. Nor should the first part of his pronouncement: "I'm the right man." Percy struggled with depression, loneliness, and physical sickness, but he was also resilient and confident. "I am never surprised at people liking me," he later wrote. "I'm always surprised if they don't. ... I feel they've made a mistake."[16] Percy was in fact well liked by others for his charm, his sense of humor, his kindness. He also liked himself. He achieved a significant measure of self-realization—of his talents, his sexuality, his gift of empathy. His was a halting, often ambivalent state of self-realization, but the evidence suggests he did not absorb the sometime disdain of his townsfolk, who called him "queer" and "sissy." "They've made a mistake," he tells us.

Percy was also strongly attached to his home and family. His parents loved him deeply, even while they did not fully understand him. He never moved out of his parents' house, even after they died. He was their only living son, his younger brother having been killed in a hunting accident at age ten. Percy walked to work with his father every day, and they talked about politics and the river and the price of cotton—all things that had concerned the Percy family for generations. Near the end of his life, Percy would begin and end his memoir with images of Mississippi soil: his story opens with the rich, alluvial dirt from which sprang acres of cotton and the livelihood of his people; it closes with the cemetery at the edge of town in which the bodies if not the souls of his loved ones lay buried in the ground. Will Percy was from first to last a white Mississippian of the planter class, an identity that sat lens-like before his eyes, coloring his perspective of everything he ever saw.

Percy's self-acceptance and love of place coexisted with his prejudice and conceit. He shared a sense of racial and class superiority with other aristocratic white people. Even as he was writing in his diary in 1910, hundreds of black sharecropper families lived in poverty, mired in debt, on the Percy plantation outside of Greenville—a labor situation Percy described as "one of the best systems ever devised to give security and a chance for profit to the simple and the unskilled." He called poor white people "peckerwoods" and "rednecks" and spoke of them as one might speak of dogs. "The virus of poverty, malnutrition, and interbreeding has done its degenerative work," he wrote. "The present breed is probably the most unprepossessing on the broad face of the ill-populated earth." Percy benefited from his position atop the racial and class hierarchies in the South, and he did much to perpetuate them.[17]

Percy's life story, then, becomes a window onto two cultural identities, "southern" and "homosexual," that were contested and in flux during his lifetime. A central aim of this book is to illuminate the history of these two frameworks of meaning through one man's engagement with them. Percy's story grounds these broader historical developments in his particular experience across the world. The landscape of Percy's world included both what has been called "the most southern place on earth," the Mississippi Delta, and what has been called the "gay male world" of the early twentieth century. In his life, these seemingly separate worlds become one.[18]

AT HOME that Monday night in December 1910, Percy was exhausted and wrote only briefly in his diary before falling asleep. He wrote of Harold Bruff, and of how he longed to be with him. He wrote of his sadness that Bruff was "to have six months vacation—without me—among divine places."[19]

The next morning, Percy went in to his office to prepare for trial—he was arguing his railroad trust case before a jury the next two days. After the trial ended with a hung jury on Thursday, he felt his arguments before the court were "worse than mediocre" and lamented: "I cannot speak other than vaguely and unconvincing." Also on Thursday, he received a letter from Bruff with details of his upcoming trip. Bruff was to leave in two days. As Percy read his letter, "it seemed to palpitate: poignant to the degree that rereading is almost an act of courage. He is going to our country. How I long to go with him." But work and his father's Senate campaign made that trip, likely to Italy, impossible. Percy felt, though, that "there is compensation" in the knowledge that "Hal is almost all mine when he gets over there."[20]

A few days later on Sunday, December 11, Percy spent two hours playing the piano and took a walk on the levee. He wrote in his diary that night that "Harold sailed yesterday to the lands overseas and the haven where I would be." Percy would see him only one more time before the following October, when Bruff checked into Park Avenue's Belmont Hotel and, alone in his room, shot himself in the head. He left two notes: one to the coroner and one to the hotel manager, both apologizing for the inconvenience his death must have caused.[21]

We will likely never know why Harold Bruff committed suicide. On the day Bruff killed himself—October 11, 1911—a man who claimed to be an intimate of Bruff's appeared at the Hotel Belmont and explained to reporters that Bruff was in love with a woman and had killed himself out of lovesickness. When Bruff's father and brother arrived at the hotel, they told reporters that they knew nothing of a woman in Bruff's life; he killed himself, they explained, because of his tubercular insanity. One of the Bruff family's neighbors conjectured that Bruff killed himself because of the negative attention brought to his family the previous summer when an embittered former mistress sued his father for $100,000. Another likely factor was that his mother had died the year before. The Manhattan coroner listed the cause of Bruff's suicide, quite simply, as "despondency."[22]

Percy was in Greece on the day Bruff committed suicide. He arrived in New York twelve days later. What he did, and what he said, in response to Bruff's death, we may also never know. He mentioned Harold Bruff explicitly in writing only two more times in his life—in his autobiography and in a 1919 letter to his friend Carrie Stern. He explained to her in that letter that Bruff had been one of two men in his life whom he "understood and who understood me, one who I knew could never fail me."[23] The finding and losing of Harold Bruff was symbolic of a larger conflict in Percy's life: his search for mutual understanding, for love, for companionship. He found these things at times, though he did not speak openly about them to most. Percy dealt with Bruff's death in part by turning to poetry; his first book, which he dedicated "To H. B.," was a poetic meditation on love between two people, on the fleeting nature of human connection, on the reality of grief and pain for those who choose to love. These conflicts weighed on him and animated his art, giving him a depth of perspective and no small measure of compassion.

Will Percy believed in the possibility that two men could share love. He believed that intimacy between men was not incompatible with moral decency, and that indeed love between men was virtuous and uplifting. He loved Harold Bruff and found in him a confidant, a sounding board, a companion, and an intimate friend. Throughout his life, he maintained intimate relationships with men, though scant evidence remains about the specifics of these relationships. But enough remains that patterns emerge: Percy surrounded himself throughout his life with queer men and women; he frequented places such as the Bowery in Manhattan, the Latin Quarter in Paris, and Taormina in Italy, among others, that were relatively tolerant of queer cultures; and he drew from the idiom of his day to write about and express homoerotic desire in his diaries, letters, poetry, and prose. To read this evidence is to read Percy's lifelong and deliberate attempt to name, understand, and vindicate his own sexuality.[24]

To read this evidence is also to read the reckonings of someone who possessed a high degree of moral seriousness. Percy's ideas about sexuality were never separate from his ethical concerns, his questions about God and the value of life. From college onward, his writings consistently engaged a series of related questions: What is an honorable life? Is there a source of moral authority outside one's own conscience? What is appropriate to do with one's own body, and what is the relationship between pleasure and purity? How can one find meaning in the absence of religious belief? How can one balance a sense of personal freedom with a commitment to the common good? These questions saturated his imagination and framed his personal search for meaning. His attempts to answer them also make up much of his life story.

When Percy wrote in his diary of "*our country*," he was writing about both a physical location and a kind of understanding he and Harold Bruff shared. When he wrote of "the lands overseas and the haven where I would be," he was writing about Italy, but he was also giving voice to a kind of spiritual and emotional citizenship that emerged during his lifetime. Over this period—quite literally represented by Percy's life span, 1885 to 1942—a monumental shift took place with regard to cultural understandings of sexuality. Specifically, homosexuality emerged as a social identity. Before the 1890s in Europe and America, homosexuality was by and large thought of as an act: people spoke of "sodomy," "buggery," and "sexual perversion." Same-sex intimacy was understood as an outward expression of deviance, not a manifestation of an inward orientation. It was a violation of God's order; it was not reproductive; it was a sinful decision. In 1885 in Great Britain, the Labouchere Amendment of the Criminal Law Amendment Act outlawed "acts of gross indecency" between men. In the United States, sodomy laws were on the books in every state.[25]

By Percy's death in 1942, these laws were still in place but a cultural shift had taken place with regard to understandings of queer sexual desire and practice. Homosexuality had become an identity—a culture, some would say, a way of thinking, believing, acting, and talking. Men and women during this era attributed to homosexuality an intellectual language, a sensibility. To a degree, homosexuality came to be seen as a manifestation of a personal disposition rather than merely a kind of sexual behavior. "Sex penetrates the whole person," British sexologist Havelock Ellis wrote in 1933. "[A] man's sexual constitution is part of his general constitution. There is considerable truth in the dictum: 'A man is what his sex is.'"[26] By no means was the matter settled, and by no means was this identity homogenous, but the effect of fifty years of writing by sexologists, anthropologists, poets, and freethinkers such as Oscar Wilde, John Addington Symonds, Edward Carpenter, Margaret Mead, Sigmund Freud, and many others—including Will Percy—was that an ongoing and widely audible cultural discussion had taken root.[27] A new vocabulary was in place. What in the nineteenth century was "the love that dare not speak its name" became by the early twentieth century, to quote one historian, "the love that would not shut up."[28]

This visibility heightened the indignation of the majority of Americans who continued to view homosexuality as deviant. One reformer in 1904, for example, fretted about "the shoals of painted, perfumed, kohl-eyed, lisping, mincing youths" that seemed everywhere in New York, but he consoled himself that at least they often received "a sound thrashing or an emphatic kicking" from other men.[29] It was against this mentality that Percy and others worked, a context that lent a sense of urgency—and danger—to their project.

Writing and talking about sexuality as a potential form of belonging that transcended local, regional, and national affiliation became common in this era, and Percy participated in and was shaped by this cultural trend. Out of the conviction that same-sex love was natural, he and his contemporaries created a framework of meaning for queer relationships, and this framework gave rise to the cultural identity later called "gay" and "homosexual." Percy and his contemporaries wrote and spoke about a shared understanding, a kind of broader spiritual kinship that was central to this emerging identity. Percy celebrated the gay world and described it as a community of belonging. He figured his own sexual awakening as an entrance into a superior wisdom, a network of human beings who recognized one another and who viewed the world from a different vantage point.[30]

This network existed not just in New York or Paris but also in small southern towns like Sewanee, Tennessee, and Greenville, Mississippi. This is significant, because with a few notable exceptions, scholars of the American South have portrayed the region as devoid of queer sexuality, particularly before 1950.[31] Work on Percy reflects this: McKay Jenkins insists that Will Percy was determined "to remain aloof from the historical pressures of his own time, and to ignore the discomfort of his own sexuality." Bertram Wyatt-Brown argues that Percy was "sexually sequestered" and "closed his eyes to the cultural maze in which he lived." Richard King reads Percy's writing as revealing "a man divided within himself and unable to express openly his essential sexual desires."[32] I have come to take a different view. The Will Percy I see in the historical record did not ignore the "discomfort" of his sexuality. He did not close his eyes to his world. In Greenville, in Sewanee, in Paris and Boston and New York and Italy, Percy immersed himself in conversations and reading about sexuality and sexual values. He involved himself in the emerging queer subcultures of the early twentieth century. He experienced and enjoyed emotional and sexual intimacy with other men. He faced his world and lived in it—and in doing so, he proved in some ways resourceful and thoughtful, in other ways close-minded and even racist; he called hierarchies of sexuality and gender into question even as he perpetuated those of race and class. His was a sensibility that seems to us at times contradictory, at times ambivalent, at times tenuously prescient.

To understand Percy's life story is to travel with him around the world. It is to track his experience of life in the South but also to journey away from it, to places like Cambridge and Florence and Japan and Samoa, then back to the South again. It is to sit in ecstasy in a Boston theatre with Percy and Harold Bruff; it is to sit in vexed watchfulness at the Washington County Historical Society in Mississippi; it is to ride on trains and steamships, to look out the windows, to wonder with Percy at the world outside. Percy invested the places he experienced with meaning: Greenville, Sewanee, Boston, Paris, New York, and the Mediterranean were not just spaces he traveled through but places that laid claim to his emotions, places whose cultures and institutions and landscapes shaped his experience and imagination. In his life, through his experience in these places, Percy considered and reconsidered, wrote and revised his stories of belonging. To tell his story is to explore a historical contest over the meaning of the words in these stories, words like "southern," "homosexual," and "sissy," among others. It is to try to understand someone who can be described as a cultural relativist, sexual liberationist, and white supremacist. It is to watch one person's engagement with God and morality, with history and his place in the world.[33]

This book tells the story of a curious man—curious not so much as in peculiar, or unusual, or queer, though Percy was all of these things. More so, this is a story about a man's curiosity. It is a story about his attempts to make sense of the world he lived in, the history he lived through. Sex, God, love, violence, beauty, war, the South, poetry, fatherhood, death—thoughts of these things kept him awake at night and textured his moral reckonings. What follows is an account of those reckonings and a history of the life that occasioned them.

1. THE STAGE OF SOUTHERN HISTORY

Those days you had to be a hero or a villain or a weakling—
you couldn't just be middling ordinary.

WILLIAM ALEXANDER PERCY, *Lanterns on the Levee*

William Alexander Percy's Mississippi Delta in 1910: a world of sprawling cotton plantations worked by sharecroppers. A disproportionately large African American population. A small but powerful white population. A political system run by white people and by Democrats yet still fiercely contentious. A land mainly of plantations but also of towns like Greenville and Vicksburg—bustling port cities, hubs of commerce, towns whose streets were lined with saloons, haberdasheries, churches, banks, mansions, and shanties, all uneasy neighbors like the black and white and poor and rich people who lived there. Stability in the world of the Mississippi Delta rested on a fine balance, and until around 1910, that balance nearly always favored the white planter elite. It was a world of gamblers betting and hoping the cotton would sell, the levees would hold, and the black workers would not rise up in rebellion.

This world was a product of a singular history. This history was the local story of Delta slaves and planters carving a cotton empire out of the wilderness, which was part of the larger story of the westward movement of Americans in the nineteenth century, which was part of the larger story of the emergence of global capitalism. The world of the Mississippi Delta was never a bounded world, though it must have seemed so to many. It was a porous world, one animated by the river, which came from St. Louis and Memphis and flowed toward New Orleans and the Caribbean. It was a world into and out of which flowed people, money, raw materials, ideas, and the steamboats and flatboats and trains that carried these things.

And indeed it had always been a porous world, shaped by migration, warfare, epidemics, and environmental change. The Mississippi River flooded the Delta almost yearly for thousands of years, creating over time rich, black, alluvial soil. Archaeological evidence suggests the Mississippian tribes of

14

Native Americans settled in the Delta and farmed on it in the centuries before 1700. Epidemics arising from European contact decimated nearly 80 percent of the native population in the American South, including many of the Tunica, Yazoo, and Chuola Tribes that had populated the Delta. In 1817, when Mississippi became a state, almost 30,000 Choctaws and Chickasaws lived within its newly established borders. They settled the Delta only sparsely. The area was a forest wilderness of swamps and hardwood trees, a thicket of vines and cane and brush, home to alligators and bears, bobcats and rattlesnakes. Sycamore trees grew to thirty-five feet in circumference. After flooding, the Delta became a vast, seething, malarial swamp. The natives did not want to live there.[1]

But many white Americans, newly cotton obsessed in 1817, did want to live there. Emerging consumer markets in Europe and America demanded seemingly limitless quantities of cotton. Technological advances such as the high-pressure steam engine, the cotton gin, and the steam-powered loom made growing, transporting, and transforming cotton into textiles more profitable. The climate of the American South was ideally suited for growing cotton, and a vast slave population provided a ready source of labor. Though Congress banned the transatlantic slave trade in 1808, some 1.1 million slaves already lived as human property in the South, mainly in Virginia and the Carolinas.[2] During the next fifty years, planters in search of fertile cotton lands would bring more than a million of these slaves and their offspring—in what historian Ira Berlin calls "the Second Middle Passage"—from the seaboard states to the southern interior.[3]

Of all the land in the South, the Mississippi Delta would prove to be singular in its productivity. In the 1820s, the land was relatively cheap and available to those who had the money and desire to clear it and plant cotton. Settlers brought slaves to the Delta by flatboat beginning in 1825 to clear lands near the river. A series of three treaties with the Choctaws during the 1820s and early 1830s, as well as the U.S. Congress's Indian Removal Act of 1830, gave control of Mississippi to white settlers. A handful of Choctaw natives stayed and became slave owners and cotton planters, some quite successfully. But most moved west to what would later be called *okla humma*, which means "red people." The Delta became home to capitalists who arrived from states like Virginia, Kentucky, and South Carolina with slaves and money and dreams of wealth. They would in time impose order on this wilderness, create plantations where hardwood bottoms used to grow, lay out towns on grids where the earth used to swell and contract in wild and tempestuous rhythm.[4]

But this was no easy task. The sycamore and walnut and mocker-nut hickory trees, not to mention the mosquitoes and copperhead snakes and almost impenetrable cane thickets, were in the way. The taming of this wilderness would become part of the mythology of the Delta. To later Mississippians such as Sam Worthington and Will Percy, the Delta of 1825 was a wilderness immemorial, and its clearing was a singular feat of courage, strength, and foresight. Percy wrote that the stage of southern history was "no ordinary stage, and the play was no ordinary play."[5]

Slaves did all the work, by and large. Slaves cut cane thickets and felled trees, built roads and levees, log cabins and landings. They drained and leveled fields. They planted cotton and corn. The first nonnative settlers and pioneers of the Delta—indeed, the majority of the population—were slaves. By 1830 almost 2,000 people lived in Washington County, and about 1,200 of them were slaves. Within ten years, slaves outnumbered white people ten to one.[6] This majority population created a slave culture that gave enduring voice to beliefs about race, God, and bondage, among other aspects of their lives. Slaves took what little freedom they had and in it invented patterns of living that informally resisted the power of their white masters. Music, foodways, storytelling, nuanced interpretations of Christianity that emphasized promises of freedom over submission to authority—these were some of the ways slaves in the Delta not only engaged in quiet rebellion but also played a role in creating a larger African American culture.[7]

In turn, a perennial concern among whites in the Delta was controlling this majority black population while still maximizing slaves' productivity. This was the balancing act of the age, the defining tension in the emerging society of the Delta. Particularly after news of Denmark Vesey and Nat Turner's plots in 1822 and 1831 to revolt against the ruling class in South Carolina and Virginia, planters throughout the South became increasingly anxious about slave rebellion. In the Delta, with its uniquely large slave population, this fear was ever present. The delicate task for planters was to prevent outright rebellion while also encouraging hard work. This required a careful balance of threat and reward. Planters styled themselves as benevolent father figures who provided housing, food, and a civilizing environment to slaves and expected in return submission, hard work, and loyalty. "On my father's plantation ninety-five percent never had a lash," Sam Worthington remembered. His words underscored a plain fact about plantation life in the South: mastery on the plantation rested on violence and the threat of violence. This truth was inscribed upon the lashed bodies of the 5 percent.[8]

Sam Worthington's father, in fact, was a partner in the first Percy plantation in the Delta. Thomas George Percy, Will Percy's great-grandfather, purchased plantation land in the Delta in 1829 with several business partners and moved his family there in 1841.[9]

Thomas George's father, Charles Percy, had arrived in the New World in 1777 having left behind two wives and a handful of children in England and the Caribbean. Some said he was related to the noble Percys of Northumberland in England; others said he was merely a ne'er-do-well and a bigamist. Very little evidence remains about his life. Will Percy referred to him simply as "the Pirate."[10] Charles Percy settled in the Louisiana Territory and created a fortune growing indigo and raising cattle. In 1780, at the age of forty, he married his third wife, Susannah Collins, who was then sixteen. They had seven children, four of whom survived until adulthood. The Spanish government took to the Percys and made Charles a magistrate. They called him Don Carlos. In 1794 Don Carlos wrote out his will and ten days later drowned himself in the creek near his house. He was said to have tied a sugar kettle around his neck.[11]

Thomas George Percy was born in 1786 and grew up, like Will Percy a century later, with money and time. He went to Princeton and after graduation devoted himself to managing his inheritance, which included a 5,000-acre plantation in Alabama and seventy-six slaves. He married a woman named Maria Pope around 1815 and by then owned plantations near Natchez, Mississippi, and Huntsville, Alabama. The Percys lived in Alabama until 1841, when they moved to the Delta. Though successful, Thomas George preferred to spend his time gardening and accumulating the library of brown-leather volumes that Will Percy would inherit three generations later. Each volume was numbered and neatly ordered in Thomas George's library: the three-volume *American Ornithology*; important Enlightenment-era journals such as *Blackwood's* and the *Edinburgh Review*; the classics translated from Greek and Latin.[12] Thomas George loved to travel and to shop. He went often to London and New York, to Paris and Princeton. He wrote home from New York to a friend that, while on Broadway, he and his wife had been "among crowds of well dress'd people, & been pretty well dress'd ourselves."[13] Will Percy noted that family members referred to his great-grandfather disdainfully as "Thomas G" because of his lack of seriousness and ambition, his lack of valor and virility. Percy, though, felt him "a familiar and a confidant of mine" for one main reason: "He isn't a demanding ancestor."[14] Percy later kept his portrait above the fireplace in his home and took comfort in his sly smile.

Thomas G's love of travel was part of a larger affinity for Europe among planters in the South. Many plantation owners self-consciously styled themselves as cosmopolitans and sophisticates. They had their children study Latin and Greek and attend foreign universities; many traveled regularly to London, Paris, and Italy. The concept of the "grand tour" gained a special purchase on the imaginations of southerners during the first half of the nineteenth century; travel to Europe was a demonstration of taste and refinement. It was also a way to study European ideas, culture, and history. Planters brought home furniture and artwork and fine silver from Paris, pistols and hunting dogs and dressing gowns from London. Thomas George Percy owned many such markers of cosmopolitan taste, such as his dining-room table with hand-carved legs and brass feet, which Will Percy would later use.[15] This kind of travel to Europe, historians have argued, was a kind of "secular ritual" among elite southerners, one that reinforced a sense of cultural superiority and granted access to a broad range of ideas and information.[16] Michael O'Brien's study of intellectual life in the Old South suggests that European travel and European intellectual currents were central to elite southerners' understandings of themselves and their world.[17] This was true for Thomas George Percy, as it would be for Will Percy a century later.

Thomas George and Maria Percy had eight children, and four of them, all sons, lived to adulthood. One of these they named William Alexander Percy, who was born in 1837. He was to become a civic leader, a Civil War hero, and a mythical figure in the Delta. He was also to become a symbolic weight on his grandson's shoulders: "When I consider all he did and all I haven't done," Will Percy recounted, "I feel the need of taking a good look at Thomas G., debonair and wistful, expecting nothing." Thomas George's life suggested the value of refinement, taste, and leisure. His son William Alexander's life evinced a more practical sensibility, a hands-on commitment to political life. Will Percy saw his great-grandfather and his grandfather as two different types of men, representing two different versions of manhood that he himself vacillated between. In the former version, the ideal man was one who loved beauty, looked beyond mere profit-seeking for the better things in life. In the latter version, men were responsible for addressing their minds to practical problems, duty bound to use their strength and talents to be productive, civic-minded, and self-sacrificing. But about being a Percy, about being a man in the South, one thing was clear to Will Percy: "[Y]ou had to be a hero or a villain or a weakling," he wrote, "you couldn't just be middling ordinary."[18]

In 1841 Thomas George Percy died, leaving his wife and four sons—the eldest, John Walker, was twenty-four—to manage the new plantation in the

Delta. During the 1840s and 1850s, William Alexander Percy came of age on their plantation at Deer Creek, about twelve miles from Greenville. During this time, the Delta continued to become one of the wealthiest regions in the country, a land of large cotton plantations, a small white population, and many slaves. The slave population of Washington County outnumbered the white population by over fourteen to one in 1850, and the average white family owned over eighty slaves.[19] When set beside the rest of the South, these numbers were wildly out of proportion. In 1850 across the South, only about a fourth of white families owned slaves at all, and of those families, only 30 percent owned more than ten slaves. Less than 1 percent owned more than eighty slaves. The Mississippi Delta, with its small white population made up mostly of wealthy planters and its large and highly skilled slave population, was an anomaly in the South.[20]

It was a situation, though, from which the Percys profited enormously. Planters like William Alexander Percy and his brothers leveraged a great deal, borrowed large amounts of money against their crops in order to plant as much cotton as possible. Most years, the gamble paid off; in some years, floods, low cotton prices, or drought destroyed the crops. Planters and plantation mistresses alternated between elation and despair. One of the Percys' neighbors wrote that her husband had "a mania for buying negroes." His ambitious plans required extraordinary risk, she said, and "it makes me feel very poor to go so in debt."[21] In contrast to the nostalgic portrayal of plantation life by some later southerners, white Delta society in the nineteenth century was marked by ambition, risk taking, and debt-laden stress.

It was also marked by a conscious effort on the part of planters to create a genteel, leisurely society; planters spent lavishly on housing and entertainment. The Percys played their part in this, hosting regular dances and dinners at their home. Theirs was a full house by the late 1850s—William Alexander Percy and his wife, Nannie; John Walker and his wife, Fannie; and another brother LeRoy, a bachelor with a reputation for gallivanting and charm. One friend remembered the antebellum Percy plantation as a hub of refined excitement, with its closely cut Bermuda grass, wide hallways, and sweeping porches: it was "a worthy retreat for a family who knew what life was and how to live it."[22]

In 1860 Abraham Lincoln was elected, and secession fervor gripped the South. William Alexander Percy opposed secession, as did many Delta plantation owners. One Washington County planter accurately summarized this position: "Wealth is always conservative."[23] War would be disruptive, and the Delta elite were wary of losing control of the land and labor that had made them rich. And the Mississippi Delta was among the richest regions in the nation: with a total wealth per freeman of $26,800 in 1860, Washington's neighboring Issaquena County was the second-wealthiest county in America. That wealth, though, was concentrated in slave property, and hence maintaining the status quo was imperative to Delta planters. The vision of northern armies marching through cotton fields terrified planters, one of whom warned that war would create a Delta "where the slave should be made free and the proud southerner stricken to dust in his presence." The possibility of slaves becoming empowered citizens also haunted white Delta residents: in Washington County in 1860, there were over 14,000 black slaves and barely 1,000 white people. There was not one free black man or woman in the county.[24]

William Alexander Percy arranged to send his friend Jacob Shall Yerger to the Mississippi secession convention. Yerger owned over a hundred slaves and a plantation in Washington County. He argued at the convention that constitutional protections for slavery would be more effective than southern nationhood as a means of maintaining their way of life.[25] He suggested Mississippi meet with other southern states to try and find a way to avoid secession. When it came time to vote, though, the delegates voted eighty-four to fifteen to leave the Union.[26]

Once his state voted to secede, William Alexander Percy committed himself to the Confederacy. He organized a local militia unit he called the "Swamp Rangers," which became a part of the Army of Mississippi. Percy fought in Mississippi until the fall of Vicksburg in July 1863. He was then transferred to Robert E. Lee's Army of Northern Virginia and fought in the battles of the Wilderness, Spotsylvania, and Cold Harbor, where Confederate soldiers killed 7,000 Union troops in half an hour. Percy joined Jubal A. Early's cavalry advance up the Shenandoah Valley, almost reaching Washington, D.C.; it was during this operation that William Alexander Percy was nicknamed "The Gray Eagle of the Valley" for his heroism in battle.[27]

While Percy was at war, his wife, Nannie, managed the plantation and took care of their four young children, Fannie, William Armstrong, LeRoy, and John Walker. Like other white women in the plantation South, Nannie Percy's wartime experience consisted mainly of inventing ways to survive. When the Emancipation Proclamation took effect in 1863, it was she who was the first to negotiate with the freed slaves. Many of them had left. A few remained but did not want to work for free. Family legend had it that she "ordered" the former slaves to work and sat in her rocking chair at the edge of the field to watch them. It is likely there was more give-and-take than this, but the story does point out her resilience and capability. Later commenting on this family lore, Will Percy rightly noted: "Indeed, indeed, the lily-of-the-field life of the Southern gentlewoman existed only in the imagination of Northern critics and Southern sentimentalists, one about as untrustworthy as the other."[28]

After the Civil War, the Percys became a city family. Though Thomas G. Percy's sons had settled on the Percy plantation in the 1840s, after the war, William Alexander Percy swapped 100 acres of plantation land for a house on the corner of Locust and Washington Streets in Greenville. He opened a law practice downtown. He, and his white counterparts in Greenville, set about trying to reestablish planter authority in the Delta. The late 1860s was a period of fluidity in which some former slaves became landowners, many voted, and a few held political offices. To Percy and other white planters, these free blacks posed a significant social, political, and economic threat.[29]

In 1873 Percy organized a "taxpayer's convention," a coalition of white landowners, in order to create a strategy to unseat Republicans and their African American allies in the elections of 1874. Percy's main task was to figure out how to convince local blacks, a vast majority, to vote the Democratic ticket. To do so, Percy capitalized on a feud between Washington County's two leading black politicians, William Grey and J. Allen Ross. Ross was moderate and friendly to planter interests, while the local elite viewed Grey as a radical. Both men announced their intent to run for sheriff of Washington County in the summer of 1874. The local white newspaper, the *Greenville Times*, reported that Grey's announcement of his candidacy amounted to a call to race war. "He was bound to be sheriff," the paper reported. The Republican governor, Adelbert Ames, "was going to send him a thousand stand of arms, to secure his election, and, if necessary, he would kill all the white men, women and children and even children in their cradle in Washington County." The article finished with an exhortation to its white readers: "You must all load your shotguns and have them ready."[30] A few days after his announcement of his candidacy, Grey and his followers mounted what the *Greenville Times* called a "murderous attack" on Greenville. In the melee, for which historical evidence is thin, J. Allen Ross was shot and killed and a local militia organized by whites ran William Grey out of town.[31]

With these two powerful men out of the way, Percy began to assemble a political machine more palatable to planters. In order to do so, he had to resort to corrupt methods, which were not recorded in detail. In the stories white Deltans told themselves about Reconstruction, those details were not as important as the end itself. Will Percy reported: "That work required courage, tact, intelligence, patience; it also required vote-buying, the stuffing of ballot-boxes, chicanery, intimidation. Heart-breaking business and degrading, but in the end successful. At terrific cost was white supremacy re-established."[32]

In 1874 William Alexander Percy created a fusion ticket for the Democratic Party in Washington County that included himself as a state senator. His cohort won the 1874 election, and Democrats throughout the state followed suit. When Democrats regained a majority in the state legislature in 1874, they immediately created a committee to investigate the Reconstruction governor Adelbert Ames's administration. On March 14, 1875, William Alexander Percy read twenty-one articles of impeachment to the state senate, and Ames resigned.[33] A Delta planter and friend of the Percys, John Marshall Stone, was placed in the governor's mansion.[34]

The "Mississippi Plan," as this strategy for the redemption of the state has come to be known, centered on the use of violence and intimidation to keep African Americans away from the polls.[35] It began in the late 1860s with the Ku Klux Klan warning blacks to stay at home come voting day. During the election of 1874, a primary tactic of the White League, the White Line, the Regulators, and other Mississippi white groups was to show up at multiracial Republican events and provoke and heckle the crowd in order to draw them into violent confrontation. In 1874 and 1875, race riots broke out in Vicksburg, Clinton, and Yazoo City in which a handful of whites and hundreds of blacks were killed. The strategy worked. In Yazoo County in 1875, for example, which had a black population of 12,000, there were precisely seven votes cast for the Republican Party. Governor Adelbert Ames, the most hated man in Mississippi, was prescient in his summary of what had happened: "Yes, a revolution has taken place—by force of arms—and a race are disfranchised—they are to be returned to a condition of serfdom—an era of second slavery. ... Time will show you how accurate my statements are."[36]

IN PERCY FAMILY LORE, Reconstruction was the main act on the stage of southern history. It was a moment of disjuncture, a period in history in which the wealth and power and patterns of living among white planters were at risk. The hero of this play, to Will Percy, was his grandfather. Percy's understanding of who his grandfather was, and what he did during Reconstruction, saturated his views of history, politics, and the South. Percy later wrote that the stories he heard of this period and this man gave him a point of view, a mindset he could not disinherit. The central theme in these stories of Reconstruction was that of southern men defending their honor and their homes.

The mentality Percy believed them to embody, he said, "while certainly not appreciated or understood by me in my childhood, seeped into me, colored my outlook, prescribed for me loyalties and responsibilities that I may not disclaim."[37]

The common narrative of Reconstruction that circulated in Greenville and was codified by professional historians in the early twentieth century was this: Reconstruction was a tragedy of Republican political corruption, Yankee economic opportunism, and newly freed slaves who cheated their way into power and prosperity.[38] The interests of lawful, tax-paying, land-owning southern whites like the Percys, the story went, were subjugated to those of northern opportunists called "carpetbaggers" and newly freed slaves. Mississippi's official textbook for elementary schoolchildren, for example, proclaimed this view: after the Civil War, "the entire political power of the state was thrown into the hands of a few adventurers from the Northern States and a host of ignorant Negroes," and "the inhabitants of the state were compelled to submit to the presence of armed bodies of Negroes, commanded by officers of their own color of the most dangerous and turbulent type."[39] Indeed, all the sources available to Will Percy told this familiar narrative of Reconstruction.

Historians have recently shown that this story left a great deal out, skewed some facts, ignored others, and was fundamentally racist.[40] Demographically, though, the traditional narrative of postbellum Mississippi was accurate: the state was flooded with new citizens, as 600,000 former slaves were now legally enfranchised in Mississippi as a result of the Fourteenth and Fifteenth Amendments to the U.S. Constitution. The prospect of "Negro domination," combined with the harsh economic realities of the postwar South, created grave anxieties within the minds of planters. One Delta planter captured the climate among Mississippi whites during Reconstruction. "We are so oppressed with carpetbag and negro rule and with all the Yankees," he said, "that we the southern people feel we have quite gone out of existence except to work very hard for bare subsistence."[41] William Alexander Percy was one of many white Mississippians who capitalized on this fear in order to reestablish white supremacy.

With the power of the state back in the hands of white southerners after Reconstruction, William Alexander Percy turned his focus to three interrelated problems: building and maintaining levees, bringing railroads to the Delta, and preventing the black labor force from moving away. Levees, railroads, and labor were the three features of Delta life that, when they functioned correctly, ensured the region's growth and fortunes. The trains integrated the Delta more fully into the world's cotton markets; the levees held back the floods that would destroy the crops; and African American sharecroppers turned the soil, planted the seeds, tended the plants, pulled the weeds, and picked the cotton.

Cotton, it turned out, did not bring most southerners the riches they dreamed of after the Civil War. Cotton from India and Egypt saturated Europe's markets; a downturn in the global economy in the 1880s further weakened demand for cotton. Southerners, in turn, grew even more cotton. Throughout the South, the system of sharecropping developed, whereby landowners allowed sharecroppers to farm their land for a share of the profits. In order to farm the land, though, sharecroppers needed seeds, fertilizer, tools, housing, and animals, among other things. Generally, the landowner advanced these things against the value of the cotton crop and added interest. When the crop came in, the sharecroppers often found they did not break even. Many of these African American and poor white sharecroppers became poorer and poorer, mired in debt, unable to move or pay their debtors or buy land of their own.[42]

But not so the planters of the Mississippi Delta, and not so the Percys. Though living in the poorest state in the country, they became some of the wealthiest people in America. Their land was fertile enough, their quest for efficiency calculated enough, their labor cheap enough and strong enough to wrench profits from the land.

It is not entirely accurate, though, to call William Alexander Percy, or his sons, planters. After the Civil War they became corporate lawyers, players of the stock market, investors in railroads and real estate who also owned and managed plantations. They did not live on them. They did not tend to their day-to-day operations. Like Thomas G. Percy before them, they inherited them (or bought them with inheritance money). They made sure they were profitable, but the majority of their working lives was taken up with these other matters that ensured the plantations made a profit: practicing law, working on the Levee Board, organizing railroads, and thinking long and hard on what they called the "Negro Question."

William Alexander Percy, the Gray Eagle, died in 1888, and his official legacy was immediately enshrined. The Episcopal Church's obituary captured the mood of Mississippi: "In the death of the Honorable William A. Percy, the Diocese, in common with all the people of the commonwealth, has sustained a loss that cannot be expressed in words. ... The example of his noble life is a priceless legacy as a model for those who survive him, and which we commend to the young men of Mississippi as the best type of manhood, that of a Christian gentleman."[43]

William Alexander Percy's sons inherited both his land and his ambition. The three boys—John Walker, LeRoy, and William Armstrong—came of age in the Reconstruction South and watched as their father shrewdly dismantled Republican leadership in the state. They watched as his landholdings increased, as his law practice grew, as his influence in local and state politics expanded. They also watched their father suffer—his older brother John Walker died in the Civil War; his younger brother, LeRoy, killed himself with an overdose of laudanum the day before his niece Fannie died. William Alexander Percy's way of managing grief seemed to have been to sink himself ever deeper into his work. His sister, also named Fannie, took a dose of morphine every day.[44]

Among the Gray Eagle's sons, LeRoy and John Walker would follow most closely in his footsteps. The youngest of them, William Armstrong, was less driven though still quite successful. While growing up in the 1870s in Greenville, William Armstrong took comfort in a romantic friendship with a neighbor, Henry Waring Ball. Ball would later write in his diary that "Will Percy was my first love, my original Damon and Pythias. There has been a long line of them since—Will Percy, Will Mays, Sam Bull, Will Van Dresser, Tony Russell, and now Eugene, with many lesser names scattered between."[45] Ball described their relationship in classical terms. "I used to love Willy Percy as David did Jonathan," he wrote. "In our letters we called each other Orestes and Pylades."[46]

In the nineteenth century, there existed a wider tolerance for intense, affectionate, same-sex, "romantic friendships" among both men and women. Historians have documented a wide range of correspondence and diaries of men such as Henry Ball who maintained emotionally loving relationships with other men.[47] These men did not self-identify as "homosexual," and most were not suspected of the crime of sodomy. Rather, the ability to sustain emotionally intimate same-sex relationships was a sign of maturity and well-being. "Friendship and love were inseparable notions," writes historian Donald Yacovone. These notions found expression in "passionate intellectual exchange as well as in homoeroticism."[48] This homoeroticism was in some cases sexually chaste, in some cases not. But because homosexuality was not yet conceived of as an identity, an either/or sexual preference, men were free to share romantic love without the stigma of *being* homosexual.

One outgrowth of this cultural pattern was that men who did conceive of themselves as homosexual used the widely condoned language of "romantic friendship" to communicate homoerotic sexual desire. In a tradition that would become very important to Will Percy, many men understood the intimate friendships of men such as Damon and Pythias—two friends in Greek mythology whose names symbolized loyalty and true friendship—as legitimizing homosexual male relationships. In the case of Henry Waring Ball and his love for William Armstrong Percy, Ball's short diary entry is the only evidence that is extant, so we will likely never know the details of their relationship unless new documents emerge. But it is important to point out that the language of romantic friendship, couched in homoerotic expression, was circulating in Greenville, Mississippi—indeed even within the Percy family—in the late nineteenth century. Will Percy's understanding and vindication of his own sexuality would to some degree grow out of cultural patterns existing within the American South.[49]

William Armstrong Percy's older brother, LeRoy, fitted more neatly the mold of his father. Born in 1861, LeRoy Percy grew up in Greenville and attended the University of the South and the University of Virginia School of Law. He returned to Greenville after law school and joined his father's law firm, as well as his other business interests: running the family plantation, working for the Levee Board, and urging northern investors to invest their money in Mississippi railroads.

LeRoy Percy was a serious man. He was a Gilded Age capitalist: practical, efficient, ambitious, and resolute. He earned a great deal of money from his law practice and plantation and invested this money in stocks, real estate, and railroad companies. He became the director of the regional Federal Reserve Board in St. Louis, counting among his friends men such as President Teddy Roosevelt, railroad tycoon Stuyvesant Fish, and Governor John Parker of Louisiana. But he was not merely all business. He was a hunter, a gambler, and an admirer of expensive bourbon. Those who knew him thought him a decent man, and he was well respected in Greenville's white community. Though he never joined the military, he was a regular defender of Greenville in the Levee Guard—a group responsible for protecting the levees from miscreants who would dynamite the levees on the Mississippi side of the river in order to lessen the pressure from the Arkansas side. Levee Guards walked the levees at night with lanterns. To locals, these lights symbolized protection; they symbolized the collective sacrifice people made for their community; they symbolized manhood, the ways in which white men were responsible for the well-being of their people. These lights would come to resonate in Will Percy's imagination, too, throughout his life.

Camille Bourges Percy (1862–1929), Will Percy's mother (Courtesy of the Mississippi Department of Archives and History, Jackson, Mississippi)

Not far away from Greenville's levees lived the Bourges family. A Frenchman named Captain Ernest Bourges, who had served under General Beauregard in the Confederate army, bought a plantation called Woodstock in 1867.[50] He renamed it "Camelia" after his wife, and they moved in with their four beautiful daughters. One of these daughters was Camille, who would in time become Mrs. LeRoy Percy. Ernest Bourges eventually lost the plantation and moved his family to Greenville, where he tried and failed at several

*LeRoy Percy (1861–1929), Will Percy's father (Courtesy of
the Mississippi Department of Archives and History, Jackson, Mississippi)*

different business ventures. He was remembered as a success only at raising
roses and daughters.[51]

In 1884 a twenty-three-year-old LeRoy Percy began courting Camille
Bourges despite her family's reservations. The Bourgeses were suspect of
the Percys: how could one account for their ancestry, which began with the
thrice-married, mysterious Don Carlos who flung himself into a creek? The
Bourgeses were a proud French family, Catholic, upright, and proper. They
spoke French in the home. They might have preferred that their daughter
marry another Catholic. While the young couple courted, the elder Camille
Bourges sat in the parlor and chaperoned.[52]

Camille Bourges was by all accounts a beautiful woman. She had fair
hair and a distinctively round face that framed her blue eyes and dimpled
chin. She was demanding, forgiving, astute, and composed of fragile nerves.
Because of her constitution, or because of the stress of a debt-encumbered

lifestyle, or because of her anxieties over her family's well-being, she would be in and out of the hospital all of her life with nervous breakdowns, neurasthenia, and exhaustion. Doctors from Greenville to Baltimore prescribed convalescent stays in the hot springs of Arkansas, the mountains of Virginia, and the Caribbean climate of Cuba.

Despite her nerves, Camille Bourges was a strong woman. She would come to maintain order in the Percy house. During LeRoy Percy's travels for business and politicking, hunting and hobnobbing, she ran the home and gave structure to daily life. She was a hearty gardener and cook, a lover of travel, a thrower of parties. Henry Waring Ball wrote often in his diaries about the fabulous parties at the Percy house, such as the one at which there was "unlimited champagne punch (nearly everybody there was half drunk when I left) and the very crème de la crème of society present."[53] Camille Percy snuck into LeRoy's wallet and stole his poker money to buy food for her cats. "Confound Cam's Kittycats!" LeRoy Percy would yell, walking to work in the morning and realizing he had no cash in his pockets.[54]

The young couple married in December 1884; six months later, Camille Percy gave birth to a baby boy, whom they named William Alexander, after his grandfather.[55]

2. CHILDHOOD, REMEMBERED QUEERLY

Heaven help parents worrying over what to do with children a
little out of the ordinary!
—WILLIAM ALEXANDER PERCY, *Lanterns on the Levee*

In May 1885, the month Will Percy was born, Greenville, Mississippi, was still a frontier town with muddy roads and wooden sidewalks. The pages of the *Greenville Times* displayed notices of land for sale and industry in need of capital. Merchants advertised their plows and razors and pistols and chandeliers in large black font. The newspaper urged its readers, "If you have goods to sell, advertise in the *Greenville Times*. If you have goods to buy, read the advertisements in the *Greenville Times*." Greenville was a business town, a place for profit seekers and moneymakers, a dais in the New South cotton kingdom. In time, it would become a place for artists as well, "the Athens of the Delta," but this was not so in 1885. As if to give a signal of unwelcome to the future poet Will Percy, the Greenville newspaper noted on the day after his birthday: "Stories of fiction, and poetical contributions always declined."[1]

William Alexander Percy was born on May 15, 1885. Much of what we know about his early life—especially the first fifteen years—comes from his autobiography, which means that any telling of his childhood will also be a telling of his adulthood. Percy wrote *Lanterns on the Levee* in his fifties, and the memoir reveals a great deal about his youth but also about several themes that animated his adult imagination: his relation to people of color, his relationship with his home and family, and his emotional and intellectual connections with other men. We can only access his childhood through his memory of it, and the dominant motif in his recollections is his own difference, his queerness as a boy growing up in Mississippi.[2]

Percy's recounting of the early years of his life lacked significant mention of his parents. In fact, he commented that even as his birth "overjoyed no one"—a subtle reference to his early arrival—his parents "impressed me not at all. ... I have no single memory of them dating from the first four years of my life." The erasure of their memory is telling, especially because Percy said that the primary figure who replaced them was his black nursemaid, Nain. In what was a common trope in his view of African Americans, Percy figured Nain as the possessor of a special spiritual and emotional wisdom. Percy's perspective on black-white relations was that of a white supremacist; but within his racial prejudice was the conviction that blacks as a race possessed a special brand of interior freedom and peace.[3]

Percy's experience as an affluent white child being raised by a black woman in the late nineteenth-century South was at once normal and exceptional.[4] It was common for such children of the wealthy to be tended to by black domestics; it was common, also, for these children to grow up and sing retrospective praises of their "mammy." What was not common in Will Percy's case was the extent to which he identified with her. He felt they shared a particular type of inner sadness. He described her body as a repository of wisdom and pathos. He felt he shared with her a space on the margins of southern society, a knowing bond of alienation, a kindred spirit of outsider status. We will never know what she felt toward him.

The "black mammy," Percy wrote, was supposed to be "fat and elderly and bandannaed." Nain, though, was sixteen years old and "divinely café-au-lait." She was beautiful, he said, and she sang to him. Percy believed that he likely loved her for her youth and zeal and sympathy, though he mentioned the possibility that "in her I found the comfort of the womb, from which I had so recently and unexpectedly been ejected." Having been ejected from his mother's womb, he recounted over fifty years later, he found acceptance from Nain: "Chiefly I remember her bosom: it was soft and warm, an ideal place to cuddle one's head against." Percy recalled that his first memory of his life was of Nain singing to him; she would hold him in her arms and rock him, and though Percy said he did not remember the words or the tune, he could not forget "what they did to me."[5]

The effect of Nain's singing, and her presence in his young life, was indeed long lasting and resonant with Percy's conception of himself and his relationship to people of color. "It made me feel so lost and lonely that tears would seep between my lids and at last I would sob until I shook against her breast," he wrote. She would try to comfort him, but her singing filled Percy with a vast loneliness. Specifically, her singing awakened "kindred compassions in the core of my being." The experience of being held against Nain's bosom while she sang imparted to Percy what he felt was a true empathy with the loneliness and alienation of black people. He figured his literal contact with her body as a moment in which she transferred to him a special wisdom: "she innocently endowed me with a sense of the tears of things," but she also filled "a baby's vacant heart" with music that "guided me more sure-footedly and authoritatively through life than all ten of the commandments." She taught him about music, about the body as containing not only flesh and blood but also traces of the sublime. He contrasted Nain's mysteriously powerful body with white southern society: the "Negro spirituals" in her bosom were more effective in guiding him through life than the Ten Commandments; her singing voice was more effective in transmitting love than was his own mother's.[6]

We will never know the veracity of Percy's first memory, but its significance lies not in its literal truth about his childhood experience. Percy even admitted that Nain existed in his memory "more as an emanation or aura than as a person." Percy's representation of his infant experience was a narrative of parental rejection and subsequent acceptance into the bosom of a black woman. Significantly, Percy explicitly pointed out that this black woman was not "fat and elderly and bandannaed." Nain was a sexual creature, her "café-au-lait" body even being a marker of interracial sex. The juxtaposition of his own mother's womb and Nain's breast suggests a theme that repeats itself throughout Percy's autobiography, indeed his life: Percy often wrote of white family life in terms that suggest rejection, and in contrast he portrayed blacks as accepting and spiritually, emotionally, and sexually free. It was Nain, not his mother, who filled his vacant heart with music.[7]

Just as Percy claimed that "every respectable white baby had a black mammy," he also pointed out that "any little boy who was not raised with little Negro children might just as well not have been raised at all." (And of his adult life, he would say, "In the South every white man worth calling white or a man is owned by some Negro.") Though Percy had a younger brother who was doubtless his companion and playmate, he did not include him as a character in his childhood. Instead, Percy imagined his childhood as primarily learning the finer points of life from his black playmates. Of his friend Skillet, he wrote: "He is all my memory records of what must have been long months of my childhood; all others it seems were lay figures." His white friends enter his narrative later; his parents are a fleeting presence; but his servant's children played a central part in his portrayal of childhood. Percy described playing with these friends in the early 1890s—a few years after black citizens had been disfranchised by the Mississippi constitution of 1890, and a few years before the U.S. Supreme Court would decree the lawfulness of racial segregation in *Plessy v. Ferguson* (1896). From Percy's memoirist perspective in the early 1940s, the racial strictures created in the

1890s had hardened into the "southern way of life," which included interracial friendships that ended with puberty.[8]

Skillet was the son of the Percys' cook and a world-class crawfisher. After an overflow of the Mississippi River, Greenville's roadside ditches filled with mud and crawfish. From Skillet, Percy learned that crawfish could often be found inside a hollow bone lying in the bottom of a ditch. From Skillet, Percy also learned of conversation and imagination. Skillet "outdistanced any white child in inventiveness, absurdity, and geniality" in conversation and had a penchant for the fantastical. One day, the two boys were sitting in a rowboat in Percy's grandmother's backyard, and, looking up at a pack of circling buzzards, Skillet told Percy that if they landed on the ground, the world would catch on fire. Percy doubted him like a "horrid little white realist," but as the buzzards moved closer and closer to the earth, his anxiety and expectation heightened. When a buzzard landed and the world did not catch fire, Percy demanded an explanation; Skillet shrugged and told Percy that the buzzard had landed not on the earth but on a wood chip.[9]

Percy wrote that the retelling of such a story was "one of the few pleasures that endure." His enjoyment of this recollection as an adult, though, rested on a specific hope. "I like to imagine that Skillet is not in jail or dead," Percy commented, "but that he lords it in a Pullman car or a pulpit, or perhaps he has a farm of his own." Percy's childhood narrative relies at once on the glorification of black childishness and the impossibility of black adult economic and civic participation. Percy's memory illuminates not only Percy's identification with and love of black people; it also demonstrates a psychological conceit necessary for the maintenance of segregation: blacks were fit for childhood companionship but not for adult political equality. Percy's tale of Skillet's imaginative excellence reveals race and class prejudice as well as a distinct admiration for black access to the supernatural. Percy ascribed to people of color a primitive connection with the earth: Skillet was not a "horrid little white realist" but had the capacity for wonder.[10]

Percy extended this theme in discussing his trips to his Aunt Nana's farm in Virginia, where his parents "deposited" him during the summers of his childhood. Again, Percy portrayed his contact with blacks not just as a coincidence of southern society but as a result of his parents' absence. His representation of his black friends in Virginia is marked by real affection interspersed with white-supremacist conceits. The servant Amelia's children—Ligey, Martha, Cora, and Friday—on the Virginia farm, for example, were otherworldly, like "satyrs and fauns," even though Percy "often wondered who and where their father was." A brief inquiry led him to believe the children's "father or set of fathers" was some sort of traveling salesman. The rhythm of Percy's narrative is characterized by call-and-response in his own mind between racial prejudice and what he believed was luminous black otherworldliness. However, the primary motif in Percy's portrayal of his interracial childhood experiences is that of spiritual content, even redemption. While he playfully told of his Virginia summer games—the hunts for treasures in the river, the making of apple cider—in the end, a more profound consequence of Percy's black friendships emerged: "From Amelia's children I learned not only gaiety and casualness and inventiveness, but the possibility that mere living may be delightful and that natural things which we ignore unless we call them scenery are pleasant to move among and gracious to recall. Without them it would probably never have occurred to me that to climb an aspen sapling in a gale is one of those ultimate experiences, like experiencing God or love, that you need never try to remember because you can never forget."[11]

Percy represented his friendships with black children as a portal to spiritual awareness. For him, childhood was a space in which interracial friendship on naïvely equal terms was permissible. Unlike adult blacks, who were illegitimate fathers or, at best, porters and preachers, black children (and mammies) were the repositories of spiritual and emotional knowledge. (Later in his life, Percy would describe Samoans in the same way.) Percy's imagining of this spiritual freedom had much to do with his own discomfort with the moral and economic strictures of white bourgeois society. Black children, like Samoans, were comfortably outside the reach of the deadening effects of modern capitalism and Western morality. The irony of Percy's positioning of himself as superior in terms of race and class, yet spiritually inferior because of his race and class, was one he lived with. Indeed, it was an enduring contradiction for someone who claimed to be both a white supremacist and a cultural relativist.

LeRoy Percy's first appearance in Percy's narrative of his own childhood is a loaded exchange between father and son about how a boy should act. The father wins. Aunt Nana Percy was reading to the young boy from a sentimental novel called *In Silken Chains*, which Percy called "the most moving book ever written." At "an unspeakably poignant climax," LeRoy Percy appeared and demanded they stop reading. "'Nana, what in the world do you mean by reading such trash to that child?'" he asked. Will Percy recalled, "Aunt Nana was crushed, I was desolate, he was adamant. We asked weakly what please could we substitute, and unhesitatingly he answered: 'Ivanhoe.'" Thus

Percy was inured to the fictional world of martial valor and gallant heroism. However, "far from being inspired to knightly heroism," Percy wrote that he "grew infatuated with the monastic life, if it could be pursued in a cave."[12]

As he often did when referring to his father in his memoir, Percy followed this depiction of his father's callousness with a compliment. In his compliment, though, there was ambivalence: "It was hard having such a dazzling father; no wonder I longed to be a hermit. He could do everything well except drive a nail or a car: he was the best pistol shot and the best bird-shot, he made the best speeches, he was the fairest thinker and the wisest, he could laugh like the Elizabethans, he could brood and pity till sweat covered his brow and you could feel him bleed inside."

To Percy, his father was "dazzling." As with a dazzling light, one can admire it from a distance but not get close to it. He described his father's appearances at the Virginia farm during the summers as "electric advents," and said that his returns from bird hunts had "a home-from-the-wars, home-from-the-seas, ballad brilliance."[13] He felt his father was baffled by him. "It must have been hard for father," Percy wrote, to have a "sissy" for a son. He remembered his father looking at him "quizzically" with "a far-away expression."[14]

LeRoy Percy's silence was often oppressive in Will Percy's life, but his presence was also stabilizing. As a boy, he looked to his father with wonder. He sat at his feet as LeRoy and his cronies talked politics and hunting on the front porch; he sucked the mint sugary whiskey from the bottoms of mint julep cups when the men were finished with them; he looked to these men as the embodiment of wisdom and virtue even as he increasingly sensed that he could not fully occupy their world. They talked of politics—"It is bitter as gar-broth, LeRoy," General Catchings, the local congressman, would say—and of levees, the cotton crop, their travels to far-off lands where they hunted boar and elk and antelope. Percy recalled their hatred of William Jennings Bryan and his free-silver platform in the 1896 presidential election; their love of Grover Cleveland; their never-ending resolve to build up levees in order to prevent floods. Class interests were central to their political views, which Percy largely adopted as his own.[15]

Percy learned the history of Reconstruction—that story so central to southern belonging—from these men during the 1890s. They were storytellers, to be sure, but the stories they told echoed those told by academic historians of the time. The dominant national myth of the late nineteenth century with its white heroes and black villains came from the mouths of men Will Percy loved and respected. "A Small Boy's Heroes," he called them: LeRoy

Percy, Captain J. S. McNeilly, Captain W. W. Stone, General T. C. Catchings. They would sit and talk, and Percy recounted that to him as a boy, they were not just men sitting and talking about politics; they were heroes in an "epic": "They were leaders of the people, not elected or self-elected, but destined, under the compulsion of leadership because of their superior intellect, training, character, and opportunity."[16] Not only were they central actors in this history, but their experience also saturated their very language, the stories that they told. One night after listening to them on the porch when he was older, Percy recorded in his diary: "About the speech of that older generation there is a tense muscularity, a vigor, a classic quality which constantly delights and surprises me. The effort is gained I think by the heroic lives they have led which influences their very speech."[17]

LeRoy and Will Percy shared a loving but not emotionally intimate relationship. LeRoy had a business approach to seemingly everything in his life save hunting and traveling. He signed his correspondence "LeRoy Percy" whether the letter was to a cotton merchant or to his young son.[18] He tolerated his son's difference, it seems, by trying half-successfully to ignore it. His ambivalence about his son's manliness was captured perfectly by a friend who later reported to an interviewer that LeRoy loved his son but was uncomfortable with his literary and artistic bent. "It was just the poetry, he was a little bit uneasy about that," the friend said. "But he knows ... He knew Will was a good man. He was a manly person, had his courage and everything like that."[19] Southerners like LeRoy Percy tolerated effeminacy, but it made them nervous.

Beginning around 1890, a series of personal tutors gave Will Percy a very different education from the one he received from his father and his friends. The distinction between his father's sensibility, which was utilitarian, political, and economically motivated, and that of his educators, which was idealistic, humanistic, and liberal, was a tension that Percy carried with him throughout his life. Though Greenville had the best public schools in Mississippi, his parents—like many elite Delta parents—insisted he be educated privately. It was at this point in remembering his childhood that Percy remarked, "Heaven help parents worrying over what to do with children a little out of the ordinary! It's a dark problem even with the recent assistance of Doctors Freud and Jung." He continued, "I was a sickly youngster who never had illnesses, who hated sports partly because they didn't seem important and mostly because I was poor at them, who knew better what I didn't want than what I did, who was sensitive but hard-headed, docile but given to the balks, day-dreamy but uncommunicative, friendly but not intimate—a frail problem child, a pain in the neck."[20]

That Percy portrayed himself as "sickly," "sensitive," "docile," and "frail" is significant. The decades on either side of 1900 were marked by a widespread fear in America that education was creating effeminate and weak young men. The preponderance of female teachers had created, according to one observer, "a feminized manhood, emotional, illogical, non-combative against public evils." To leave young boys primarily under the tutelage of women, it was thought, was beginning to "warp the psyches of our boys and young men into femininity." Masculine virtues such as virility, reason, strength, and valor were at risk of being replaced by purportedly feminine vices such as illogicality, impulsiveness, emotional instability, and indecision. The "specter of the sissy" was everywhere threatening in the 1890s and 1900s to fill the nation with what one writer called "flabby, feeble, mawkish … chicken-hearted, cold and fearful" men.[21] Doctors, educators, clergy, reformers and politicians alike displayed pressing concern that men become more active, strong, athletic, and virile—what they called "manly" and "masculine." LeRoy Percy could often be found appealing to the "manhood of Washington County" in his civic speeches, exhorting his listeners to be more "manly."[22] LeRoy Percy's friend and hunting buddy, Teddy Roosevelt, was the most prominent advocate of what he called "strenuous manhood." "We do not admire the man of timid peace," Roosevelt famously exclaimed. "We admire the man who embodies victorious effort." Roosevelt advocated military service, athletic prowess, and physical strength as antidotes to becoming "the over-civilized man, who has lost the great fighting, masterful virtues."[23]

Feminized men were especially threatening as more Americans came to associate effeminacy with homosexuality. At the turn of the century, gay male subcultures became increasingly visible in cities such as New York and Chicago, among others.[24] These subcultures had systems of meaning, places of meeting, and methods of self-identification. One such method, historian George Chauncey has noted, was for men to present themselves as effeminate. A prevailing medical theory about homosexuality held that "inversion," as it was called, resulted from the embodiment of feminine qualities. Though homosexual men did not necessarily believe this (and though this theory fell out of respectability in the twentieth century), they did seize on the stereotype as a means of self-identification. "Effeminacy was one of the few sure means [homosexual men] had to identify themselves to others," Chauncey writes. "Adopting effeminate mannerisms represented a deliberate cultural strategy, as well as a way of making sense of their sense of sexual difference."[25] The visibility of these subcultures played a role in the widespread concern about American manhood at the turn of the century, and it also shaped Will Percy's gender presentation in his memoir.

Percy's self-characterization as a "sickly youngster" who "hated sports" meshes with the rest of his memoir, in which he variously describes himself as "a sissy," "a spoiled darling," "a pewee," a "pale runt," and "small, weakly, and ignorant as an egg."[26] One might describe this as self-deprecation, but that is only partly true and misses an important point. In the preponderance of Percy's writing—his memoir, but also his diaries and correspondence and especially his poetry—he presents himself as gendered feminine. He drew from the dominant gender metaphors of his day to portray himself as embodying female characteristics.

The significance of this is twofold. On one level, this was common strategy among men in the early twentieth century to fashion a queer identity. As Chauncey and others point out, effeminacy was a marker of queerness, a common method of gender presentation. On another level, in his writing, Percy implicitly argued for a more expansive conception of manhood. Because the truth was that Percy did not believe himself to be a weakling or a "sissy." He expended a great deal of energy and effort into solving practical problems. He became a decorated war veteran and a local hero. "I wasn't meek and I wasn't afraid," he wrote in *Lanterns on the Levee*. "I am proud to be a man."[27]

To Percy, one did not have to be effeminate or virtuous, overcivilized or strong, idealistic or accomplished—one could be each of these at the same time. One could live at once inside and beyond prevailing gender categories. In addition to providing a critique of these categories, Percy's gender presentation reveals his strategy for navigating the cultural currents of his time: in an era when gender identities were coming to be associated with sexual identities, Percy could both protect himself and identify himself. Presenting himself as feminine allowed him to use a well-worn idiom that served as a signal to like-minded men; other readers could simply interpret this as self-deprecation, weakness, or "over-civilization." This played out among Greenvillians and allowed them to imagine Percy as either sufficiently masculine or homosexual. Recall the Greenville neighbor who insisted Will Percy was "a manly person." In contrast, another Greenville neighbor imagined Percy in her novel as living with his gay lover, "an old, poor fag."[28] Percy's success with regard to gender was to be at once manly and queer, courageous and homosexual.

So Percy's characterization of his childhood as a contest between an effeminate child and parents increasingly anxious to place him in all-male settings is ironic and humorous. To begin with, his parents sent him to a local Catholic convent as a five-year-old and dropped him off, according to Percy, "with a basket of lunch and no advice." At the church school, Percy found "cruel, nasty, bullying" classmates; a teacher named Sister Evangelist who was a "midget of a nun with the valor and will-power of an Amazon"; and the personal truth that for someone with a "third-rate" body, pistols were more effective than fists in self-defense. In addition to these martial aspects of his education, Percy found religion.[29]

Sister Evangelist was in fact an ardent evangelist, and in Will Percy she found fertile soil. He came home from school one day and announced to his mother that he had decided to become a priest. That he had to announce this at all suggests the incongruity it represented: Percy men did not grow up to be celibate priests; they grew up to be planters, politicians, and soldiers. As a family, the Percys were nominally religious, but not zealous believers. Percy's memory of this encounter with his mother was vivid: Camille Percy was tending to a Cape Jessamine flower, wearing a ribbon to keep her hair out of her eyes, when he walked up and announced his intention to enter the priesthood. She looked up from her flower bed, and the young boy saw in her eyes, perhaps for the first time, "scorn." She was "too late" in hiding it, he later wrote; her expression—which must have communicated her consternation with his eccentricity—was branded into his memory. As was his practice, Percy quickly moved the focus of his narrative off his mother and onto himself. "I must have been an unbearable little prig," he exclaimed. Despite his mother's disapproval, though, he pursued God with fervor; he went to confession and mass, prayed and even fasted "on the sly." He was determined, he said, to be perfect.[30]

His parents pulled him out of the convent and placed him under the tutelage of Judge Griffin, a neighbor of the Percys who had never taught and who insisted there was no God. He was "the town atheist." In time, Will Percy came to see Judge Griffin as a saint. His house was an oasis of inventiveness and excitement to the curious young boy. It was littered with stacks of books, the judge's half-finished inventions, old dogs, and roller skates. In Judge Griffin, Percy found a model of learning, an older man who both loved him and challenged him, a guide to "knowledge of every world but this one, and much wisdom." He taught Percy about "eternal verities" and truths "the spirit seizes on and transmutes into its own strength." Percy figured the passing of knowledge from an older man to a younger man as a spiritual exchange—a theme that ran throughout both his life and his writing. Resonant with the Greek conception of education, pedagogy was not just intellectual enterprise but was also erotic. Percy wrote of the judge's "beautiful benign face" and the blissful but torturous "spasm of enjoyment" he felt when the judge read to him from *Othello*. Of Iago's lines in the first act, Percy wrote: "I knew in my soul it was pornography and I enjoyed it exquisitely." But it was too much for the ten-year-old Percy, still devoutly Catholic and striving for perfection. When Judge Griffin reached for the play the next morning, Percy said to him, "I don't want to read any more *Othello*. It's—it's immoral." The amused judge respected his wishes.[31]

When Percy's parents sensed their son was "growing a trifle remote from ordinary doings" under the judge's teaching, they placed him under two new tutors: Father Koestenbrock and E. E. Bass. Bass was the superintendent of Greenville's schools and today remains a town hero for the work he did in building what was then the state's best school system. In the mid-1890s, Percy went to him for afternoon tutoring. Bass was redheaded (though balding), intemperate, emotional, and generous. When his thoughts crescendoed as he sat, he flapped his knees together "very fast as if a grasshopper's sound-box ought to be between them." He was above all a gardener, and the love and capacity for wonder that he displayed in his garden translated into his affect as a teacher. His care for his students was akin to his care for his diverse plants: "it only mattered that they were living things mysteriously standing in the earth and reaching for the sun." One summer, he took Percy on his first trip away from Mississippi—to Arizona, where the two rode in a stagecoach pulled by ten horses from Flagstaff to the Grand Canyon. "It is God's most personal creation," Percy wrote of the canyon. "[Y]ou feel he's just walked off and is expected back any minute."[32]

Father Koestenbrock was the local Catholic priest, and before he began to tutor Will Percy, he had already heard the boy's confessions, delivered him sacraments, and prepared him for confirmation. Unlike the atheist Judge Griffin, Father Koestenbrock "was not a saint and nothing shocked him." He gave rambling discourses on Haydn's superiority to Mozart and Beethoven and asked uninterestedly if Percy could conjugate his Latin verbs. Percy took to his easy, abstracted manner and came to love him. Every so often, Percy would come for his lessons to find Father Koestenbrock sitting alone in his bedroom in his undershirt, and the priest would tell the boy to go away. He was a drinker, Percy learned, and this was his "first lesson in reconciling the irreconcilable." Father Koestenbrock would binge for several weeks at a time, and in Mississippi, men who did this were outcasts; yet, to Percy, the priest was not a bad man. Percy came to believe he was not immoral, just lonely. This realization was not merely about Father Koestenbrock, though, but also about himself: "I thought Father was single and unique in his loneliness: it was only the beginning of wisdom."[33]

Will Percy's childhood, at least as he remembered it, was peopled by diverse and often charming people—inventors, imaginers, travelers, and drinkers. His parents were background figures, his younger brother not a character at all, his closest companions black servants and their children. Percy identified himself as both on the inside and the outside of his home, both belonging to his family and his hometown and longing to escape them. He portrayed himself as an effeminate child in a hypermasculine place and time, a gender presentation that aligned him with emerging queer identities and suggested a broader range for how men could act and talk and think. His childhood experience was marked by several important relationships with men such as E. E. Bass and Judge Griffin, and probably others hidden from the historical record.

Percy left Greenville in 1900 and was gone for the better part of eight years. But he would never leave Greenville for good. He always came back to it, always called it home. This was due to a loving family who provided him wealth, education, and a degree of comfort. It was due to his father, a model to his son of civic sacrifice and service if not emotional intimacy and open-mindedness. It was due to the presence of his caring, fragile mother who would love her only son with both loyalty and heartache. "She would have enjoyed so a lot of normal children," Percy later explained to a friend. "It's an awful pity I have such a wild queer streak in me."[34]

3. SEWANEE

To me, my kinship with immortal things
Hath been too clear revealed.
—WILLIAM ALEXANDER PERCY, "Sappho in Levkas"

In July 1900 Percy boarded a train bound for Tennessee. He was alone; his parents had left for a two-month tour of Europe a few weeks before. His father sent him with a letter of introduction. "His mother and I, of course, feel some solicitude about him, as he has never been away from home alone before," LeRoy Percy wrote of his son. "If anything should happen to the small chap I shall be some distance away." He asked a local man to keep an eye on his son and promised he was good for the bank draft should he need any money.[1]

Some days after Percy left Greenville, he arrived in Cowan, Tennessee, where he switched to a small train called the Mountain Goat that bumped and smoked and groaned a thousand feet up onto the Cumberland Plateau, where it deposited him at the edge of the hamlet of Sewanee, home to the University of the South. One can imagine him standing on the train platform with a trunk full of clothes and a letter from his father, a betrousered fifteen-year-old boy looking out onto a dusty southern town. Tennessee in 1900 may seem to have been an unlikely place and time for a sexual and spiritual awakening, there in the Jim Crow South in the midst of segregation, racial violence, agricultural poverty, and the folks who would put John Scopes on trial. Sewanee was a rural and conservative place. It was in the woods and in the mountains, faraway from any city; students read liturgy every morning in chapel; professors wore robes and tutored in Greek and Latin. These qualities, though—the physical beauty of the world, the constant talk of God, the emphasis on classical learning—opened up new ways of thinking and relating for Will Percy.

Episcopal bishops, planters, and educators conceived of the University of the South at the height of the cotton boom in the mid-nineteenth century as a place to educate sons of the southern gentry. They raised over half a million dollars to establish a university that would be "the Oxford of America."[2] These early leaders articulated the ideals of the school in terms of gender: "Sewanee was founded to make men," recalled an early Sewanee chancellor. Its founding generation of planters and priests included men like Leonidas L. Polk, Stephen Elliot, and James Otey: "men in every way themselves, who had known ultimate experiences of physical, intellectual, and spiritual manhood in periods of war and peace, they sought the education and development of the whole man."[3]

When the war came, the university invested its endowment in Confederate bonds. The money disappeared, but the hopes for the school did not. Sewanee admitted its first class in 1868, and the character and ideals of the school remained much the same when Percy arrived in 1900: it was a school devoted to cultivating physical, intellectual, and spiritual manhood. These three strains composed the larger aim of education at Sewanee, which was to make men whole. As a student editorial exclaimed a few years before Percy's arrival, no man "feels his manhood unless he is physically, as well as morally and mentally strong."[4] Sports teams—especially football—developed the bodies of men. Compulsory chapel enriched their spirits. And most important for Percy's story, Sewanee modeled itself on the Oxonian and classical pedagogical traditions in order to cultivate intellectual manhood. The founders of the university believed that Oxford was the most worthy university to emulate, and they did: the structure of Sewanee's administration, the campus architecture, and the Order of the Gownsmen all harkened back to Oxford. And also like Oxford, Sewanee placed heavy emphasis on the classics. One Sewanee historian wrote of the faculty of the late nineteenth and early twentieth centuries: "These men had much Latin and more Greek. They breathed the bracing air of the civilization that was Athens and they kept alive on Sewanee Mountain Socratic wisdom, Platonic idealism, Aristotelian balance."[5]

Before we return to Will Percy, standing at the edge of town with his trunk and his letter, we need to understand the contours of the intellectual world he was about to enter. Sewanee's emphasis on the classics takes on a great deal of significance when placed into a broader context. The cultural conversation about manhood and sexuality that would be centrally important to Will Percy, the conversation that would shape his values and benefit from his input, originated largely at Oxford. Some background is necessary.

The systematic study of Greek philosophy, history, and poetry came to occupy a central place in British culture during the nineteenth century, a shift that had profound consequences for later expressions of love between men in Europe and America. To nineteenth-century British intellectuals like Benjamin Jowett, Matthew Arnold, John Stuart Mill, and George Grote, the study of ancient Greek society suggested powerful correctives to what they saw as the cultural stagnation created by modernity. They viewed modernity, and the nineteenth century in particular, as a distinct period of history in which industrial capitalism, urban life, and possessive individualism circumscribed the potential for full human experience. The result of this was a deadening of the senses, a spiritual, intellectual, and emotional decay. Men were not thriving in the modern world; they were corrupted by it. As historians like Jackson Lears and Linda Dowling have so ably shown, though it was officially "the Age of Confidence," it was also an era marked by anxiety, restlessness, and doubt. In the eyes of many Victorian intellectuals, human progress had not been very progressive.[6]

In contrast, many at that time felt that the culture of ancient Greece offered an antidote. Refinement, simplicity, communal harmony, and intellectual and spiritual richness were among the many virtues that seemed to have flourished there. They saw in its history a wellspring for their own tired times. This brand of Hellenism—the celebration of classical Greece as the ideal society, distinct from modern life but with the power to transform it—became a dominant strain of nineteenth-century European thought. Throughout the Western world—and, indeed, throughout the American South in this same period—Hellenism was an intellectual tradition that enjoyed significant cultural legitimacy. To a large extent, to be "civilized" implied a mastery and appreciation of the classics. This was a conservative way of thinking—that society needs to look back to ancient Greece in order to preserve timeless values essential to human civilization. But as we will see, many people found in this conservative milieu ingredients for a liberatory perspective on sexuality.[7]

Throughout the century, educators revamped the university pedagogical system—and Oxford in particular—to make Hellenism the centerpiece of British higher education. An unintended consequence of placing the study of Greece at the center of the all-male culture of the university, Linda Dowling has persuasively argued, was that many students' immersion in Greek texts led them to develop a "homosexual counterdiscourse" that justified and valorized love between men. Men from Walter Pater and John Addington Symonds to Oscar Wilde, Charles Kains-Jackson, Edward Carpenter, and, in America, Will Percy and others found abundant evidence of culturally sanctioned same-sex expression within what they regarded as the natural and honest culture of ancient Greece. The ideal of "Greek love," as it came to be known, found its most public expression in Oscar Wilde's famous sodomy trials of 1895, as a result of which he was convicted and imprisoned. During cross-examination, Wilde famously articulated a philosophy of same-sex relationships that had been developing in Europe throughout the nineteenth century. "The 'love that dare not speak its name' in this century is such a great affection of an elder man for a younger man as there was between David and Jonathan, such as Plato made the very basis of his philosophy, and such as you find in the sonnets of Michelangelo and Shakespeare," Wilde testified. "It is that deep, spiritual affection that is as pure as it is perfect. … That it should be so the world does not understand. The world mocks it and sometimes puts one in the pillory for it."[8]

Though Wilde's trial contained perhaps the most sensational testimony of Greek love, he was giving voice to several generations of intellectuals who had been studying ancient Greece and finding in it a history through which to understand and affirm their desire. Like their British counterparts, German and Swiss Hellenists such as Karl Otfried Müller, Heinrich Hossli, and Karl Heinrich Ulrichs had documented and celebrated the history of Greek "pederasty"—a form of "spiritual love" between an older and a younger man. This pederastic relationship was neither always nor merely sexual. Though most of these men doubtless desired and experienced sexual relationships with other men, the concept of Greek, or pederastic, love was an ideal type that emphasized intellectual and spiritual fervor in greater measure than sexual intercourse. Pederasty was not simply a structure for male relationships; it was also a concept men employed as a broader justification for the legitimacy and, indeed, the superiority of homosexual love. To the men of this generation labeled by Victorian culture as "inverts" and "sodomites"— and for whom criminal charges for homosexual activity were a real possibility—pederasty, as an erotic expression inseparable from "spiritual love," possessed obvious appeal.[9]

Pederasty should not be conflated with pedophilia. For Will Percy in particular, the historical record suggests his intimates were roughly his own age. But the concept of pederasty, which often focused on the love of male youths, was a central feature of Percy's thinking. The significance of this lies primarily in the relationship between gay love and pedagogy: in discussing and defending homosexual desire and practice, Percy focused less on the physical act of sex than on the transmission of spiritual and intellectual wisdom. The pairing of men with boys symbolized the teacher/student relationship and emphasized the ways in which homosexual love was uplifting and empowering. Many thinkers of this generation drew from this concept to articulate what they viewed as the purity of love between men—in contrast to the current and historical emphasis on gay love as corrupt and corrupting. This understanding of pederasty was most often grounded in a reading of Plato's "erotic dialogues," the *Symposium* and *Phaedrus*, texts that help shed light on this tradition of Hellenism that profoundly influenced Will Percy.

The *Symposium*, a set of speeches on the topic of erotic love, particularly influenced the Hellenists with its frank discussion of love between men. Socrates, Plato's teacher, presides over this discussion and amends his pupils' various views on the true nature of Eros. After the pupils have spoken and attempted to make sense of love in general, and the love of men for other men in particular, Socrates engages the issue by describing a conversation he once had with Diotima, an expert on love. Diotima had explained to him that the god Eros was conceived at a celebration of the birth of Aphrodite, the goddess of beauty. Eros was thenceforth a follower of Aphrodite—so all Eros is "love of what is beautiful." What is truly beautiful, Diotima said, is reproduction, both physical and mental. Mortals have an innate desire for immortality, and they satisfy this desire by reproducing. "Those whose creative urge is physical," Diotima explained, "tend to turn to women, and pursue Eros by this route. . . . In others the impulse is mental or spiritual—people who are creative mentally, much more than physically." This type of creative man, whose desire is to seek beauty and to reproduce ideas, will likely find a younger man he finds beautiful. When he does, "He'll drop everything and embark on long conversations about goodness. . . . Now that he's made contact with someone beautiful, and made friends with him, he can produce and bring to birth what he long ago conceived. . . . They form much firmer friendships, because they are jointly responsible for finer, and more lasting, offspring." Diotima puts a higher value on such "intellectual friendship," free from the biological exigencies of physical reproduction, as the source of art and creativity in Greek culture. Socrates gives his approval of this explanation of male love, and the group applauds its ingenuity.[10]

Socrates's apparent endorsement of love between men was liberating for many and became a cornerstone of male homosexual culture in the late nineteenth and early twentieth centuries. To men such as Will Percy, the key words in Diotima's explanation of Greek spiritual procreancy were "beauty" and "friendship," concepts central to the "coded counterdiscourse" that Dowling describes as well as the language that pervades Percy's writings. Beauty came to symbolize devotion to earthly ecstasy and aesthetic perfection, and in homosexual writing its ideal form was male love. The British historian and classicist John Addington Symonds, for example, declared: "I love beauty with a passion that burns the more I grow old. I love beauty above virtue, & think that nowhere is beauty more eminent than in young men." The figure of the male youth was not necessarily a sexual object but was symbolic of the purity and beauty of the male body and love between men. Friendship, or comradeship, was the corollary to love of beauty and signified a relationship between two men. Because these relationships were sometimes but not exclusively between an older man and a younger man, writers often conflated terms such as "friendship," "pederasty," and "Greek love" in order to reflect the broader legitimacy of gay desire. Many homosexual men in this era celebrated, in the words of Oscar Wilde, "the intellectual loves or romantic friendships of the Hellenes." The primary literary journal for pederastic poetry was entitled *The Quorum: A Magazine of Friendship*, while the first English anthology of homoerotic verse was entitled *Iolaus: An Anthology of Friendship*. A standard vocabulary was almost ubiquitous in homosexual writing in this era—one scholar has called it a "barely obscured code" that allowed communication about such illegal matters—and Will Percy's correspondence, diaries, and poetry are replete with its language and related themes.[11]

The philosophy of nourishing the artistic and creative soul through male relationships was already present in the British pedagogical system, and it manifested itself at Sewanee as well. Students developed close intellectual friendships among themselves and with their professors. These were not necessarily homosexual, but they did contain a homoeroticism that grew out of a mutual love of beauty and respect for learning. One of Percy's favorite professors was William Porcher DuBose, a theologian, classicist, and legendary Sewanee teacher. In his memoir, DuBose tried "to account for the peculiarly close and personal relations which from the beginning grew up between myself and my immediate students." He described the intellectual relationships that created trust and led to an increased sense of personal wholeness. "I was finding and making myself in and with and through and by, as well as upon, them," he wrote. "They both took more from me and gave me more than I ever asked or deserved. ... I became in many instances the intimate personal friend of many of my students, their confidant in love, their counselor in difficulty or trouble, their companion, so far as presence and sympathy could go, in amusement or play."[12]

This is not to say that William Porcher DuBose was "a homosexual." That category of identity was not widely used at the turn of the century, though homosexuals and homosexual cultures were increasingly visible in American culture at the time. It is to say, however, that when Will Percy picked up his things and walked to campus in 1900, he was walking into a place where a specific language of male friendship was in circulation. He was walking into a place where intellectual friendships were valued, where some professors viewed pedagogy as a process of mutual spiritual growth, and where the love of beauty was a chief virtue. One classics professor in particular, Huger Jervey, explicitly linked his teaching of Greek with his own homosexuality. Percy, as we will see, followed the lead of his American and British counterparts in interpreting classical history as legitimizing and celebrating homosexual love.

The extant evidence from this period suggests that college was a significant turning point in Percy's life with regard to spirituality and sexuality. At Sewanee, Percy lost his faith in Catholicism but gained a different form of spiritual awareness that grew primarily out of the mutual love of beauty among and between men. This love of beauty was inextricably linked with homoerotic desire. Percy described his experience at Sewanee as one in which he came to a new understanding of himself as a sexual being, and he did so in concert with several others.

So in July 1900, Will Percy got a room at a boardinghouse and unpacked his trunk. "I had never known a confidant or been in love," he later wrote of himself as a fifteen-year-old boy arriving at college. His instructions from his father were to enter the military prep school next to the university and prepare for college. But Percy took one look at the prep-school boys drilling and marching in their "dusty ill-kept uniforms" and decided it was not for him. "I suspected they smelled bad," he concluded.[13] He took the Sewanee entrance exams and passed. On August 10, 1900, he signed into the school roster: "William Alexander Percy, Age 15, Weight 90, Height 5.'"[14]

"There's no way to tell of youth or of Sewanee," Percy wrote. "It must be done obliquely and by parable." Percy's parable of Sewanee engages the Hellenist themes of community, mutual love of beauty, and intimate intellectual friendships. "It is Arcadia," he explained. "Not the one that never used to be, but the one that many people always live in; only this one can be shared."[15] Percy's oblique reference becomes more direct when his key words and themes are placed in context. The metaphor of "Arcadia" has long been central to homoerotic male writing. Arcadia is a mountainous and remote region in Greece that historically was the province of shepherds and herdsmen and one of the reported birthplaces of Zeus. The historian Byrne R. S. Fone rightly points out that the "Arcadian ideal" has been a consistent theme in the homosexual literary tradition employed for three primary reasons. First,

> to suggest a place where it is safe to be gay: where gay men can be free from the outlaw status society confers upon us, where homosexuality can be revealed and spoken of without reprisal, and where homosexual love can be consummated without concern for the punishment or scorn of the world; 2) to imply the presence of gay love and sensibility in a text that otherwise makes no explicit statement about homosexuality; and 3) to establish a metaphor for certain spiritual values and myths prevalent in homosexual literature and life, namely, that homosexuality is superior to heterosexuality and is a divinely sanctioned means to an understanding of the good and the beautiful, and that the search for the Ideal Friend is one of the major undertakings of the homosexual life.[16]

Classic homoerotic texts, Fone argues, such as Virgil's *Second Eclogue*, Thomas Mann's *Death in Venice*, Edward Prime Stevenson's *Imre*, E. M. Forster's *Maurice*, and others all use Arcadia as both a metaphor for homosexual love and a site for homosexual encounter. Rustic forest settings, often called "greenwoods" and peopled not only with humans but also with satyrs, nymphs, and pans, have historically been prevalent in gay male writing in cultures where men could not write of their intimate selves without social and legal reprisal. It was in just this manner that Percy wrote about Sewanee, combining the sexually charged atmosphere of the bucolic male college with a narrative of his personal awakening.

The University of the South enrolled about 300 students and was set atop Sewanee Mountain. During his freshman year, Percy joined a fraternity, studied hard, and adored his professors, especially John Bell Henneman and William Porcher DuBose, whom Percy described as "a tiny silver saint who lived elsewhere, being more conversant with the tongues of angels than of men." These men would hold forth in classes about Aristotle, Chaucer, Shakespeare, and Beowulf, and DuBose at times would become so rapt at his own profundity that he would suspend his monologue and stare off into the distance. The students would "tiptoe out of the class, feeling luminous."[17]

Percy's most influential professor was Huger Jervey. Jervey was twenty-two years old in 1900 and was teaching Greek at his alma mater before he would eventually go on to become a dean at Columbia University in New York. Percy and Jervey became close both in Jervey's Greek classes and through the Alpha Tau Omega fraternity, of which Percy was a member and Jervey

Huger Wilkinson Jervey (1878–1949), ca. 1900. Huger Jervey was Will Percy's professor of Greek at Sewanee and later became dean of the Parker School of International Studies and professor of law at Columbia University. After 1925, Jervey and Percy were co-owners of Brinkwood, their summer home in Sewanee, Tennessee. (Courtesy of the archives, Jessie Ball duPont Library, University of the South, Sewanee, Tennessee)

an alumnus. They remained close throughout their lives, traveling often to Greece and Italy and purchasing a summer home together in Sewanee in 1925. Jervey was remembered by Sewanee locals as having been charismatic, full of wit and charm, and not a little controversial. Remembering back to her childhood in Sewanee in the 1930s, one local woman assumed Jervey "was most likely gay with Mr. Will."[18] Another woman wrote in her diary about Jervey's openness about his own homosexuality, and how he seemed always to steer conversations with her toward contemporary attitudes about sexuality. He was always interested if she had lesbian friends, she said, and "he says that he would almost advise young people to be as wild as sin and coquettes as well as lesbians."[19]

Percy and Jervey may or may not have been "gay" together, which in this recollection implied they had sex with one another. More accurately, in the context of Sewanee in 1900, Percy and Jervey's relationship should be viewed as pederastic. Jervey was seven years older than Percy and was primarily responsible for teaching him Greek. They shared a mutual love of the ancients, and it is not difficult to imagine them embarking on "long conversations about goodness." In his memoir, Percy wrote that Jervey was "brilliant and bumptious then, brilliant and wise now, and so human."[20] Jervey and Percy's relationship was doubtless pederastic; one can also safely conjecture it was sexual at some point.

Before college, Percy explained, he had been "utterly without intimates." At Sewanee, though, he found himself "among young creatures of charm and humor, more experienced than I, but friendly and fascinating." Percy wrote delicately of the friends he made at Sewanee and the profound connection they shared. He described them as imparting to him an otherworldly wisdom, a new angle from which to view life: "The springtime was on them and they taught and tended me in the greenwoods as the Centaurs did Achilles— I don't know how I ever recovered to draw my own bow." Percy's description of them indicates something of their importance in his young life:

> Percy Huger, noble and beautiful like a sleepy St. Bernard; Elliot Cage, full of dance-steps and song snatches, tender and protective, and sad beneath; Paul Ellerbe, who first read me Dover Beach, thereby disclosing the rosy mountain-ranges of the Victorians; Harold Abrams, dark and romantic with his violin, quoting the *Rubáiyát* and discoursing on Shaw; Parson Masterson, jostling with religion, unexpected and quaint; Sinkler Manning, a knight who met a knight's death at Montfaucon; Arthur Gray, full of iridescence, discovering new paths and views in the woods and the world.[21]

Sinkler Manning in particular became one of Percy's best friends; he was the other person, in addition to Harold Bruff, Percy described as "one I understood and who understood me, one who I knew could never fail me."[22] Manning was born on a large and prosperous plantation in the South Carolina low country, his father a wealthy planter-businessman and his mother a descendant of one of the South's oldest families, the Merediths. His father would eventually become the governor of South Carolina during World War I, one of six South Carolina governors the family produced. The Manning family, one friend said, "represents everything that is best in the Old South." They were refined, well connected, wealthy, and genteel. Sinkler Manning studied English at Sewanee and became a reporter for the *New York Times* after graduation.[23]

Sewanee was an ideal place for young men like Percy and Manning to form deep friendships; there was time for long conversations, space for long walks. Sewanee was "a long way away," Percy explained, "in the middle of the woods." And those woods, to Percy and his friends, were beautiful. The dusting of snow in winter was replaced in springtime by dogwoods, anemones, hepaticas, azaleas, and violets; the limbs of trees shrouded "puffs of ghost," and the perfume of wild honeysuckle, Percy said, was "actually dangerous, so pagan." These delights of the woods were the province of Sewanee youths. The "faun-like" students read poetry to one another in the forest, searched out sellers of mountain whiskey on nearby farms, and gathered in one another's rooms to play poker and piano. One time, Percy watched another student, wearing only his slippers and a wet towel on his head, read aloud from *Ode to a Nightingale*. Another time, a friend recited a poem to Percy on a hillside near campus, and the poem made the "two lads in a greenwood more shimmery and plumed."[24]

Percy described his college intimates, the Arcadians, as otherworldly. Their ears were "slightly more pointed and tawny furred, a bit of leafiness somewhere in their eyes." He called them "Pan and Dionysos," the Greek gods of wild nature and pleasure, respectively. They were "sweet" to their cores, and their charm was of the lineage of "Socrates and Jesus and St. Francis and Sir Philip Sidney and Lovelace and Stevenson." Their intimate contact with the beauty of the earth, the transcendent language of the King James Bible read to them each morning, and the environment of learning created "the tremulous awe and reverence you find in the recesses of the Arcadian soul—at least you can find them if you are wary and part very gently the sun-spotted greenery of Pan." By portraying his intimates as gods and his college setting as Arcadia, Percy tapped into a long-standing tradition in homoerotic writing that used classical and bucolic metaphor to suggest male intimacy, knowingness, and goodness.[25]

Percy's "sojourn in the greenwoods," as he called it, was a challenge for him to later write about in part because what he learned there were "the imponderables." Percy portrayed coming of age at Sewanee as a journey toward spiritual knowledge. This is particularly important because this journey included, at the age of sixteen, the loss of his faith in Christianity. While a freshman, Percy rode a horse ten miles to the nearest Catholic church to go to confession and mass—a practice all the more remarkable given Sewanee's heavy Episcopal emphasis and its daily compulsory chapel. As in Greenville, though, Percy ignored the perplexity of his peers and pursued his faith, albeit with anguish. "I'm certain Shelley never sank upon the thorns of life and bled nearly so often as I did between ten and sixteen," he wrote. "To be at once intellectually honest and religious is a rack on which many have perished and on which I writhed dumbly, for I knew even then there were certain things which, like overwhelming physical pain, you must fight out alone, at the bottom of your own dark well, beyond ministration of assuagement or word of advice, incommunicado and leper-lonely." Throughout his freshman year Percy went to receive communion, and as he did he examined his conscience. He questioned the church's ability to give meaning to his life and provide community, the ability of Christ to forgive him his sins—and whether forgiveness was what he needed. Silently and sadly, he left the church: "I knew there was no use going, no priest could absolve me, no church could direct my life or my judgment, what most believed I could not believe."[26]

Throughout his life, Percy expressed admiration for Jesus, but he felt that the church had corrupted Jesus's message of grace and turned it instead into a prescription for morality. The church, he believed, was interested in control, not love. The end result for Christendom was a society that limited the possibility for authentic human experience—the ability to truly give and receive love, exhibit kindness, and behold the beauty in the world. Percy illuminated this theme in his poem "An Epistle from Corinth." He wrote from the perspective of a first-century Corinthian who had recently read the letters of the Apostle Paul. The narrator laments:

> Paul, Paul, I'd give
> My Greek inheritance, my wealth and youth,
> To Speak one evening with that Christ you love
> And never saw and cannot understand!

He admonishes Paul for limiting the richness of Christ's message, for overemphasizing the afterlife and underemphasizing "the perfumed, warm, corporeal parts of us." Paul was blinded to the body and its wonders, he felt. "Forgive me follower of Jesus," the poem concludes,

> I
> Am Greek, all Greek; I know the loveliness
> Of flesh and its sweet snare.

To Percy, the Greeks loved their bodies and the Christians did not. The Greeks sought the sublime while alive and the Christians afterward. Percy cast his lot with the Greeks.[27]

Percy's struggle for faith should not be construed as merely torment over sexuality. Sexual desire was a regular focus in Percy's mind—to explain it, to provide context for it, to act on it. But his existential dilemmas were those of many a modern intellectual: how to find a source of meaning outside the self; how to explain the range of emotion inside one's body; what to do with beauty and love and grace as well as doubt and lust and loathing. His loss of Christian faith while in college marked a loss of religiosity but not of spirituality, nor of the struggle for existential explanation. The spiritual realm was one with which Percy wrestled throughout his life. The themes in his poetry in particular suggest that rather than lose faith altogether, he transferred his faith to a kind of aestheticism—the love of beauty as a portal to the sublime. For Percy, this was love without dogma and faith without a church, though it did provide a community of like-minded people.

And as for many others, the ideal manifestation of beauty was the human body. Percy's most common manner of articulating beauty and the sublime was through his depiction of men and male bodies. The fusion of spiritual wholeness and homoerotic desire is the main theme of a poem he wrote about Sewanee. "Sappho in Levkas," Percy often said, was one of his favorites.[28] The poem is set in ancient Greece, and one reader wrote to him after reading it to ask if Percy wrote the poem in Greece. Percy replied, "I had not visited Greece when I wrote 'Sappho,' and I am afraid the scene of Sappho is Sewanee."[29]

"Sappho in Levkas" is narrated by the poet Sappho, who was born in the seventh century BCE on the Greek island of Lesbos. Sappho is often depicted as either lesbian or bisexual in classical mythology and, according to myth, she committed suicide because of her torment over her love for a shepherd boy, Phaon. Percy's poem is an imagining of Sappho's last moments, during which she confesses her carnal sin to the god Zeus as she stands at the edge of a precipice. Several of Percy's poems employ female narrators who sing of male beauty—a technique that allowed Percy to write about same-sex desire under the guise of heterosexual pairings. In this case, the poem becomes a meditation on the beauty of Phaon and the ecstasy of physical love—even as it is marked by Sappho's anguished hope for harmony between physical sex and spiritual love. "Sappho in Levkas" should be read with an eye to its distinctly pederastic themes and language. It is a poem in which Percy himself was considering the spiritual and physical nature of sex. It is useful to follow Percy's suggestion and imagine that Levkas is Sewanee and, by extension, that Sappho is Percy. As such, it narrates an important story about an important moment in Percy's life: it is a retelling of his sexual awakening. The poem's confession is detailed, erotic, and thorough, but, as one of Percy's friends noted, "there is no repentance."[30]

"Sappho" is a poem about lovers meeting in the woods. The poem is marked by Sappho's struggle to love and understand beauty, which she feels she has done: her life has been "high and full of joy" and she thanks Zeus "that in all life / 'Twas mine to see goodness." She also celebrates her friendships, her companions who are "heroes and kings, sea-wanderers, poets, priests," all of whom

> fervent, pass
> The flame of righteousness and truth
> To sequent generations yet asleep.

Indeed, the poem is a celebration—of beauty, of music, of the loveliness of the gods and god in man. "Thou has made beauty mine own element," Sappho tells Zeus, "taught me to drift, a burnished leaf, / Down the long winds of ecstasy."[31] The poem echoes Percy's prose writings about Sewanee, where his friends "taught and tended [him] in the greenwoods" and showed him "new paths and views in the woods and the world."

Conflict enters the narrative with the appearance of Phaon, "A slim, brown shepherd boy with windy eyes / And a spring upon his mouth!" As often as possible, Sappho steals away, "up from the quiet village from the hills," to the mountain meadows where she can watch Phaon. She sits on a hill above him and watches,

> gazing—
> Drinking the poison of his loveliness.
> For he was lovelier than the youthful day;
> More beautiful than silver, naked Ganymede!

Sappho becomes filled with lust, a feeling she is troubled by but cannot suppress. No earthly thing, Sappho recalls, is

> plumed with wilder rapture than my heart!
> Nor was the earth's red longing for fruition
> More hot than mine for Phaon.

Sappho becomes obsessed with the sight of his body; she takes every chance to "glimpse his loveliness" and confesses that her "utmost intellect was bent to plan / Assurance of chance meetings."

The poem is fraught with sexual tension, and its climax comes when Sappho awakens in the middle of one night:

> Haggard and parched, love's frenzy caught me up
> And bore me from my dream-hot bed into the night.
> My feet unconscious chose those pastures known
> to love.

When she arrives in the pasture, she sees Phaon, "And on the visioning lept all the pity of / My life—vexing and hounding me." She tells Phaon of her love for him and awkwardly asks for a kiss. The radiance leaves Phaon's face, and she feels "pain steal up like age. Within me died / All fire." Sensing rejection, she turns to leave, filled with anguish and guilt. But he takes her in his arms, "all gentleness, and on my mouth lay his, a long, long kiss." The two share a "snatch of starved, impossible delight" in the moonlight.

The language Percy chose to describe this sexual encounter recalls Diotima's idea that all humans desire immortality through reproduction, and some men achieve this through relationships with other men. Indeed, Sappho describes her relationship with Phaon as a kind of rebirth: "Unto perfection I was born," she says, remembering their consummation. Phaon "recalled me to myself." The poem is replete with metaphors of love as regeneration: Phaon is lovelier than "the first strong tulip" of April and reveals to Sappho "my kinship with immortal things." Following the pederastic model of love that uplifts the younger man, Sappho claims that

> Out of the evil of my passioning came good!
> For Phaon, Phaon loved me as a goddess sent,
> And, curbing grossness, looked to me for praise.

And the uplift is mutual. Sappho becomes invigorated by the retelling of their encounter:

> Oh, let the anguished crimson of his mouth
> Seek fire from mine, and all his brown, light grace
> Flame into strength to crush my paleness.

"Sappho in Levkas" can and should be read as a recounting of Percy's sexual awakening, a poem about a nighttime lovers' meeting in the woods near Sewanee around 1900. Perhaps Percy was writing about Sinkler Manning, perhaps another Sewanee student, perhaps a local teenager. In addition to this narrative content, the poem should be read as an apologia for same-sex love and a statement of the difficulty Percy had in coming to terms with his desire. Recall Percy's fervent Catholicism, his devotion so intense that he rode a horse ten miles through the woods to go to mass. Sappho's lament echoes Percy's anxious quest to be perfect, to find purity in being. "O night, am I the only struggling thing?" Sappho asks. "Mine eyes blur, and my throat is hurt / With welling pain." In a line that recalls Percy's Catholic childhood, Sappho says: "I could not quite escape that holiness / The sacred years had bred!" The crux of the struggle for Sappho, for Percy, was to know and understand what is truly holy, what is sacred, while at the same time resisting what is vulgar. It was to come to a workable understanding of love, regardless of what others thought it meant.

The tension created by loving perfect beauty while occupying a human body (and living in human society) was the anguish of Sappho and, by extension, of Will Percy. The poem speaks of the reality of pain and the fleeting nature of ecstasy. But while the poem is realistic about suffering and distrustful of mere lust, it expresses no ambivalence about love. It was love that recalled Sappho to herself, that gave her grace. It was love that uplifted Phaon and allowed them both, if only for a moment, an entry into the sublime. "Sappho" is suggestive of Percy's larger ambition to fuse homosexual desire and experience with moral legitimacy. His emphasis in the poem, and throughout his life, was not on sex for the sake of mere physical pleasure but on male relationships as an ideal type that increased love in a world defined by its lack.

When we read this poem alongside Percy's other writings about Sewanee, it becomes all the more clear that it was there that Percy came to think of homosexuality as a superior form of love. As Fone suggests, queer men often saw their sexuality as a "divinely sanctioned means to an understanding of the good and the beautiful," and Percy did just this in his own writing.[32] At the end of his recollections on Sewanee in his memoir, he figuratively positioned himself in a tower looking out of a window onto the world. He preferred this perspective, he said, because it was the perspective of Arcadians, who had special access to the good and the beautiful. They were eternally leaning out of the windows of their tower, viewing the world with an enchanted eye: "watching the leaves shake in the sunlight, the clouds tumble their soundless bales of purple down the long slopes, the seasons eternally up to tricks of beauty, laughing at things that only distance and height reveal humor in, and talking, talking, talking—the enchanting unstained silver of their voices spilling over the bright branches down into the still happy coves."[33]

Percy portrayed his sexual awakening as a hard-earned discovery of true delight, an introduction to a network of people who recognized and understood one another. "Sometimes you of the valley may not recognize them," he wrote of Arcadians, "though without introduction they are known of each other." These men also viewed the world from a different vantage point. Peering out onto the machinations of everyday life with the ability to transcend it was, to Percy, a central task of life: to be able to see and appreciate the shimmering leaves of autumn and take joy at the passing of winter, to talk to another who *understood*—this was victory in a world full of lonely monotony and emptiness.

Percy graduated from Sewanee in 1904, but before he did, he learned a great deal about the kinds of relationships he valued, the kinds of people he would live the rest of his life with. To place his writings about Sewanee in the larger context of homoerotic writing during this period is to understand the language he spoke, the idiom of Greek love, the coded vocabulary through which he both revealed and protected himself. It is to understand a measure of his delight at loving beauty, his possession of what he felt to be a superior wisdom in a world where few recognized or appreciated it. It was in Tennessee during the first years of the new century where he learned that there were many who did. It was knowledge he would take with him throughout the world.

4. SOUTHERNER IN EUROPE

The Greeks practiced bisexuality honestly
and simply without thought or condemnation.
—WILLIAM ALEXANDER PERCY, *Lanterns on the Levee*

LeRoy and Camille Percy traveled to Sewanee in June 1904 to attend the graduation of their only son. Their other son, LeRoy Percy Jr., died in a hunting accident in 1902. He had loved to hunt and fish and play sports. He seemed destined to follow in the hearty, sturdy footsteps of his namesake. Even after the ten-year-old was shot in the stomach with a rifle, his first words to his father were, "Hello Pop, I am alright." He died eight days later. LeRoy Percy wrote to Will Percy at Sewanee: "I knew that the flare would be gone from the sky and the music from the laughter of children forever."[1]

LeRoy Jr.'s death seemed to bring the family closer together. It certainly deepened Will Percy's devotion to his parents. They were a family of three now; as his parents' only son, Percy's feelings of duty toward them intensified. The three of them spent the summer vacationing together at Aunt Nana Percy's farm in Virginia. By this time, Percy's childhood playmates Ligey, Martha, Cora, and Friday were too old to be playmates. Percy was nineteen years old and had a college degree; Ligey, Martha, Cora, and Friday by this age would have been working. If they saw one another at all, they would likely have now called him "Mr. Will." Rather than play with them in the creeks and Aspen stands, he spent the summer of 1904 discussing his future with his parents.

Part of the family's task that summer was to determine Will Percy's plan of action. "Father thought I'd overstudied," Percy recalled, knowingly and with irony—though he did concede, "I was undoubtedly puny." He was barely five feet tall, barely 100 pounds. LeRoy Percy shared the anxiety of the age that American education was turning men into sissies. He agreed with his friend Teddy Roosevelt, with whom he had recently been bear hunting, that young men needed physical challenge—warfare if it was available and just—and strenuous activity. Will Percy had not spent his years at Sewanee playing football or improving his physical strength but rather reading poetry and studying the classics. LeRoy likely suggested something rough. Percy recalled of the summer: "Had there been dude ranches in those days I don't doubt I should have landed on the back of a Broncho and swung a lariat with the worst of them."[2]

But Will Percy had a different idea. "From first childhood," he wrote, "I had saved every penny of birthday and Christmas money for a trip abroad. It was my obsession, my one mundane objective." He convinced his parents that he should move to Paris for a year. They either implicitly or explicitly asked him what kind of physical challenge this would bring him, because he promised them he would take fencing lessons. The compromise worked and they consented, he recalled, "dubiously."[3]

In August Percy boarded a steamship bound for Europe. The Paris he arrived in was a historic metropolis characterized by industrial modernity and *belle époque* creative culture. The Eiffel Tower, constructed in 1889, stood on the bank of the Seine, a spectacle of technical achievement and a radical disruption of the Paris landscape. In the middle of the river stood Notre Dame, for over 700 years a symbol of the Catholic faith, the keeper of moral law, the mediate between God and man. Just across the river, where Percy rented a room, was the Latin Quarter and Montparnasse on the Left Bank, the secular cathedral of literary salons and socialist clubs and artists like Pablo Picasso, Max Jacob, and Natalie Clifford Barney. Across the entire city, historians have shown, Paris had a highly developed queer sexual subculture that was characterized by public visibility and recognizable behavior patterns.[4] Percy was doubtless aware of this subculture, and his time in Paris was a continuation of that process he had begun in Mississippi and Tennessee: trying to understand and to realize himself as a full spiritual, intellectual, and physical being. Evidence from his year abroad suggests Percy's enduring concern with the relationship between sexual desire and cultural authority. What was appropriate to do with one's own body? What authority determined sexual values? In a time and place where Christian sexual ethics predominated, what did that mean for those, like Percy, who had left the faith? As we will see, Percy engaged these questions by looking to art, to literature, and to history.

Will Percy moved into a four-room boardinghouse on Rue de Vaugirard. His room had a red-tile floor, a cracked ceiling stained with candle smoke, and a view of chimneys, rooftops, and clotheslines. He furnished his room with a piano. He wrote to his mother that the room had "snail-green wallpaper, tortured with a pattern which at times you imagine chrysanthemums, but at others you are sure must be spiders."[5] Despite his efforts to improve the place, he concluded that the furniture was "neither sittable nor lyable," and that nothing could be done about the moist, dowdy air. "It was a fit habitat for a rubber plant," he wrote.[6]

Percy shared this habitat with three others: a Polish medical student with one green and one yellow eye, the *femme de chambre* Marie, and a prostitute. At first, Percy felt moral revulsion—"I had the American contempt for whores," he remembered—but in time, he softened his view. His housemates referred to her as "*la pauvre*" and felt bad for her when business was down. "He [the Pole] and Marie taught me a great and needed lesson in compassion," Percy wrote.[7]

Immediately after his arrival, Percy signed up for two other lessons: French and fencing. "Monsieur Wagner (classical name, isn't it?) comes every day at ten," Percy told his mother, "and I make a violent attempt to pow-wow in French."[8] He also approached his fencing lessons with irony: "Tomorrow is my first fencing lesson. If I am not slain in our first combat I will report in further detail." He explained that his fencing master "is a decided disappointment, hasn't got any waxed mustache or any gótee (spelling unknown), in fact appears to be quite a sane ordinary mortal and is married! Now any fencing master who has a wife would eat snails."[9] A week later, he described the master as "a huge man with an enormous chest, who sputters so fast and furiously that I am left in a stunned condition after each outbreak."[10] Percy never excelled at fencing and later concluded that he only did it "to please father." The result: "I developed my single visible muscle on the inside of my right leg, for which I have never since found any use."[11]

But fencing was a small part of Percy's life in Paris. His primary ambition was to see and learn, to experience and to watch. He later wrote that his aim was "to study, to school my eyes and ears, to train the sensitive and unruly bondsman in my body."[12] His time in Paris was one of self-refinement, reading, and contemplation. He went to free lectures at the Sorbonne, read aloud to himself in French on park benches, and watched the leaves turn from green to gold to red in the Luxembourg Gardens. He practiced his piano for several hours each day. He went with his French instructor Wagner, who was "a young literary man," and his Polish roommate Magewski, whom Percy described as "a courageous noble creature," to the Opera Comique, the Concerts Rouge, and the Concerts Collonne.[13] One might also conjecture that, living on the Left Bank at the turn of the century and being interested in literary culture and sexual values, they attended salons such as Natalie Barney's. The record does not tell us specifically. But it does tell us that Percy made every effort to insert himself into Parisian literary and artistic culture. "I have been exceptionally gay and giddy," he wrote to his mother, "going to the theatre every night." "There is hardly a day that I am not in the Louvre at least an hour," he wrote in another letter, "and every time I discover something new."[14]

Percy's visits to the Louvre are particularly instructive regarding his ever-broadening perspective on gender and sexuality. He declared that cumulatively he must have spent "months" in the Louvre, "the longest, tallest, widest, worst-hung, most exhausting, irritating and magnificent gallery in the world." He came to love paintings of the Holy Family and the Virgin Mary and claimed to hate everything Dutch except Rembrandt, everything Spanish except Bartolomé Murillo, and everything French except Jean Ingres. His was always a visceral encounter with art. But what most filled him with "horror and fascination," he said, was Greek hermaphroditic sculpture. A human figure with both male and female anatomy seemed to him "sleazy" and "false." Why would the Greeks, whom he thought "so healthy and frank" and who "practiced bisexuality honestly and simply without thought or condemnation," create these "slick symbols of love divided in its objectives"?[15]

Percy's explanation is significant. The Greeks did not create those statues, he learned—it was the Romans. It was a later, "more prurient age, the age of the nasty *Crouching Venus*." There are many statues of Venus, but the Crouching Venus Percy referred to was likely sculpted sometime in the first or second century CE.[16] It is a sculpture of Venus covering her body, having been surprised while bathing. She has an arm across her breasts and looks over her shoulder in such a way that implies shame about her naked body. Percy's point here was explicit: the Crouching Venus was an expression of Christendom's anxious beliefs about the body. It was to be hidden and covered, private and shameful; it needed to be controlled; it was that which one fought against in the battle against sin. Percy believed that this age, the age of the Crouching Venus and the Roman hermaphrodite sculptures, "titillating and ahing, symbolized what they understood and were ashamed of by these sentimental decadent man-woman creatures, false art and false biology."[17]

This is a rare moment in Percy's writings in which he explicitly articulated his critique of Christian sexual ethics. The passage comes in his memoir, so it is the voice of Percy as an adult, not that of the nineteen-year-old Percy in Paris. But it is fair to say that his memories of the Louvre suggest the importance of this moment in his life, in his development of a grounded set of beliefs about sexual values and their place in history. To Percy, the history of sexuality was not a triumphalist story, a narrative in which human society evolved toward greater freedom, understanding, and wisdom. Indeed, it was at times quite the opposite: Percy felt it was the ancient Greeks who created a unique, honest, and healthy culture in which beauty was the chief virtue and truth the great object. This culture also had a wider range of sexual practices that were thought to be normal—such as homosexuality. The body was not an object of shame but of celebration. The later coming of Jesus was heart-shaking and beautiful, Percy felt, and his message of love and forgiveness was profound; but his followers corrupted his message of immeasurable grace and transformed it into a mechanism to control people's behavior. In doing so, the church created a culture that was distinctly oppressive and unfree in comparison to that of the earlier Greeks. Sex and the human body became the particular regulatory emphasis of the church. Recall Percy's poem, "An Epistle from Corinth," in which the narrator admonishes the Apostle Paul for his "blur of words" that "completely hide the God I sense." Paul—and subsequently the Christian church in Rome—made impossible the open, honest enjoyment of the "warm, corporeal parts of us."[18]

So when Percy described the "mock-modest" hermaphrodites in the Louvre, he was making a specific historical commentary. What the Roman church called "modesty" was really shame to Percy. The values put forth by the Apostle Paul—not Jesus, who never spoke of homosexuality—grew out of a cultural impetus to regulate sexual behavior. This did not reflect, Percy felt, the truth of God but rather the values of that particular culture. Percy later wrote a poem called "A Canticle," which suggested that transcendent ideals such as beauty and love were due to some unchanging, unknowable essence, and that all the gods of men were merely attempts to name that essence. These gods came and went. "Dead is Astarte, Astoreth is dead, and Baal; / Zeus and Jehovah share a single grave and deep," the narrator explains, but "there is a loveliness outlasts the temporal gods." When a reader wrote to Percy and asked him to explain this, Percy responded: "I mean that the god of the Jews is just as dead as the god of the Greeks. That which we call the god is I presume eternal and unchanging, but our conception of him always changes."[19]

A society's conception of God, Percy felt, was always contingent upon values specific to place and time. Percy came to see in ancient Greece and (as we will later see) contemporary Samoa places where there was less cultural pressure to conform to rigid notions of moral sexual behavior. This belief, which Percy began to develop in college and which evolved in Europe, was central to his version of cultural relativism: cultural values, and specifically expectations about sexual behavior, manifested themselves differently in different places and different times. So when Percy pointed out that "the Greeks practiced bisexuality honestly and simply," he was holding them up as an example of a culture with a more tolerant framework for sexual values.

Percy was not alone in this view in the early twentieth century. His interpretation of sexual values, Greece, and classical art owed a great deal to his location in the epicenter of a very visible, widely circulated cultural conversation about same-sex love. The idiom of "Greek love" was in the air in both Europe and America. Throughout the nineteenth century, men developed this interpretation as an affirmation of same-sex desire. John Addington Symonds, who would become important to Percy, was one of the nineteenth century's most articulate apologists for homosexual love. He was a British art critic, biographer, historian, and pamphleteer who lived from 1840 to 1893. Toward the end of his life, he wrote two important tracts on sexuality and "Greek Ethics" and a long introspective memoir centered on the question of sexual desire. Though these pieces were not widely circulated (and his literary executor made every effort to suppress them after his death), Symonds was a well-known and widely read literary figure. He insisted that the idea of Greek love "has been the light and leading of my life," and his preoccupations with Greek sexuality were not merely a fixation on the past, but on the present. He wrote to the sexologist Havelock Ellis about his sense that "there is lurking in manly love the stuff of a new spiritual energy, the liberation of which would prove of benefit to society."[20]

While in Paris, Percy discovered and became enamored with Symonds. Of his time of reading and contemplation in the fall of 1904, he wrote: "I saw and spoke to no one, I was completely unconscious of human beings. I lived with John Addington Symonds, Ruskin, Cellini, and Shelley."[21] He was particularly taken by Symonds's aestheticism—his careful renderings of the European landscape; his profound appreciation for architecture and poetry and music; his love of beauty for its own sake. Symonds's idealism and romanticism resonated with Percy's own feelings. Percy wrote to his father: "If you come across a book called 'Sketches in Italy' or 'Sketches in Italy and Greece' by Symonds don't fail to read it or them. They are the most thrilling descriptions of Italy, Sicily and Renaissance life I have ever read. His sketch on Mentone is a masterpiece."[22]

These two books would serve as travel guides of sorts for Percy. Toward the end of 1904, he began to plan a trip through southern Europe, though he hated to leave the Left Bank. He wrote to his parents about his excitement about seeing Europe but also about the comfort he had developed in the Latin Quarter, the strange energy of the culture. "Everywhere are long-haired students in outlandish red and green hats and enormous corduroy pants," he exclaimed. He told his mother that he too had become a "bohemian" and wondered if southerners would be shocked at life in the Latin Quarter. A Sewanee friend, Huger Elliot, and Elliot's sister had come to visit in November 1904 and were to be followed by their aunt. "They are awaiting in terror," he wrote, "the arrival of their aunt who comes today. She is a lovely little old maid ... and thoroughly imbued with old South Carolina ideas. How she will stand this hap-hazard Latin Quarter life is more than I can see."[23]

Despite Percy's love of Paris, and its contrast to what he now called "old" ways of thinking, he also wanted to experience more of Europe. He left after Christmas for southern Europe. He went to Nice and the Riviera on his way to Italy. "Of course I had Symonds' books along with me," he wrote from Italy, "and read as much as I could."[24] Indeed, one notices Symonds's influence in Percy's letters from this period. In such books as *Sketches in Italy*, which Percy was reading at the time, Symonds's emphasis is on the experience of natural beauty as a form of ecstasy. He luxuriated in the naming of flora and descriptions of the landscape. "The narcissus sends its arrowy fragrance through the air," Symonds wrote of the Italian countryside, "while, far and wide, red anemones burn like fire, with interchange of blue and lilac buds, white arums, orchises, and pink gladiolas."[25] Likewise, Percy told his parents that while on walks in Italy, he "went off into ecstasies over the scenery": "I never saw anything like the tulips, red, white, and yellow, and anemones that fill the fields and orchards." He added: "It makes our Mississippi spring seem dreadfully commonplace."[26]

In early 1905, Percy followed much of the same path Symonds described in *Sketches in Italy*. Like Symonds, Percy traveled from Paris to Nice to Mentone, then down the west coast of Italy until he reached Rome, where he would meet up with Huger Jervey. In traveling down the Italian coast, Percy was for the first time immersing himself in a geography that would become literally and symbolically important to him. Historians have shown that Italy, and the Mediterranean more broadly, had long held figurative significance in the queer literary tradition as a metaphor for sexual freedom; Robert Aldrich argues that the image of a homoerotic European South, comprised of the Mediterranean basin, "is the major motif in the writings and art of homosexual European men from the time of the Enlightenment to the 1950s."[27] The physical beauty, the warm climate, and the seemingly more tolerant sexual values combined to make "the south" a fixed point in the homosexual imaginary. This was true, as we will see, in Percy's poetry and prose.

But Italy was also widely known to be a gathering place for queer men. A long line of Americans and northern Europeans from Johann Winckelmann to Lord Byron, Henry James, Walter Pater, E. M. Forster, and Norman Douglas, among many others, looked to Italy not just as a metaphor but also as a place to find sexual fulfillment. Capri, Venice, Rome, and Taormina were particularly well known for thriving male homosexual cultures. Aldrich goes so far as to argue that traveling to Italy "was the way many homosexuals 'came out' and the desire to go abroad linked with a homosexual's self-realization."[28]

Percy's experience of Italy suggests that this is half true. He went to Italy and Greece regularly, and he presumably realized some measure of sexual fulfillment. But it is important to point out that he did not need to go to Italy to achieve self-realization. His first sexual experiences were in the American South; he began to develop an intellectual paradigm to explain and vindicate homosexual desire in Tennessee and Mississippi. Italy—and travel more broadly—was one of several spaces in which he experienced male intimacy.

Percy's trip to Italy in 1905, immersed as it was in his reading of Symonds, was also formative in his thinking about spirituality. One finds in *Sketches in Italy* and *Sketches in Italy and Greece* ideas that Percy would reiterate clearly in his own writings. Symonds's influence on him was more than just as a prose stylist; his connecting of physical beauty, sexual desire, and spiritual well-being was a fusion that would animate Percy's imagination as well. Symonds advocated oneness with nature and an open criticism of cultural values. "Limitations of every sort have been shaken off during the last century; all forms have been destroyed, all questions asked," Symonds wrote in *Sketches in Italy and Greece*. He described "a new renaissance" of thought and feeling and urged his readers to be "unbiassed [sic] by prescription, liberal as the wind, and natural as the mountain crags." The greatest spiritual state, he explained, was to be in sympathy "with the inanimate world; we have learned to look on the universe as a whole, and ourselves as part of it, related by close ties of friendship to all its other members." This, he said, was "ecstasy."[29]

This spiritual framework was to Percy a source of both meaning and melancholy. He, too, desired wholeness and connection with what he viewed as beautiful, honest, and natural. "Above all things we desire to be united and absorbed," Percy wrote in his memoir. "At the intensest peak of our emotions—lying on the bosom we love, or lost in a sunset, or bereft by music—being then most ourselves, we dissolve and become part of the strength and radiance and pathos of creation."[30] This wholeness with the natural world, this pathos of creation, was a central feature of Percy's spiritual hopes. In *Lanterns on the Levee*, he wondered aloud about the possibilities of being connected to a source of meaning outside the self. Science offered none, he felt, and Christian religion was "outworn rubbish." In the final analysis, Percy concluded, "It is given man to behold beauty and to worship nobility." Only when one experiences this "does the air taste native and the place seem home." Human beings, Percy felt, suffered above all else from "apartness" and "isolation" from this spiritual home. "To become part of this creating essence and of all things created by it," Percy wrote, "in this alone might be found fulfillment, peace, ecstasy."[31]

To be one with the creator and to be one with another human being—these were the twin wellsprings of Percy's spiritual desire. To be "lying on the bosom we love," to "behold beauty and to worship nobility"—these were the great ideals and also the great impossibilities of Percy's life. His melancholy and his abiding sense of spiritual alienation were symptoms of his "apartness," he felt, from god and man.[32] Wholeness and connection were possible, and he achieved them in moments throughout his life; but his regular traveling companion, in 1905 and later, was loneliness. "Loneliness," he wrote, "was so familiar I came not to hate her but to know whatever happened in how ever many after years she alone would be faithful to me and, departing a little way for some brief beatific interlude, would always return."[33]

Percy's physical loneliness was temporarily relieved in Rome, where he met up with Huger Jervey in January 1905. He was happy to see Jervey, Percy told his mother, because while traveling alone, he had no one with whom he could share his excitement: "if enthused it had to be to my own secret soul for want of a better listener." When they met up, Jervey told Percy that he had never seen him look so well, so Percy decided to have himself photographed "when the present crop of bumps disappears."[34] After his acne cleared up, he sat for a picture and was pleased: "I was unusually handsome," he told his mother, "and if the photograph does justice to my charms you may expect to receive one."[35]

One evening in early January, Percy and Jervey went to a dinner party in Rome, and Percy sat next to a "young nice-looking German." He spoke only French and German, so Percy had to take "heroic measures ... to make myself understood." The two became friends, and a few days later, the young man gave Percy a ticket to have an audience with Pope Pius X. Percy tried to

Will Percy, likely in Italy during his year abroad in 1904–5 (Courtesy of the Mississippi Department of Archives and History, Jackson, Mississippi)

politely decline but, as he explained to his mother, "the affair ended up by my decking out in my very best bib and tucker of black and white of course, and sallying forth to the Vatican." When he arrived, Percy was shocked to hear himself introduced as "Signor le baron." He described his state as "invariably almost caving in with fear lest my baronship should be found to be a fake and I hauled ignominiously away." But no one found out, and Percy knelt down in a room decorated in red and gold and lined with officials in velvet knee trousers and long robes. The pope entered and walked around the room, "giving each person his great emerald fisherman's ring to kiss." Pius X, dressed in white with a large gold cross around his neck, delivered a blessing and then retired.[36] Percy's description of the pope's blessing is worth quoting at length: "A more beautiful, a more absolutely sad face I never expected, I never wish to see again. As he bent slightly forward and blessed the people without the ghost of a smile on his lips, there was something infinitely digni-fied and noble, but infinitely sorrowful in his whole attitude. He looked like a man who had known all the misery of the whole world and whose life was filled with a vast pity for his fellow sufferers."[37]

For a nineteen-year-old on vacation after college, Will Percy was very serious-minded, very much focused on understanding themes like dignity, nobility, and sorrow. His encounter with the pope struck these chords and left a deep impression on him. He described and redescribed the event in his next three letters home. Meeting the pope seemed to bring into stark relief the spiritual progression of Percy's short life—from his childhood ambitions to the priesthood to his gravitation toward a nonreligious yet still spiritual young adulthood. He clearly had great admiration for the pope and his capacity for pity, but he had also moved away from his faith in Catholic doctrine. Percy hoped for the love of God but doubted if the pope was its only purveyor. Yet childhood faith is not lost easily. One wonders what this encounter meant for Percy in 1905, if his kiss of the pope's ring contained a prayer or a farewell.

Percy and Jervey soon began to tire of Rome. It seemed to Percy that on every street corner there were "guides spouting yards of inaccurate Tommy-rot in one ear while some miserable urchin squeals 'want to buy postcards!' in the other."[38] In addition, three Sewanee families—the Grays, the Elliots, and the Bradfords—were vacationing in Rome at the time. Percy enjoyed seeing his old friends but felt Mrs. Gray was a bit pushy; she had two daugh-ters and felt the younger one was an ideal match for him. Percy felt other-wise. He wrote to his mother: "Mrs. G. insisted that I loose [sic] my heart to the younger one, but finally gave me up as hopeless."[39]

Percy and Jervey discussed their travel plans but disagreed about where to go: Percy wanted to go to Egypt and Jervey wanted to go to Greece. They agreed to go their separate ways and meet back in Florence in April. Percy traveled alone from Rome to Naples, where he set sail for Port Said. While on the boat, he thought of his father. "I had head-ache, stomach heaving, and back-ache," he told his mother, "all at once and the same time. I imagined father standing on the top deck and admiring the beauty of the waves break-ing over everything, but for me each wave demanded an ounce of flesh."[40]

Indeed, when Percy reached Egypt, his mind often returned to the United States. His ship docked at Port Said—"A most miserable, unattractive town that looked like Flagstaff, Arizona"—and then he traveled on to Cairo, Luxor, and Aswan. On the train, he sat next to "a Sir Something Somebody, one of the biggest men in Egypt," and he also met a "pleasant, usual-looking, middle-aged Englishman" who became his traveling companion. Upon the pair's arrival in Cairo, Percy wrote to his mother: "I just arrived today on the banks of the Father Nile. I will drop you a line to let you know that I have not fallen in."[41]

His most enduring impression of Egypt seems to have been the people, for it was about them that he wrote in his one surviving letter home. "The Egyptians are without doubt the most picturesque people I have ever seen," he told his mother. He loved the shape and flow of their blue-and-white gowns, he said, and "sometimes one runs across a really splendid looking Arab (a Sheik I always imagine) with fine features and pale yellow skin." But the majority of Egyptians, Percy felt, did not look this way. He lamented that "picturesqueness always seems to demand the forfeiture of cleanliness ...' the average Egyptian is a mongrel creature varying from ebony to cream." Percy's reflections on race while in Egypt were the beginning of a regular practice of using his time abroad to write about race in America. Presumably speaking of one of their house servants, Percy wrote that those Egyptians who were black made "Minny ... resemble Persian marble in comparison."[42]

In March Percy returned to Italy. He took a train from Rome to Florence, during which he continued to read Symonds on the Mediterranean: "[I] read as much as I could of the history and romance of the thing—and there is a never-ending supply of both."[43] The romance of Italy was all the more apparent in Florence, which combined the natural beauty of Tuscany with the art and history of the Renaissance. Percy rejoined Huger Jervey and settled in for a two-week visit. He described their hotel room as a tangle of "clothes of all kinds, letters, pictures, Egyptian relics, and books," and he told his mother how nice it was to be with Jervey again: "He has been a great deal of company for me as he knows all about the art and architecture of the place, and is a very pleasant fellow to boot."[44]

Percy and Jervey involved themselves in the Florentine art culture, through which Percy met a group of "spiritualists and several artists." At a dinner party that Pope Pius X would not have been happy with, one of the spiritualists called forth evil spirits. Percy wrote home that while they were all gathered around a table invoking "spirits, past, present and to come," "a very pretty Swiss girl and myself got the giggles and were disgraced." Despite their cynicism, the table began "skipping about" and floating in the air. "All us unbelievers decided that an old lady of spiritualistic tendencies was the one doing the pushing," Percy explained. But then, one by one, they all moved away from the table except Percy and his Swiss friend. The table continued to bounce and float. Percy checked for tricks but found none. "There was no fake about it," he wrote, and proudly added that "we were immediately dubbed 'very mediumistic' and from this time on it is not proper for us to say we are tired, we are 'depleted in our magnetism.'"[45] God had not revealed himself to Percy in church, but the devil certainly seemed real enough. Indeed, for the rest of his life, Percy dabbled in spiritualism, particularly Ouija boards. It seemed to bring him comfort to experience that which he could not explain.

Percy and Jervey split up again in mid-April, and Percy joined another Sewanee friend, Huger Elliot, and traveled to Venice. "Venice! And spring and full moon, all at once!" Percy exclaimed to his mother. "Can you imagine anything more delightful? Between pictures and palaces and gondolas and the feel of summer in the air Elliot and I are rapidly verging on a state of lunacy." The two rented a room in a house with a "picturesque canal beneath, and looking into the garden of a palace filled with wisteria and yellow Jessamine and the walls hidden behind climbing roses. We are the sole guests in our house and the Italian family thinks we are the greatest things in Venice and treat us like Lords, all of which pleases us immensely." Percy and Elliot explored the canals, sat in cafés that "suit the tastes of artists," and one day took a trip to nearby Ravenna. "The great thing about Ravenna," Percy wrote in a letter home, "is the fine forest which Dante and Dryden and Byron sang about—particularly Byron who lived at Ravenna for a long time and had several interesting love affairs there." What Percy did not mention to his mother was that several of these love affairs were likely with men. In this and other letters like it, Percy seemed to want to test the limits of his mother's awareness; or, perhaps, this was his way of communicating his queer feelings to her even as he knew she would not understand. In the absence of full mutual understanding, Percy and his mother opted for indirection, obliqueness.[46]

For Percy's year abroad, the historical record drops off after his mid-April trip to Venice. He would work his way back up to Paris and then over to England, and from there he would sail for home in May 1905. But in his memoir, Percy provided some retrospections that serve to tie together the significance of this year of his life. It was a year of prolonged engagement with European art, writing, and history; Percy wanted to understand himself in relation to these things, and he did. Just after his comments about Greek bisexuality in *Lanterns on the Levee*, he wrote: "It's a grievous and a long way you travel to reach serenity and the acceptance of facts without hurt or shock." Percy's teenage years had a great deal to do with what he called "the acceptance of facts." At Sewanee and in Europe, Percy surrounded himself with men and with writing about male love; he chose to visit places like the Latin Quarter and Ravenna; he thought about God, he thought about history, he thought about himself. He emerged with some "imperishable memories," he said, as well as a measure of serenity and a firmer sense of the things he wanted in his life: dignity, nobleness of heart, someone to be with. He wanted to be at peace with God, and with himself.[47]

Yet for all this, he "missed Mother and Father," and he missed "the Centaurs"—presumably a reference to the relationships he had had at Sewanee. He was fundamentally a relational person, he wrote, someone who needed love, who needed an ally and a confidant: "At sight or sound of something unbearably beautiful I wanted desperately to share it, I wanted with me everyone I'd ever cared for—and someone else besides. I was sick for a home I'd never seen and lonely for a hand I'd never touched."[48]

Percy was speaking here, in part, about Harold Bruff, whom he would meet after he traveled back across the Atlantic Ocean.

5. HARVARD

I have enjoyed spells of more intense happiness but never three years of
uninterrupted happiness as I did at the Harvard Law School.
—WILLIAM ALEXANDER PERCY, *Lanterns on the Levee*

On May 20, 1905, Percy boarded the SS *Saint Paul* in Southampton, England.
The *Saint Paul* was an icon of the Gilded Age—a fast, luxurious steamship
that ferried travelers, merchants, and immigrants from Europe to New York
City. American and European steamship companies had been competing
for decades to make the biggest, most lavish ships to entice "saloon custom-
ers"—travelers other than immigrants—to travel between continents. Families like the Percys paid top dollar for first-class tickets across the Atlantic
and enjoyed carpeted berths and saloons on the top deck. But the majority
of passengers on these ships between 1880 and 1920 were those crowded in
the hull below, "steerage aliens" coming to America—Slavs, Poles, Greeks,
Russians, Italians, Armenians, and Estonians who slept in bunk beds in the
bowels of the ship. The year 1905 was the first in American history during
which 1 million passengers arrived at Ellis Island, most of them coming from
southern and eastern Europe.[1]

On the SS *Saint Paul*, Percy traveled on the top level, carefully segregated
from the people below—people like Catterina Marchetti, a twenty-five-year-
old housekeeper bound for Pittsburgh; and Carlo DiGiorgi, a mason with
$40 in his pocket who, upon arrival, would be deemed of sound mind and
body by the U.S. government and found not to be an anarchist or a polyg-
amist. At Ellis Island, Percy signed his name on the manifest and moved
through customs and on to the railway at Penn Station in Manhattan. His
luggage would have been handled by porters. Passengers like Marchetti and
DiGiorgi may have had to wait weeks at the quarantine for clearance. They
carried everything they owned. They were inspected for their cleanliness
and their politics.[2]

Percy took the train south, likely stopping in Sewanee for a visit on his
way to Mississippi. He spent the summer of 1905 in Greenville, again wring-

ing his hands with his parents about his future. "I agreed uneagerly with father that a man should earn his keep," he remembered, but when he looked within, he found himself without "any quality convertible into cash." He had a solid knowledge of the classics; he loved poetry and sculpture and painting; he was possessed of the desire to travel and to read and to experience the beauty of the world. He had many avocations, but no vocation. He had a growing desire to become a writer, but *poet* was not historically a prosperous career, nor was it one LeRoy Percy encouraged. LeRoy encouraged law school—he had gone, his father had gone, his brothers had gone. His law firm, then called Percy and Yerger, was enormously successful litigating corporate disputes, writing contracts, and overseeing the formation and dissolution of business partnerships. By this time, at age forty-four, LeRoy Percy had established himself as one of the most prominent attorneys in the region. Will Percy, though, had little enough interest in his father's corporate clients. He was a humanist, he felt, not a moneymaker. But he also felt that his father and others had for years "been pouring out money, skill, time, devotion, prayers to create something out of me that wouldn't look as if the Lord had slapped it together absent-mindedly." In the end, he wrote, "I did not choose the law, it chose me." LeRoy Percy and his brothers had gone to Virginia, but Will Percy chose Harvard. This was his compromise: "I wanted to be near Boston with its music and theatres, which I would miss the rest of my life in my future Southern home."[3]

In August Percy and his parents boarded a train in Greenville for the week-long trip to Boston, a city mythical and romantic in Percy's imagination: here waited the Boston Symphony Hall and the Columbia and Orpheum and Majestic and Colonial Theatres—the last of which just opened in 1900 and boasted a lobby of mirrors and white marble and Corinthian columns, seats upholstered in dark green leather, and proscenium and pilasters gilded and leafed in gold. Here in Boston waited the opera and the theatre and the symphony, which regularly performed Wagner and Brahms, Bach and Beethoven. Here was the city of painters like John Singer Sargent, pastors like John Winthrop and Phillips Brooks, and novelists like Julia Ward Howe and William Dean Howells. Boston was the "Athens of America," the seat of cosmopolitan culture, the exemplar of the beneficent largesse of the Gilded Age.[4]

The scene that greeted the Percys when they pulled into South Station, though, would likely have been different from the Boston of the imagining southerner. Downtown Boston was alive with noise and with physical energy: the city streets were crowded with wagons and carriages interspersed with the occasional automobile; the Italian and Russian and Irish immigrants who dominated the working class doubtless were busy building and paving and unloading and digging as the Percys made their way from South Station to Harvard Square. As the Percys crossed the Harvard Bridge over the Charles River, they would have seen to their north hundreds of workers finishing the Longfellow Bridge, which was nearing completion in the summer of 1905. In the streets and trains and dockyards they passed, the Percys would have seen a portion of the vast immigrant population that undergirded the city's elite veneer.

Harvard Square, though, would have been less diverse, with the Boston laborers replaced by white Harvard students, their professors, and a supporting cast of cooks, cleaners, and carpenters. Percy's boardinghouse, Winthrop Hall, was a short distance north of Harvard Square. Winthrop Hall was a stone building that sat just behind the Henry Wadsworth Longfellow home, a few blocks off of Cambridge Common. It was a favorite boardinghouse of Yale graduates, and one of the most expensive: the building was finished in 1895 and all of the rooms were large singles with a sitting room and a bedroom; each room had its own fireplace and hardwood floors. One can imagine Will Percy's excitement looking out of his second-story window onto Henry Wadsworth Longfellow's former backyard. One can imagine his sense of newness and anticipation as he met his neighbors: Bob Black from Cincinnati; Richard Hunter from London; George Roberts and George Reynolds and Harold Bruff from New York.[5]

Harold Bruff was born in Brooklyn in 1884 and, like Percy, grew up amidst wealth and comfort. At Yale, he was a member of the Linonia debating society and the banjo club. In the exit survey all Yale graduates filled out, Bruff wrote that he preferred cube-cut tobacco and beer, that compulsory chapel should be abolished, that he was a Republican, and that his favorite college course had been "19th Century Poets." He said that his strong point was "being a student" and his weak point was "laziness and tobacco." When asked for his "Opinion of New Haven Girls," he wrote: "Not qualified to judge."[6]

Harold Bruff's father, William Jenkins Bruff, was in the gun business. In the late nineteenth century, an era during which industrial production of guns and ammunition changed the nature and quantity of violence in human life, William Bruff grew vastly wealthy as president of the Union Metallic Cartridge Company—one of the largest manufacturers of ammunition in the world. In the early 1890s, Union Metallic invented a smokeless cartridge that became widely coveted in the military and among gun enthusiasts. Buffalo Bill Cody had a standing order for 40,000 bullets a month for his Wild West show. After the sinking of the USS *Maine* in 1898, the War Department allotted $50 million to buy "all that can be turned out" by manufacturers such as Union Metallic. William Bruff, in turn, owned homes in Brooklyn Heights and on Bay Shore, Long Island, and had access to the most exclusive clubs in New York.[7]

At Harvard, Harold Bruff lived at 18 Winthrop Hall, just below Will Percy, who lived on the second floor in room 27.[8] The two immediately formed a bond and spent afternoons walking along the Charles River or through Cambridge neighborhoods; they spent evenings in each other's rooms talking and reading aloud to one another. They made friends with their other neighbors, and as classes began in September, they took the trolley downtown for dinner and concerts. They no doubt shared anxieties about the first-year curriculum: contracts, criminal law and procedure, property, torts, and civil procedure.[9]

Percy bought a piano for his room and decorated his walls with Navajo tapestries and paintings he had brought home from Italy—the beginning of a lifelong practice of what one historian calls "cosmopolitan domesticity."[10] Percy, Bruff, and their friends stayed up late in Percy's room talking, reading aloud, and playing music. On such occasions, they forbade any discussion of the law. One night, Percy made a fire and settled down to conversation with George Roberts and Harold Bruff. "Enter two evil spirits," as Percy described it to his mother, "i.e. Johnnie S. Reynolds and soon followed Tommie, bent upon asking odious questions about guilt and burden of proof and other unknown legal honors. Therefore I told them that they must leave either their doubt or their presence without my threshold. They preferred the latter course, so we turned out the lights, threw on more logs and settled ourselves to the enjoyment of youth's greatest privilege and delight, much talk arising from a mass of nebulous ideas."[11]

To an extent, Percy revealed their topics of conversation in his letters home: music, art, and literature, spoken with what he later described as "a minimum of inhibition and a maximum of gusto."[12] One night in conversation, someone belittled the accomplishments of Wagner and Beethoven, and Percy bragged to his mother how he "shone forth like a splendid knight in protection of a damsel in distress," coming to Wagner's defense.[13] When they tired of conversation, they each had different methods of diversion: Stanleigh played ragtime on the piano; George Reynolds fantasized about working for a railroad; George Roberts (who was a debater at Yale) found someone to argue with; Tommy got drunk; and Percy locked himself in his room to play piano and read Shelley.[14] One time, all the northern boys pinned Percy to the floor, sat on him, and loudly read passages from *Uncle Tom's Cabin*, particularly "Mrs. Stowe's more sadistic and blood-boiling passages, with Simon Legree gestures."[15]

Depending on who was in the room, we can assume conversations also turned to broader issues of moral authority and sexual values. It would be wrong to presume that these students were uninterested in the significant shifts in cultural values around them at that moment in the first years of the new century. John Reed, later to become a famous journalist-cum-revolutionary, was a student at Harvard during these same years and recalled: "There was talk of the world, and daring thought, and intellectual insurgency; heresy has always been a Harvard and New England tradition."[16] Percy's description of his and his friends' lack of inhibition echoed this claim and also resonated with the spirit of his and Bruff's relationship. Their relationship was one that pressed against boundaries, challenged one another and those around them. Late-night conversations in Winthrop Hall, among Percy and Bruff and their friends, doubtless followed this trajectory. They also doubtless alighted on the subject of the age: American manhood.

Historian Kim Townsend has argued that central to the Harvard experience in the early twentieth century was a high degree of self-consciousness about becoming a "Harvard man." She suggests that Harvard and Harvardians played a central role in constituting the ideal of modern manhood for the rest of the nation. The dominant version of this model posited that manhood meant fighting for the practical application of ideals like justice, well-being, and liberty. Manhood did not mean aloofness, abstraction, or idealism; it meant solving problems, it meant fighting for good, it meant *doing*, not *being*. At stake for Harvard men was no less than the nation itself. The governor of Massachusetts explained this in a speech at Percy's commencement ceremony: "Whatever patriotism of American manhood comes to the fore, Harvard memory, Harvard ideals, instinctively rise, because Harvard is not merely Massachusetts, Harvard is not merely New England, Harvard is the ideal of America."[17]

Indeed, early in law school, Percy and Bruff went to see Teddy Roosevelt deliver a speech on Harvard manhood entitled "The College Man." Roosevelt was delighted at the recent construction of Harvard Stadium, which at 43,000 seats was the largest sports venue in America. It was dedicated to "the joys of manly conquest." But many, including Harvard president Charles William Eliot, were calling for the abolition or at the least significant reform of the violent game of football. Roosevelt was said to have privately called

Eliot a "mollycoddle" because he felt the football field was the ideal forum for proving one's toughness.[18] "I emphatically disbelieve," he explained in his speech, "in seeing Harvard or any other college turn out mollycoddles, instead of vigorous men." Vigorous men, the president felt, were necessary to a thriving democracy. These men did not "shrink from physical effort or a little physical pain" because physical courage was a necessary corollary to moral courage. "Thoroughly manly" sports like football and wrestling were crucial in developing a manly citizenry; he felt that manly sports would serve as a safeguard against effeminacy. "Above all, you college men," he exhorted, "remember that if your education, the pleasant lives you lead, make you too fastidious, too sensitive to take part in the rough hurly-burly of the actual work of the world … then you had better never been educated at all."[19]

Percy appreciated Roosevelt's version of hurly-burly, practical manhood, having seen and admired it in his father and uncles. But he did not see it as incompatible with refinement and sensitivity. In Percy's view, which he drew from the Greeks, education was a central means for the achievement of virtue, and virtue had diverse manifestations. Virtue produced warriors as well as poets, and not a few who were both warriors and poets. So Percy's reaction to Roosevelt's speech was positive with a hint of irony. He told his father that Roosevelt's "voice is bad, often breaking with falsetto," and that the president was fixated on physical activity and its relationship to American values. "What he said bore chiefly on college athletics and the duties of citizenship," Percy wrote. "He took particular pains to ridicule the attitudes of the Harvard professors on sports" and mocked the "educated ineffectuals." "He has a wonderful way about him of convincing his hearers of his own sincerity," Percy declared. "While scarcely a genius he is one of the biggest, the biggest, I believe, man I have ever seen outside of private life."[20]

Roosevelt's visibility was undeniable, as was his fixation on manliness. It was a fixation grounded in anxieties about his own manliness but also in his anxieties about the moral fabric of the nation. The decline in manly virtue, he perceived, was not just a generic decline but one that came largely from a specific source: homosexuals. "As a whole we are still in the flush of our mighty manhood," he said in 1901, but there are "signs of senility … of gross vice and moral weakness. Nobody can tell when or how soon disaster will come." He insulted his political opponents by calling them "hermaphrodites," and he disdained "certain dreadful qualities of the moral pervert" and those "men who were not men." Roosevelt, historian Sarah Watts has rightly argued, was focused "obsessively on sexuality as the source of social breakdown."[21]

This obsession was due in part to the increasing visibility of homosexuals and discussion of homosexuality in American culture at the turn of the century. Indeed, at Harvard throughout the nineteenth century—but especially in its latter half and in the early twentieth century—there existed a visible counternarrative concerning American manhood. Douglas Shand-Tucci has documented the progression of Harvard men from Walt Whitman, Charles Warren Stoddard, and Owen Wister to James Mill Pierce, Henry Wadsworth Longfellow Dana, and Arthur Kingsley Porter, among others, who posited quite different possibilities for expressions of manhood. The range was broad: Whitman's epic poetry suggested a radically expansive, homoerotic masculinity; like John Addington Symonds, Whitman's ideal men were not abstracted artists but tough, chivalrous athletes and warriors. Henry Wadsworth Longfellow Dana was a pacifist and later a Soviet sympathizer who felt that manhood should include a fight against those very ideals Roosevelt so vocally advocated. Arthur Kingsley Porter was a medievalist and architectural historian who equated manhood with intellectual seriousness and scholarly work. These men preferred sex with men, but there was diversity in their conceptions of gender and masculinity. One could be a warrior, a radical, or a scholar and still be a man. In their own ways, these Harvard men and others worked to suggest that men could be men—indeed, useful, virtuous men—regardless of their choice of sexual partner or their proximity to the dominant model of vigorous, practical manhood.[22]

Perhaps the most famous contributor to this conversation was James Mill Pierce. Pierce was an astronomer, mathematician, and dean of the Graduate School of Arts and Sciences and lived two blocks from Will Percy in 1905. Along with William James and George Santayana, he was one of the most accomplished members of the Harvard faculty. Shand-Tucci rightly describes Pierce as "one of the most progressive advocates of homosexuality in the nineteenth century," particularly after he published a piece in Havelock Ellis's landmark study, *Sexual Inversion* (1897).[23] In it, Pierce wrote: "I have considered and inquired into this question for many years; and it has long been my settled conviction that no breach of morality is involved in homosexual love." Pierce felt that love between men was not only a pure type of sexual passion but also a true expression of manhood. "I have known many persons more or less the subjects of this passion, and I have found them a particularly high-minded, upright, refined, and (I must add) pure-minded class of men." Like Percy, Pierce drew from personal observation as well as from history. "I clearly believe that the Greek morality on this subject was far higher than ours, and truer to the spiritual nature of man," he wrote. "We ought to think and speak of homosexual love, not as 'inverted' or 'abnormal,' as a sort of color-blindness of the genital sense, as a lamentable mark of inferior development, or as an unhappy fault, a 'masculine body with a feminine soul,' but as being in itself a natural, pure, and sound passion."[24]

In Cambridge—like in Sewanee and the Latin Quarter—Will Percy was in a place where people were questioning and attempting to reconfigure cultural values regarding gender and sexuality. While the historical record does not always tell us the specifics of his conversations or his acquaintances, it tells us without a doubt that these cultural currents shaped his attitude, his sensibility, and his perspectives. We see in his poetry echoes of Whitman's capacious homoerotic ideal; we see in his ardent patriotism during World War I echoes of Roosevelt's practical manhood; we see in his comments on Greek bisexuality echoes of Pierce's defense of "Greek morality." In his consideration of all these ideas, Percy was using the material available to him to understand what it meant to be a man in his time and place. Though some of his contemporaries may have seen contradiction in his views, Percy himself did not—one could be a patriot and a poet, a fighter and a lover, a man and a homosexual.

IN ADDITION TO conversations with friends, trips to the symphony, and walks along the Charles, Percy managed an above average but not exceptional career as a law student. Percy's first year of law school set the pattern for his relationship with the profession during the rest of his life. That is, the law was necessary for him to make a living, but more importantly, it afforded him time and money to do what he wanted to do: be with his friends, travel, hear music, and write poetry. He never loved the law, though he was good at it. He wrote to his mother about his lack of enthusiasm for his courses— "I got my usual B," he mentioned after one semester.[25] The day after going to the opera with Bruff (they had season tickets each year), he wrote: "Last night was the oratorio and in spite of a lecture in contracts this morning I am still thrilled over it."[26] Throughout his life, Percy never had great ambition for legal fame or wealth. He was afforded this luxury, of course, by his family's affluence and his father's ambition. His father, and *his* father before him, had built the Percy law practice from scratch and literally seemed to work themselves to death. They enlarged their legal practice, they enlarged their landholdings, they enlarged their reputations and their bank accounts. Will Percy, in contrast, made a compromise with this ethic: he would work hard enough to maintain the family business, but no harder. "I wanted to do whatever piece of work fell to my care as well as I could," he remembered, "but beyond that I wasn't concerned over what opinion my brethren of the bar held of me."[27]

One area in which Percy did not deviate from his father's ethos was in his view of race relations. With regard to race, he seemed always to find evidence that reaffirmed rather than questioned his southern roots. In the spring of 1906, Percy wrote home from Cambridge about a magazine article that "has created much astonishment and a great deal of comment up here."[28] Written by Charles Francis Adams Jr., a Boston businessman and former colonel in the Union army, the *Century Magazine* piece was entitled "Reflex Light from Africa." Adams had recently traveled to Africa, where he found proof of "the existence of an uneradicable and insurmountable race difference." Black people, Adams felt, were by nature lazy, savage, and incapable of self-improvement. Their only advances as a race were due to the guidance of white colonialists and Americans. What Adams felt was a "scientific" difference between black and white people created a problem for Americans: "If true, this strikes at the very root of our American polity—the equality of man before the law. We cannot conform to it." He pointed to the granting of equal rights to freedmen during Reconstruction as an example of the folly of thinking people of African descent could be political equals. This was "work done in utter ignorance of ethnologic law and total disregard of unalterable fact." All but throwing up his hands in despair, Adams suggested the best course was to treat the African American "as a ward and dependent—firmly, but in a spirit of kindness and absolute justice."[29]

Will Percy encouraged his father to read the article, saying that the piece "strikes me as being very good sense."[30]

Percy's hierarchical views of race—in which he was positioned at the top—no doubt played a role in the sense of solidarity he felt with his white Harvard classmates. Whether from Mississippi or New York or New England, they shared privileges and opportunities afforded to them by their whiteness—and by and large, they neither questioned nor challenged this. To read that black people were fundamentally different justified, in their minds, the vast inequality around them. To read that they had a responsibility to treat blacks with "kindness and absolute justice" reaffirmed their sense of their own magnanimity. They were highly conscious of themselves as Harvard men, as American men, central to which was to be white, to be prosperous, and to believe in the righteousness of the American way of life.

Whereas Percy and his friends' racial bond was largely unspoken, they bonded more directly over their shared experiences. What animated Percy's first year of law school more than anything else was the culture of camaraderie among the residents of Winthrop Hall. They played tennis, they went snowshoeing, they took weekend trips to Maine and Vermont and Gloucester.[31] His northern friends tried once to teach Percy to ice skate, after which he reported to his mother that "a large rude audience gathered in the road and watched my gyrations with noisy exclamations and mirth."[32] After their January exams, Percy and his friends took the trolley into Boston "to obliterate our sorrows in a good dinner and—need I say!—in the flowing bowl." By the time Percy arrived a bit late, his friends were already drunk, or, "to speak figuratively, had vine leaves in their hair. The immediate effect, far from being aesthetic, was to make them call loudly and oft, 'Garcon, open the window, it's too hot! Some more champagne!'" They were singing Yale songs loudly and out of key, and a particularly tipsy George Roberts waved his napkin at an old man across the room and shouted, "Hello, Paddy-rooski!" Percy concluded the story to his mother: "It was truly tragic when the said old gent walked over and shook George's hand and George in a fit of intelligence recognized him as an old friend of his father's. Apologies! Tableau, curtain."[33]

Percy was happy to receive a visit from Huger Jervey in the spring of 1906. He introduced "Hugger" to his friends before the two southerners took off on a walk to Lexington. One can only imagine what they talked about, or what they saw, on this walk that took at least four hours. Jervey surely filled him in on Sewanee news, part of which was that their mutual friend Sinkler Manning was considering marriage. In the same letter in which Percy mentioned his walk with Jervey, he told his mother that "Manning was still infatuated with Mary Moore and to all appearances had been persuaded not to try for the Rhodes scholarship. That miserable girl will ruin him completely and what in the world can she expect to gain!"[34] A month later, Percy said that he wanted to bring Sinkler Manning home with him for the summer, "so for a while he'll be out from under the baleful eye of Mary Moore."[35]

His plan worked. Percy spent part of the summer of 1906 in Sewanee with Manning and Jervey and the rest in Greenville with Manning. There, they spent time with LeRoy and Camille Percy, played tennis, and read poetry and Greek drama.[36] They must also have talked about Sinkler's future; he decided not to pursue Mary Moore but rather move to New York and become a journalist. We do not know a great deal about Percy and Manning's relationship; there is only one extant letter from Manning to Percy in Percy's papers. This is curious considering Percy's 1919 comment that Harold Bruff and Sinkler Manning were the two most important people in his life, people whom "I understood and who understood me."[37] Regardless of what happened to Percy and Manning's correspondence (maybe they did not write to each other much; maybe Percy threw his letters away; maybe the family later destroyed them), a few significant details emerge. First, it is important to point out that most of their relationship took place in the South, and that they bonded in part through a mutual love of the classics and a mutual friendship with Huger Jervey. Manning, more than Percy or Jervey, felt pressure and/or a desire to marry a woman. (Indeed, he did eventually marry.) This was common among queer men in this period, when, according to one historian of sexuality, "given the pressure to marry, it meant nothing in terms of sexuality to do so but everything not to."[38]

Also significant in piecing together the queer world of Percy and his contemporaries is that when Manning moved to New York, he moved to the Tenderloin in Lower Manhattan. At the time, the Tenderloin was host to the city's "red-light" district and home to an almost exclusively working-class, immigrant population. Historian George Chauncey has shown that if middle-class men and women went to the Tenderloin (and its larger neighborhood, the Bowery) at all during this period, it was most often to go "slumming" or to solicit sex at a brothel. As Chauncey has shown so compellingly, New York at the turn of the century had "an extensive, organized, and highly visible gay world," and the section Sinkler Manning moved to was central to that world.[39] His motives for moving there were not recorded, but we can assume that the affluent, white southerner—the son of the governor of South Carolina—made a deliberate choice to move to the Tenderloin.

Sinkler Manning found a small apartment, and Percy went to New York to help him settle in the fall of 1906. Percy left Boston at midnight on a Friday. "Sinkler was awfully glad to see me," he told his mother, "and received me into his little fourth floor room situated somewhere near the center of the Tenderloin as tho it had been the most elegant of ancestral southern homes."[40] Percy and Manning went to a play, drank a bottle of champagne, and ate at the nearby Child's restaurant—one of the most widely known meeting places for queers during this period, Chauncey has shown.[41] In addition to enjoying New York, their primary diversion was Percy's favorite: talking. "With the exception of a few hours when he was interviewing various newspapers," Percy wrote to his parents, "we talked steadily the entire day."[42] Again, we will never know what they talked about, but it is important to emphasize this repeated theme: in his letters home, in his memoir, in his diaries, Percy made regular note of his pleasure in conversation. To relate to another person, to come some small distance closer to understanding and being understood— these were moments Percy relished. And it is all the more significant given that Percy came from a family that valued emotional restraint, practicality, and hard work in men. Male friendship to LeRoy Percy most often involved hunting, gambling, and drinking, and often grew out of a mutual, practical concern—a business partnership, a political arrangement, a civic duty. But for Will Percy and his intimates like Huger Jervey, Harold Bruff, and Sinkler Manning, male friendship most often involved art, travel, and conversation. Though they took practical concerns like the law and employment seriously, they tended to idealize being over doing, relating over accomplishing.

Percy did accomplish one important thing in his conversations with Manning. "By the time I was ready to take the train back to Boston," he wrote to his mother, "I had persuaded Sinkler to stay a month longer in NY instead of going Lord knows where."[43] Manning got a job as a reporter for the *New York Times* and lived in New York for several years until he moved to Washington, D.C., to cover national politics for the *Times*. He married in 1913, had three children, and joined the army in 1917. He was killed in battle in 1918 at Montfaucon, France.[44]

PERCY'S SECOND YEAR of law school followed the pattern of his first. His letters home reveal very little about his studies but a great deal about his leisure time. He joined "The Southern Club" at Harvard, took weekend trips with his friends, and spent his money on tickets to the theatre, opera, and symphony. He conspired with his mother to get LeRoy Percy to send more money to fund his outings. "Kindly explain," he suggested, "that law books are as expensive as they are uninteresting."[45] With Harold Bruff, George Roberts, and others, he watched *King Lear* performed in Italian, George Bernard Shaw's *You Never Can Tell*, and a Belasco production, *The Girl of the Golden West*.[46] They went downtown to hear the Boston Symphony on Saturday nights, evenings that enlivened his imagination even years later. He recalled: "To have the great masterpieces of music, matchlessly performed, poured into your fresh ears with Harold Bruff or George Roberts or Harley Stowell in the seat next to you—well, one could ask nothing more of life—that was ecstasy."[47] He wrote home to his friend Carrie Stern after one such evening: "It is midnight and the symphony concert I've just heard has left me reduced emotionally to the state of a jelly-fish."[48]

These moments of sublime experience began to translate into poetry in Percy's mind. For the first time, he began to write poetry in earnest. He sent drafts and sketches to Carrie Stern and Huger Jervey. "What I wrote seemed more essentially myself than anything I did or said," he later explained. "It often gushed up almost involuntarily."[49] From the beginning, the themes of

Percy's poetry engaged his broader struggle to understand the good and the beautiful—which for him most often meant knowing and loving another person, music, the natural world, and human courage—while living in a place and among people who did not. His poem "After Hearing Music" serves as a useful meditation on these broader themes, as well as his more specific experience as a twenty-one-year-old law student and budding poet in Boston. "Give me a breath of air!" it begins,

> There is too much of sweetness here,
> Too much of pain, pain blent with loveliness.
> I am allured from all that we call living
> and sickened of the harsh necessities.[50]

It was the practical necessities, it seemed, that always seemed to impose upon the sweetness of experience. To see into this core of experience, with its pain and its loveliness, was what Percy hoped to do, both in his poetry and in his relationships.

His relationship with Harold Bruff deepened in 1906 when Percy went home with him to Brooklyn for two weeks over the holidays. Percy and Bruff went to the New York Opera and spent time with the Bruff family at their brownstone on Pierrepont Street. "They are the loveliest people," Percy told his mother, "thoroughbreds to the core and unusually intelligent." Percy enjoyed himself and found the Bruffs hospitable and kind, but the trip was cut short: just after the New Year, Harold's mother had a stroke and came close to death.[51] She became paralyzed and would never fully recover. In trying to understand Harold Bruff and his relationship with Will Percy—as well as Bruff's eventual suicide—it is worth noting the direction that his family life took over the next several years. His mother became incapacitated and eventually died in the fall of 1910 from complications developing from her stroke. During this period, William Jenkins Bruff also was carrying on an affair with another woman and promised to marry her on the day after his wife died. When Edith Bruff died, William Bruff did not follow through with his promise. His mistress sued him for $100,000, and the story was widely reported in the newspaper.[52]

The death of his mother and the public embarrassment of his father can partially explain the intensity of Bruff's relationship with Will Percy. Both Percy and Bruff came from prominent, wealthy families, and they shared a similar ambivalence toward them; a sense of familial love coexisted with a sense of alienation. Both Percy and Bruff had mothers with fragile nerves and fathers with outsized ambitions. Both of their fathers (as we will see in the next chapter) became embroiled in publicized controversy during this period. In one another, Percy and Bruff found a confidant, a sympathetic friend, a quiet listener. They likely also found a sexual partner.

At the end of their second year of law school, Percy and Bruff planned a walking trip through Germany and Switzerland. In June they finished their exams and spent a short weekend away together before Bruff went to New York to intern at a law firm for a month before their trip. While in New York, he wrote to Percy, who was spending the month in Greenville. "It was a most bright spot in my days of 'dark toil and grevious labor' to get your twilight fancie today," he told Percy. "Wish I could have heard that mocking-bird with you also Butterfly." Bruff described his new job to Percy and complained that their being apart had left him with a less stimulating intellectual life: "I rely on you to discover for me the things worth thinking." He concluded: "Write soon Billy your inmost thoughts and even if it's a sonnet (an elegy or ode would probably be more polite) don't be afraid to pour it out." By this point, their relationship had developed to the point that even a few weeks apart was too long to go without sharing "inmost thoughts." These may have had to be written in code—such as a poem—but Bruff demanded them nonetheless. He also demanded less self-deprecation from Percy and more confidence. He urged him not to be afraid to communicate with him, and he scolded him when he belittled himself. "You speak in your letter in a most shameful way William," Bruff admonished, "as if you could be anything but 'standable' on our short trip—after a whole year together!"[53] Bruff's use of the phrase "a whole year together" is significant here, since they had known each other for two years. It seems likely that he was using the word "together" to describe their romantic relationship (which perhaps began sometime during 1906), not their relationship as a whole (which began in August 1905).

In mid-July Bruff and Percy boarded a steamer for Europe, where they spent a portion of the time alone but also met up with friends. In Berlin they spent every night at the Bier Gardens. "We never go to bed before 2 AM or get up before 10:30," Percy wrote to his mother. "Everything has been merry as a May morn." When they did wake up, they went to museums. "We have visited four galleries," he wrote, "wept over all the Botticellis, scoffed at the Greuzes, basked and fettered with delight at the Böchelins." He assured his mother that he and his friends were making good use of LeRoy Percy's money, which was funding his trip. "Tell father this scion of the noble house of Percy is not squandering his substance fruitlessly."[54]

From Germany, Percy and Bruff traveled south to Switzerland, where they met up with some American friends. One night in Zurich, they stayed out late drinking, and when they went back to their hotel, Percy and Bruff played a game with some girls, whistling back and forth from their balconies. Percy's description of the game's outcome reveals something of the sense of freedom he felt with Bruff, as well as his apparent desire to test his mother's tolerance: "It all ended by my suddenly appearing on Harold's balcony clad in pink pajamas, with the moonlight a spot-light on me and imagining that I was completely hid by the shrubbery. A number of shrieks and giggles and scamperings discovered to me my mistake and ended our game so well begun in a disgraceful anti-climax."[55]

Percy's pink pajamas suggest a hint of the campy relationship he and Bruff had when they were alone, but also another important fact: Percy and Bruff shared not only their pain with one another, but also their joy. They laughed together, they got drunk together, they made the most of their time. They did not hide themselves away but rather aimed to live fully in the world. "Mother dear its glorious," Percy wrote home, "and I'm awful glad I'm living and young."[56]

Walking and talking was the main feature of their trip. They walked for hours and saw what there was to see, said what there was to say. Percy had specific ideas of what a walk should be. These were moments, he felt, for conversation and the shared appreciation of the world's beauty. In all of Percy's writings—his poetry, his correspondence, his memoir—he depicted his moments of greatest happiness while well-companioned and in a beautiful setting. His ability to experience beauty, he felt, required another person. And in the summer of 1907, he had what he wanted. His letters home reveal nothing of unhappiness—except, for instance, when a walk's destination proved a disappointment. "After walking the last two hours in the rain," he wrote in one, "besides getting lost, it was too discouraging to find that the village contained four Americans besides ourselves, all women. We went to bed in a very bad humor."[57]

Percy and Bruff's trip neared its end in early September, when they had to return to Cambridge for their final year of law school. Before they left, Percy wrote his mother a letter that reveals something of the wide range of experiences he had in Europe, as well as the playful nature of his relationship with Bruff and their friends: "On this trip I find myself endowed with a list of names indicative of various, widely differing moods. Companionable, Bill; humorous, Billikins; killingly funny, Billykint; mock-dignified, William; affectionate, Billy; scornful, Alexander; when I refuse a second stein of beer, Child; after they have had six steins, Bilee. But when I awoke and made known my latest sorrow [he had lost his steamer ticket], I was greeted with '——Will——!'"[58]

Percy eventually found his ticket, for he was back in Cambridge for the first day of classes in September 1907. As his final year of law school progressed, Percy began to consider his future. The thought of moving back to the South—after Paris, after Boston and New York and Venice—pushed and pulled in his mind. He missed his parents. He missed the patterns of living that from his earliest memories had shaped his experience. He wrote loving letters home to his parents and begged them to visit. In those same letters, though, he worried about what he would actually *do* in Greenville, Mississippi. "I look forward," he wrote to his father, "to several years in which 'The Clansmen' at the Grand will be the height of my theatre expectations."[59]

Meanwhile, he made the most of his days in New England. In November he and Bruff took dates to the Harvard-Yale football game and then to the symphony, a day he described as "eleven hours of steady fussing." He described to his mother how "for two days almost without pause Harold and I were left busy acting the unaccustomed role of gallants to Helen Bruff and Bessie Boswell," but now he was pleased that "the week strenuous is past and once more we breathe the easy air of masculine student life."[60] Set in the midst of his Navajo and Italian art, with his piano and fireplace, Percy preferred the company of men. He enjoyed women, and throughout his life several of his most important friends would be women. But his time at Sewanee and Harvard was largely homosocial. He ate, drank, traveled, and came of age in the company of young men. They sorted out their priorities and preferences, taught one another, in Percy's words, how to "proceed into the frightening concourse of men at least awake and not wholly unarmed."[61] He wrote home to his mother about his happily insular world that others might not (or could not) appreciate: "I am having a splendid time which I find hard to describe. College life to the participants is the rarest, most varied, most romantic, most delightful possible. We are heroes of a little play which has too little of either tears or universal laughter to be of dramatic interest to the rest of the world. Our comings-out and our goings-in are to us grand exits and entrances while to the outside they appear wanderings singularly lacking in purpose."[62]

In almost every letter from the fall of 1907, Percy asked his parents to come visit for the holidays. But as December began, LeRoy Percy was so involved in a legal case he told his son that a Christmas visit was impossible and sent him a large check instead. Percy thought it crass. "I suppose there's not any use in talking about how disappointed I was and am," he wrote to his mother. "For the past few days I've been rather miserable, so disappointed that I hardly cared what happened or where I went for the holidays. ... All day [Christmas] I shall be thinking of you and wishing you and father were with me or I with you." He wrote that if they wanted to get in touch with him he would be at 60 Pierrepont Street in Brooklyn with the Bruffs.[63]

After Christmas in New York, Percy returned to Cambridge for his January exams and final semester of school. Bruff developed a case of insomnia, and Percy stayed up with him at night. During the day, he wrote, "I have advised a series of long walks and to see that he takes the advice have been accompanying him." When not walking, Percy played piano, sometimes as many as six hours a day. He let his hair grow long and performed *La Bohème* at the Harvard Union. "In a little less than a quarter of an hour," he told his parents, "I had cleared the room."[64]

As the end of the semester approached, Percy celebrated his twenty-third birthday in part by preparing for exams and whatever lay beyond. Studying the law, he told his mother, created in him "a weary brain, a weird disposition, and a conviction of the futility of life." Worse than the prospect of finals, though, was the prospect of a career in law. "Most of us," he wrote, "dread the thought of what's coming after exams worse than the exams themselves."[65] Law school had been a sideshow to the main events of the past few years, which Percy summed up by drawing a mental picture for his mother. He and his friends had spent the day on the Charles River. "Not being an adult," he wrote, "at the art either of paddling or swimming I was propped Cleopatra-like on many cushions in the middle of the boat and borne luxuriously down the crowded stream with George and Bobbie doing the heavy work."[66] His friends had supported him, taught him, made him who he was. Now it was time to make a decision about the future: move to New York and be with Harold Bruff and his closest friends or move home and join his father's law firm. Clearly, to Percy, becoming an "adult" meant assuming the responsibilities of his home and family. Though he would waver in his commitment in his first few years, and though he insisted that he first take a European trip in the summer of 1908, he informed his father he would join the law firm of Percy and Yerger.

Percy passed his exams with his "usual B" and graduated from Harvard Law School in June 1908. His parents traveled to Cambridge to attend the graduation ceremony, which took place on June 24. One can imagine Percy sitting in the audience with his parents, sweating in his dark suit and starched collar. Scattered nearby would have been George Roberts, Harley

Stowell, Harold Bruff, and others, most with their parents, some not. Students like Harold Bruff may have been recognized for their high marks or their editorial work for the *Harvard Law Review*. But all would have heard the exhortations of Governor Augustus E. Willson of Kentucky, the final speaker of the day. He called the graduates to action by exhorting them to become great Harvard men. The Harvard man, he explained, had a singleness of purpose and a toughness of spirit. "He is the real thing," Willson said, "all wool and a yard wide. He is in earnest; he has courage; he is sometimes a little hard-headed ... but he is a man all the time, wherever he is, and a real man who intends to do things."[67]

Willson's message did not fall on deaf ears. Percy and his friends believed in "doing things," and they believed in courage. Many of them, including Percy, would in their lives do things that addressed real problems and achieved practical ends. But for all their sympathy with this call to action, they felt an equal amount of resistance, of discomfort with this emphasis on practicality, results, and progress. What was practical about classical music? Where was the place for beauty in a man's life? Could practical manhood coexist with same-sex love? Surely these questions and others were circulating in the minds of more than one listener in Harvard Yard. Will Percy would meet Governor Willson halfway: he would address himself to the problems of the real world, and he would do so with courage; but he would work to merge this ethic with a broader notion of manhood as potentially inclusive of same-sex desire, sensitivity to art, and work habits that made ample room for travel and leisure.

He began, a week after graduation, with a trip to Europe with a group of law-school friends. Unfortunately, no evidence survives from this trip except for a postcard Percy sent to his mother as his steamer embarked from New York on July 2. "We're off!" he wrote. "New York is fading in a quiver of heat and we find ourselves alone unchaperoned, ready to be perfect dare-devils."[68]

Harold Bruff was unable to go this time. He took a high-paying, intensive job at the Manhattan law firm Byrne & Cutcheon. He went to work at nine in the morning and worked through the evening—sometimes until 1:00 AM—seven days a week. He lived at home, where his mother's condition had not improved. In late August, he wrote a letter to Will Percy, who was still in Paris. His letter illustrates his passion for Percy, as well as an impending sense of melancholy that would hover over their relationship during the next three years. Bruff's letter also serves as a fitting marker for a turning point in Percy's life: his transition after law school from the "easy air of masculine student life" to the decidedly more difficult life as a lawyer in Mississippi. For eight years, Percy had lived unencumbered by professional responsibility; he had formed relationships with men like Sinkler Manning, Huger Jervey, and especially Harold Bruff that were marked by joy and by love. In Bruff's letter to Percy, we see a measure of their love for one another as well as a real sense of sadness about the future. "Dear Billy," Bruff began, "If I have not written sooner it is not from selfishness for I have had to forego all pleasures under pressure of contencious [*sic*] business and you know my convenient vice of forgetting my conscience. (This is a vile pen). I have missed you tremendously and perhaps there is sour virtue in suffering in silence. Your letters have been whatever is appropriate to an aching soul—and I'm so glad for you that the trip is a success and Italy is in sight."[69]

Bruff was eager to hear about the trip, telling Percy that his letters had brought him great comfort. Bruff had recently been to dinner with Harley Stowell, who had been in Europe with Percy. Stowell told Bruff a bit about Paris, but they could not talk openly in the restaurant. Bruff wrote: "He is going to take me out in his motor tomorrow and discourse on what modesty (?) made you omit." He filled Percy in on "les amies de Winthrop" who now lived in New York, and he described his one lonely trip to the ballet: "I saw Isadora Duncan dance a Tchaikovsky waltz," he said. "I wish you had been with me." He insisted that Percy stay in New York as long as possible when he returned from Europe, "for I want a good many of your evenings myself."[70]

Percy and Bruff would see one another regularly over the next three years, but there was still the sense of an ending in the summer of 1908. Bruff, waiting in New York for Percy's eventual return, his mind focused daily on "refunding bonds and convertible notes and other of your pet aversions," tried to tell Percy of his love. "You have done much for me in three years Bill, leading the way to something higher and the better things in life (and I don't mean morals)," Bruff wrote. "You know that you have a place that no one else can ever quite fill."[71]

6. THE SENATOR'S SON

Perhaps it is a strengthening experience to see evil triumphant, valor
and goodness in the dust. But whatever the value of the experience, it is one
that comes sooner or later to anyone who dares face facts.
—WILLIAM ALEXANDER PERCY, *Lanterns on the Levee*

September 1908 found Will Percy again on a train bound for Mississippi.
Much had changed since he boarded a train in Greenville in July 1900, a
fifteen-year-old southerner bound for college. He had lost his faith in Christianity, though not necessarily his faith in God. At Sewanee he developed
the beginnings of a historical and philosophical explanation of same-sex
desire that made sense to him. His exposure to this knowledge coincided
with sexual experiences that he wanted to view not as crass and lustful but
as honest expressions of a natural desire. In Paris he immersed himself in art
and literature that further expanded his aesthetic sensibility—his faith in the
world's beauty as the fingertips if not the face of God, his belief that the fullest embodiment of that beauty was in the human body and in the physical
and spiritual connection between two people. He experienced this connection with Harold Bruff at Harvard. Being with him "was ecstasy," he said.[1]

On the long train ride south in the fall of 1908, Percy must have felt that
he was entering a new phase of his life. And he was. Cities like New York and
Philadelphia and Washington, D.C., passed outside his window, replaced
with long stretches of rural farmland and forest. He no longer saw Irish and
Italian and Greek workers outside the window, but black sharecroppers and
white tenant farmers plowing and pulling, wrestling to coax some small
profit out of the earth. He saw fewer automobiles and more mules, fewer
buildings and more trees. As he traveled toward Mississippi, the resolve with
which conductors segregated white and black passengers on the train would
have hardened. From where he sat, Percy would not have heard it, but on the
last leg south from Memphis to Greenville, blues music was even then beginning to thicken the air inside plantation cabins and juke joints. During the
eight years Percy had been gone, Mississippi averaged one lynching every

twenty-five days, some of them in Percy's hometown. The Mississippi Delta was a very different world than the one he was leaving behind.[2]

But it was also the same world. The things Percy had learned in Massachusetts he would bring home to Mississippi, just as he had taken with him to Sewanee and Paris and Cambridge the things he had known as a child in Greenville. Percy moved between these seemingly divergent places and cultures and found in each of them something of home. Significantly for Percy's story, sexual values and practices were transportable. It would be a mistake to simply equate New York and Paris with freedom and Mississippi with oppression. These places were different, to be sure, but Percy's experience suggests—not surprisingly—that there were queer folks in the South, too, and that they knew how to recognize one another, where to meet, and how to navigate various obstacles in order to fulfill basic human desires for things like companionship, love, conversation, romance, and sex. The fragments that emerge from the historical record indicate that Percy would come to play an important role in the emerging queer subculture of his hometown.

As Percy got off the train in Greenville, he brought with him a trunk full of new memories, experiences, and ideas, but he also looked out onto a town whose social structure—indeed, even its physical appearance—reaffirmed his deepest prejudices. Greenville's urban black population lived in poverty below the levee; they took jobs as cooks, cleaners, haulers, drivers, and occasionally as preachers and teachers in black churches and schools. Their houses in the shanty section were by and large not level with the ground, their roofs and floors and walls leaning and sagging from the weight of years. The majority of the black population, though, lived on plantations in the countryside, where they too lived in sagging wooden cabins and grew cotton in hopes of profit and new opportunity, though they almost always gained neither. As black people were situated on the hierarchy of wealth and opportunity, so they were situated in Percy's mind: beneath him, beneath his family, and beneath all white people save a few. What Percy saw as a young man reinforced what he had learned as a child—that way of organizing society in the South that historian David Delaney has called "inherited geographies of race and racism."[3]

Though doubtless inferior, Percy felt, black people had soul. They could sing, they could laugh, they could tell stories and jokes in a way no white person ever could. These were a few of the many ways black people dealt with a life filled with oppression in Mississippi, but Percy saw them as innate racial qualities. "The brother in black is still the tiller of our soil, the hewer of our wood, our servants, troubadours, and criminals," Percy wrote. "His manners offset his inefficiency, his vices have the charm of amiable weakness, he is a pain and a grief to live with, a solace and a delight."[4] Toward blacks, Percy's was a condescending, paternalistic, self-indulgent love.

But he had no love whatsoever for poor white people; "peckerwoods," "rednecks," "hill-billies," he called them. Standing on the Greenville train platform in September 1908, looking out over his hometown, he would have seen very few of them. Greenville's white population was demarcated by an elite planter class; an ethnically diverse middle class of merchants, shopkeepers, and entrepreneurs; and an almost nonexistent white working class (since blacks provided most of the cheap labor). The "peckerwoods" more often lived on small farms outside of town, where they rented land or sometimes owned small plots. "I can forgive them as the Lord God forgives," Percy wrote, "but admire them, trust them, love them, never. Intellectually and spiritually they are inferior to the Negro, whom they hate."[5] Like all prejudices, this one had historical roots. Though Percy may have been pre-disposed to class snobbery, the events of the next three years would harden his snobbery into hatred.

SO PERCY UNPACKED his things and became a Greenvillian again. He moved into his old room upstairs in the mansion on Percy Street. He paid ten dol-lars for a Privilege Tax License to carry on the business of attorney-at-law and joined the law firm of Percy and Yerger. Though it was a time of new beginnings, Percy had misgivings.

The evidence that remains about the fall of 1908 suggests that Percy's reen-try into Greenville was less than easy. "I hated it," he wrote in his mem-oir. "Eight years of training for life, and here I was in the midst of it—and my very soul whimpered." The things that men did in Greenville held no appeal to him. "Drunkenness made me sick," he explained, "gambling bored me, rutting per se, unadorned, I considered overrated and degrading. In a charitable mood one might call me an idealist, but, more normally, a sissy." Those things that occupied the lives of the men around him for the past eight years—conversation about art and beauty, long walks through the woods, emotional trips to the symphony—here seemed the doings of "a sissy." And his physical expressions of desire thus far had not merely been "rutting" but relationships, adorned with love and what he felt was noble intent. Percy felt uncomfortable, unable to join fully the culture of Greenville, yet he was still drawn into it.[6]

Much of Percy's difficulty lay with his father, whom he loved. LeRoy Percy by this time had become a leading power broker in the region, so much so that he would soon be nominated for a vacant seat in the U.S. Senate. People trusted him, including his son. "Father was the only great person I ever knew," Percy wrote in *Lanterns on the Levee*. "No one ever made the mistake of thinking he wasn't dangerous, and to the day of his death he was beautiful." LeRoy Percy's presence in the house, in the office, and in the town loomed large in the fall of 1908. Though Will Percy had a difficult time, he realized that he was not alone: "It must have been difficult for father too. Enjoying good liquor, loving to gamble, his hardy vices merely under control, he sympathized quizzically and said nothing. But his heart must often have called piteously for the little brother I had lost, all boy, all sturdy, obstreperous charm."[7]

Percy began to take long walks at night. He would sit on the levee and smoke and write and listen to the Mississippi River. Sometimes he stayed out all night. During these nights, Percy began to write in earnest, mostly poetry. It was probably during one such night that he wrote a fictional sketch called "Fifth Autumn." "Fifth Autumn" is a short reflection, told in the first person, about lust, desire, and memory. It is also about a family's values, about the moment when parents can no longer control their children. It seems very much to be about Camille and LeRoy Percy, who last lived with their son when he was a fifteen-year-old boy and who were now coming to terms with him as a twenty-three-year-old man—a twenty-three-year-old man who interrupted their perspectives and expectations. It is an important document in Percy's unpublished record, for it speaks much more explicitly than other sources about the conflict he felt in Greenville—how to be himself in the South, how to manage his feelings and desires while living in his parents' home.

"Sometimes at night when I had been walking for many hours in the quiet streets," the narrator recounts, "perhaps sitting on the bank of the river watching the dark movement of the water, I would return home very late. I would hear my mother crying out in her sleep and my father in his room pacing the floor. I would sit down beside the open window, drawing a bathrobe around my shoulders, and smoke cigarettes in the darkness." The narrator explains that to him, autumn called forth tangled feelings of lust, desire, and sadness. "Desire in autumn is a bitter thing," he says, "because lust first came upon me in the fall of the year." But now, during the "Fifth Autumn," he had to reconcile the desires of his body with the desires of his parents. "My father and mother looked at me strangely," he says. "My mother gave thanks to God that I was untouched by sin, but she would stop in the midst of her words and weep bitterly." The parents would talk about their son, try and explain him to one another, "but my mother would cover his lips with her hands. 'Do not speak,' she would say, 'we do not know what we may be saying.'"[8]

"Fifth Autumn" speaks clearly to the burden that weighed on Percy—and on his parents—after law school. The Percy home was a place marked both by love and pressure, support and consternation. Camille and LeRoy Percy loved their son, they enjoyed his company, and they wanted to have him near them. They wanted him to settle in Greenville and marry a woman. They also had expectations for how he should behave. It was his gender they were troubled by, his manhood. People called him "sissy" and "queer," and he acted in ways that cut across their expectations. His effeminacy likely raised in their minds the possibility of his homosexuality. Significantly, in "Fifth Autumn," Percy linked their concerns to his sexual desire. The narrator juxtaposes his own lust with his father's pacing and his mother's "crying out." He makes it clear that he is the source of their pain and his "sin" the root of their angst. It is all the more remarkable, then, that though the narrator is troubled about his own place in the family home, though he is "stricken and confused with memory," he comes to this conclusion: "the body of my desire has remained fixed and without change." The concluding note is one of calmness and melancholy peace in the midst of family unrest.

We may never know the extent of Camille and LeRoy Percy's knowledge about their son's "sin." "Fifth Autumn" captures something of two parents on the verge of *naming* their feelings, but they cannot bring themselves to do it. Instead, they weep and pace. They speak, they cover one another's lips; they know, yet they do not understand. Perhaps the most extensive evidence about the Percys' feelings about their son's queerness comes from Percy himself, who wrote a great deal about his parents. This evidence, of course, may or may not have captured their true feelings, but it certainly captured his. "Fifth Autumn" clearly dramatizes an almost impossible home arrangement—though in the end, the narrator sits with his pain, turns it into writing rather than self-loathing. He insists that "the body of my desire" would not change. Throughout Percy's poetry and memoir, his depictions of his parents are similar: portraits of fundamentally good people who were disappointed with and unable to understand or appreciate their son. Recall Camille Percy's "scorn" for her son's decision to become a priest and LeRoy Percy's "far-away expression" when he looked at him.[9] Percy wrote a poem about his mother, "To C.P.," that tried to capture both his and her feelings. It is only four lines:

Her spirit's loveliness was such
Her body's loveliness I could not see;
I only knew her eyes were heavenly blue
That now are grey with tears for me.[10]

It is hard to imagine, in the face of these feelings, why Percy chose to live at home and not elsewhere in some other house or some other city. Possibly, he chose to live at home not in spite of his parents' ambivalent feelings, but because of them. He was drawn to their love as well as their consternation, their goodness as well as their vexation. Recall Percy's portrayal of his own queerness to his mother—his pink pajamas, his being borne "Cleopatra-like" down the Charles River, his being given up as "hopeless" to fall in love with a woman in Italy. Throughout his life, he never stopped trying to please his parents, nor did he abandon that which displeased them. This vertiginous range of pleasure and indirection seems to have been a wellspring for Percy, a crosswise arrangement he was drawn to. "Fortunately I wasn't meek and I wasn't afraid," he wrote of this period. "But it wasn't fun. I had attacks of nausea, but not of tears."[11]

All the more difficult was the fall of 1908 with Harold Bruff over a thousand miles away. In October Bruff wrote down his life story, in two volumes, and sent it to Percy. Not hearing back quickly, Bruff wrote to Percy: "What's the matter Billy? I'm naturally a bit anxious not having a word from you since you received my autobiography (in 2 vols.—both of which required answers). Was it too much for you or is it that you are ill?" Bruff, as usual, was working long hours and worried that Percy would fall into the same trap. "Your last letter sounded ominous Bill—you were never born for a life of colorless toil and worry," Bruff wrote. "You mustn't let anything happen that might shake your confidence in your capacity to achieve your destiny."[12]

Bruff rightly sensed Percy's feelings of anguish, which seemed to be taking a toll on his health as well as his happiness. He worried about him. "There's too much at stake to take any chances," he admonished. He demanded, as was his practice, complete honesty from Percy: "The point is that you owe it to me to take care of yourself, and if you are not entirely well, I have a right to know." Bruff softened his edge as he concluded his note and urged his partner to take solace in his sympathy. "I know how hard it is to find time to write the kind of letters I like to get from you," he said. "But if an eager listener is any inspiration, sit down and talk to me, even though you are tired."[13]

Unfortunately, Percy's letters to Bruff have not surfaced in the historical records; nor did Bruff's autobiography survive in Percy's papers. In fact, there

The Alpha Tau Omega Fraternity, University of the South, in 1909. Will Percy and Huger Jervey served as faculty advisers to the fraternity. Percy is in the back row, standing second from the right, and Jervey is next to him at the far right. (Courtesy of the archives, Jessie Ball duPont Library, University of the South, Sewanee, Tennessee)

is an almost complete gap in the historical record for the next year of Percy's life. Only one letter survives from the year 1909, and what it tells us is this: we do not know Percy's deliberations during the fall of 1908, but we know he decided to move away from Greenville. A member of the English department at Sewanee died and the university asked Percy to fill his spot. This was possibly at the suggestion of Huger Jervey, who still lived in Sewanee, and Percy likely accepted the position in order to consider an alternative career and to be closer to Jervey. The surviving letter, a thank-you letter from the Sewanee "Class of 1909" to Percy, suggests he was an excellent teacher. "By your enthusiastic efforts and well-proven competency," the class wrote, "you have saved the English Department from the temporary deterioration to which it seemed doomed and made the loss of our late beloved Professor much less keenly felt."[14] For his part, Percy enjoyed it as well; a year and a half later, he wrote in his diary that teaching at Sewanee was "my best achievement so far."[15]

Percy only taught at Sewanee for one semester. Perhaps the reason for this was because Jervey decided to leave Sewanee for New York. After having taught Greek at Sewanee for over a decade, he enrolled in law school at Columbia. Percy also went to New York after the spring semester, where he and Harold Bruff embarked on a trip to Europe from June through September 1909. No records survive for this trip, save the notation of their arrival back into the United States in the fall of 1909.[16] Percy once again boarded a train bound for Mississippi. He once again left Bruff in New York. He once again compelled himself to be a lawyer and a son in the Delta.

It proved a momentous decision. Over the next two years, the Percy family was swept into a national political drama that would land LeRoy Percy a seat in the U.S. Senate. Only too quickly, he would lose it. The story of this period in Will Percy's life begins in the fall of 1909, with him once again living in his parents' home, struggling to establish himself as an attorney and an adult in his hometown. To understand the stakes of the story, some background is necessary.

IN 1903 James K. Vardaman was elected governor of Mississippi and at his inauguration pronounced the Fourteenth and Fifteenth Amendments stains on the otherwise virtuous history of America. To have granted citizenship and the right to vote to former slaves was a collective mistake that stood out "naked to all the world in all of its stupid ugliness." Vardaman hoped that the people of Mississippi, along with other white citizens throughout the South, would lead the way in righting this wrong by repealing the amendments. He explained that Negroes "never felt the guilt of sin, the restraining influence of moral scruples, or the goading of an outraged conscience" and were not fit for citizenship. In fact, for the American Negro, "slavery is the only process by which he has ever been even partially civilized." Mississippi's few intelligent blacks, said Vardaman, were "mix breeds and freaks of the race." The real threat to American democracy and the American way of life, he explained, was the presence of black people. Black men in particular, with their insatiable sexual appetite for white women, posed a constant threat and mandated the segregation of the races in all public space.[17] Vardaman's inaugural address echoed his campaign promise that if he became aware of a black rapist in town, he "would head up the mob to string the brute up, and I haven't much respect for a white man who wouldn't."[18]

In 1909 James K. Vardaman was a leading figure in Mississippi politics. Within a year, he would become a bitter enemy of the Percys. Vardaman and his political career played an important role in shaping the way Will

Percy came to view race and class in his southern world. Percy wrote that Vardaman was a "vain demagogue unable to think, and given to emotions he considered noble. ... He stood for the poor white against the 'nigger'—those were his qualifications as a statesmen." In 1910 and 1911, Vardaman was LeRoy Percy's opponent as a candidate for the U.S. Senate. The story of this political contest illustrates a turning point in Will Percy's life and in Mississippi history, as well as several of the most important themes in southern history: how race shaped politics; how class shaped politics; and how the careers of white politicians came to depend largely on the rhetoric they employed concerning African Americans.[19]

After the Civil War and until the civil rights movement, the Democratic Party dominated the American South politically—an environment historians have called the "Solid South." The Republican Party was the party of Lincoln, the party of emancipation and Reconstruction, and white southerners wanted no part of it. By the turn of the twentieth century, white southerners had effectively disenfranchised African Americans by initiating poll taxes, literacy tests, and all-white primary elections. Though the nuances of local politics in southern towns and counties were myriad, two dominant strains emerged within the Democratic Party: the conservative, probusiness plantation elite and the reform-oriented, populist demagogic wing.[20] The two strains agreed that whites should have absolute economic, social, and political superiority over blacks, whom they thought inferior. But they had very different expressions of white supremacy. As Barbara Fields has explained, white racism was far from monolithic throughout southern history. "From the democratic struggles of the Jacksonian Era to the disfranchisement struggles of the Jim Crow era," she wrote, "white supremacy held one meaning for the back-country whites and another for the planters."[21] The contest between LeRoy Percy and James K. Vardaman would lay bare this rift among southern whites.

The conservative strain, exemplified by LeRoy Percy, felt that blacks were an inefficient but necessary source of labor and as such should be treated fairly, educated to some extent, and not threatened with violence lest they strike out for work elsewhere. Leaders like Percy fashioned themselves as paternalists, a guise that put a kindly, fatherly face on white supremacy and the quest for profit. The populist strain, comprised of men like James K. Vardaman, did not advocate black education, felt that the status quo could effectively be maintained by the threat and use of violence, and sought to garner support among constituents by inciting racial hatred (as Vardaman did in his inaugural address). "Race-baiting," perfected by Vardaman and practiced by generations of southern politicians from Louisiana's Huey Long to South Carolina's "Pitchfork" Ben Tillman, became a central part of the southern political landscape and led many such southern demagogues to local and even national leadership.[22]

Another central theme of southern demagogues such as Vardaman was class. Not only did these demagogues fan the flames of racial hatred in their rhetoric; they also assured their white constituents that they were being oppressed by corporations, bankers, financiers, and the elites in their own neighborhoods. They promised reform that would benefit the people, not the elites. During his term as governor of Mississippi, for example, Vardaman disassembled the powerful vestiges of the convict-lease system (whereby planters could use prisoners for farm labor), increased taxes in order to improve schools for orphans and handicapped people, and approved laws regulating big businesses such as railroads, timber, and utilities—all reforms distasteful to wealthy families such as the Percys. Though often quite wealthy themselves, many such southern politicians learned to cast themselves as plainspoken, hardworking men of the people. In contrast, leaders such as LeRoy Percy felt themselves endowed with a special virtue that allowed them to lead the people; they were not motivated, they felt, by profit or power but by a sense of responsibility and honor.[23]

Early in his career, Vardaman was not as virulently racist as he would become. He moved to the Mississippi Delta in 1884 and bought a newspaper, the *Greenwood Enterprise*. In his editorials, and from his seat in the state legislature in the late 1880s and early 1890s, he advocated progressive change in his town: a new public high school, a fire station, and electricity and telephone service. In one instance, he lashed out at the treatment of a black man who suffered unjustly at the hands of Mississippi's convict-lease system. In another, he argued that his readers should support "improvement and elevation of the negro" through education.[24] However, during the late 1890s and early 1900s, his views on race solidified around a more spiteful platform. This transition was an outgrowth of a larger shift in southern politics in which politicians more explicitly campaigned as protectors of a white race under constant threat of annihilation.[25] Seeing potential for broad audiences and an increase in his own power, Vardaman developed a standard campaign speech that he gave thousands of times called "The Impending Crisis." The crisis was the presence of blacks, whose moral and intellectual advancement halted, he argued, at puberty. Despite this, their ambition was to be equal to the white man, and Vardaman warned it would unfold in this way: Negroes had been granted citizenship and the vote by the Fourteenth and Fifteenth Amendments; these rights would lead to progress in political equality; political equality would lead to social equality; and social equality would lead to intermarriage between whites and blacks and would thus pollute the white race forever. Thus the best way to "smother in his native savage breast the fury of his passion" was to repeal the amendments that granted the black citizen his political equality. He packaged this platform to his audience within the rhetoric of fear, patriotism, and rape. "The white women of the South are in a state of siege," he exclaimed. "The cloud of this black peril hovers about them as a deadly vapor. Their very hearts are perturbed and they live in constant fear and painful apprehension. . . . The pestilence is spreading."[26]

Vardaman's venomous idiom might not have gained the traction that it did had it not been for a development in Mississippi politics in 1902 called the Noel Primary Election Law. Before 1902, a committee in the Democratic state convention selected nominees for state offices. Since the populous Delta counties had the largest representation at the convention, Delta interests had dominated state politics since the Civil War. "Bourbons," as they were called, made up of planters, bankers, and lawyers such as LeRoy Percy and his friends, maintained disproportionate power since they maneuvered to have their candidates placed before the people in state elections. Political observers had long spoken of the antipathy between "the Delta" and "the Hills," which though not precisely accurate geographically nonetheless pointed to a clear division within state politics. With the passage of the primary law, however, politicians would thereafter have to canvass the state and be selected by the people as a candidate for state office. This system gave more power to non-Delta voters and also emphasized oratorical skill, charisma, and the ability to connect with a wider range of people. In addition, the convention mandated that only whites could vote in the primary elections, thus placing another barrier (in addition to poll taxes and literacy tests in the general election) between African Americans and their right to vote.[27]

James K. Vardaman was perfectly suited to politicking directly with the people: he was dynamic, tall, and well built, and he habitually wore a white suit, white boots, and a black Stetson hat. He combed his jet-black hair straight back and let it hang down over his shoulders. He held audiences spellbound for hours at a time and often had the stamina to speak four times a day. Will Percy, despite his disdain for Vardaman's politics, had to admit the man was entertaining: his oratory was merely "bastard emotionalism," but Vardaman "was such a splendid ham actor, his inability to reason so contagious. . . . [And] besides he had charm."[28] This energy and charisma—

and his fear-mongering, racist diatribes—carried him into the governor's mansion in 1903. Because Vardaman was sympathetic to levee interests, and because his opponent was part of an anti-Delta cabal, LeRoy Percy supported Vardaman in 1903. Vardaman served one term as governor and then lost in the 1907 race for U.S. Senate to John Sharp Williams, a close friend of Percy. He turned immediately to traveling the nationwide lecture circuit (delivering "The Impending Crisis" day after day) and to editing a Jackson newspaper, the *Issue*. He then set his sights on the 1911 U.S. Senate race.

On December 22, 1909, though, the other Mississippi senator, Anselm J. McLaurin, died suddenly with three years left in his term. In Mississippi, LeRoy Percy was hunting ducks and James Vardaman was writing editorials for the *Issue* in Jackson. Vardaman immediately announced his plans to run for the newly vacant seat. Percy began to confer with his political friends as to who should run against Vardaman. Vardaman's popularity with the people was unsurpassed, and it was unlikely that anyone could beat him. With this in mind, the elite power brokers hatched a shrewd plan. Since there was not time enough to hold a statewide election, Governor Edmund Noel charged the Mississippi legislature to choose the new senator. That body convened on January 6, 1910, and found that in addition to Vardaman, six other candidates had entered the race. Percy and his like-minded associates had decided that since no one person could defeat Vardaman, they would put up several candidates, each of whom would gradually drop out of the race when he was sure his votes would go to another anti-Vardaman candidate. LeRoy Percy was one of the six.[29]

When the first vote was taken on January 7, Vardaman garnered seventy-one votes and none of the other six candidates more than two dozen. The victor would need the eighty-six votes that represented the majority. The vote was to be taken by secret ballot. This infuriated Vardaman, who increasingly felt that this "secret caucus," as it came to be known, was a conspiracy against him, since he was the most popular candidate with the people. In a way, he was right. Governor Noel, as well as many others in Mississippi politics, felt that Vardaman was too radical and unstable for the U.S. Senate, as well as too reform oriented. His views on constitutional amendments, they felt, could possibly rekindle northern sympathies for blacks and lead to more outside meddling in southern affairs. And to probusiness planters like LeRoy Percy, Vardaman's race-baiting tactics were bad business: when faced with the threat of violence, many blacks would seize the chance to move elsewhere for work.[30]

Every day for several weeks, the legislators voted again with no real change.

During this time, Jackson bustled with activity: barrels of whiskey were unloaded off trains and delivered to campaign headquarters; burlesque women were seen coming and going from hotel rooms at all hours; votes were being bought and sold, handsome dinners given, and fistfights fought in the streets. When Vardaman learned of a legislator on the fence, he invited him to his room for some sherry and conversation, which he called "missionary work." The pro-Vardaman press published regular editorials calling for an open vote, proclaiming that an elite cabal was conspiring to undo the will of the Mississippi people. Vardaman himself wrote in the *Issue* on January 29 that the sovereign will of the people was being jeopardized by railroad lawyers and big-money lobbyists. The next day, LeRoy Percy boasted in another newspaper that though he was in fact a railroad attorney, at least he was not, like Vardaman, "a briefless barrister" and a "reckless agitator" who had to rely on friends and creditors for money. Vardaman played his hand perfectly, writing a few days later: "I have no desire to indulge in personalities, nor shall I stoop to notice Mr. Percy's thrust at my impecunious condition. If poverty is a crime, then I am guilty." In a state full of impecunious farmers, Vardaman knew how to win at politics.[31]

But with a secret ballot, popular politics did not matter. The majority of state legislators did not want James Vardaman in the U.S. Senate, and they were the ones casting ballots. After almost two months of deadlocked balloting, anti-Vardaman supporters began to drop out of the contest and LeRoy Percy emerged as the strongest candidate. On February 22, 1910, before a packed gallery of Percy's and Vardaman's supporters, the final vote was cast, and LeRoy Percy won, 87–82. The Percy people cheered and the Vardamanites sat in silence as Vardaman reportedly ran back and forth on the senate floor with his hands on his head yelling, "Black as the night that covers me!" Rather than the end, though, it was the beginning of a long and bitter fight. Vardaman's paper, the *Issue,* promised: "People of Mississippi, the fight between the classes and the masses, between the corporate influences and the people is on, and it will be a fight to the finish."[32] On the other hand, many throughout the country celebrated the result as a victory over radicalism; the *New York Times* proudly noted that the senator-elect from Mississippi was not a populist demagogue but a descendent of the English "Northumberland family of which Harry Hotspur was a member."[33]

Also in New York, Harold Bruff was sending positive thoughts to Will Percy and his family. He had sent Percy a telegram on New Year's Day: "[T]he dawn is here I think may you have at least half the happiness you deserve."[34] As the political caucus heated up, Bruff wrote to make sure Percy kept his priorities straight. "Why haven't you written me? Are you still at Jackson engrossed (that's legal enough) in practical politics?" Bruff chided. "I wrote you a long letter (mine have that habit) *weeks* ago—did you get it? You see I've no pride at all but only a great desire for a letter." Bruff reminded Percy of the fun they had the previous summer in Paris—"Don't you wish you were there?"—and wondered when they could see one another again. He reported that he had been to see Wagner's opera *Tristan and Isolde* ("Are your eyebrows turning green?"), seen the symphony perform Debussy ("You know where my thoughts were"), and been to a Harvard Law reunion dinner ("[E]veryone was dreadfully middle-aged and legal and stupid and glum"). He said that he wished Percy had not returned to Mississippi, concluding sarcastically: "O lucky one in the pleasant ways of Greenville, doesn't your conscience ever smite you?"[35]

In fact, Percy seemed to be finding a measure of peace in his life in Greenville. His father's political career gave him a specific set of goals. He believed in LeRoy Percy's candidacy. He felt his father's viewpoints were humane, thoughtful, and honorable, and he worked with him to ensure Vardaman did not reach the Senate. LeRoy Percy's political ambitions also meant that Will Percy had more responsibility in the office. He took on some of his father's cases. He found that the busyness of legal work could be oddly pleasurable. "There is," he wrote in his diary later in the year, "a sort of joy of efficiency in being a lawyer to the exclusion of all else and not only am I more intelligent but am actually more content when an accumulation of business forces me to work every hour, day & night." But he also knew that such joy was tenuous and second-rate: "During such periods a crash of music from an open window or a sunset is liable to tumble the house of my oblivion about my ears and leave me shivering with longing."[36]

A month after LeRoy Percy's victory, Theodore Bilbo—a man who would become one of the most famous politicians in southern history but who was then a thirty-two-year-old state senator from Pearl River, Mississippi—came forward and said that he had accepted a bribe to vote for Percy during the caucus. He did it, he said, solely to uncover corruption and in the end still voted for Vardaman. He still had the money—$645 in cash—that had been paid to him in installments during the caucus by a Delta plantation owner named Lorraine Dulaney. The state senate immediately launched an investigation into the charges of bribery, and the proceedings of that investigation uncovered much finger pointing and one truth: Mississippi politics, in the words of journalist George Creel, was a "carnival of corruption."[37] During the caucus, state legislators were wooed by promises of patronage and barrel after barrel of liquor, and in at least one case a Percy aide paid the property taxes of a state representative. But the state senate, eager to defend its election of Percy, found no evidence of wrongdoing on Percy's part and made a resolution to expel Bilbo from the senate. That failed to obtain a majority vote, but after the pro-Vardaman legislators walked out, the senate passed a resolution asking Bilbo to resign and calling him "unfit to sit with honest, upright men in a respectable legislative body."[38] For his part, LeRoy Percy pitched in that Bilbo was a "moral leper" and "a characterless man, a self-confessed liar, a self-accused bribe-taker."[39]

This resolution had the unintended consequence of galvanizing the support of the electorate on behalf of James Vardaman and Theodore Bilbo. Bilbo and Vardaman's supporters successfully—and accurately—portrayed the "secret caucus" as a series of backroom deals between the state government, big-money bankers, and corporate lawyers. Furthermore, the charge of bribery, as Will Percy put it, was "a lie with a thousand lives."[40] LeRoy Percy's name became tainted with corruption, elite prejudices, and political chicanery. His battle to be reelected in the regular primary election, set for August 1, 1911, would be all uphill.

LeRoy Percy did not help himself by being tiresomely intellectual in his campaign speeches, which began immediately in the summer of 1910. In speech after speech, he began by introducing himself and promising that he was neither as corrupt nor as wealthy as Vardamanites charged. Boll weevils ate most of his cotton, he said, and though he had served as counsel for the occasional railroad, most of his business consisted of serving his community. He then explained that the appropriate candidate for the U.S. Senate needed to have a working knowledge of business and law in order to best represent the people. To prove he was such a candidate, he delved into the intricacies of cotton futures, the machinations of Mississippi's Department of Agriculture, and the methods by which the federal government collected revenue and reapportioned it to the states. Rather than be moved to support Percy, many of his audiences heckled him and threw tomatoes.[41]

Will Percy, for his part, loved his father's speeches. When work allowed him time off, he rode trains around the state and listened to LeRoy Percy's campaign promises. "Father's genius in speaking lies in his power to make an audience see that he is fervently sincere and deeply thoughtful," he wrote in his diary. "His English is wonderfully clear but he employs no rhetorical devices; his style is masterful but not eloquent, impassioned but not passion-stirring, appealing to the mind but not the emotions, dramatic but in no way theatrical."[42] Percy was actually identifying not his father's genius, but his miscalculation: politics *was* theatre; it demanded rhetorical devices, show-manship, and passion. Mississippians found Percy dull and uninspiring at best, haughty and pretentious at worst.

LeRoy Percy assured his audiences that he was not a racial liberal. Varda-man, he explained, was too extreme and actually posed a danger to white supremacy. "There was never a time since the war," he told audiences, "when the relations between the whites and the blacks were more pleasant or bet-ter. Never was white supremacy surer or safer or more complete. No Negro votes in Mississippi, nor sits on a jury. And this, without Federal aid, in fact in spite of Federal opposition."[43] With Vardaman in the senate, the federal government would be forced to take notice of the race question, and due to Vardaman's extremism, officials in Washington might actually take punitive action. Percy was not trying to persuade anyone to abandon white suprem-acy; he wanted his audiences to adopt his interpretation of it. He wanted them to believe he was the protector of their values. Vardaman, he told them, was the real threat to white supremacy.

LeRoy Percy never connected with the people. Part of this was because he had a serious air and a personality that was all business. Unlike his son, he had little charm or patience for people, and he often did not remember faces or names. "He just couldn't remember folks," the son of his campaign man-ager remembered.[44] A large part of this, though, must have sprung from the fact that he did not admire "the people" or want to connect with them. He and his contemporaries referred to the masses of poor whites in Mississippi as "the bottom rail." Will Percy described the audience at a campaign stop in Black Hawk, Mississippi:

> I looked over the ill-dressed, surly audience, unintelligent and
> slinking, and heard him appeal to them for fair treatment of the
> Negro and explain to them the tariff and the Panama tolls situation.
> I studied them as they milled about. They were the sort of people
> that lynch Negroes, that mistake hoodlumism for wit, and cunning
> for intelligence, that attend revivals and fight and fornicate in the
> bushes afterwards. They were undiluted Anglo-Saxons. They were
> the sovereign voter. It was so horrible it seemed unreal.[45]

In his campaign, LeRoy Percy evinced this planter mentality, his social standing, and his education. The University of Virginia grad was suspicious of democracy, of "the sovereign voter." As Will Percy said idealistically of his father and his political friends, "Being convinced no system of government was good without good men to operate it, they considered it their bounden duty, their prime obligation as members of society, to find such men. Concerning democracy they had no illusions. ... Anybody who was anybody must feel *noblesse oblige*."[46] But most voters of Mississippi in 1910 were not looking for "good" men to lead them with disinterested virtue. To them, LeRoy Percy's disposition did not look like noblesse oblige—it looked like condescension.

So they heckled him. At campaign stops, crowds cheered "Hurrah for Vardaman! Hurrah for Bilbo!" In one town, Will Percy found baskets full of rotten eggs that were to be thrown at LeRoy, so he stood next to them with a pistol in his pocket, he said, "which I intended to use."[47] On July 4, 1910, the Percy entourage stopped at Godbold's Wells in the piney woods region of south Mississippi. The crowd was so noisome and cantankerous that Percy could not speak. He stood on the platform waiting for the crowd to silence. As minutes went by, Percy grew angry. As his attempts to begin speaking were met with jeers and laughs, he grew furious. Finally, in his anger he shouted at the crowd, and what the crowd heard was: "Cattle!" To a polity already suspicious of Percy's airs of aristocracy, this was just the charge needed to create a groundswell of support for Vardaman and Bilbo. Pro-Vardaman newspapers and campaigners seized on this reference and never let crowds forget that Percy thought them nothing but hillbillies and rednecks, no different than herds of cattle. Vardaman's newspaper, the *Issue*, caricatured LeRoy as "the dead-game plumed knight of the Poker-table, the Crowned Victor of the Rotten Secret Caucus."[48]

During the summer of 1910, James Vardaman was away delivering "The Impending Crisis" on the California lecture circuit. In his absence, Theodore Bilbo, who was himself running for lieutenant governor, campaigned for himself and for Vardaman. Though Bilbo was barely five feet tall and often campaigned in borrowed suits, one journalist wrote that "on the stump he's 7 feet 10 inches tall."[49] Like Vardaman, he electrified crowds with his invective. In one such speech, he painted a political enemy in these colorful terms: he was "a cross between a hyena and a mongrel; he was begotten in a nigger graveyard at midnight, suckled by a cow and educated by a fool." (The man subsequently cornered Bilbo on a train and beat him with his pistol, fracturing Bilbo's skull and sending him to the hospital for a week.)[50]

In addition to his own offbeat charisma, Bilbo had the added benefit of being at the center of the Dulaney bribe controversy—people wanted to see him, wanted to hear the inside story of Delta planters buying votes with money and liquor. He titled his campaign speech "Jim Vardaman, the Radical; LeRoy Percy, the Conservative; Grandma Noel, the Sissy; Senator

Bilbo, the Liar." In it, he gave salacious details about the ways Governor Noel orchestrated the secret caucus and Percy's election; the dark rooms in which he received corrupt money from Dulaney; the sordid designs black men constantly made on white women. When he spoke, his followers shouted "Hit 'em, Bilbo! Amen! Hallelujah! Good ol' Bilbo! Goddam!"[51]

In July 1910 Bilbo invited LeRoy Percy to an open political rally. Percy rejected the invitation, and Bilbo published a letter to the rally's organizer, saying: "I am very sorry, indeed, but presume the Hon. LeRoy Percy was afraid that he would not have his secret caucus legislature along to 'applaud' when he cussed Bilbo."[52] After this, Percy changed his mind and prepared to attend the rally. LeRoy's brother Walker, a Birmingham lawyer, was fed up with the attacks on what he saw as his brother's honor and decided to challenge Bilbo to a duel. Walker came into Will Percy's hotel room the night before the speech and told him that "one of our group would have to kill the bribe-taker" and instructed him to meet him on the morning of the rally in the hotel dining room, where Bilbo would be eating his breakfast. After target practicing in front of the mirror all night, Will Percy met his uncle and his seventeen year-old cousin LeRoy at six o'clock the next morning. Bilbo was across the room eating oatmeal. Walker pointed at Bilbo and "boomed out the epithet which makes an American fight if he's a man." Bilbo did not look up.[53]

At the rally that afternoon, Bilbo riled the crowd of a thousand into such excitement they hoisted him onto their shoulders and danced after he spoke. They howled for Percy, and when Percy stood up to speak, they cried "Vardaman! Vardaman!" Though one of Percy's aides had urged him to speak briefly about the tariff and cotton futures and be done with the bloodthirsty crowd, Percy did not. He began to fling insults at the crowd and at Bilbo, calling him a "vile degenerate" and a "consorter with lewd women and frequenter of assignation houses." He claimed that the only person who would corroborate his bribery tale was "a poor, broken-down shameless woman of the streets." Bilbo was quaintly sitting on a rocking chair on a porch listening to Percy's caustic speech—he was a master of public relations and mass appeal.[54] When LeRoy Percy was finished, his son recalled, "the bear-baiting cowardly crowd, wild with excitement, cheered and cheered and cheered."[55] It seems likely that they were cheering at the sheer spectacle of the campaign: the "man of honor" insulting the state senator's sex life and morality; the presence of bribery and scandal; the electric advent of Bilbo onto the political scene.

The summer 1910 campaign ended with an electorate energized to work on behalf of Bilbo and Vardaman. LeRoy Percy returned to Washington, D.C., weary from campaigning. He wrote to his wife: "[S]ome day this cruel war will be over and then we will try to pick up the broken threads of our lives … [A]nd if we can come out of it in good health, with honor, and not a [*sic*] bankrupt I will be satisfied."[56] Vardaman, on the other hand, returned to Mississippi ready to jump into the fray. In California he had delivered "The Impending Crisis" almost daily for five months and had it honed to near perfection. His first act upon his return was to stage a masterful rally at the Jackson fairgrounds. Five thousand Mississippians flocked to the capitol to see the White Chief. With Bilbo successfully managing his identity as martyr for the people, and the pro-Vardaman press issuing daily reminders of the corrupted power of those like LeRoy Percy, much of Vardaman's work had been done for him. As Vardaman finished speaking at the fairgrounds in October, an excited listener grabbed his black hat, cut it into shreds, and passed it among the crowd. The mob hoisted Vardaman in the air and carried him through the fairgrounds.[57]

IT WAS LIKELY also in the summer of 1910 that Harold Bruff was diagnosed with tuberculosis. He took time off from work to go to the hot springs in Virginia, a regular destination for convalescents at the time. From there, he wrote to Percy: "Dear Billy—I haven't written sooner because I've not been in the mood and I'm not now." Bruff's tone was decidedly less sensitive than usual, and he wrote despairingly about returning to "New York and work and Hades," though a letter from Percy—which mentioned a trip north—had "raised great hopes. Can't you come to or at least through N. Y. for a day or a week or a month?" He asked Percy to write him about his plans and concluded: "You must take a month now and later the Gods may smite us both at once."[58]

A few weeks later, in early September, Percy wrote and told Bruff that he was on his way. In that letter, he must have posed some sort of question to Bruff—perhaps about where Percy would live after the election, or about their relationship, or about Bruff's health—because Bruff wrote back: "Dear Billy—Thanks for your letter—It did me lots of good. This is not an answer to it but merely to say I'll expect you Monday surely and even if you stay at the Manhattan or some equally frivolous places we can arrange to see lots of each other and possibly even talk 'De Profundis'—but that is very difficult."[59] The phrase "de profundis" means "from the depths" and was the title of Oscar Wilde's famous letter from prison, where he was serving his sentence for "gross indecency." Wilde wrote the letter to his former lover Alfred

Douglas, and in it he ruminated on love, art, and forgiveness. Though the letter was a confession, he refused to admit that his sexual conduct was wrong; rather, he pointed out that the laws of Great Britain were unjust. At 50,000 words, the letter was a great many things, but for many of its readers it was a final statement on love and loss by one of the greatest artists of the time. *De Profundis* was published in 1905, and Bruff and Percy almost certainly read it—it was widely read during this period, particularly by those interested in Wilde's spectacular downfall. References to Wilde, Dorian Gray, and "de profundis" became part of the homosexual idiom of this period, and in fact Bruff mentioned reading Oscar Wilde in a letter to Percy.[60]

Bruff concluded his letter on a curious note. "You must stay here many days," he wrote. "I know N. Y. is not the place for <u>us</u> and there are so many distractions that seem to frighten away the desired mood but maybe—who knows?"[61] In the past, New York had been a place where Percy and Bruff found space and time to be together—to see shows, to talk to one another, to walk amidst the noise and the energy and the possibility of the city. This was "the desired mood"—to be alone, to be able to talk freely and express themselves physically. Presumably what had changed—the "distractions" Bruff spoke of—was his mother's health. By the time of this letter, her condition must have been tenuous. Percy arrived in mid-September, and within two weeks, Edith Bruff was dead.[62]

Percy's trip to New York in September and October 1910 must have been intensely emotional. Bruff, recently diagnosed with tuberculosis and soon after losing his mother, likely also knew about his father's mistress. Soon enough, the newspapers would publish excerpts from his love letters to her, most of them signed "lots and lots of love and kisses." Soon enough, William Bruff would be in court, facing a $100,000 lawsuit for breach of contract.[63] Harold Bruff must have been grateful to have Percy with him during the two weeks after his mother's death, filled as it must have been with visitations and a funeral—and likely also sadness and confusion and rage.

When Percy returned to Greenville in mid-October 1910, he began to keep a diary. This was perhaps because of the intensity of his trip to New York, or possibly because of his increasing desire to become a writer. Regardless of his reasons, he decided that "the present year promises to be for me peculiarly vital, perhaps a real turning point in my life."[64] The two-month period from mid-October to mid-December 1910 is the only period in Percy's life during which he kept a daily diary—or at least the only diary he kept that survives in an archive. The themes and topics that emerge most regularly in Percy's diary are a concern for Harold Bruff, a sense of perplexity about how to manage being both a poet and a lawyer, and ambivalence about where he should live—Greenville or New York. He also wrote a good deal about his father's senate campaign. When Percy wrote about men, he tended to describe their physical appearance and their attractiveness (or lack thereof), and in one instance he recorded sleeping with a local teen. A "confessional of misdemeanors and fancies," he called his diary, and, quoting Shakespeare's *Twelfth Night*, he wrote: "I shall keep a nightly tab of events in this book, the words here-with being to my eyes 'divinity, to any other profanation.'" It is a singularly illuminating piece of evidence in his extant records.[65]

Not surprisingly, many of Percy's nightly notes included descriptions of his legal work. He was working on a railroad trust case and a lawsuit against the Knights of Pythias. He did not include details of the cases themselves but rather thoughts about how work made him feel. "Life was drab today," he wrote in mid-October. He wondered why he was "pretty unhappy in the profession" and "guilty of a continual discontent," answering his own question: "I seem to be happy only when writing what seems to me beautiful." What he wanted was more time to write; practicing law dimmed his creative energy and made him less able to contemplate beauty. He wrote of his rare moments of poetic energy: "If the keen hours of afflatus came oftener I should almost have courage to chuck all and seize them." But something about Greenville squelched his creativity, he felt, made him more a lawyer and less a poet. His town's ethos seemed to demand practicality and usefulness, and the culture around him "made rapture seem contemptible." "More soul and less liver," he decided, "would make me in Greenville itself a singer."[66]

Percy did not particularly enjoy legal oratory, and his opponents on the bench reaffirmed his political and class conceits. On the same day James Vardaman had addressed the Jackson crowd at fever pitch, Will Percy was in court arguing against a "hill-billy." He noted of his legal adversary: "His style of speaking is a bastardized rococo of pure oratory, much in vogue in the hills and seldom heard in the Delta; characterized by flamboyant and frequent gestures and by loud vocal ornamentation. A quaint ridiculous old person he was obsessed very naturally with Vardamanism."[67] Percy chafed at the thought that his days were spent arguing railroad cases in a provincial town, against "ridiculous" old men, rather than writing poetry. He was busy, and constant work did not allow him time for his art. "This business of living everyday life," he wrote, "completely makes art impossible because with its hurly-burly it makes a weighing of values and an appreciation of the absolute impossible."[68]

One thing that regularly disrupted the seemingly stolid atmosphere of

Greenville was the Mississippi River. On October 17, 1910, it brought a man named "Roth." Roth, as described by Percy, was a wanderer, "a nomad in practice and in theory" and also "an Englishman, a Socialist, an Agnostic, a Lover of Wagner, a Dentist, an Aspirant to be a Prose Artist without having read any Literature, a Reader of Phylosophy [*sic*]. And a Stimulant." "A remarkable fellow of great charm," Percy wrote. "He has a youthful intensity and good looks, but no physical attraction." Percy hinted that the reason Roth was in town was to see him, because despite his constant travel, "a sudden affection for this place and perhaps for an inhabitant has made him wish to stop his wanderings." Unfortunately, Roth got caught up in some sort of scandal that Percy described obliquely: "The discovery of a flaw in his code of living together with the [illegible] his desire by an accidental fet [*sic*] has left him considerably perturbed within." This discovery also made it clear that it was time for him to "move on."[69]

It is unclear exactly what transpired with Roth or who he was, but a few details about Percy's note warrant some explanation. First, it is worth pointing out that Greenville was not an isolated, homogenous, conservative town untouched by outside influence. Rather, it was a place where a nomadic, socialist, agnostic dentist might stop to visit; and he stopped to visit because he knew what he would find there—presumably Will Percy. That Percy described Roth as good looking but without "physical attraction" suggests that Percy did not find him sexually attractive. Perhaps Roth's "flaw" involved sexuality, perhaps it did not; perhaps it involved Percy, perhaps not. But one thing was clear: "He must move on." Roth's arrival and departure suggests a liveliness to Greenville that must have been attractive to Percy on some level. Of Roth, Percy concluded in his diary: "I shall miss him."[70]

The day after Roth's departure was for Percy "all day work." That night, Percy took a long walk alone on the levee, "watching the full golden moon float up into a hot, vividly purple sky." A "bright spot" during the otherwise unhappy late October day was the receipt of a letter from Huger Jervey. "My correspondence with him causes only satisfaction," Percy wrote in his diary, and seeing him in New York recently had imparted "that proud calm delight that being with such a friend should call up. Ours must be 'a marriage of two minds.' The maelstrom of New York sucks in more and more of the people I love."[71] Percy was reminded daily of his loneliness, of his distance from those he loved like Bruff and Jervey and Manning, in his Mississippi life. A few days later, he wrote in his diary: "This morning I was intensely and delightfully alive, delicious fancies coursing thro me like birds thro an open window. While dressing a day or two ago I noticed our new calf was feeling the same way, full of whimsical observations ... lacking but one thing—someone to romp with."[72]

In late October, Greenville held its first ball of the season, and Percy went with a date named Sue Myers. "Dancing is a debatable amusement," he wrote in his diary, and "I felt quite old. Most of the girls were very young and very silly." He used the occasion to invite a young man, Walter Sillers, to spend the night with him. Unfortunately, "something was wrong with the supper at the dance because almost everybody was sick," and Sillers spent the night sick in bed at the Percy house. The next morning, Percy left to hear his father deliver a speech in Jackson.[73]

After his speech, LeRoy Percy put his campaign on hold for the winter and returned to Washington, D.C., with Camille.[74] In Greenville, Will Percy filled his days with work and reading. His boredom permeated his reflections in his diary: "One of the days I hate, lacking any kind of passion or thrill, the tide of feeling within as drab as the tide of events without. No gusto. No pang of sympathy"; "Another day with no noble deed done"; "Tonight I read from cover to cover Bailly's The Divine Minstrels (English translation) and found it 'to my purpose nothing'"; "To me came as comforter no poetry all week, but instead indigestion and headaches aplenty which this afternoon culminated in an authentic attack of the blues." One evening, he read and was taken with Percy Bysshe Shelley's drama *Cenci*. He felt the heroine, Beatrice, was comparable to Shakespeare's best heroines, and Percy evinced an implicit feminist perspective when he wrote: "She is the only heroine in all poetry who independent of love remains a heroine." Other than reading Shelley, his most notable "mental experience" in November was a "conversation with Francis on the necessity of belief in a Beneficent Purpose at work in the universe and the reasonableness of that belief. I held that for the race to go forward such belief must exist and that, further, contemplation of the universe, especially infinite of space and time, led irresistibly to the conclusion that there was behind it all purpose, design, which if at all must be beneficent."[75]

In late November, Percy used the opportunity of his parents' absence for male companionship. He attended a local showing of Israel Zangwill's popular play *The Melting Pot* with a date, Sue Myers. "After the play," he wrote the next night in his diary, "W.H.G. who went with Tanque spent the night with me—a sweet, untrained child with a hint always of prankish Pan, and handsome."[76] We do not know the identity of Tanque or W.H.G., but this entry is significant for several reasons. Percy's use of the words "untrained" and "child" speak to his pederastic conceptions of homosexuality. W.H.G. was most likely a teenager, or he may have been Percy's own age. But by describing him as "untrained," Percy portrayed himself as the partner with more knowledge and sexual experience.

In addition, it is important to note that Percy, Tanque, and W.H.G. were not meeting secretly but out in public. It was often the case that Percy took women on dates where he met up with men; at several social functions like plays, dances, and operas, he went with Sue Myers but invited men to come home with him afterward. Percy and W.H.G. perhaps met for the first time at *The Melting Pot*, or perhaps they knew one another previously through Greenville's small but growing arts culture. At some point, though, they *recognized* one another. They clearly had ways of communicating—manners of affect, patterns of dressing and self-presentation, coded vocabulary (such as "prankish Pan"), or shared interests in authors or artists—that formed mutual understanding. This is important not just for understanding Percy but also for understanding the ways that, despite the oppressions and limitations in the South, queer people connected with each other.

In early December, the Mississippi River brought a surprise visit from a law school friend, Bob Black. Percy took the day off from work and spent it with him. Though Black had tended to be combative and temperamental at Harvard, something had softened in him. At one point, his eyes filled with tears at the mention of a former girlfriend, and Percy was strangely touched. Black was able to express feelings that Percy was "unacquainted of." "I am envious," he wrote in his diary. "Joy I have felt in all its stir under many different provocations; but never sorrow. Bob thinks he will never marry, but he has loved. There too he terrifies me: I fear that perhaps I shall never marry or more terrible I shall never love."[77] This poignant moment in Percy's diary points to the tangle of feelings he had about Greenville and his ability to thrive there. A month earlier, he had written of Harold Bruff and Huger Jervey, of how "New York sucks in more and more of the people I love." Without question, Percy loved Harold Bruff, so why now was he writing of his fear that he would never love?

My sense is that in this instance, he was speaking of love as it related to marriage to a woman. It was common for queer men to marry women, and indeed in many cases to love them. Percy no doubt felt pressure to do so, and perhaps he had some desire to do so. The prospect of life as a bachelor in Greenville held for Percy both possibility and pain. He could never live openly in a loving, committed relationship with someone like Sinkler Manning or Harold Bruff. Yet he could find companionship and sex with someone like W.H.G. He could also be more mobile, experience the world away from Greenville. Percy made the most of his limited options; he cultivated and participated in a queer network of people in Greenville and traveled in order to be with men in other places. But he was not content with that. When he wrote of his fear that he would never marry or love, he was expressing a complex of sadness that included not having the comfort of a long-term, rooted relationship; not having his love or his relationships validated by his family and neighbors; and having the person he loved most a thousand miles away, suffering from tuberculosis and grieving the loss of his mother. Percy was a lover of men in a place where that was only possible in limited and carefully planned situations. For a person who found his greatest joy in relationships, a lifetime of love on the sly was not what he wanted.

It was also in early December 1910 that Harold Bruff wrote to Percy with news of his impending trip to Europe. "Today work, tedious even more than usual because of the dark and soggy day," Percy wrote on December 5. Bruff's letter arrived, and Percy noted that Bruff was "to have six month's vacation—without me—among divine places," a fact that created within him a "longing which for want of leisure to indulge turned sour."[78] Three days later, Percy received another letter from Bruff, Percy's description of which is worth repeating: "It seemed to palpitate; poignant to the degree that rereading it is almost an act of courage. He is going to our country. How I long to go with him." Percy wrote of his sadness that Bruff was "not taking me with him" and how he missed his "tangibility and rather physical tactility."[79]

Percy was in the midst of a stressful trial and spent an "unrestful" weekend worrying about the case and about Bruff. He went to visit a friend, Will Hardin, who was in the hospital: "Hardin is splendid, sincere, clean, brave to an extraordinary degree, also good to look at."[80]

Percy's final lines in his only remaining diary were these, on December 11: "Harold sailed yesterday to the lands overseas and the haven where I would be."[81]

THE SPRING OF 1911 witnessed the climax of James K. Vardaman's political career. The band played "Dixie" as he opened his campaign for the August primary on February 24 in Canton, Mississippi. The crowd buried the music with its cheers and whistles. Vardaman's popularity was such that he did not have to slander LeRoy Percy; though he referred to him as the man "spawned in the cesspool of the secret caucus," he rarely mentioned him by name. Also, since he had established his views on the race question so thoroughly in the previous decade, he often limited his racial diatribes to a call to amend the Constitution to ensure that America remain a white man's nation. Primarily during the spring and summer of 1911, Vardaman made himself visible, created an atmosphere of excitement, and spoke again and again of his platform for the common man: railroads and corporations should be regulated; a graduated income tax should be passed; the people should elect U.S. Senators directly; prohibition of intoxicating liquors should be federal law; and America should not intervene in foreign affairs. He pointed to his success as governor and never let his constituents forget that he was the victim of bribery and a carefully orchestrated secret caucus.[82]

Vardaman's campaign capitalized on LeRoy Percy's one recorded condescending epithet. At rallies, many men, women, and children carried signs that read "Cattle," "Hillbillies," "Rednecks," and "Low Brows." In Meridian on Independence Day, 2,000 Vardaman supporters marched through the town with these signs and with lighted pine-knot torches and red neckties. Several bands played "Dixie" and Confederate battle marches. In the middle of the procession, a high wagon pulled by eighty oxen carried the White Chief himself, and the crowd thronged around it to touch the wagon or get a glimpse of Vardaman. LeRoy Percy and his supporters read about such theatre with disbelief. Of Vardaman's Meridian parade, John Sharp Williams wrote to a friend: "There was a fanaticism about the fool performance that rather frightened me. When men get to fighting about who shall touch the stupid car, upon which a man almost as stupid is riding, there enters into it a factor of fanaticism that I don't understand and am not capable of measuring."[83] The Percys had a sense of what this "fool performance" and others like it meant. Coming home one day after campaigning in the summer of 1911, LeRoy Percy asked his son what he thought of the election. "Not a chance," he replied.[84]

On election day, Vardaman won a landslide victory, garnering almost 60,000 votes more than Percy and carrying seventy-four of Mississippi's seventy-nine counties. Bilbo, too, won his race for lieutenant governor by a large margin, and the state senate became filled with Vardamanites. Historian Bertram Wyatt-Brown poignantly notes that LeRoy Percy spent $20,000 on his campaign in order to garner about 20,000 votes; Vardaman spent $2,000 and garnered almost 80,000 votes.[85] This election was significant in southern political history because it was one in which whites voted almost strictly along class lines: farmers and laborers voted for Vardaman, planters and businessmen voted for Percy. The Mississippi Delta elite, which since the Civil War had maintained dominance in state politics, was losing its grip on power and being replaced by a new generation of populist politicians. This shift coincided with a dramatic increase in racial violence in the 1890s and

1900s and a solidification of Jim Crow laws throughout the South. A new brand of politician, symbolized perhaps most fully by James K. Vardaman, sought to create solidarity among white voters by inciting racial fears and animosities, assuring audiences they would maintain the absolute dominance of the white race by any means necessary. Vardaman said: "We would be justified in slaughtering every Ethiop on the earth to preserve unsullied the honor of one Caucasian home."[86]

Deltans such as the Percys found Vardaman's racial views maddening. LeRoy Percy wrote to a friend of Vardaman's manner of creating "horrible pictures of the assaults of negroes upon white women ... only to inflame the passions and hatred of his audience. ... Playing with dynamite, arousing the bitterest of race feelings, to accomplish nothing—only to get a few votes." But Percy's perspective was not shaped by his sympathy for African Americans or by a progressive political agenda. He felt black people were inferior and politically incompetent but highly valuable for the production of wealth. The considerable riches of the Delta depended on the vast majority of black field hands, and racial agitation would do nothing but drive them out of the state. He felt that Vardaman's agenda would only make "the Negro more difficult to reason with and control." Blacks with their own volition, especially when this meant out-migration, spelled disaster for "not only the future prosperity and development of the South, but its very civilization."[87]

For Will Percy, the political developments in Mississippi were central to his conception of race and class. His view of black people as otherworldly, pitiful, and tragic depended at least in part on his view of poor whites as violent, stupid, and susceptible to demagoguery. He had nothing but scorn for them, especially after 1911. He blamed them for corrupting the Delta and the South more broadly. "Today," he wrote thirty years later, "Mississippi is like the rest of the South and the South is like the rest of the nation: the election of demagogues horrifies nobody." LeRoy Percy's loss was symbolic to him of the rise in power and presence of a group of people that were wresting control from honorable men—not just in Mississippi, but throughout the world. Vardaman's election in 1911, he wrote in 1941, was "my first sight of the rise of the masses, but not my last. Now we have Russia and Germany. ... The herd is on the march, and when it stampedes, there's blood galore and beauty is china under its hoofs."[88]

Thus in August 1911, inured to defeat, filled with contempt not just for James Vardaman and Theodore Bilbo but for the "masses" in Mississippi, LeRoy, Camille, and Will Percy prepared to board a steamer for Greece. Just before leaving Greenville, Percy received a telegram from Harold Bruff:

"Much disappointed on your account but cannot believe your father really cares to represent such stupid people. Hope this means you will all come north at once." Percy had invited Bruff to come with them to Greece, but Bruff wrote that at present it was "impossible for me to go away."[89] Ten days later, Bruff wired again: "[W]ill expect to bring you down to Bay Shore or stay with you in New York as you prefer, come soon, Harold."[90] The Percys arrived in New York in late August, stopping for a few days before sailing for Europe. They left behind them the pain of the recent political loss and sailed across the Atlantic and through the Mediterranean. Arriving in Greece, Percy and his parents stepped on the beaches of Patras with "considerable peace of soul."[91]

While the Percys were in Greece, Harold Bruff's condition worsened to the point that he felt compelled to die. His suicide in October confirmed what Will Percy wrote in his diary precisely one year before: "The present year promises to be for me particularly vital, perhaps a real turning point in my life."[92] His father's defeat and Bruff's suicide were central moments in Percy's experience; the evidence from his first twenty-six years suggests very little of the melancholy stoicism that marked the later parts of his life. The sadness and restlessness that historians have so often pointed out as the result of sexual frustration or misplaced longing or an abstract belief in stoic ideals was actually the result of real-life events: the death of his lover, the humiliation of his father, the prospect of a long life alone. Percy explained this in his memoir, echoing his earlier phrase. "It was a turning point in my life," he wrote of this period. "Since then I haven't expected that what should be would be and I haven't believed that virtue guaranteed any reward except itself. The good die when they should live, the evil live when they should die; heroes perish and cowards escape; noble efforts do not succeed because they are noble, and wickedness is not consumed in its own nature."[93]

It is difficult to speculate about Percy's state as he returned to Greenville at the end of 1911 without cheapening it. Remarkably little evidence survives for the next few years of his life. The evidence we have, though, suggests that Percy faced the facts and lived with them. Bertram Wyatt-Brown has documented the peculiar regularity with which members of the Percy family committed suicide in the face of trauma, despair, and persistent depression.[94] This must have seemed an option. What happened, though, was that Percy returned to Greenville and resumed practicing law. And more important to him, he wrote poetry.

Shortly after Bruff's death, Percy wrote a poem called "Longing," which captures something of his feelings at the end of the long year 1911. In it, the narrator sits alone watching a sunset, longing for the presence of his lover. Rather than vibrant red and purple, "the sky is limpid loveliness," and "Grey as slow tears, the dusk blurs out the trees." The narrator speaks to an absent person and says that this night, unlike in the past, "we no more shall come together home" after watching nightfall. The poem concludes:

> Oh, for one hour to-night,
> One little hour with you—
> To touch your hand—
> To lean within the halo of your perfume—
> To watch, as those sweet many times,
> Together, love, the young, white moon,
> Like some strange petal blown into our round of space
> From out the cool abysms of the night,
> Where unknown blossoms bloom for unknown eyes
> To gaze upon in wistfulness. . . .
> A little while to watch,
> And then, together, home.[95]

7. ON LOVE, POETRY, AND WAR

> When you feel something intensely, you want to write it down—if anguish,
> to staunch the bleeding; if delight, to prolong the moment.
> —WILLIAM ALEXANDER PERCY, *Lanterns on the Levee*

Percy had been writing poetry since law school, but after Harold Bruff's death in 1911 his work became more focused. Over the next few years, he wrote a series of poems he published as a book in 1915: *Sappho in Levkas and Other Poems*. Taken as a whole, the poems in *Sappho in Levkas* amount to an extended meditation on love, death, and loss. Percy dedicated the book "To H. B." Many of the poems, such as "Longing," are addressed to a dead lover. The title poem, as we have already seen, is a narrative poem about sexual awakening. Other poems in the volume address Percy's regular preoccupations: the elusive love of God, the beauty of man, the longing for peace. Poetry should never be reduced to mere autobiography, but *Sappho in Levkas* demands to be read as occasioned by a specific juncture in Percy's life—one in which he was grieving the loss of Harold Bruff, trying to establish a workable pattern of living in Greenville, and continuing his meditations on love, sex, beauty, and art.

Percy left this chapter of his life out of his autobiography, which stops in August 1911 and picks up in August 1914. One possible explanation for this is that, sandwiched between the Vardaman campaign and World War I, Percy felt these years lacked narrative tension. After all, *Lanterns on the Levee* is more a series of thematic reflections than a strict chronological account of Percy's life. My own sense, though, is that Percy may have found these years difficult to write about. This was a significant period in Percy's life for several reasons. In addition to grieving for Harold Bruff and writing the poems for *Sappho*, Percy developed a relationship with a woman that seemed as if it might end in marriage. Rather than lacking in importance, the years between 1911 and 1914 were marked by deep sadness, creative energy, and multiple, conflicting desires. It was precisely these tensions that structured his love and his poetry.

WILL PERCY and Janet Percy Dana met in New York City, probably during Percy's trip north in the fall of 1910. They shared a great-great grandfather, Don Carlos Percy, the oft-married planter who arrived in Louisiana in the 1780s. Janet Dana descended from Don Carlos and his first wife, Margaret, and Will Percy from Don Carlos and his second wife, Susannah. Percy and Janet Dana joked to one another about their shared ancestor, whom they called "the Pirate," and wondered if it was he who endowed them with such similar interests: literature, classical music, sculpture, travel, conversation. When they met, Percy and Dana immediately formed a deep connection. They enjoyed one another's company, talked openly and vulnerably, and sparred about music and politics. Percy sent her drafts of his lyric poems, and she sent him gifts. She breathed new air and positive energy into his life in the years after Bruff's death.

Janet Dana was beautiful, intelligent, and sensuous, and she possessed a penchant for idealism. Her grandfather, Charles Dana, had been the undersecretary of war in Abraham Lincoln's cabinet. Her father, Paul Dana, was the editor of the *New York Sun* and had inherited a small fortune from his father and a large fortune from his father-in-law. The Danas lived on Fifth Avenue in New York City and summered at a property in Glen Cove, New York—one of only two houses on Desores Island, the other of which belonged to J. P. Morgan.[1] The New York social arbiter Ward McAllister included the Dana family in his infamous list "The Four Hundred," which named the select families in New York City who had "the poise, the aptitude for polite conversation ... the infinite capacity of good humor and ability to entertain or be entertained that society demands."[2]

The Dana family mansion stood at 1 Fifth Avenue in the heart of Greenwich Village on Washington Square Park. Just a few doors down, at 23 Fifth Avenue, lived the iconic bohemian Mabel Dodge. When Mabel Dodge moved to Fifth Avenue in 1912, she demanded to live apart from her wealthy husband as an experiment in free thought and free love. She painted over the drab Victorian walls of her home until the interior shone bright white, from the porcelain chandeliers down to the polar bear rug she placed in the living room. She held a regular salon at her home that was frequented by such visitors as feminist and birth-control advocate Margaret Sanger, labor organizer "Big Bill" Haywood, muckraking journalist Lincoln Steffens, and political radical Max Eastman. At these affairs, the forward-thinking Bohemians spoke freely of topics such as sex, jazz music, socialism, and modern art and sometimes experimented with hallucinogenic drugs. "It seems as though everywhere," Mabel Dodge later remembered of the period, "barriers went down and people reached each other who had never been in touch before; there were all sorts of new ways to communicate as well as new communications."[3]

To place Will Percy and Janet Dana in the context of this "new spirit" of the 1910s illuminates their relationship to the shifting terrain of American cultural norms. Percy and Dana shared much in common with many bohemians: they were born in the mid-1880s; they were reared in affluence and comfort in an age of enormous inequality; they read widely and traveled extensively; and they felt discomfort with the confines of Victorian morality. Dana and Percy were remarkably open with one another and shared idealistic and open-minded temperaments. They wrote to one another a great deal about wanting more from life, about feeling trapped by convention. But whereas Dana's neighbors called for open, deliberate revolt against convention, Percy and Dana were more restrained. They questioned, but they did not revolt. They still clung fast to some of the traditional values that Greenwich Village intellectuals rejected, such as patriotism, reticence, duty, propriety, and honor.

Dana's intelligence and adventurousness come across vividly in her letters to Percy. Before Percy left for Greece in 1911, she wrote him: "I think I want to go to Greece more than anywhere else in the world—except maybe, Italy, and the Great Wall of China, and Constantinople, and a few other places that I have no chance of seeing. So come and rouse envy in my heart and let me charge you with special messages to the Gods." She spoke excitedly about their future visits: "As for poetry, and music, and The Pirate, please add politics to the order of business at our next meeting."[4] Percy was attracted to her remarkable energy and her deep sympathy. Her letters pleased him, and he demanded more of them. From Greenville, he wrote: "[O]f course I've considered long lyric outbursts to you these many days. … It is a constant grief to me to know that letters from you automatically cease when I fail to bid for one." In the same letter, likely written sometime during 1912, Percy told Dana that his parents were traveling to New York and would call on her family. "I hope you'll see them and like them," Percy wrote. "All my best is inherited, only in the wrong proportions."[5]

As Percy and Dana's relationship developed during the early 1910s, he was also writing poetry that grieved the loss of Harold Bruff. In "Arcady Lost," Percy engaged similar themes as the ones in "Longing": the physical beauty of the world and sadness at having to experience it alone. In the poem, the cherry trees bloom and robins sing

the dire divine
Music, that once, beyond the violet rim
Of pain, could waft us clear to where, our own,
Th' unstable faery shores of ecstasy
Burn in the twilight of an April sea.

Now, though, the sound of birdsong stirs not ecstasy but grief, for "our music came last night to me alone." The poem ends on a melancholy chord that suggests ecstasy and delight may no longer be possible, that such moments will always be freighted with memory. Such moments can only recall "the days / We clung together here," can only bring

the pain of hearts that, glamorous still with spring,
Break, and the dread of star-lit, lonely ways
Where once, O comrade mine, we heard them sing.⁶

Likewise, "The Happy Isles" is addressed to a dead lover. The narrator imagines his lover in a beautiful afterlife and wishes him well. Again it is twilight, "This hour that we loved most," an hour that always reminds his heart of "its lack of you." He hopes that

perhaps, there, too, in those far lands of yours,
Springtime comes flowing like a tide of dreams,
Mysterious, on bluer wings.

The poem is marked by love and longing; it is an attempt to imagine the absent lover in heaven, to imagine him at peace. But it also hopes for mutuality, for the possibility that the dead also long for the living:

Yet, even there, perhaps,
Your unaccustomed eyes yearn back
Across the spirit-footed ocean of the air,
And you are homesick for the earth ... Homesick, perhaps,
    tho' Paradise be yours,
For me.⁷

In "A Sea-Bird," melancholy transitions to despair. In the short poem, a bird flies "a haunted flight" over the ocean in search of the dead. The poem begins, "I cry, I cry / Into the night," as the bird flies out over the sea. The sea, though, reveals not the dead but the loneliness of the bird. It ends:

Lone, alone,
And the Sea is mad.

Mourning, mourning,
Broken and strown,
It nurseth the dead,
The dead alone—
And my heart that is mad.[8]

Significantly, one finds in *Sappho in Levkas, and Other Poems* not just grief and mourning but also a reflection on art as a potentially redemptive process. The prevailing motif in the poems is that of loss, but several poems begin to measure the possibility that poetry itself can unify and uplift. For example, the first poem in the volume is called "Song," and it begins, "O singing heart, think not of aught save song; / Beauty can do no wrong." The poem is an exhortation to the poet himself to give himself to art, to set his focus on beauty. One sees in "Song"—and indeed in other poems in *Sappho*, such as "Ecstasy," "Soaring," and "For Music"—a sustained attempt to find in art that which religion failed to deliver: comfort in affliction, a vision for beauty, moments of calm. The poet in "Song" tells himself:

Deaf to immortality or gain,
Give as the shining rain,
Thy music pure and swift.

The emphasis is on the here and now, on art for its own sake. Percy found in poetry not only a medium for conveying his perceptions and desires but also a process that created emotional comfort and a framework of meaning.[9]

In addition to writing, Percy spent these years lawyering and traveling. He traveled to New York three times in 1913 to see Janet Dana and Huger Jervey.[10] Though little evidence survives regarding these trips, we can surmise that Percy's experience was divided between the New York of Huger Jervey and the more conventional world of the Dana home on Fifth Avenue. After Percy's trip in December and January 1913–14, Dana wrote to him, presumably speaking of Huger Jervey: "I almost ransacked New York for your music-loving friend—although you say he wouldn't like me!"[11] Percy likely mentioned Jervey to Dana after he had seen him in New York, but clearly he was not eager for them to meet. The truth is probably that Huger Jervey would have liked Janet Dana very much; she was eminently likeable, open-minded, and had similar tastes in opera and classical music. Percy's comment to Dana that he "wouldn't like" her was probably made half-jokingly, but it also seems to have been an oblique attempt to prevent them from meeting. Perhaps Percy was not ready for them to meet; perhaps he feared Jervey's censure over their budding relationship; perhaps he wanted time to think things through for himself, since Jervey had been such an outspoken and important influence on him.

It is clear, though, that Dana and Percy's relationship was developing a more romantic character. After his visit in the summer of 1913, she wrote: "Of course, it is vastly forward to say so, but I must confess that I vastly enjoy talking to you." She hoped the chance would come again soon. "I am on my knees," she wrote, "praying busily that the new year will bring you very early in its course."[12] Percy did visit again in late December and early January, and the two went to see the opera *Tristan and Isolde* and stayed up late into the night talking. After Percy left, Dana wrote to him: "You made yourself much too agreeable during those four days you spent 'under my mother's roof'—I really miss you." She continued: "With all the miles there are between us, I don't even blush to make that frank statement—or to tell you that I shall wait impatiently for your next visit. ... Nothing will keep me from pursuing you." She told Percy about the art shows and operas she planned to see, and that she would prefer to have him as company. "I also wish to 'rub it in,'" she wrote, "that you made a great mistake to go when you did, for no less than three opera boxes descended on us last week." One of these was for *L'Amore de Frere*, which Percy had seen and gushed about to Dana. She chided him: "Woe be to you if my anticipations aren't realized."[13]

A month later, LeRoy and Camille Percy traveled through New York and visited the Danas for tea. After their visit, Janet Dana wrote to Percy: "We were awfully disappointed Wm Percy could not come too, and I don't need to tell you that I shed tears for your sake." She sent him a gift—a framed photograph of a Venus statue—and pleaded for another visit sooner rather than later. "Oh!" she concluded, "why are miles between Greenville and New York—it would be so nice to see you at this moment and tell you Easter greetings and spring greetings instead of stupidly covering a pretty clean page with little black scrawl."[14] Percy responded: "I'm so glad you saw mother. She's one lovely and lovesome person."[15]

In Greenville in the spring of 1914, Will Percy was wrapping up several legal cases and planning a summer trip to the Mediterranean. He was also revising poems for *Sappho in Levkas* and writing new ones, and he would use his time in Italy to put finishing touches on the volume before sending it to Yale University Press. He apologized to Janet Dana for his infrequent letters: "How it is I immediately get so snoggled up in affairs ... YMCA's, beer parties, auto rides, commercial clubs, drainage meetings—I never know." He was restless, he said, and stressed about his part in maintaining "the family fortunes." Boll weevils were eating all the cotton, and he knew nothing of how to stop them. His father might, but he was off in Alaska hunting wild game. "Do you know a nice pawnshop for heads and steins?" he asked. "If so his return might help." Regardless, he felt some comfort at the thought of getting out of town for the summer. "I'm beginning to get thrilled over the prospect of a European trip," he told Dana, "tho, to be frank, the thrill is not so much anticipation of what I'll see as of what I hope to get away from. But it is discouraging to remember that in the end the thing you run away from is always yourself." He suggested that she try to join him. "Can't you somehow manage a flight at the same time? It's a crime against things as they should be that we never have tripped together."[16]

In June Percy took a train to New York, where he spent a week before boarding the SS *Saxonia* for Europe. While there, he went out to Glen Cove to visit Dana (who was not able to join him on his trip) on her family's summer estate. The night after his visit, she dashed off a quick note—addressed to him at the "Cunard Pier," from which the *Saxonia* was leaving the next day—that suggests any ambivalence about their relationship was his, not hers. "My dear Will," she wrote, "I fully realize how base it was of me to wail so indigo-ly after you had given up some of your precious New York hours to a country visit. I'm ashamed, but nonetheless appreciative, although when good-byes were said, I did not seem so! Will you remember your word to come and tell your tale, on your way home? In that case, I will try not to be so selfish. Anyway, dear Will, I wish you Bon Voyage and many adventures & may the sea and Sicily at least answer some of <u>your</u> questions. Thank you again for coming. Au Revoir."[17]

THREE WEEKS LATER, Percy was atop Mount Aetna in Sicily with a group of drunken donkey boys. Unbeknownst to him, Archduke Franz Ferdinand had been murdered the day before in Sarajevo, Bosnia. Percy was merely happy to be traveling in a beautiful place. His Baedeker travel guide double-starred the sunrise view from the volcano, so he had hired a crew of guides to take him to the top. But the night before the final ascent, they drank too much and were keeping Percy awake. Perturbed, he asked his tipsy guide "if Aetna donkey-boys always got drunk." The guide said no, but this was the first trip up since the last eruption; furthermore, the guide explained, his last client was the archduke himself. "I was not interested in Austrian grand dukes and wished he would shut up," Percy recalled. "One duke more or less—what time did we start up the crater for sunrise?"[18] After the Aetna sunrise, Percy traveled to Syracuse to find solace in the Sicilian countryside.

He dashed off a postcard to his friend Carrie Stern: "Was piped asleep by a shepherd at Girgenti."[19] He wrote to Janet Dana: "I wish this very minute you were perched beside me under this olive tree."[20] Within a month, this Europe of sunrises and shepherds would be altered forever.

While Percy traversed the Sicilian countryside in search of bucolic idyll, the political alliance system that had held Europe in a balance of power since the 1890s began to come apart, leading quickly to a war that changed the world. A month after the murder of Franz Ferdinand, the German army invaded Belgium. In turn, Great Britain, France, and Russia declared war on Germany and its ally, Austria-Hungary. Britain initiated a naval blockade of German seaports, hoping to starve the Germans into submission. The Germans, in turn, sent out U-boats to sink Allied naval and mercantile ships. On both sides, civilians and political leaders believed the war would be short and decisive. Instead, the war lasted four years, involved over forty countries, and left over 8 million people dead. Rather than a decisive confrontation that would alter the political landscape, the war became a machine of death. The slaughter of modern warfare mocked ideals like heroism and gallantry. Sacred values became profane. Soldiers died face down in the mud. Churches donated tens of thousands of pounds of steeple bells and organ pipes to the war cause to be melted down into bombs and bullets and land mines.[21]

Historians have long argued about the role of the Great War in shaping a "modern" consciousness among its participants—one that rejected the notion of history progressing peacefully toward perfection; one that valued questioning over dogma, experimentation over tradition, and irony over romanticism; one that saw art not as a tool for moral and spiritual uplift but one used for plumbing the mysterious depths of the human psyche and the violent randomness of history.[22] With regard to war, modern thinkers came to reject the ancient notion that *dulce et decorum est pro patria mori*—that "it is sweet and fitting to die for one's country." By the end of the war, British war poet Wilfred Owen was firmly convinced that Horace's dictum was "an old lie."[23] War and its outcomes could now only be written about with irony.

This debate is useful for framing Will Percy and Janet Dana's experience of World War I. The conflict in Europe aroused within them—as it did within many Americans—deep patriotic sentiment and deep feelings that they had a noble responsibility to the war cause. In addition to their other mutual pleasures and interests, they now shared a passion for the war. Percy sailed to New York on August 1, three days before Germany invaded Belgium, and stayed with the Danas before traveling back to Mississippi. When he returned to Greenville, Percy wrote to Dana: "To miss this war is to miss the opportunity of living in this century." He wondered aloud about how they could become involved. "How can one get to the front?" he asked. "How can two? For instance could we get the Red Cross to take us as nurses?" At this point, in the fall of 1914, the war remained a distant abstraction to Percy; he imagined it not a violent, deadly affair but an honorable one. He was still able to write about it lightheartedly, as someone who had never experienced it. "To lie in a trench (particularly if filled with cold water) and shoot a fat kindly blond German doesn't inspire me," he wrote, "and I couldn't drive a machine or fly an aeroplane, but in sound and sight of the titan horrors there must be work. Allons!"[24]

The onset of the war brought Percy and Dana closer together. They wrote each other more frequently, and they wrote of the war as something that bound them together in common cause. Dana enrolled at Barnard College for the fall semester and wrote that college was uninspiring, but "it will keep me from running off to England, or to Mississippi, as I am sore tempted to do." She and Percy had both been practicing a difficult Brahms piece on the piano, and she pointed out that "it is a rather difficult thought to reconcile oneself to the fact that all the most glorious music is German—when Germans are doing the horrors we read of every day." She told Percy their floors were sagging under the weight of newspapers about the war, and that the walls were covered with maps of Europe, pushpins noting the daily movements of the armies.[25] Percy wrote back that he admired her family's fervor and that her letter was "a fine autumn cry above the dissolving empires and domestic retrenchments." He, too, could think of nothing except the war, and his only consolations were letters from her: "Word from you, anyway, these days seems peculiarly golden, for I am overwhelmed with work and at night am too tired for either writing or reading—unless you are the author."[26]

The winter of 1914–15 was marked by several disappointments for Will Percy. He increasingly felt himself on the margins of world history, bogged down in legal work in Mississippi while British and French soldiers were dying for a cause he believed in. In addition, his mother's condition was not well. "Just before Christmas father took mother to Johns Hopkins Sanitarium, Baltimore, for an incipient nervous breakdown," he explained to Dana. "She is there now, slowly mending, allowed to see no one and neither receiving nor sending mail." A central part of the difficulty, he explained, was that "when she goes the bottom quite drops out of our family establishment." Percy's choice of phrasing suggests that it was not the first time Camille Percy had had a breakdown and that the family dynamic required her presence. With his parents in Baltimore, Percy spent Christmas at a hotel in Pass Christian, Mississippi.[27]

"What are you doing spending Christmas in Pass Christian?" Janet Dana demanded to know. "I take it very unkindly that you should take holiday flights in any direction but towards New York." She told him she was concerned for him and wanted to better understand his restlessness. "I wish I knew what you most wanted," she wrote, "so that I could importune the fates of 1915 for your benefit." She wanted him to be happy, she said, and she insisted he look to her "if you wanted an unquestioning supporter for any private and particular prayer."[28]

It was likely around this time that Percy met Tommy Shields, who would become a very important person in his life. The historical record is almost completely silent about Tommy Shields, though a few significant details emerge. Shields was six years younger than Percy and lived in Greenville all his life. Percy dedicated *Lanterns on the Levee* to him (along with several others) and had him buried in the Percy family plot in the Greenville cemetery when Shields died in 1941. In addition, Shields is listed as living in the Percy home in the *City Directory* for at least one year during the 1920s.[29] One Delta resident remembered Shields as "a misfit who drank excessively but whom Percy loved," and a distant Percy family member described him as Percy's "boyfriend."[30] Shields emerges for the first time in Percy's papers as a traveling companion in 1915. Theirs was a decades-long friendship that seems also to have been at times—if not the entire time—a romantic relationship. Percy was probably not alone on Christmas Day, 1914, but with Tommy Shields.

It also seems likely that Shields went with Percy to New Orleans several weeks later. Percy wrote to Dana from that town, telling her: "I'm down here, instead of on my own native hearth, without any good sufficient cause. My temper day by day became more unendurable so I just packed up and ran away, with an unfinished manuscript and a toothbrush under my arm." Percy was finishing his revisions of *Sappho in Levkas*, but not without ambivalence and negative pressure from his parents. Of his poetry, he wrote: "My poor family regards it as a poor way of spoiling a perfectly good career (tho this is learned merely from divination), I suffer they are right." He wondered how he had become endowed with gifts and interests so different from, and often at odds with, his parents. Referring to their shared ancestor, he asked Dana, "Do you suppose the Pirate, before Le Belle Louisiana sniped him, filled the fo' castle with ribald rhymes hot off his chest?"[31]

Janet Dana sympathized with him. "It must be almost unbearably hard," she wrote, "to stick at the law when you so long to be entirely a priest after the order of Apollo."[32] She wrote that there were four spring concerts coming up and that he should come to New York to see them. "I am greedy for them all and I would so like to thrill in your company. There's just a cool, damp, hint of spring in the air that calls us to break rules & duties." She urged him to put aside his concerns and come be with her, experience the music. "For the moment," she wrote, "I want to be bare to every beauty of sight or sound that is within reach."[33]

Percy and Dana's correspondence illustrate a confluence of desires and responsibilities that pulled Will Percy in at least four directions at this point in his life. First, he felt compelled to commit his physical energies to his family, his work, and Greenville civic life. He worked doggedly at the law; he went to flood control meetings and fund-raisers and dinner parties in Greenville; he worried about his mother. When he grew weary of life in the South and wanted to move away, he listed the reasons he could not: "Father without anyone to help him, money fearfully scarce, mother on the verge of nervous collapse."[34] Other times, he told Dana of his genuine love for his place. "I really do love the life here," he wrote. "It is so unrushing, so natural, even when drab so human. And our skies are immense. Summer is on us now, smotheringly, but the trees and the river and the flowers are of dream-like beauty and the mockingbirds day and night are gushing song."[35] All at once, he felt that he must live in Greenville, that he loved Greenville, and that Greenville made him restless and tired and eager to travel.

A second competing desire was poetry. "Poetry makes me happy," he told Janet Dana, "and that aside from all else is gift enough from the gods."[36] What he wanted to be was a poet, not a lawyer. Writing the poems for *Sappho* had awakened in him a wellspring of creative energy and had been cathartic and redemptive; poetry was a delicate and beautiful form, Percy felt, the ideal medium for expressing doubt and faith, love and lust, grief and joy. It pleased him, and it scared him. He conveyed his fears to Dana: "I believe there is some real poetry in my verse, but taken together it is too intense, too personal, too unrestrained, too un-objective."[37] In another letter to her, he confessed: "I may be taking the verse I write much too seriously; indeed, that's very probable, but there's just enough of it in me to ruin me hopelessly for anything else, so when I doubt the worth of what I write, the doubt shakes everything I'm built on and altho no one else feels the jar, to me it's an earthquake."[38] Percy's doubts were enhanced by his parents' skepticism and the fact that his legal work left such little time for writing. And when he wrote that his verse was "too intense, too personal, too unrestrained, too un-objective," he was expressing some measure of his angst that he was about to publish a book that narrated his sexual awakening, plumbed the depths of his grief for Harold Bruff, and celebrated the beauty of the male body and homoerotic love. This was no small matter to him, a thirty-year-old man living in his parents' home in Greenville, Mississippi.

Percy may also have felt himself at a crossroads with regard to sex and love in 1915. In his life, he had experienced romantic and sexual relationships with Harold Bruff and "W.H.G.," and possibly also with "Roth," Sinkler Manning, Huger Jervey, Tommy Shields, and others whose names did not make it into the archives. These relationships emphasize his willingness and desire to meet men in the South, his ability to communicate with like-minded men and form liaisons despite the potential for legal recrimination and public humiliation. This, too, was no small matter to him. Nor is it a small matter in understanding the history of the South itself. Percy's experience suggests that what John Howard and others have shown about the second half of the twentieth century—in Howard's words, that "queer sex in Mississippi was not rare. Men-desiring-men were neither wholly isolated nor invisible"—was also true for its first half.[39] Percy did and would continue to accept and act on his homosexual desire in Mississippi.

But at this point in his life, this desire seemed to coexist with genuine affection for Janet Dana. As we will see, Dana eventually forced the issue and—though we do not know what Percy said—the relationship became explicitly a friendship and not a romance. But it seems possible that Percy had some desire to marry her. Particularly in 1915, his letters to her suggest a great deal of endearment. "You probably don't know just what a place you have come to occupy in my thoughts, my life," he told Dana. Thinking of her, he wrote, had a profound effect on him: "I become calmer & breathe the salt cold air from the foamy sea. ... It's bad for you to be so far away. ... I only want to hear from you and of you."[40] A month later, he told her that her letters to him "are my only consolation for not being with you." If she were to stop writing them, to stop thinking of him, "I could almost tell these thousands of miles away & I know you'd catch the ensuing wail. To know that you are thinking of me is more than a tonic, it is a drink of whiskey to a half-frozen wayfarer."[41] The tenor of Percy and Dana's correspondence was tender, sympathetic, and understanding. We do not know what Percy *thought* precisely, but it seems that if he ever considered marriage, it was in 1915 to Janet Dana.

All of these feelings, pressures, and desires weighed on Percy. The evidence from roughly 1910 to 1915 shows an increasing sense of sadness and restlessness in his life. This comes across clearly in his poetry, but also in his correspondence. He confessed to Dana that regularly "I get a case of the uttermost dumps—& that baleful disease has become almost chronic."[42] "I get all droopy, sickly with thought or near-thought, discouraged," he said. "I have no lark qualities."[43] Though he was sacrificing so much to be home, to work for his father, to do right by his family, he still felt "the necessity of my presence believed in by no one except myself. ... The taste of life is very braccish [sic]."[44] He echoed these sentiments in a letter to another friend, the queer poet Witter Bynner: "I write because I love it and I practice law because I must live. To be in a small southern town means to engage in all sorts of activities. It's a pretty energetic life, but some day I hope I can get out of it."[45] This was not merely abstracted sadness, nor was it the self-loathing of a closeted homosexual, as has been suggested by some. The death of Harold Bruff, the difficulty of living in Greenville, the as-yet-unrealized ambition to be a full-time writer, the prospect of companionship and family with Janet Dana coexisting with sexual desire for men—these things combined to create a sense of dislocation and unease. Percy wanted to remake his life. "I'm about convinced that my usefulness down here is ended," he lamented to Dana, "and certainly all chance for happiness is. From now on it would be a 'petering' out process, which of all things I most despise."[46]

Adding to this sense of restlessness was that, in the spring of 1915, Janet Dana announced that she would begin training with the Red Cross in order to serve as a nurse in France. Percy felt at once proud and useless. He saw himself as sitting complacently "in comfortable aristocratic surroundings" while Dana had acted on her ideals. She had shown "a true knight's courage," while he had not. "I'm proud of you," he wrote, "and—this almost disappoints me—so too are my mother and father."[47] Stuck in Mississippi doing legal work, he tried to experience the war vicariously through her. He stole time to write to her from his office in the middle of the day. "I'm almost anxious for you to get to the front," he told her in one letter. "It's the next best thing to going myself and your vision has, I love to fancy, the same slant as my own. So please drink twice of all the terrible and the beautiful you will find there, once for you and once for me."[48]

When Janet Dana did arrive in France, she found much more terrible than beautiful. While Percy wrote from America, "Have you seen the heroic armies?," from France Dana wrote of the tedium of her twenty-four-hour nursing work, the chaotic and dirty hospital, and the eyes of the men she hoped would die so they did not have to suffer for the rest of their lives as invalids. She wrote of amputating infected arms and legs. In one case, a soldier had his shattered arm amputated and was shortly thereafter informed of the death of his best friend. Fogged with ether and grief, "He kept calling to his friend—'*Raymond, mon ami, au revoir, au revoir … Ah, pourquoi tu ne me reponds pas?*'[49] "No one who has not seen it," she wrote, "can realize the sheer material horror of it, let alone the spiritual side—which is a sharper knife."[50]

Percy, having not seen this material horror, continued to read gallantry into the war. "How I glory in your sketches of French heroism!" he wrote. "Please tell me more & more & more!"[51] To him, the war was more than fighting; it was a source of meaning. He told Dana that her letters from the front "are the only things that seem to radiate vivid life & connect me with some vital force."[52] He was absolutely convinced of the rightness of the Allied cause. It was a war of ideals, he said, and specifically a war against Germany's "hideous ideals": "Her victory is the defeat of liberty, individualism, and brotherly love." Significantly, he made a moral comparison: "How fearfully a wrong idea may be imposed upon a people and how eternally it may effect that people may be seen in the workings of Puritanism on the English and to a less extent on us."[53] That he would connect German authoritarianism to Puritanism speaks to his developing beliefs about the oppressive values of his own culture, a topic he would write more explicitly about later. "Lord, Lord," Percy concluded, "if one stops to think there is nothing of moment to the individuals of this generation except the war."[54]

As much as he loved Dana's letters, Percy did not reciprocate fully her outpouring of emotion. As Janet experienced the terror of battle, she remained frustrated by his silences. "After I had bombarded you with letters almost as heavy as the shells that struck Dunkirk," she rebuked, he had not even bothered to write "to inquire whether I had been blown up to heaven by the Germans."[55] Her letters were laced with chastisement for his inattention, but also with longing for his companionship. "I've needed your company badly, Will," she wrote. She described the beauty of the countryside and the destruction wrought upon it by war, declaring that only he, the poet, could capture its pathos. She described walking through the countryside and finding a church behind the front lines. Outside, swarms of women and old men tended to wounded soldiers. She joined in to help. Eventually, priests and a robed choir emerged from the church with a crucifix and led a procession of people, "to the music of a strange wailing chant," to a nearby chalk cliff to perform a mass: "*pour la paix, pour le salut de notre pays, pour les soldats sur le champs et pour nos morts glorieux.*" "The Gods of Battle may not have heard," Janet wrote, "but surely the Son of Mary did. There were so many mothers there." She told Percy how she longed for him to have experienced it with her. "But do you know, dear Will," she wrote, "I find myself wishing that in nearly all my experiences." She concluded: "I am beginning to wonder, at least my New England conscience is beginning to wonder, just how long you will stand being appreciated in the spirit in this cavalier fashion. I leave it to you to say quite honestly whether you object."[56]

While Dana was in France wishing for Percy's company, Percy was growing closer to Tommy Shields. In the summer of 1915, Percy and Shields traveled to Utah and Wyoming together for two months. From the Teton Lodge, Percy wrote Dana about the Aspen trees, the Snake River, and seeing moose and elk and bear and beaver. "The fact that the season isn't yet open and so one can't shoot makes it even more fun," he wrote. He did not tell her he was with Tommy Shields. A few weeks prior, he had written Carrie Stern from Utah and told her that he and Tommy were having a nice trip and were headed for Wyoming.[57] But in his letter to Dana, he figured himself as a chaperone. "Three Greenville youths ('children') are with me," he wrote, "and if they don't furnish companionship at any rate they are very sweet and amusing."[58] It is unclear whether Shields was one of these youths (Percy was thirty years old, Shields twenty-four) or whether there were no youths at all. Perhaps Percy and Shields met up with the "children" in Wyoming. Given the absence of evidence, it is difficult to conjecture about the specifics of the arrangement. But it is evident that Percy rendered the situation carefully, and that in his relationship with Janet Dana, he wanted to keep some things to himself.

Percy returned to Greenville just as *Sappho in Levkas* came out in the late summer of 1915. Janet Dana told him how happy she was for him and insisted he send her a copy, which would be the next best thing to being with him. "Oh, I want so much to see you," she wrote.[59] She also sent him a purple scarf that she had knitted; he wrote in response that purple was his favorite color and that the scarf was "as beautiful as a jewel or a flower." "When I think of you working on it at night, in France, during the lonely hours, and for me," he wrote, he felt "unworthy, utterly, but still very proud and very happy." He told her that despite his book's appearance, being in Greenville and not in France left him depressed. The sadness, though, was manageable: "This very sadness is less melancholy and more splendid than the sadness of spring days—just as death is so much less sad than most life. Soon the wild geese will be flying down the river: I wish you could see them with me."[60]

Percy's sadness was certainly lessened when the first reviews of *Sappho* began to appear. He hired a newspaper clipping service to monitor book-review sections around the country and send him reviews. Many were favorable. Alongside a full-page picture of Percy in the *Boston Transcript*, William

Stanley Braithwaite wrote that Percy "does exactly what I desire done when I read a poem. I want my pleasure stimulated, my emotions aroused. I want a mystery defined, a secret revealed."[61] He said that although Percy's themes were classical, his poetry was fresh and emotionally honest. Likewise, the *New York Evening Post* wrote of his "unusual restraint of expression and the real depth of his feeling," while the *Hartford Times* noted that "Mr. Percy has written a number of poems which are filled with the love of the classical Greek for the beauty and brightness of life, his keen delight in the harmonious union of body and spirit."[62] From Scotland, the reviewer for the *Glasgow Herald* wrote that Percy's poetry "glorifies in opposition to meek acceptance of the world."[63] Over a dozen largely positive reviews appeared, most commenting on his erudition, delicate phrasing, and deeply felt emotion.

At least a few readers, though, were not moved. Harriet Monroe founded *Poetry: A Magazine of Verse* in 1912 and was an influential editor and important voice in modern American poetry; she was an early advocate of modernist poets such as William Carlos Williams, Ezra Pound, and T. S. Eliot. Of *Sappho in Levkas*, she wrote: "This book has been so much praised by highly respected reviewers that I have taken it up a number of times with a firm resolve to read it. But each time I have failed." She felt it was pretentious and coy, its outmoded diction a veil for Percy's true feelings: "It is full of everything that I most dislike and resent in poetry." Percy's focus on dead myths and heroes, his use of treacle language like "empurpled air" and "methinks"—it all added up, she felt, to mere doggerel. She concluded with a word of warning to other poets. *Sappho in Levkas* "represents certain tendencies which the modern poet should avoid with every fibre of his being and every effort of his art," she wrote. The book is "an absolutely artificial product, with neither simplicity, sincerity, nor emotion, three qualities indispensable in poetry."[64] Likewise, O. W. Firkins, writing in *The Nation*, wrote that Percy's book was "devoid of feeling."[65] When Percy read the review, he wrote Janet Dana that Firkins had "crucified me: a very cruel criticism which I hope I did not deserve." Of Firkins's comment that he wrote without feeling, Percy said, "Why should a poem be written if the words aren't struck from you like a cry?"[66]

Privately, however, Harriet Monroe evinced more ambivalence about Percy's poetry. In a letter to a friend, the critic S. T. Clover, she wrote, "I think Percy has something in him but is covering it up as completely as he can." Clover sent her note to Percy.[67] Percy wrote back that, given Monroe's taste in poetic form, it was not surprising that she did not like his verse. However, he explained, they had something very important in common that she seemed not to understand. "Although she would be very surprised to know it," Percy wrote, "many of her pet hobbies win a considerable amount of sympathy from me and with her fundamental idea of greater freedom and greater naturalness, I am entirely in accord."[68]

This correspondence highlights an important tension in Percy's poetry and its reception. His poetry was not modernist—he preferred classical themes, formal language, and adherence to traditional forms. But his larger intellectual project—to honestly understand and express sexual desire in his poetry, to find meaning in human experience without religious dogma, to consider art itself as a source of meaning tantamount to spirituality—was very much in line with that of modernist intellectuals like Harriet Monroe. What Monroe did not recognize was that Percy was working out of a different tradition—that of Walter Pater, John Addington Symonds, and Charles Kains-Jackson, among others—whose experimentation was in theme rather than form. When Percy wrote in "Sappho in Levkas" about "those pastures known / To love," or in "Arcady Lost" about "the days / We clung together here," among other examples, he was trying to portray homosexual relationships not as sodomy but as love. When he wrote, in "Longing," "Oh, for one hour tonight, / One little hour with you— / To touch your hand— / To lean within the halo of your perfume," he was writing about a real person— Harold Bruff—whom he had loved and lost.[69] His was a delicate balance: he could not write openly about Bruff or about his specific ideas on "greater freedom and greater naturalness" without reprisal from his family and community. So he wrote in such a way that at once protected himself and laid bare his ideas and desires. As we will see, in the coming years, many readers would understand precisely what he was doing and find it liberating.

Percy was emboldened by the appearance of *Sappho in Levkas* and decided to act on a long-held desire: to move to New York and become a full-time writer. He wrote to Janet Dana, who was soon to return from France: "I'm in the throes of a decision—shall I come to New York, set up in a garret, and experiment in writing for six months or a year or—more? I won't have to tell you all the missives such a decision involves. Well, it's about decided I shall go, for a while anyway. It's a leap in the dark, but somehow I can't help feeling a leap for life."[70]

Before he moved north, though, his relationship with Dana changed considerably. She returned home in September 1915, having served in France for almost six months. Coming home to comfort and convenience was a difficult adjustment after the terror of the war. "I am puzzled to know," she wrote to Percy, "whether this present, or what has just been, is the dream—surely both cannot be real—& I am inclined to think that this concrete, common-place, three-meals-a-day-served-by-a-butler (i.e. a waitress) existence is the illusion."[71] Much like before the war, she associated her affluence with malaise and purposelessness and faulted herself for freely enjoying its comforts. To her, the war was real; the war was authentic and full of meaning even as it was terrifying and grotesque. To be so close to death, she felt, brought her usually submerged humanity to the surface; experience and ideals were joined, for the first time in her life, in the crucible of war. And once home from Europe, she wished to go back: "Every mail brings me letters from France and I am positively homesick for that atmosphere of high endeavor, that marvelous blend of courage and *joie de vivre*."[72]

In October 1915 Janet Dana became reacquainted with a doctor named Warfield Longcope, whom she had known as a friend for four years. Longcope, almost ten years older than Dana, was the head of Presbyterian Hospital in New York City and professor of medicine at Columbia University. Within a month of their reacquaintance, Longcope proposed marriage to her. She was deeply ambivalent. In a long and tormented letter to Percy, she made one last attempt to speak clearly of her feelings. The letter is worth quoting at length:

All my life I've lived awfully much in my mind—even done my loving and enjoying and suffering with it—but with a queer feeling that some day I could <u>feel</u> overwhelmingly—I think my most intense longing has been for that day to come. I always thought it would come when someone loved me that I could love back—for the past two or three years I must say that I've been more alive—happier—than ever before & in my mind there has grown up an indefinite feeling—Will, has any woman ever shown themselves to you like this before?—that either one of two men who were my friends might be the flint & steel which might strike the living spark in me—one has spoken—I'm thrilled but not aflame. Now my puzzle is—shall I blow the bellows hard myself & possibly help to light my own fire—or shall I wait on—I'm not even sure the other man could light me, even if he cared to try—O Will, the heart is a strange thing & our selves still stranger. We're bound about by longings & ideals & fears & high restraints—we are so awfully lonely—so proud—so humble—so chary—you've hit it right—to be needed utterly—that is the touchstone to tell the truth from the illusion. Have you never cared—what kept you from your hearts desire—fear—or duty—or a mistaken idea of sacrifice. I seem to have bared myself to you. Won't you speak the truth on your side. We live so veiled perhaps you will be repelled by what I am saying.[73]

Percy wrote back and told Dana that her letter "completely sapped the carefully built fortifications of my friendship." The letter was "surcharged with hidden meanings," he explained, and he asked her to "write plainly what I've had to read, so far, between the lines." He understood, though, what she meant, and he replied with indirection. He explained that he was "unmothered of Aphrodite" but would "pray to the most beautiful gods I know that your decision whatever it is will bring the happiness you so deserve."[74] Still unsettled, he wrote to her the next day: "even when we know what we mean the difficulties of saying it seem almost insuperable."[75] Percy could not find a way to tell her, in a letter at least, that he loved her but was not sexually attracted to her.

Janet Dana, for her part, decided to accept Longcope's proposal, despite her concerns that he did not "light" her. Their courtship was a whirlwind, and she explained to Percy that "I never realized he cared until I came back from France—& then it happened. There is nothing exciting about it." However, she said, "my doctor is a very wonderful person, Will, so kind and fine—so sensitive, so human."[76] Nonetheless, doubts remained. Just before her wedding, she told Percy that "you don't know how often my thoughts go to you—in spite of a wedding in ten days time."[77] And even while on her honeymoon, she wrote to him and confessed: "On that day that was in some mysterious way the happiest and most serene I have ever known—I missed you."[78]

Despite Dana's marriage, Percy persisted in his plans to move to New York. Indeed, he and Janet seemed to become even closer and remained so for the rest of their lives. In January 1916 Percy rented an apartment at 110 E. 22nd Street, just outside of Greenwich Village, a block off of Gramercy Park, and less than a mile from 1 Fifth Avenue. He lived next door to Huger Jervey. When he arrived there, he wrote to Carrie Stern: "Well here I am—what's left of me, & 'taint much. ... I do hope I can do some good work."[79]

The poetry that Percy wrote in New York is the only evidence that survives from this period of his life, and it suggests that on his mind were enduring preoccupations: the loss of religion and the struggle to replace it with an adequate framework of meaning; the longing for emotional and sexual human connection; and the hope for a meaningful orientation to home and family. Percy's poem "In New York" poignantly captures the multidirectional, often contradictory impulses Percy wanted to convey in his writing and serves as a fitting conclusion to this chapter in his life. The poem moves from the church to his mother to emptiness to longing to lust to home; it combines themes seemingly at odds with one another in hopes of creating a multilayered poetic of desire. It speaks at once of dread impossibility and impossible delight, and it attempts not to resolve these contradictions but to understand them. "In New York" is one of the most significant of Percy's poems, one of the most successful in expressing the complex of desire and regret and love and despair that animated his imagination.

The poem is divided into five sections, each of which moves in a different thematic direction and ends with an unresolved image. In the first section, "On Sunday Morning," the narrator is in New York thinking of his mother, "one I dearly love," going to church. His thoughts are delicate and peaceful as he thinks of her.

> The sunlight falls in slanting bars
> and fills the church with light.
> And I remember when I knelt
> Beside her, in delight.

But his memory of himself as a child, kneeling next to his mother, reminds him of his distance from her and from the faith of his youth.

> There's something lost, there's something lost,
> Some wisdom has beguiled!
> My heart has flown a thousand miles
> And in the sunlight mild
> I kneel and weep beside her there
> As she prays for her child.

The delight of his youth has been replaced with weeping; the narrator acknowledges his loss and represents it with an impossible image: though he is in New York, he is also weeping beside his mother. The image is that of a divided person whose "heart has flown a thousand miles," a heart that is at once in both places and in neither of them.[80]

The second section, "The Song You Love," speaks to the hopes of the poet who seeks to capture beauty and meaning in poems but is limited by finite vision. Speaking to a beloved, the narrator laments:

> When I have sung the sweet songs and the sad,
> The songs of magic drifting from above,

. . . Still there will be one song I have not sung—
The song you love, the song you love.

The narrator again expresses his melancholy, unsatisfied desire—to fully convey the experience of him and his lover. In the end, "Long after it is dust, one heart there'll be / Restless with words it could not sing."[81]

In "Weariness," the poet longs to be known and loved.

To-night I have the need
Of human tenderness; not hovering wings,
But one warm breast where I may lay my head
And close my eyes.

Loneliness is a tangible quantity in this section of the poem, with each image reminding the narrator of the things he lacks:

The park was full of lovers,
And such a slender moon looked down on them. . . .
For one kiss of one mouth, free-given, I
Would give—what's left of me to-night.

Addressing God, the narrator concludes: "Thou dost deny me what's of life most sweet, / The bending head and lovely eyes of love."[82]

Indeed, it is love, "human tenderness," and physical intimacy the poet hopes for. The next section of the poem, "In the Night," questions mere lust and sex without love. The section is marked by tactile, erotic images, which are then called into question.

Drifting, groping
For delight;
Longing, hoping
All the night.
Perfume of
Blossomed hair—
Where is love?
Ah, no, not there!

This fleeting sexual encounter, set merely in the night and aiming merely for "delight," is not love but lust. Significantly, though, the poem then questions itself. Feeling "something burning" next to him, the sleepless narrator turns to see

winds that sweep
Poppied hair,
Where is sleep?
Ah, no, not there! . . .
Not there?

The section ends not with a resolution but with a question mark, with an image of a confused lover hoping for rest and for love. Finding neither, he wonders if he has found both.[83]

The final section of "In New York" looks homeward. The poet considers rootedness, the landscape he knows, and the rhythms of his home. It is the most resolute section of the poem, though it gives voice to an enduring sense of rootlessness. It returns to the conflict the poem began with: the poet's inability to *be* in one place, his inability to inhabit fully either the world of his youth or some new world of his adulthood. "I have need of silence and of stars," the section begins. "Too much is said too loudly; I am dazed." The world of the big city is filled with energy but also with illusions. As the narrator looks around him, he sees

these ears that hear all save silence,
These eyes that see so much but not the sky,
These minds that gain all knowledge but no calm.

In such an atmosphere of unrest, he is drawn home.

Oh, I must go
Back where the breakers of deep sunlight roll
across flat fields that love and touch the sky;
Back to the more of earth, the less of man.

In the poem as a whole, "Home" operates as one fixed source of meaning in the midst of unrest and instability. Religious belief had come and gone; his mother felt him in need of prayer; God denied him love; sex left him wanting. Even poetry was restless in its inadequacy. In this shifting constellation of unrequited desire, the specter of home provided some sense of constancy. The poem ends with a resolve: "I will go home."[84]

Taken as a whole, "In New York" provides a compelling portrait of Percy's motivations and hopes at this point in his life. The poem considers five sources of meaning—religion, poetry, love, sex, and home—and finds in each of them an inadequate wellspring. It suggests also the impossibility of remaking oneself in a new place. The poem ends with images of Delta soil and trees and the Mississippi River, the physical landscape that from his birth had shaped his experience. The irony at the end of the poem, then, is that there is hardly a more volatile physical landscape than the Mississippi Delta, with its inevitable but unpredictable floods, the soil that is layer upon layer of washed-up silt. Even home, the most stable image in the poem, is contingent, constantly shifting, and arbitrary. "In New York," finally, is about Percy's inability to be *in* New York—or anywhere else.

The themes in this poem can go some distance toward explaining Percy's particular restlessness, his multiplicitous and sometimes contradictory desires. But the desire he acted on next—the desire to be near the war, to find a more authentic experience through the war effort—was one he shared with many others in his generation. And like many others, he would be disappointed with the ability of war to give lasting meaning to his life.

8. THE SOLDIER

One must be a soldier these days—
there is no other part a man may play and be a man.

—WILLIAM ALEXANDER PERCY to Camille Percy, September 25, 1918

In early 1916 the war in Europe was nearly two years old. Trenches stretched from the North Sea to Switzerland on the western front, the main theatre of a war also being fought in Russia, Turkey, Italy, and other places and now involving over forty countries. British, French, Russian, and Italian armies struggled to stop the expansion of the German Empire, which in January 1916 extended from Berlin to Bagdad in the east and threatened always to press toward Paris in the west. Allied defenses had thus far proved resilient, though resilience was measured in bodies—over 3 million soldiers had been killed during the first two years of the war.[1] In 1916 morale began to fracture on the home fronts, particularly as the battle of Verdun took place in eastern France. From February to June 1916—roughly the same dates Will Percy lived in New York—over 600,000 soldiers died at Verdun.[2] From July to October, over a million more would die at the battle of the Somme. Neither of these battles was decisive. It was becoming apparent that the machine gun, a recent invention, so filled the air with bullets that no number of human bodies could satisfy its appetite.

In America, opinion remained divided. A majority of Americans supported the Allied cause, though not yet enough to declare war on Germany —despite the sinking of the *Lusitania* in May 1915 and increasing U-boat attacks on American merchant ships during 1916. The most vocal supporters of the war tended to be educated, elite, white northeasterners, such as Teddy Roosevelt. They cast the war in terms of moral idealism and promised it would deliver glory and manhood to its participants. Roosevelt assured anyone who would listen that war was "the Great Adventure," the defining moment of a man's life.[3] Popular writers like Arthur Empey traveled to France and wrote that "the spirit of sacrifice is wonderful," describing "the deep sense of satisfaction felt by the man who does his bit."[4] The dominant

American patriotic idiom in 1916 drew from the romantic tradition of the nineteenth century to portray war as cleansing and purifying. A long way from the killing fields of Verdun, this was still believable.

In New York, Percy certainly believed in the war. He watched the war's developments and waited for his opportunity to serve the cause. Despite the relative success of *Sappho in Levkas*, he told Janet Dana that "even the book is no anodyne for not being connected even menially with the war. I've nearly prayed for our country to enter the maelstrom so I might volunteer, but I hope I've resisted such a hellish prayer."[5]

His opportunity came not in the form of fighting, but philanthropy. In the summer of 1916, Percy applied to serve in Herbert Hoover's Commission for Relief in Belgium. Hoover was then a wealthy businessman and engineer who felt it his duty to orchestrate a relief effort for Belgian citizens, who since August 1914 had been particularly hard hit by the war. Hoover was in London when the war broke out and immediately set to helping American travelers caught in the crossfire; his efforts eventually led to the creation of the Commission for Relief in Belgium, which he hoped would be "the greatest charity the world has ever seen" and perhaps even "the greatest job Americans have undertaken in the cause of humanity." Indeed, Hoover's effort was unprecedented and enormously successful, eventually providing 5 million tons of food for over 9 million Belgian and French civilians trapped between the German army and the British blockade.[6] One historian has suggested that because of his humanitarian efforts, Hoover was responsible "for saving more lives than any other person in history."[7]

Percy felt that Hoover's commission was his best chance to get involved. His enthusiasm, though, was tempered by his feeling that he was abandoning his parents. He believed that they needed him. He explained this to Janet: "In a way I feel utterly guilty at the thought of going—it seems as if I were sacrificing nothing except the feelings of mother and father. If I get the place—a very uncertain matter—it will be I'm afraid with no great feeling of gusto. Isn't it fearful how one attains freedom only at the expense of the blood and tears of others?"[8] But as he had done with his move to New York, he pressed on with his plans despite his tangled feelings of guilt, excitement, and family loyalty.

Percy was accepted to the commission and arrived in London as a civilian in December 1916. It seemed that everywhere around him were young soldiers. Soldiers home from war, soldiers preparing to go to war, soldiers whose eyes seemed to Percy to be filled with purpose. Every able-bodied man seemed to be prepared to make the ultimate sacrifice, and he was envious.

When he made the journey across the North Sea and eventually arrived in Brussels, he found that "the romantic pioneer period" of Hoover's project had ended. Now there was only administrative work and boredom. Percy lamented later that "there was nothing dangerous or onerous about our tasks" and that "the simple truth is we were the spoiled darlings of Belgian society."[9] The American ambassador to Belgium also resented the unuseful presence of so many young men of Percy's class and status, writing that Belgium was "filled with a lot of impulsive, ignorant young doctors of philosophy."[10] The Americans were provided with upscale homes and servants and were entertained with food, wine, and evening parties. They spent the weekends walking in the pastures and golf courses of opulent country estates. In the far distance, they could hear the sounds of mortar shells and airplanes. Percy wrote home to Carrie Stern: "I hope you haven't lain awake nights thinking of wars and horrors and my bones bleaching on the bottom of the channel. This is a very curious life over here but it's safe enough and my state of mind even thro these combustions is quite tame." What he really desired, he said, was to return to his writing. "I'm—as usual," he wrote, "longing for about two months of pure leisure with the muse."[11]

In addition, Percy could not come to peace with the idea that others were fighting for a cause he believed in while he was not. He wanted to be a soldier, not a "spoiled darling." Beyond that, Percy clung to the romantic notion of death in warfare. He did not just want to be a soldier, he wanted to die a soldier's death. "Probably," he wrote in his memoir, "although I had no liking for hardships, a soldier's hardships and his likely end seemed to me a better poem than I could ever hope to write." A soldier's death was particularly romantic in what he felt was the war that would define his generation, indeed the war that would punctuate world history. It was the Great War. He viewed the two sides of the conflict in stark terms and had no doubts as to the moral superiority of the Allied cause. He noted, with no sense of irony regarding his own family's history in the plantation South, that the Germans treated the Belgians as "slaves" and herded them off to work in munitions factories in a process of "wholesale enslavement of the able-bodied males of a helpless little country." The German treatment of Belgian civilians was, Percy felt, "wicked stupidity that Germans alone could have been capable of." In his memoir, written years later during the Nazi occupation of Poland, he declared that what the Germans were doing in 1916 "was only a miniature venture into slavery, a preliminary to the epic conquest and enslavement of whole peoples in 1940."[12]

That Percy likened the German occupation of Belgium to the institution of slavery is not insignificant. Percy knew the history of the slave South intimately—it was the history of his own family. Furthermore, in Mississippi Percy lived in a postemancipation society in which former slaves and their descendants lived with little social, economic, or political opportunity. Freedom and self-determination—the ideals that undergirded the Allied cause in Percy's mind—were, in his home region, distinct privileges of those who had never been enslaved. Freedom was more than an abstract principle; Percy lived daily with visible reminders of its tragic opposite. When Percy looked out and saw the "indignity," the "actually and literally" starved Belgians, the trainloads of "slaves," he had a potent and very personal frame of reference. He did not, however, associate his lofty ideals with southern blacks. "Americans at home," he wrote, "cannot possibly appreciate the freedom so abundantly theirs."[13]

WHEN AMERICA declared war on Germany on April 6, 1917, Percy was overjoyed. He also had to find a way to get home. Now that America was a belligerent, he could not travel freely. He worked his way to Switzerland, to Paris, and eventually to an English port, from which he traveled safely home. Immediately, though, he wished to return. He wrote to Janet: "My escape from Europe, if I actually wanted to get away, was extraordinarily fortunate. … But to leave Paris at such a time was really to miss the opportunity of a lifetime, almost of a flame's lifetime." Concluding with a well-worn patriotic trope, Percy wrote: "I knew you'd feel the cleansing elation of the horror of it all."[14]

In Mississippi he set out to find a way to support the American cause. He was thirty-two, a year over the draft age, and the next officer's training camp was not for several months. So he signed on to become a fund-raising speaker for the Red Cross. Throughout the summer of 1917, he traveled across the South and told stories of Germany and Belgium and the rightness of the Allied cause. Audiences adored him. One listener wrote to his father about Percy sharing a platform "with those big army officers" addressing 4,000 soldiers. Percy, he wrote, "was calm and collected and made a great talk, by far the best of the day, and the best I have ever heard. I wish you could have heard him. He was cheered all through his speech and when he concluded he was given a fifteen minute ovation."[15] Another man, D. W. Houston, wrote to LeRoy Percy about his son's eloquence and noted "you must be proud of such a son." Houston's letter illuminates a great deal about the ways many Mississippians understood Will Percy in their context: he was a man, a Percy, fit to lead and to serve as a role model. Houston continued: "He knew his subject thoroughly, and was a master of the situation from beginning to end. Nor was this due alone to his intellect, eloquence and charm of manner, all of which he has in abundance, but, as it struck me, it was due largely to something better and deeper still—to the soul of the man—his absolute sincerity and simplicity and his consuming desire to serve others, and forget self, which my father has told me was so characteristic … of all men who are really and truly great."[16]

For his part, though, Percy felt that to be anything less than a soldier at the front was second-rate. "I was hailed as a young hero," he wrote to Janet Longcope after one speech, "and felt of course the worst of imposters."[17]

In the fall, Percy sent an application to the U.S. Army. Despite the patriotic fervor that gripped the nation, Percy's parents made it known that they did not think he was suited for soldiering. He wrote in his memoir that "mother and father looked as if they had just taken communion: there was a stillness in them which covered, I suspected, a great sadness."[18] At the time, he told Janet Longcope, "all my friends—and family—here were against my trying for it; the usual argument—great intellect that could be used elsewhere to better advantage, general unfitness, no physique (?), duty to stay home, etc." But Percy was determined. He explained to Janet that what he did have was "heart and soul for the cause, the offering of nothing except one's own body seems in the least to satisfy."[19]

It was his body, though, that presented the next problem. To qualify for officer's training camp, one had to weigh at least 135 pounds. Percy was 112. He had a long way to go. He began to eat raw eggs, cream, and spoonfuls of tanlac. For a month, he did little but lie in bed, not wanting to exert himself in any way that might cause him to lose weight. Before he stepped on the scale, he ate four bananas and drank a quart of water. It paid off—he had gained twenty-three pounds in just one month. "I was at last about to be a soldier," he wrote.[20]

Percy viewed his opportunity to train as an officer as a monumental test of his manhood. In his writing about it, he portrayed himself and his friends as "peewees" who faced long odds and enormous pressure. "If any of us failed," he wrote, "he would have wasted the government's time and money, he would have disgraced his family, and he would have failed in the supreme test of his whole life." Most American men who served the war cause were enlisted; to become an officer meant authority and prestige. It meant a leadership role in the fight to save democracy. "I don't suppose any of us ever felt," Percy said, "so necessary to God and man."[21]

He reported to training camp at Leon Springs, Texas, in September 1917 and was assigned to the "pewee squad" of Company D. He described him-self and his friends as "pale runts," "insignificant" in comparison to the big "husky young Southerners" who comprised most of the camp. They struggled to keep up and tried to make up with brains what they lacked in physique. In one instance, the company was "broiling" in the Texas heat as they lay on the ground doing push-ups. Percy was exhausted and could not do another. Lying in the dust, near the point of fainting, he gave up. "I gig-gled," he remembered. "Mr. Percy," the captain yelled, "this ain't no kinder-garten."[22]

Despite the physical hardships, the constant drilling and running and bayonet charges, Percy won his commission as a first lieutenant. He and his friends felt that "we'd rather have had those single bars on our shoulders than celestial wings" and bade each other farewell as they set off on their assignments. The army instructed Percy to report on December 15 to Camp Pike, Arkansas, where he would begin preparations to move to the front. While at Camp Pike, he composed a poem, "Poppy Fields," that gives some indication of his hopes for the war:

And would it not be proud romance
Falling in some obscure advance
To rise, a poppy field of France?[23]

On the steamship that took him to Europe, Percy read a novel and met a man named Gerstle Mack, an art critic and architectural historian who would become a lifelong friend and traveling companion. (As with most of Percy's bachelor friends, very little evidence about Mack's life remains.) The novel, Percy noted, was one that had been "forbidden by father."[24] That Percy began his depiction of the war in Europe with these two details is significant. Recall that when Percy was a young child, his father demanded that any nov-els he read be chivalric tales such as those of Sir Walter Scott. Otherwise, he should read practical, useful books and not mere fictions. But Percy punctu-ated his memoir with images of himself as a different kind of man than his father. Percy grew up in a household where novel reading—and indeed the idea of the artist-writer—was deemed effeminate. It signified passivity rather than action, intellectualizing rather than practical work. But Percy wanted to conjoin the two; he wanted to couple his artistic ideals to the work of war, aesthetics to action. For him, the war was a moment in his life where practicality, creativity, and male companionship could meet. He also wanted to depict the ultimate test of manhood—soldiering at the front—as being accomplished by queer men such as himself and Gerstle Mack.

In France, the army assigned Percy to Tours, which was well behind the front. His job was to inspect housing that locals offered to the American officers. He lessened his disappointment somewhat by securing himself a room "fit for a major general" in a doctor's house. He loved the family's French civility and fine meals with wine from their own vineyard, and he delighted when the famous sculptor François Sicard visited from Paris. Another regular was soon-to-be Nobel Prize winner Anatole France, who took a liking to Percy and invited him to his home. (Percy's superior, who had never heard of the writer, declined his request for a leave.) At the doctor's house, the group laughed and drank wine and passed the winter nights by reading aloud from "naughty" eighteenth-century memoirs. At one large dinner party, a kindly French woman turned to Percy and asked him to tell them about the American South. "Panic enfolded me," he remembered. "What can you say about the Delta? I became distraught in my search for a Southern theme." The word that would not leave his mind was "rattlesnakes," though he did not know the French translation. "In my country there lives a serpent," he began. "He is three or four kilometers long. ... He always carries little chimes." He continued his fumbling description of rattlesnakes until he attempted to describe the tail of the snake and alighted instead on a French profanity. The dinner party was shocked and then erupted into uproarious laughter.[25]

After his job as a billet inspector, Percy was assigned as an aide to a commandant who had no real job for him, so he asked Percy if he would fix his stove—something that Percy did not know how to do. Into this not-very-heroic war experience in early 1918 entered LeRoy Percy, who had joined the YMCA board and was on a fund-raising tour. Percy wrote that soldiers loved his father's speeches and that LeRoy, in his "Y" uniform, looked like General Pershing himself. LeRoy Percy told his son that he was proud of him. Will Percy later explained that it must have been his father's innocence that made him regard his son as a hero, because, he wrote, "I had never seen a trench."[26] Janet Longcope echoed LeRoy's insistence that his son was a hero. She could not envision Will Percy as anything but a noble warrior; she told him that in his army uniform, he looked like a "crusader," and she said: "I know you have already been through fire and conquered in your soul and I thank God I know you. Will, you must have seen the Holy Grail with the eyes of your spirit. ... Go out to battle dear knight and may god and our lady keep you."[27] She contrasted Percy to her new husband: "When Barbara asks later, 'Daddy, what did you do in the great war?' his only trophy will be a very shiny pair of breeches worn smooth in a revolving chair!"[28]

In late spring, orders came for Percy to be moved to Paris for more aide

Will Percy and his father, LeRoy, ca. 1918. Will Percy is wearing his army uniform and LeRoy his YMCA uniform. (Courtesy of the Mississippi Department of Archives and History, Jackson, Mississippi)

work. He protested, insisting that he wanted to go to the front. His colonel "observed that as far as he was concerned I could go to hell, but for the present I might try the next train to Paris." So Percy got on the next train to Paris, where he found himself in charge of organizing civilian labor for the American army. Because most Frenchmen were fighting at the front, he was forced to put together teams of masons and carpenters and painters out of "the scum of Paris." He wrote that the spring of 1918 was an unhappy one. Artillery and gunfire thundered in the distance, bombs fell from airplanes, and he was in Paris doing administrative work. All around him, on the streets of Paris, were soldiers on furlough—soldiers from Australia and New Zealand and Great Britain, soldiers with battle-worn uniforms and heavy eyes. "I began to believe these true soldiers knew that I worked in an office," Percy wrote, "like a damn civilian." Percy felt his work as an aide behind the front lines hung from his uniform like a "badge of disgrace," and he "became convinced that without suffering there was no real soldiering."[29]

It was Huger Jervey, who now held an army administrative post in Paris, who saved him. Percy begged Jervey to use his influence to get him a transfer, and Jervey put in a request. When Percy's superior officer refused the request, Percy went to him with wet eyes and said: "Think how I must feel. . . . This is my only chance." He begged him for the chance to fight, the chance that "every real American wants." When the major consented, Percy barely restrained himself from kissing his bald head. "I walked on air," Percy wrote, "down the Champs-Elysees repeating: 'My heart is like a singing bird whose nest is in a watered shoot' and wondering what a watered shoot might be."[30]

Since Percy had been out of the infantry for six months, he trained briefly at the officer's school at Gondrecourt. He worked hard in anticipation of going to the front as a platoon leader. Upon completion of the course, the officers received their orders: Percy was not to go to the front. He was ordered instead to be an instructor in the Ninety-Second Division, America's first all-black military unit.

"I decided that in a fit of homesickness I had lost my mind—the landscape was speckled with Negro soldiers!" The enlisted men were black. The lieutenants and sergeants and captains were black. Percy went to the head of the Ninety-Second, General William Hay, and said, "Sir, I didn't ask to be sent here and I don't want to be here." The general was not amused. Percy explained that he was a soldier, not an instructor. "I'm one of these new officers out of civilian life," Percy insisted. "I know nothing at all, sir."[31] The general appointed him to teach black officers, most of whom outranked him, how to read French maps. When Percy wrote to Janet Longcope about his new position, she responded: "I can imagine your feelings when you found yourself in command of colored troops. No one but fate herself could have perpetrated that little jest, I'm sure."[32]

The few months with the Ninety-Second Division in France in the summer of 1918 was the only time in Percy's life that he was forced to face the impermanence of his sense of racial hierarchy. He had to salute black officers. He had to maintain military deference despite his deeply held belief that black people were different from, and inferior to, white people. His time with the Ninety-Second in France did not change his thinking. He felt that although there were some good officers, most of the black troops were "lazy, undevoted, and without pride." He kept his distance from them and did not eat with them at meals. He even wrote a Mississippi friend who was an aide to General Pershing that he did not think the troops were fit for battle at the front. Years later, he wrote disdainfully that when the Ninety-Second returned to America, they were treated as heroes; they marched down Fifth Avenue in New York (past the Dana mansion) in front of a flag-waving crowd, despite only having had one engagement and performing, Percy felt, badly in it. He quoted General Pershing's comment that during one battle, "the 92nd Division attacked but did not hold all its gains," and he called Pershing's words "a masterly example of the glacial tact of understatement."[33] He simply could not accept that a black man performed his notions of the heroic work of a soldier.

LeRoy Percy wrote his son a letter in the summer of 1918 that highlights this tension of Will Percy's situation in France. In his letter, LeRoy Percy filled him in on Greenville's news, the state of the cotton crop, and his friends— Tommy Shields, for example, who was in New Orleans for sinus surgery. The letter also includes knowing references to black Mississippians, comments that suggest a shared sense of racial superiority between father and son. LeRoy Percy mentioned that he had recently gathered all the tenants of their plantation together and explained to them that they should buy war savings stamps. He implied that the tenants were capable of neither understanding this need to invest in the war nor of genuine patriotism, so they needed to be prodded. "I do not know that they were thoroughly convinced," he wrote, "but Hardie [the plantation manager] will see that they take the requisite number of stamps." Patronizing coercion was the only way LeRoy Percy could conceive of black participation in the war effort. He concluded his letter by mentioning a recent tragic episode. Alfred H. Stone, a family friend and prominent local planter, was under fire for the treatment of blacks on his plantation. "After all of Alf Stone's careful and just treatment of darkies," he wrote, "the first Negro on his place was killed yesterday unnecessarily by one of his managers."[34]

LeRoy Percy's letter underscores a plain fact of this story: LeRoy and Will Percy's racism assigned a lower value to the dignity and worth of a black life. To describe the murder of a black farmer as "unnecessary" implies that sometimes such murders were necessary; to mention the episode merely to express frustration that it had shed bad light on a good friend suggests a shocking nonchalance about the lives of African Americans. Will Percy did not speak out against this. Despite being among black soldiers in France, some of whom would die fighting for their country, Will Percy could still regret with his father that a black farmer was killed *unnecessarily* in Mississippi. For all of his self-awareness, for all his well-developed habits of introspection, he could not see the artificiality—indeed, the insidiousness—of his family's and his own views about race. Percy perceived and critiqued what he felt to be relative cultural values concerning same-sex love, but he did not do so with cultural values concerning race.

While teaching black officers about the French army's military tactics, the ways of sending messages to and from the front, and how to use a compass, Percy missed action at the front that was the beginning of the end of the war. The German army had, in the spring of 1918, made a frantic gamble. In the Ludendorff offensive, the German army mustered all of its strength for a series of attacks intended to break through Allied lines and capture Paris. Since the Bolshevik Revolution of 1917 had eased the pressure on the eastern front, the German army transferred thousands of its troops to the western front. The Germans made significant advances and even began to shell Paris in June; by July 1918, the German Empire stretched from near Paris in the west to the Ukraine in the east—its largest extent ever. But these gains were Germany's last gasp. Between March and July 1918, the German army suffered 800,000 casualties. Desertion was a problem, and revolution among war-starved civilians seemed imminent on the home front.[35]

Allied commanders decided to capitalize on what they rightly perceived as weakness and launched a counteroffensive that would be the death knell for the German army. On July 18 the Allied forces launched what would become the Second Battle of the Marne, and Percy did not take part. His resentment toward the black troops went beyond racial prejudice; he believed that they were robbing him of his chance to lead a platoon into battle. They were demanding his time and energies during the first major fighting the American army was involved in. While nine American divisions took part in the Second Battle of the Marne, the Ninety-Second was well beyond the front lines. What was worse, many of the American infantry gained the heroic status that Percy so ardently desired. One war observer in France wrote that the American soldiers looked like "Tommies in Heaven ... so god-like, so magnificent, so splendidly unimpaired." In July and early August, the Allies gained such significant ground and caused so many German casualties that Ludendorff called August 8 "the black day of the German army." He predicted his soldiers would not be able to fight much longer.[36]

In mid-August, though, Percy got a break. Colonel William P. Jackson, with whom Percy served in the Ninety-Second Division (and who was white), was promoted to brigadier general of the Thirty-Seventh Division—which was at the front—and he asked Percy to serve as his aide. "Thanking him, I said I understood that an aide was the lowest form of military life and all I aspired to was to be a platoon leader at the front," Percy wrote. But Jackson told Percy it was either be his aide at the front or remain as an instructor with the Ninety-Second. Percy agreed to go. He wrote to his Greenville friend Billy Wynn that despite his decision, "still I'll never cease regretting not being a platoon leader."[37]

The Allied armies were planning what would come to be called the Meuse-Argonne offensive, which would take place in late September and October. Percy's Thirty-Seventh Division was to play a vital role. On September 13, Percy wrote home to his mother that "everyone is overjoyed" about the offensive and "the French are kept busy congratulating us." His duties with his new assignment were primarily to attend to the needs of General Jackson; he went with him on trench inspections, he sent messages, he organized the general's administrative affairs. But at last he was at the front: shell holes, barbed wire, abandoned canteens and field glasses and boots littered northern France. Lights were not permitted at night, and in the "inky darkness" the prospect of death could be felt, though rarely seen. "Don't worry about me," Percy wrote. "Lots of love to you and Father."[38]

A few nights before the battle, Percy lay in bed in a makeshift command post—a bombed-out farmhouse behind the front lines. In the bedroom above him, he heard a couple making love, their noise the only thing that could be heard over the artillery fire. This juxtaposition of love and death was jarring and, it seemed to Percy, pitiful. Perhaps thinking of Harold Bruff, Percy wrote: "I remembered that love had once seemed tender and beautiful. It wasn't anymore."[39]

As with love, so it was with art. The next night, Percy again lay listening to the sounds of killing in the distance. His candle illuminated an Italian print of the Virgin Mary on the wall. He tried to recall the painter, and as he did, "a wave of anger and nausea swept over me." Lying there mere miles from the trenches, in which men were dying at that very moment, and in which perhaps he would soon meet his own death, he questioned his idealism. "Art? What was art, painting, and poetry," he asked. "Child's play, the pastime of weaklings, pointless, useless, unmanly, weak, weak, weak."[40]

These two vignettes illustrate an ongoing tension in Percy's life that the war laid bare. On the one hand, to be a man was to be strong, to be practical, and to sacrifice one's body and mind and abilities for the larger good of society. Teddy Roosevelt and LeRoy Percy, among others, would have given table-pounding approval to Percy's portrayal of poetry as child's play next to the work of war. On the other hand, the Greeks and the romantics and his own teachers had taught him that to be a man was to love beauty, to be fully alive was to understand art as the most fundamental expression of the human spirit. Love, relationships, sex, empathy, beauty—these things were real and lasting and would certainly outlast the arbitrary borders between nations for which millions lay dead or mutilated. Percy's war experience reflects his ongoing struggle to combine these ideals, which to others may have seemed incompatible.

The night before the battle was to begin, Percy wrote again to his mother. Now his tone was more somber. Though he still anticipated a "glorious big battle in a few hours," he reminded her that "battles of course aren't safe things." He explained to her, and perhaps to himself, the meaning of what he was doing:

> One must be a soldier these days—there is no other part a man
> may play and be a man. Should anything ever happen to me over
> here, you and Father must, and I know you will, feel that it was a
> great privilege for us to be allowed to go forth with the heroes. I've
> had too much and too keen happiness out of this life to want to leave
> it or to leave it without regret, but this cause is too great to count the
> cost or speculate on the outcome to the individual. All that's good in
> me comes direct from you and Father, and my only ambition in
> this business is not to be unworthy of you. And whatever happens
> we'll be together in the end.[41]

Early in the morning of September 26, the American, British, and French armies launched a coordinated attack in hopes of disrupting German communications, destroying German morale, and breaking through the German line that for so long had seemed impermeable. The American army, including the Thirty-Seventh Division, attacked the center of the German line in the Argonne forest. Percy watched the initial barrage from an observation post with General Jackson. He wrote to his father that through the fog, he could see almost nothing, and "my only sensation as the sun came up was listening to the wild canaries which suddenly and strangely moved to music could be heard above the thunder of the guns." As the troops began to advance, Percy and Jackson followed. The road was choked with traffic—ambulances, mules, motorcycles, medics, and messengers clogged the street, on which bombs fell intermittently. One shell landed fifty yards in front of Percy: "An ambulance went up in a puff of cotton; horses and men fell." He and the general had to make their way, on foot, through the forest. As they did, Percy saw for himself the texture of war: dead German and American bodies, living men with missing jaws or legs or arms, former German trenches in which diaries and letters and bottles of water had been abandoned in haste. In one trench, he told his father, he found a copy of Sir Walter Scott's novel *Waverly*.[42]

The first day of the American attack was a success. But on the second day, the German army received reinforcements, and in addition a downpour turned American supply roads into mud. Progress slowed, and American casualties began to mount. Percy's job was to coordinate the movement of wounded soldiers behind the lines, as well as to locate all the "cowards and deserters and malingerers" and send them back to their platoons. There were many of each type: soldiers who had been gassed, shot, or hit by shrapnel; and soldiers who were scared, exhausted, or "gone mad with shell-shock."[43]

On the third day, General Jackson decided to go to the front lines to encourage his soldiers. When Percy learned of this, he set off to find the general, but while he was searching the German army began an artillery barrage. "To be shelled when you are in the open is one of the most terrible of human experiences," he wrote to his father. "You hear this rushing, tearing sound as the thing comes toward you and then the huge explosion as it strikes, and, infinitely worse, you see its hideous work as men stagger, fall, struggle or lie quiet and unrecognizable."[44] As Percy waded through these bodies and holes, a nearby company of soldiers broke, and Percy noticed a colonel trying unsuccessfully to rally them. Percy and another officer took over the company, organized them, and bunkered them in makeshift trenches, all while men were being "smashed and killed" around them. Percy went forward to find that the advance had stopped, so he got down in a hole next to a French lieutenant and sat for four hours as bombs fell all around them, spraying dirt and shrapnel into their hideouts. "We sat there laughing and talking and wondering if the next one would get us," Percy wrote. "He had a wife and child and had seen four years of this hell."[45]

In a week of fighting in the Argonne forest, the American army suffered 100,000 casualties and advanced only eight miles. History has not judged the battle a success but rather, in the words of one historian, "a severe check if not defeat."[46] However, at the same time, British and French forces gained considerable ground, and by early October, German officials began negotiating for peace. During October, Percy's division inched forward, following the retreating German army down the River Lys. General Jackson and his staff stayed in abandoned farmhouses whose windows had been shot out and whose occupants had long been displaced. Percy was aware of his relative safety compared to the platoons on the front lines. "I've suffered personally none of the agony that the men and line officers have been called on to endure," he told his mother. But having seen the front lines, his perspective was decidedly different than it had been even six months before. Though he still believed in the cause, he said, war was evil. "No one can ever hate war as a soldier does," he wrote. "It is the wickedest, most hateful thing man was ever guilty of."[47]

When the news of the November 11, 1918, armistice reached Percy, he was elated. "Today is the impossible great day for which the world has been waiting four years," he exclaimed to his mother. "This physical relief is so great that I can't begin to appreciate the enormous spiritual results, this wave of gladness sweeping over the world."[48] Four days later, he wrote to his father: "It is impossible to realize that the most enormous fact in history has happened and the wrecked world is once more at peace." After four months of solid bombardment, the silence was thick with meaning.[49]

For his efforts in rallying the troops in the Argonne forest, the French army awarded Percy the Croix de Guerre, which it bestowed on those who showed heroism in battle, and King Albert of Belgium awarded him La Medaille du Roi Albert for his service protecting the nation of Belgium. The American army promoted him to captain.[50] General Jackson wrote to LeRoy and Camille Percy telling them how indispensable their son was, and that "I was very much taken with him the first time I met him." General Jackson told Will Percy that he was brave, efficient, and courageous. "You may rest assured," he wrote, "that you will always hold a very high place in my esteem and the remembrance of your courtly courteous manner will always be a pleasure."[51]

Five months passed before Percy returned home in mid-April, and as he waited, his elation turned to despair. On January 7, he learned that Sinkler Manning had been killed in battle at Argonne on November 6—five days before the armistice. The story Percy read of Manning's death doubtless deepened his personal investment in the ideal of martial glory. The newspaper reported that after three days of intense fighting near Montfaucon, Manning had attempted to rally the troops. At the head of the battle-wearied Third Battalion, reported the *New York Times*, "strode the tall, lean figure of Major Manning, with a flowing black cape over his shoulders, flying in the wind that emerged from the woods behind, a heavy cane in one hand and an American .45 in the other." He had no fear, the story read, "for if ever a man was utterly, completely, and whole-heartedly wrapped up in the cause he espoused, it was this son of South Carolina's Governor." Manning led the battalion into a barrage of machine-gun bullets and was immediately shot in the neck and killed. His company eventually captured the outpost, which was strategically insignificant, coming as it did in the final days of the war. This did little to temper the enthusiasm of Manning's former colleagues at the *New York Times*. "Who can say," they asked, "how much of that victory was due to the example of one man, scorning camouflage and leading his men in the good, old American way—out in front and standing up."[52]

To Percy, Manning had died the perfect death—he later described him as "a knight who met a knight's death"—but it was death nonetheless.[53] For the second time, Percy had lost an intimate friend. He wrote to Carrie Stern about Manning. "You, probably more than anyone else," he told her, "know how much he meant to me: after Harold, he was my best friend, one I understood and who understood me."[54] He confessed that "the mental and spiritual let-down" he felt "is immense and seemingly continuous."[55] In his life, Percy had lost two men that he loved, and now the prospect of the old life in Mississippi seemed bleaker than ever. He told his mother to prepare the library for him: "I intend sitting a solid month in my red chair without getting up except for meals."[56]

In his autobiography, Percy captured this feeling of emptiness. He wrote that his happiness and serenity over the war's end was "only the superstructure over a hidden tide of desolation and despair." It is over, he told himself, "the only great thing you were ever a part of. It's over, the only heroic thing we all did together. What can you do now? Nothing, nothing. You can't go back to the old petty things without purpose, direction, or unity—defending the railroad for killing a cow, drawing deeds of trust, suing someone for money, coping again, all over, with that bright rascal who rehearses his witnesses. You can't go on with that kind of thing till you die."[57]

Upon his return, his parents met him at the harbor in New York. "They were so happy," Percy remembered, "so filled with pride and thanksgiving, it was embarrassing. I tried, too, to be glad and proud and thankful, but I have never before or since felt so incapable of emotion, so dead inside."[58]

Feeling dead inside but wearing the uniform of a soldier, Percy boarded a train headed for Mississippi, his Croix de Guerre hanging from his chest in silver and gold.

9. THE NAÏVE AND NOSTALGIC POET

We are homesick for "the glory that was Greece."
—RAYMOND GANGER to William Alexander Percy, November 12, 1921

In April 1919, Percy returned home to a Mississippi that was similar in some ways to northern France—a farming region, a religious culture, and a place once torn apart by war. But Percy set himself to neither farming nor faith. Instead, he set himself to finishing a book of poems, *In April Once*, which he had been writing over the past four years. He finished the book in a changing America in which women would soon vote, liquor would soon be available only from outlaws, and the Ku Klux Klan would soon be the nation's largest and most violent social club. Throughout 1919, race riots broke out across the country as black soldiers returned from France wearing their uniforms and demanding jobs and fairness in this new world safe for democracy. In Greenville, Percy wore his uniform home as well. The local newspaper celebrated the return of "the brilliant son of former Senator LeRoy Percy." Greenville could be grateful, it read, for his "bravery and heroic sacrifice."[1]

Percy no doubt spent much time in his red-leather chair in the parlor during the spring and summer of 1919, reading and writing. Soon, though, he grew restless. He had not lived at home or practiced law since 1915, before New York, Belgium, and the army. Perhaps he felt it was time to leave Greenville for good. Perhaps he wanted to finish his book in a place free from the demands of family and community. An opportunity presented itself when a teaching post again came open in the Sewanee English department that summer. He decided to take it. As usual, Janet Dana Longcope grasped the significance of his leave-taking. She commended him for his decision but knew it had not been an easy one: "Somehow, you and the law don't seem to belong. And yet Will, I know this choice hasn't been made without real heartache. It hurts to chop off the loving tentacles of life-at-home and take a path outside training and the pain is so complex and vicarious."[2]

Once in Sewanee, Percy seemed to settle well into teaching and writing. As in 1909, he was a popular teacher, and he enjoyed being among the students. However, something went wrong during the fall semester. Percy wrote to Carrie Stern, somewhat obliquely, that "[I] have lost a friend or two but am feeling first-rate and classes are coming along pretty well."[3] These lost friends may have been related to the fact that after the semester ended, Percy was dismissed from his post. As is too often the case with Will Percy, no evidence from the time has surfaced about his dismissal—either in the Sewanee archives or in Percy's own papers. But a Sewanee alumnus, Arthur Chitty, later explained to a friend that "a member of our Board of Trustees used his influence to prevent Percy's contract being renewed." This dismayed Chitty, because Percy "was greatly beloved and admired as a teacher here. He had enormous influence among the students."[4] Another Percy family friend later remembered members of the Percy family being "cool" toward Sewanee because Percy was "fired" in 1919.[5]

The dynamic of this episode warrants comment. We do not know from the evidence exactly why Percy was dismissed. But we do know it was not because he was a poor teacher, nor was it because he wanted to leave. Something happened that caused at least one board member to fight strongly against retaining Percy. Perhaps the trustee had a vendetta against the Percy family; perhaps it was a financial move; perhaps Percy was caught having an affair with a student. It seems, though, that to suddenly dismiss a popular and effective teacher required a good reason. That no reason was given is a significant silence. The contours of that silence suggest the unsuggestable; they imply that the "good reason" could not be written down, and certainly could not make it into the archive.

Six months later, the board of trustees adopted a resolution commending Percy for his excellent service to Sewanee and regretting that "the call to other activities" led him to leave the school.[6] Again, we can only speculate as to the meaning of this. When placed in the broader context of southern history, Percy's dismissal and later commendation illustrates an important dynamic between class and scandal in the South. The trustees did not want to involve themselves in what could have developed into a controversy with Percy; on the other hand, they did not want Percy to remain at Sewanee. So they dismissed him quietly, gave no reason, and passed a resolution that gave the episode a veneer of respectability. Here, it seems, Percy's class status protected him from recrimination. Sewanee's interest in protecting its own reputation also must have been a concern. Whatever happened was hidden beneath politeness and silence. Southerners were well practiced at reticence concerning the "misdeeds" of the elite.

Perhaps the Sewanee trustees had in mind the case of William Rice Sims, a Vanderbilt and later University of Mississippi professor found to have a "vicious tendency" and a "perverted sexual mania." In 1895 Mississippi's chancellor Robert Fulton learned that Sims had had sexual relations with several male students. Fulton wrote to the board of trustees that Sims should be dismissed quietly and sent to the Johns Hopkins University Hospital for treatment. He wanted to prevent "undue publicity," and the trustees agreed with Fulton's "quiet way of guarding the interests of the university." Sims was dismissed and did not return. Perhaps the Sewanee trustees likewise urged medical treatment for Percy; perhaps they suggested it and he declined. Until new evidence surfaces, if it ever does, we can only speculate.[7]

Despite Sewanee's official praise of Percy's efforts, the school—or at least one member of the board and possibly more—continued to privately work against his association with the school. Two years later, Percy's former students nominated him to become a trustee. The day after they submitted Percy's nomination, the board of trustees passed a resolution requiring all trustees to be members of a church. Percy was indignant. He wrote to a board member: "I do not care to serve where I am not wished. I hope a fight will be made on the resolution at the next meeting of the Board of Trustees, but I can take no part in that fight."[8] There was clearly at least one member of the board who wanted Percy to have nothing to do with Sewanee. He would not say why, except perhaps in private.

Another former Sewanee professor, Huger Jervey, likely had a special sympathy for Percy's experience. In January 1920, just after Percy's dismissal, he wrote to Percy and asked him to come to New York to talk things over. "Love to those that love me and I hope that means much to yourself," he wrote.[9] Rather than fleeing Sewanee, Percy and Jervey bought a house there in 1925 and spent most of their summers there for the next fifteen years. They loved Sewanee and found it beautiful. It was an important place to them. Though not churchmen, they still laid claim to Sewanee as sacred space.

PERCY'S DISMISSAL from Sewanee seemed to have given him a sense of urgency regarding his writing. He spent the late spring and summer of 1920 in Jackson Hole, Wyoming, finishing his revisions. Percy had written in his diary a decade earlier that "the only writing worth doing is the result of long brooding on one idea, or set of ideas."[10] The set of ideas on which Percy brooded should be clear by now: he was interested in understanding himself fully as a spiritual, relational, and sexual creature located in a specific moment in history. More specifically, to engage these questions, he looked to the classical tradition and to the homoerotic Hellenism laid out in the *Symposium* and other works, as well as its modern variant expressed by European Hellenists in the nineteenth and twentieth centuries. What Percy developed in his poetry was a meditation on love and desire that drew from the concept of Ancient Greece as a kind of "home." Through his verse, nostalgia became something of a wellspring for Percy, a way of writing about and legitimizing his sexual and spiritual longings.[11]

Nostalgia is generally described pejoratively as a tool of escape, a mode of imagination that allows an individual to sidestep discomfort with the present by imagining an ideal past. While this contention contains some truth, it also has the effect of simplifying the complexity of human emotions by stereotyping nostalgia as a kind of weakness. The concept of nostalgia originated in the seventeenth century to describe a debilitating homesickness among Swiss mercenaries distant from their homeland. From the Greek roots *nostos*, meaning "to return home," and *algia*, meaning "longing" or even "bodily suffering," the word evolved from a descriptor of physiological illness in the seventeenth century to a psychological concept in the twentieth—a fruitless yearning for an idealized and irrecoverable past. More recent theorists, such as Christopher Lasch and Svetlana Boym, have characterized nostalgia somewhat more positively as the "ideological twin" to the concept of "progress" and an essential component of the modern mentality. Boym's contention that nostalgia is a "romance with one's own fantasy" implies a larger interpretive possibility: the relationship between nostalgia and the erotic. More than longing for a lost time, more than resistance to historical change, nostalgia can create a space distant in place and time onto which one can script emotional and sexual desire. In turn, this idealized portrayal serves as an ethical statement, a positive vindication of queer longings. Will Percy did just this in his poetry.[12]

Students of southern literature have generally ignored Percy's verse or described it as romanticized and anachronistic, echoing William Faulkner's oft-cited review of Percy's *In April Once*. Faulkner wryly pointed out a few positive qualities but mainly catalogued the weaknesses of Percy's poems. He noted the "naïve" elements of Percy's tone and suggested that his sentimentality was evidence that Percy unfortunately "suffered the misfortune of having been born out of his time." "He is like a little boy," Faulkner continued, "closing his eyes against the dark of modernity which threatens the bright simplicity and the colorful romantic pageantry of the middle ages with which his eyes are full." Jay Tolson has called Faulkner's critique "searingly apt" because it articulated "the greatest weakness of Will's character—a willed blindness to certain realities."[13]

One passage in Faulkner's review, however, has never drawn comment. Faulkner wrote: "The influence of the frank pagan beauty worship of the past is heavily upon him." This comment is a more useful reference point for understanding Will Percy's intellectual influences—as well as the erotic aspects of nostalgia for Percy—than assertions that he was merely waxing sentimental when composing verse. Percy's poetry indicates that he was committed to a very specific ideal of "frank pagan beauty worship" that drew from a long and important history of European thought; in engaging this tradition, he was addressing his own contemporary concerns about modernity, creativity, and sexuality.[14]

The intellectual tradition Percy drew from as he was writing *In April Once* was not new. Almost 100 years before Percy was born, the German intellectual Friedrich von Schiller declared modernity a failure and ancient Greece the apex of human civilization in an essay called "Naïve and Sentimental Poetry." To Schiller, the prevailing conception of the human being as separated in soul and body was a failing of modern thought. The notion that the soul belonged to the heavens and the body to the earth led to a fundamental disconnect between humans and nature. Poets of his own day, then, wrote with an essentially *sentimental* disposition borne out of their disconnectedness from the world. In contrast, ancient Greeks believed that body and soul were one, and this consequently infused their poetry with a sensibility that Schiller called naïve, which, translated literally, means "natural": it was intimately connected with the simplicity and beauty of the natural world. Schiller wrote of "the beautiful nature that surrounded the ancient Greeks" and admired "how very much closer their mode of conception, their manner of perception, their morals, were to simple nature, and what a faithful copy of this their poetry is." Schiller's essay is an early example of a tradition of thought in Europe that posited ancient Greece as a society unique in its freedom and frankness. Greeks lived in accord with nature, and their creative expression indicated they were free of false duality between spirit and body.[15]

As we have seen, throughout the nineteenth century, several strands of Hellenism developed in Europe and America. The dominant strand of classical thought became central to university curricula, which immersed students in the study of Greek and Latin as well as classical poetry, philosophy, and history. A less visible strand was one in which some male students—most famously Walter Pater, John Addington Symonds, James Mill Pierce, and Oscar Wilde—read classical texts not merely as a vindication of their own queer desire but also as a critique of modern sexual ethics. Repressive bourgeois morality, some felt, was not good for anyone, and a remaking of sexual values would go a long way toward revitalizing modern society.[16]

Likewise, Percy's use of Hellenist language and themes was not merely a vessel through which he covertly expressed his sexual longings; it was also a medium through which he grappled with fundamental questions concerning art and society. The interrelationship of nostalgia, Hellenism, and sexuality in his poetry demonstrates Percy's belief that a society's sexual mores shape its art. Percy himself made the case for linking creativity and sexuality. "The situation is fundamental and eternal," Percy wrote to an editor, describing his poetry. "Much of our greatest art is directly traceable to the sex instinct and all of it is influenced by that instinct. ... I do very deeply believe in facing the facts, and I know of no love in which the overtones of beauty and nobility are not discernible." A society's conception of sexuality, he maintained, affects the authenticity of its creative culture. His reflections on Greek sexuality in *Lanterns on the Levee*—that "the Greeks practiced bisexuality honestly and simply without thought or condemnation"—indicate that Percy felt the beauty and nobility in Greek art was derived in large part from that society's frankness regarding homosexual love. In his poetry, Percy was both giving voice to his own sexual desire and implicitly critiquing the sexual mores of the society he lived in. He wrote as an individual, but he also wrote squarely within a significant literary context—central to which was an idealization of a homoerotic past free of the moral strictures of the modern bourgeois world.[17]

Scholars such as George Chauncey, E. Patrick Johnson, and John Howard, among others, have shown that even in repressive environments, gay men strategically carved out spaces of sexual freedom—analysis that has significant bearing on Will Percy's experience, as we have seen. Evidence suggests Percy experienced and enjoyed intimate relationships with men, both in the American South and elsewhere. Sexuality, though, is not merely composed of physical experience. Historians of sexuality pay attention not just to structures of relationships and varieties of sexual experience, but also to the ways longing is expressed in literary and material culture, the ways desire is articulated in historically specific language, the ways knowledge about sexuality is constituted and transmitted within particular social and political frameworks. Exploring the concept of nostalgia usefully engages these questions of sexual longing, desire, and knowledge. Nostalgia, evoked through a particular idiom in Percy's era, was one of many vehicles through which men understood and legitimated their homoerotic desires. This idiom featured several characteristics: the celebration of "Greek love," "Grecian beauty," and "Greek pederasty"; key words such as beauty, friendship, comradeship, and ecstasy when describing the uplifting nature of male relationships; and the portrayal of ancient Greece as a moral and spiritual home for men with queer desire. Examining this idiom and this context is useful not merely for understanding Percy's poetry, but for understanding a broader intellectual framework that created meaning and a degree of solidarity among many in the early twentieth century.[18]

Yale University Press released Percy's new volume, *In April Once*, in the fall of 1920. The idea of Greek love animates much of the book, and whether the poems are set in ancient Greece or elsewhere in the distant past, the concept provides the framework for male relationships in his poems. Percy articulated the uplifting nature of love between men in "Mr. W. H. to the Poet," a short poem in which Percy imagined a communication between friends Will Hughes and William Shakespeare—a relationship that many Victorian homosexuals viewed as pederastic. Percy portrayed their relationship as such. The sonnet is an imagined letter of gratitude from the younger man after Shakespeare sent him a copy of *The Tempest*. "My thanks, dear friend, as always!" the poem begins, but the speaker confesses that none of Shakespeare's writing

> can speak to me
> As those swift words you breathed first in my ear.
> They were your heart; this but your wizardry.

The young man says in gratitude that in his life, "There's nothing shines but took its light from you," but the poem ends with the lament that others could not understand their love:

> I wondered if the world, so prone to slight,
> Would some day slur your stainless name with mine,
> Not knowing there is ice in heavenly flame,
> And Friendship is Love's canonizèd name.

Percy sent a copy of this poem to his friend William Stanley Braithwaite, then editor of the *Boston Transcript*, and explained that despite the poem's casual tone, "I mean it very seriously as a defense against those charges of abnormality not infrequently made against the poet in these latter days." "I realize its appeal," Percy continued, "even its understanding, will be limited," and he suggested Braithwaite not publish it "if it seems to you either in subject or in treatment unsuitable."[19]

"Mr. W. H. to the Poet" is instructive not only because in it Percy valorizes a pederastic relationship as spiritually and artistically nourishing, but also because its language draws from one of the era's most important homoerotic texts. Walter Pater's *Studies in the History of the Renaissance,* which Oscar Wilde later called "the golden book of spirit and sense, the holy writ of beauty," gave voice to the Victorian Hellenist's philosophy of paganism. In the famous conclusion to the book, which Pater later had to revise rather than face scandal, he argued that the epitome of life was to experience moments of worldly ecstasy. "To burn always with this hard gem-like flame," Pater wrote, "to maintain this ecstasy, is success in life." Pater's exhortation to pagan ecstasy was inspirational to many late nineteenth-century intellectuals, regardless of their views about sexuality, though many read and welcomed Pater's work as a queer manifesto. Pater celebrated passion and ecstasy but also the particular joys found in beauty and friendship. His description of worldly ecstasy as a "hard, gem-like flame" took root in pederastic discourse as poets wrote often of male love with reference to fire and flame, symbolizing what critic Paul Fussell calls "erotic heat." Percy's reference to the "heavenly flame" of "Friendship" unmistakably reflects the Socratic Eros of late Victorian male homosexuality.[20]

Percy once explained to one of his readers that the main theme of his poem "In April Once" "grew from the conflict, frequently so poignant in youth, between the pagan joy of life and the increasing sense of duty—Guido vs. Serle." "In April Once" is a long, dramatic poem in which Guido, a religious prisoner in a castle near Florence during the thirteenth-century Crusades, confronts his youthful pagan idealism through an encounter with David, a prison guard, and Serle de Lanlarazon, an imprisoned heretic. Serle, whom Percy mentioned as representing "duty," challenges the pagan Guido to offer his heart "to something sterner than delights of youth." At the end of the poem, Guido does this by sacrificing his own life so David and Serle can go and fight in the Crusade, thus dying a heroic death in the service of good.[21]

The interaction of the characters in "In April Once," all of them male, amounts to a paean to pederasty and paganism. David is described as "twenty-two, strongly built, blond, with blue, wide-set eyes and sullen, brooding expression," while Guido is the same age and "slender, very dark, beautiful, full of high spirits and humorous gusto. His dark eyes are vivid and changing." Serle is a "tall and fearful" old man. In the course of their discussion, Guido tells romantic stories of adventure and youthful experience, but it becomes clear that what he wants is not more adventure but forgiveness for carnal sin and validation for his love of beauty. He suspects that in pagan love there is "vileness," but that in selfless belief and action there is honor. In the end, he remains at the castle to fend off attackers so David and Serle can escape with time to flee. He is stabbed and left to die, but his page, Felice, a thirteen-year-old boy, enters and takes him up in his arms. As he lies dying in Felice's arms, Guido recounts the "earthly ecstasy" of spending April evenings together. Sobbing, Felice implores Guido not to leave him, but Guido begins to fade. He tells his page:

> O littlest comrade of my heart,
> Doubt not the world is good and mankind mostly noble.
> That I have lived unstained
> Hath profited me surely by the gift
> Of deep delight. The lips of harlotry
> Can never kiss the sun
> With the light rapture that was ours.

Guido's last request is for Felice to lean closer and sing to him. Felice, holding Guido in his arms, sings to him a song, a prayer requesting Jesus to

> make
> Thy peach trees bloom for me,
> And fringe my bridle paths both sides
> With tulips red and free. [22]

"In April Once" is less ambivalent than some of Percy's earlier work, such as "Sappho in Levkas." Guido dies a hero's death in the arms of the "comrade" of his heart. The intimacy of the final scene adds depth to Guido's dilemma of trying to reconcile pagan ecstasy with masculine duty. The peach trees and tulips that may await in heaven suggest a redemptive outcome, and Guido is satisfied to remember that he "lived unstained" as he experienced the "light rapture" of friendship with Felice. The poem uses a chaste but erotically charged pairing of a man and a boy to emphasize the purity and pathos of male relationships. "In April Once" is far from hollow nostalgia; writing the poem allowed Percy to imagine a moment of charged intimacy between a man and a youth, a fleeting moment of empathy and understanding in the context of a pederastic relationship.

This moment resonated, furthermore, with Percy's readers. Felice's song to Guido was later slightly revised and reprinted in the first anthology of homosexual verse published in America. Compiled by Edward M. Slocum and privately printed, *Men and Boys: An Anthology* was a commentary on and compilation of homoerotic verse from Greek literature to the present.

Billed as "An Anthology of Verses and Poems on the Charm of Boyhood and Young Manhood," the book was "for sale only to mature and discreet persons" over the age of twenty-one. Published under the pseudonym "A. W. Percy," Felice's song appeared as "A Page's Song" with two lines revised. Felice's prayer now requested Jesus to "fringe my boyhood's path, both sides, / With lads-love fine and free." It remains unclear whether Will Percy submitted this version of the poem to be included in *Men and Boys* or whether Slocum read it, liked it, and revised it himself for the anthology. One scholar of queer poetry has argued that Slocum was less than reliable as an anthologist and sometimes changed texts to suit his liking. In addition, there is no extant evidence of connection between Percy and Slocum in Percy's own papers. Whether or not Percy intended this poem to be published in *Men and Boys* is likely to remain a mystery; in either case, though, the inclusion itself is important. If Percy submitted the poem, it indicates his willingness to semipublicly participate in a queer literary culture and his desire to make his homoerotic expression more explicit. If he did not, it remains illustrative that Slocum read the poem in print, recognized its pederastic themes, and included a form of it in his anthology.[23]

The trope of home and homesickness appears throughout *In April Once* and highlights Percy's engagement with themes of longing and belonging. "Riolama" is a poem about a distant, beautiful land whose inhabitants experience "other dreams and other loves" that the narrator recognizes: "All their dreams and all their loves are mine. / They are my people!" However, conflict arises out of this knowledge. The narrator confesses in the poem's final lines that he is "Forever homesick, baffled, yearning to / My native land that I shall never know." The poem captures a simultaneous sense of dislocation ("homesick") and rootedness ("my native land"), a combination that gets to the heart of nostalgia's emotive power: it was a form of longing that accommodated contradiction, that allowed for multiple, irreconcilable urges. To *know* home while being unable to fully inhabit it was both a problem and a possibility. The problem lay in the disconnection, the distance between the narrator and his "native land"; the possibility was that in delineating the characteristics of an ideal home, Percy was able to give voice to his most sacred desires, to eliminate a small piece of the distance between here and there.[24]

This movement toward home is also the motif of "Night off Gallipoli," a poem that imagines the voices of eight people who died during the Gallipoli campaign in World War I. Their spirits now hover over the Aegean Sea and the Greek Isles. They reflect on death and the meaning of war, among other things, but a broader theme of the poem is that to have died here was to have arrived home. An English poet celebrates this fate: "Let me find rest on that divine, sweet shore, / And have for spirit-home some strip of Hellas!" A young Turk anticipates being reunited with his lover:

> Death could not keep me from the arms of you,
> But I should die again upon your mouth
> While all the swaying garden changed from blue
> To red, and softer grew your bosom's south.
> I should not care, I should not greatly care,
> Dying again upon the mouth of you!

Finally, an English soldier imagines himself becoming part of the Greek past:

> O Grecian Stars, how oft
> At home, in the Grey sea,
> I longed to know the lands ye guard.
> . . . .
> Blow, wind of Tauris, blow!
> This is the sea that heard
> The Lesbian's cry, and further south
> The shining song of him
> Whose heart was washed with tears.
> O southward blowing wind, blow on!

Here, as elsewhere, Greece operates as a site of freedom, an erotically charged space, and an ideal home. In addition, the men who narrate the poem do not see their death as an escape but as a reward for a hard-fought, virtuous life. The narrators who arrive in this ideal home do so with no regrets and with a belief that theirs was a good fight. The poem ends:

> Strong Spirit, who has wrought
> A fighting world for men,
> Take us; like men we fought.[25]

Critics and readers of *In April Once* noticed Percy's engagement with Hellenist and homoerotic themes. Responding to a *New York Times* editorial ridiculing the state of American poetry, the poet Lindley Hubbell wrote to the editor and suggested that Americans were producing excellent poetry led by Edwin Arlington Robinson, Edna St. Vincent Millay, and "the exquisitely spiritualized Hellenism of William Alexander Percy." When a friend sent him a copy of Hubbell's comments, Percy wrote back: "That Mr. Hubbell is just exactly the kind of critic of whom I enthusiastically approve. Seriously I like the company he put me in and was pleased at his praise." Percy and Hubbell became friends in the 1920s and corresponded regularly and affectionately until Percy's death.[26]

Many other readers recognized and appreciated Percy's homoerotic verse, and some wrote to him to empathize with his longing for the pattern of relationships that seemed to thrive in classical Greece. "Those of us who have known your poetry," wrote one such admirer, "must find it very difficult to express our gratitude for that rich joy you bring us. We are homesick for 'the glory that was Greece' but we are happy for the reincarnation of that spirit in you. We love you." The reader, who was an aspiring poet in New York, wanted to meet Percy and introduce him to his friends, to sit at his feet.

> Forgive us that we long to see you and have you daily among us. Dear, poet brother, how shall we tell our love for you who have known and kept this high fellowship of song with yourself—with less result but with no less desire. Come to us soon. There shall be long enough to yearn back across the period of our creative fire—this peach bloom and this wine of youth. Then you should be glad to have touched the hands of those your disciplines [sic] who are all about the earth—you will want to remember then, perhaps, who we were who followed you. Come soon to these shores. We have much need of you.[27]

Several readers appreciated Percy's linkage of Greek ethics and contemporary ethics. One thanked Percy for drawing on "that fresh and unencumbered soil, the seed of the ideal that made Greece great" and assured him that "you have done great service in bringing about this flowering of beauty. And you have done it in the choicest and most effective way—that is, by going back to the thirteenth century and invoking its sincerity, its lightheartedness and spiritual fervor, to resuscitate and administer to this jaded twentieth century civilization." Like Percy, the reader did not need the poem to be set in Greece to invoke "the ideal that made Greece great." The reader also felt the poem's use of historical themes did not render the poem anachronistic or futile but added depth to its meaning in the present. "If we today could only catch some of the fire of those men," he concluded, "we could be surer that the crusades of the last few years would have a more permanent meaning." Another reader, the literary critic Stuart P. Sherman, told a friend in a letter that he read *In April Once* "with full delight" and that its type of "paganizing may be … a route to that vital wholeness which is the true goal of every civilization."[28]

Some of Percy's readers connected his work more explicitly to questions of sexuality. One woman cried out: "To hell with homo-sexual exhibitionistic poetry—let us have delicacy of movement, enforced by a knowledge of classicism." Another person read *In April Once* and immediately went out and bought *Sappho in Levkas*. She wrote to Percy that he was obviously "steeped in and loving ancient culture, especially Grecian beauty. ... How boyish of you to choose a theme like Sappho!" Reginald Turner—a close friend of the late Oscar Wilde and an outspoken member of Florence, Italy's expatriate English queer community—wrote from Florence that Percy's verse reminded him of A. E. Housman, the English classicist and homoerotic poet. He wrote that he especially enjoyed "Mr. W. H. to the Poet" and felt that Percy's evocations of male love were more hopeful than Housman's: "They have deeper notes with a more profound and less melancholy philosophy." Percy's verse contained a refined and intellectual expression of sexual fervor that sat well with many of his educated readers.[29]

A more impassioned response came from a younger reader named Malcolm Vaughan. Responding to a letter from Will Percy, Vaughan articulated his love for Percy and his poetry in a manner resembling the intimations in "Mr. W. H. to the Poet": "In your note is suggested that all your days are not rose-coloured. I wonder why I had never suspected it, had always thought of you as sustained in ecstasy." He continued:

> You are one of the children of dream. Whom the gods adore they
> glorify with passion for beauty: beauty whose intimations are agony.
> And the gods adore you, I know. Why, why is there so much sorrow in
> beauty, can you tell me? From time to time, I read from your poems
> to some friend, and all the poised pain of their loveliness throbs in us.
> Why is it thus? Is it that the human breast is capable of desire unre-
> quitable? Yes; I suppose so; yes; love is that, I think; and beauty too,
> no doubt. I am smiling: who am I, to talk of beauty to you!

Vaughan concluded that if Percy were to come to New York to visit, "my head would be bowed, yes, positively sagging, beneath its aureole—the radiance of you. ... Meanwhile, I shall continue to love you: poet that you are." Being the only extant piece of evidence related to Vaughan and Percy's relationship, the letter can only suggest so much. But it is important to point out that the relationship contains the elements of the Socratic Eros: an older and a younger man joined together by a mutual love of beauty and art; the older man taking an interest in the younger, and the younger man being uplifted by that interest; and an intellectual friendship that both nourishes the artistic spirit and contains erotic overtones. Vaughan's melancholic description of the sorrow of beauty and "desire unrequitable" also suggests the not-insignificant social pressures of the day regarding homoerotic expression.[30]

Percy's poetry was far more than a mere idealization of the "colorful romantic pageantry" of the distant past; it was for him and for others a medium that evoked the possibility of a shared homoerotic history. Percy wrote in his memoir that while his writing was "intensely personal," he found solace in the thought that what he was feeling and thinking "had been felt and thought by thousands in every generation. Only that conviction would have permitted me to publish without feeling guilty of indecent exposure." In this he was right: his feelings were common among men and women of every generation and, indeed, across the world. In his poetry, Percy was able to express a measure of both his joy and his anguish, all the while reaching a small but sympathetic audience.[31]

According to Schiller's interpretation of the Greeks, a naïve poet was fundamentally in accord with the natural rhythms of the world. Sentimental poets, conversely, were divided in body and soul, yearning for a lost connection with nature, honesty, and simplicity. By the time William Faulkner dismissed Percy's poetry as "naïve," the term had come to be synonymous with "sentimental." Faulkner's accusations of naïveté and sentimentalism suggested that Percy was in some fundamental way blind and weak, this weakness manifesting itself in futile nostalgia. Will Percy has too often been viewed as a man born out of his time, a man unable to deal with the complexities of modern life and resigned to long for a bygone age through his anachronistic poetry. This is not so. Percy wrote poetry in a deliberate effort to achieve naïveté in Schiller's use of the word: he desired wholeness and connection with what he viewed as beautiful, honest, and natural.

Percy was not merely escaping the present; he was trying to understand himself and his desire as part of a meaningful historical context, a context inclusive of traditionally suppressed human relationships. He figured these relationships as a natural part of creation, which, if understood, could lead to a fuller appreciation of human life. Percy drew from the work of generations of European Hellenists, and his poetry clearly demonstrates his participation in this literary context. His poetic characters' obsessions with "earthly ecstasy" and the beauty of life are distinct expressions of Pater's "hard gemlike flame" of experience. Will Hughes sings of his passion for Shakespeare, Sappho for Phaon, Guido for Felice. Some historians have noted that when Will Percy wrote of love, it was always unrequited. True, those looking for actual *sex* in Percy's poetry will not find much. Virtually no one in this era published writing about *fulfilled* homoerotic encounters. What is more important is the manner in which Percy wrote and the meaning of his writing in context. Percy wrote what amounted to a meditation on queer desire, complete with the mourning of its nonacceptance in contemporary society. He drew from the pederastic focus on the figure of the male youth to articulate the beauty of the male body, and he wrote about asymmetric pairings to emphasize the pedagogical nature of gay love. Percy's characters reflected Socrates's explanation of pederastic love as a spiritual and intellectual form of uplift. The distant past was not merely a setting in which Percy fantasized idyllic scenes but one in which he scripted desire, considered the joys and limitations of male love, and meditated on ecstatic experience.[32]

However, Percy never fully embraced the pagan ideal of the European South, even as he was clearly drawn to it. What Percy called "the conflict between beauty and duty" illustrates an animating tension in his life. He was drawn to the Hellenistic paganism of the classical past, but he also lived within the cultural framework of the American South. His pursuit of ecstasy was tempered by his sense of restraint. He wrote about, experienced, and enjoyed male intimacy, but he also worked to fulfill what he regarded as "duties" to his home and family—duties that, in part, mandated that he remain silent about his sexual desire. This he did not do. His expressions, though, were heard only by those inclined to hear; the rest insisted Percy was merely a versifier using classical themes—or they remained silent themselves.

Percy's close friend David Cohn captured this tension in Percy's life between Greek paganism and Christian morality. In a reminiscence of Percy, Cohn wrote that his friend possessed "an antique beauty suggestive of the Greece he loved and poet he was" and described Percy as perpetually longing for "pagan Greece: for the immortal beauty created there in such a moment of fruition as men have never since known." However, Cohn explained, Percy was also drawn to Christian teaching of selfless service; as such, in his bosom dwelt both "Saint Francis of Assisi and cloven-footed Pan." Despite this conflict, Cohn saw Percy as having essentially succeeded in his attempts to live in spiritual accord with the world—like the Greeks. "Worldly, traveled, widely read, no denizen of an ivory tower," Cohn wrote, "Percy nonetheless was marked by the naïveté and credulity that are nearly always the mark of the spiritually superior and truly sophisticated man." Cohn felt that this "naïveté" made Percy out of step with his times and urged his readers to think of Percy as a kind of pilgrim who was, "in a sense, going home."[33]

This reminiscence, as well as letters from Percy's readers and Percy's own comments on longing for home, suggest that nostalgia is a useful concept for understanding queer desire in the early twentieth century. Percy described his poetry as a medium in which he created a space of freedom, always set in the past. "When after years of pondering you feel you have discovered a new truth or an old one that has the excitement of a new one," Percy explained, "you write a longish poem." And in order to "keep it free from irrelevant photographic details," it is important to "set it in some long-ago time, one, of course, you love and perhaps once *lived in*." Percy's longing for home was inescapably connected to his longing to understand and vindicate his sexual desire. In using the classical past as both a setting and a source of inspiration, Percy and others were able to imagine themselves as part of a "home" that transcended place and time.[34]

When situated in its proper literary context, Will Percy's poetry was squarely in the mainstream of late Victorian homoerotic verse. Though he often employed traditional forms and archaic language, the themes of his poetry were contemporary and reflected an intellectual tradition that was centrally important to the queer idiom of the era. Percy's verse was not impotent fantasy but a deliberate attempt to find in the classical past tools for self-understanding. His poetry became a meditation on the ways in which he was not alone in the world, on his belief that others throughout place and time had felt and loved as he did. To him and to others like him, the possibilities of the ancient European South, of imagining oneself a southerner, imparted a chance of feeling at home in the world.

THOUGH PERCY'S POETRY clearly spoke to a particular audience of like-minded readers, many did not recognize the homoerotic content of his writing. Percy received feedback of all kinds—some commending him for his contribution to southern literature, some asking permission to set his poetry to music, some protesting his interpretations of the Bible. Greenville locals marveled that they lived among a published poet. One Confederate veteran stopped LeRoy Percy on the street and insisted on reading aloud from *In April Once*.[35] This highlights an important dynamic of Percy's work, which both expressed and masked homosexual desire. His achievement was a delicate one. He wrote poetry that felt true to him (and, as it turned out, to others) but also protected him from social reprisal. There were multiple available interpretations of his work—a situation Percy deliberately worked to achieve.

After *In April Once* appeared, a young southern writer, DuBose Heyward, wrote to Percy and asked him what his theory of poetry was. Percy responded that he had no theory except sincerity and "the portrayal of high nobility."

He explained that technique was less important to him than "spiritual fervor or intellectual backbone for in the long run the race will read only what comforts it, or delights it, or informs it, and a perfect technique can never be a substitute for any of these."[36]

Percy was bemused when readers failed to understand the specific "intellectual backbone" that informed his work. He was surprised at how many readers insisted he was a "southern" poet when so few of his poems were concerned with the American South. Heyward had written to Percy enthusiastically about "The Southern Poetry Movement" and said, "You are pretty much the Dean of our school you know." Percy responded: "I appreciate your crowning me dean of Southern School of Poets, but it makes me feel rather bald-headed and whiskery."[37] When another reader wrote him that his was the poetry of the classic southern gentleman, Percy wrote back: "I am not sure I want to give the impression of too southern or too gentle a poet."[38]

If some readers wanted to champion Percy as a "southern" poet, others wanted to register their disapproval of his religious themes. "As a minister of the gospel I marvel at your comprehensive grasp of the real content of the Christian revelation," wrote one Mississippian about Percy's poem "An Epistle from Corinth," in which a Corinthian rebukes the Apostle Paul for corrupting Jesus's message of grace. "You put the language of unbelief in its most subtle forms on the lips of your Corinthian, yet I cannot feel that such is your personal attitude toward God, Christ, and immortality." Percy thanked him for his letter and wrote: "I have always found the New Testament the most interesting book in the world and the teachings of Christ the most vital and the most profoundly wise." However, Percy said, "In the eyes of sure-enough-church-going folks I am afraid I am a bad actor. ... I must confess at bottom I have a grudge against Paul. With all of his eloquence and fire, I am certain he was nervous and cocksure."[39] Other readers were not as gentle as the minister. Speaking of Percy's portrayal of religious values changing over time, one Kentucky reader complained to Percy's editor that "the men's Bible class of the Methodist church here wish to enter a protest against this." When the editor sent Percy this feedback, Percy wrote that it gave him "amusement and real pleasure." He explained: "To the Orthodox I can only say, if this be treason, make the most of it."[40]

Admirers of Percy's work wrote to him to tell him that he was at the head of a literary revival in the South. He responded that he hoped they were right, but the production of art too often came into conflict with the practical work of being a citizen. He told DuBose Heyward that he only wrote "fitfully amid interruptions. I am afraid that is our usual trouble in the South.

We have always had so many practical problems, problems of common justice or citizenship that demand the attention of any self-respecting intellect that we have had only a small part of our lives to devote to any of the arts." To another reader, Percy was slightly more optimistic. "I am certain the South is capable of art," he wrote, "and I believe there is an artistic awakening, the heralding of something I hope of something really fine. So far our people have been so occupied with making a living, obtaining a decent local government and fighting for justice to the Negro, that no leisure was left for more beautiful and more lasting things. Perhaps we are at the end of that period."[41]

Percy was right on one count: there would indeed soon be a moment in southern history that would witness the creative genius of William Faulkner, Zora Neal Hurston, Richard Wright, and many others. On the other hand, as Percy would soon personally experience, southerners, both black and white, were nowhere near the end of racial injustice.

10. THE KLAN

In the Klan fight the very spirit of hatred materialized before our eyes.
It was the ugliest thing I have ever beheld.
—WILLIAM ALEXANDER PERCY, *Lanterns on the Levee*

As Percy was writing *In April Once* and subsequently enjoying its reception, he was also practicing law and living at home with his family. He maintained the pattern of living that characterized his working life: he would work enough to save money and then take a long, distant trip. He competently argued cases for companies such as the Illinois Central Railroad and the O. B. Crittendon Company, and then, just as competently, albeit with more enthusiasm, he would leave for months at a time on trips to Italy, to Greece, and to New York, among other places. In Greenville, he also began to engage more directly with what he and others called the "Negro Problem." Up to this point in his life, he had not written much about the South's particular arrangement concerning race, labor, and etiquette. But like most other Americans in the years after World War I, the race question was everywhere before him. Indeed, on a rainy night in 1923, it would come to his front porch.

Like his father and grandfather, Will Percy came to feel responsible for articulating and defending the Mississippi Delta's regime of race relations. They called their own point of view noblesse oblige, a sense of duty that led a gifted and privileged race to protect and provide for an uncivilized and inferior race. This was a structure of racial hierarchy that accommodated both a cultural style and a set of market values; it allowed families like the Percys to maintain their self-image as benevolent aristocrats, and it also aimed to maximize the labor output of African Americans. It was a system of social and economic authority packaged in the rhetoric of paternalism: elite whites, who had intellectual and material attainments, would provide fatherlike care for blacks under them. In some ways—such as the Percys' steadfast opposition to racial violence—this paternalist concern was more than mere rhetoric. But even in this, economic priorities were also at stake. Lynching was bad for business, especially in a place where Chicago-bound trains left the station every day. Greenville elites wanted the black population to stay just where they were, focused on their work while remembering their place. From the black perspective, paternalism may have created a local culture that was less violent, but it did not create one that was more hopeful.[1]

At its best, paternalism was a racial ideology that allowed for acts of kindness and a degree of mutuality between blacks and whites. There is much evidence from both black and white Mississippians that speaks to LeRoy and Will Percy's concern for black individuals—paying hospital bills, providing free legal counsel, and even paying for schooling in some instances.[2] And from the perspective of blacks working for the Percys, either in the Percy home or on their plantation, paternalism allowed them to wring concessions from their employer. They pressed their own advantage by appearing deferential and loyal, and in turn they negotiated better hours, better living conditions, and more time for family, religion, and community. The fact that most sharecroppers on Percy plantations had screens on their porches, vegetable gardens in their yards, and Christmas bonuses was not because the Percys insisted on these things; it was, rather, because the sharecroppers insisted on them (and, it should be said, because there were potential economic advantages for landowners having a relatively contented labor force less likely to move). But despite these soft edges, paternalism—and paternalists like the Percys—subscribed to the central tenets of white supremacy: there was a real and measurable difference between black and white people; white people were intellectually, culturally, and morally superior; and social inequality was the natural and inevitable outcome of blacks and whites living side by side.

This did not mean, however, that Delta planters viewed all white people as equal. Shortly after he had returned from the war, Will Percy sent an unsolicited letter to the *New Republic* explaining southern race relations. In it, he argued that the Negro Problem was not so much a matter of race as of class. The Negro race, he explained, was "a race which at its present stage of development is inferior in character and intellect to our own." They were a tragic, pitiful, and lovable race, but they were essentially lacking in development. They needed the care and protection of white men, particularly those who lived among them and possessed the "wisdom, justice, and kindness" to lead them. This higher class of whites maintained the ability to orchestrate race relations in a way that was peaceful and effective, "not quickly nor easily, but through the years. And they are the only people who can: it is their problem, their burden, their heavy heritage." The greatest challenge to peaceful race relations in the South was not blacks themselves but "the lawlessness and hoodlumism of our uneducated whites." These "inflammable, uneducated whites whom the best part of our lives is spent in controlling"—people like James K. Vardaman and Theodore Bilbo—were responsible for the violence, the lynching, the hatred, the feelings of fear and mistrust between the races in the South. Further complicating the situation, Percy contended, was the long legacy of northern interference in the South. "To you our tragic situation, calling for courage and wisdom and unselfishness and patience, is a theory, a subject for criticism, suggested panaceas, scorn. We know the solution, the only one. ... My plea to you is that you trust us who are fighting the fight in the South."[3]

Here, Percy gave voice to several key ideas among Delta planters. He was as dogmatic about the distinction between white and black as he was about that between elite whites and "uneducated" whites. He insisted that these elite southerners be in charge of race relations, as had planters since Reconstruction. And finally, he drew from the oft-used trope of the martyr: leading blacks was a "problem" and a "burden" for honor-bound, well-intentioned aristocrats. He rearticulated this lament in his autobiography when we wrote of "the pathos of a stronger race carrying on its shoulders a weaker race and from the burden losing its own strength!"[4] This combined feeling of martyrdom, racial distinction, and class superiority was a strong emotional cocktail, providing as it did a justification for the vast disparity of wealth, power, and privilege that Percy enjoyed. It gave moral legitimacy to a way of life.

But this way of thinking was also more than self-justification. It ordered and sustained a system of labor that required a large agricultural class. As we have seen, growing cotton in the Mississippi Delta demanded prodigious amounts of labor from day one. Since there were also prodigious amounts of money to be made, planters imported this labor (usually from Virginia and the Carolinas) in the form of black slaves. These slaves became the majority of the population, and after the Civil War and emancipation it was imperative, planters felt, to both keep blacks working and prevent them from becoming economic competitors. The thought of social and economic equality with these former slaves was anathema to former slave owners; however, so was the thought of barren cotton fields. Hence the Negro Problem for planters was this: how to structure a biracial society, maximize black labor while minimizing black opportunity, and control a majority population who refused to conform to their expectations.

Around the turn of the century, planters looked to immigrant labor—especially Italian and Chinese farmers—as a way of gradually replacing black workers. LeRoy Percy was especially taken with the idea of Italians. He felt Italians would make more efficient workers and more respectable citizens, and—most important—they would rid the Delta of the Negro Problem. As Italians came in, the former slaves would go out. "Let him go as he will," Percy wrote in 1907, "taking his troubles to other climes, filling his place with the best immigrants you can get, but filling it with white men, possessing the potentialities of citizenship, whose children, or whose children's children, some day in the future, will help us bear the burdens, help us solve the problems, of government. This the negro can never do."[5] LeRoy Percy recruited hundreds of Italian families over a ten-year period, but in doing so he violated federal peonage laws and nearly incurred a federal lawsuit. The Italians claimed that they were forced to work against their will and charged usurious rates of interest. Percy had to ask for help from President Theodore Roosevelt; soon after he did, the Justice Department dropped the case. But Percy's experiment in whitewashing the Delta had failed, and he and others persisted with the labor at hand.[6]

The biggest challenge regarding the labor at hand, though, was mobility. African Americans were free people, and they increasingly exercised their freedom by moving away. Nearly 150,000 black people left the state of Mississippi between 1910 and 1920.[7] The Mississippi-born black population of Chicago grew fivefold in that decade.[8] The railroad, which Colonel William Alexander Percy and his son had so tirelessly worked to bring to the Delta, traveled in both directions. The Illinois Central Railroad, which connected New Orleans and Chicago and was a client of the Percy & Percy law firm, was busy trying to lure people *to* the Delta, not away from it. Its brochure promised white readers in 1910 that "nowhere in Mississippi have antebellum conditions of landholding been so nearly preserved as in the Delta." In addition, the railroad assured potential investors and settlers that race relations had never been better: "The Negro is naturally gregarious in instinct, and is never so happy as when massed together in large numbers, as on the Delta plantations." The great irony, of course, was that those Negroes were not happy, and it would be the Illinois Central itself that took them north by the hundreds of thousands in the coming decades.[9]

African Americans left Mississippi for many reasons—to pursue opportunity, to reunite with family, to escape Jim Crow. Many blacks doubtless left because race relations in the South were too often violent. When racial violence increased after World War I, the Percys regularly spoke out against it, as Will Percy did in his letter to the *New Republic*. They did this as a matter of conscience, but also because they had a vested interest in Greenville appearing to be a peaceful, stable community. LeRoy Percy in particular went to great lengths to oppose racial violence, and his most public opportunity came when the Ku Klux Klan arrived in the Delta in 1921.

A group of Confederate veterans formed the Ku Klux Klan after the Civil War in an effort to control newly emancipated blacks. After several years of vigilante justice against freed slaves, northern missionaries, and Reconstruction politicians, the Klan disbanded in 1869.[10] In 1915, though, the Ku Klux Klan reformed. This time, Klansmen were responding to a new set of anxieties. Fifteen million immigrants had come to America between 1900 and 1915, most from eastern Europe. The Catholic church more than doubled its U.S. membership between 1890 and 1915. Catholics, Jews, immigrants, communists, anarchists, and socialists threatened to change the American way of life—and many of them threatened to take jobs as well. African Americans returned from war galvanized in their fight for civil rights, and their spokespersons penned lines like these by W. E. B. Du Bois:

> We Return.
> We return from fighting.
> We return fighting.
> Make way for democracy!

What was at stake, many felt, was nothing less than America itself.[11]

This new Ku Klux Klan capitalized on the widespread anxiety about "Americanness" at a moment when people, men in particular, were infatuated with secret societies and rituals. It was the "Golden Age of Fraternity," and by 1920 there were over 800 secret societies with a membership of at least 30 million men.[12] The Klan promised its members a secret society committed to white supremacy and "100 percent Americanism." At its peak in 1924, its membership included almost 5 million people across the country.[13]

In Mississippi, the Ku Klux Klan never grew to be a powerful force in the 1920s. It did exist, however, and like most Klan chapters, it left little record of its activities and membership. But the extant records show that the Klan entered Mississippi with the same basic aims of vigilante justice and white supremacy that it boasted in other locales. In a letter addressed to "All Flag and Liberty Loving, Law Abiding Citizens" that appeared in a Delta newspaper in 1921, the Klan warned "bootleggers, gamblers, and all other lawbreakers" that "we have our eyes on you, and we are many; we are everywhere, and you will not escape." To "the Negro" they only said, "We are your best friend, but we wish you to do right."[14] As with elsewhere, the Klan appealed to Mississippians' sense of patriotism, morality, and decency in the broader service of white supremacy and the notion of America as a Christian nation.

The Percy family also viewed themselves as patriotic, moral, and decent people, but their perspective differed from the Klan's in several important ways. LeRoy Percy was married to a Catholic and encouraged Italian immigration to the Delta; he was a gambler, a drinker, and a corporate conservative. Will Percy was a cosmopolitan poet who believed that love between men was noble and beautiful. The family fortune of both father and son depended upon a ready supply of labor supplied by black workers, all of whom were aware of the Illinois Central Railroad and the possibility of a different life elsewhere. The Klan's message of fear and intimidation threatened labor stability and planter authority. The group's reactionary, populist appeal to white southerners came into conflict with the Percys' economic and cultural priorities. A common belief in white supremacy was not enough to bind these white men together in solidarity.

In March 1922 one of the Klan's traveling speakers, Colonel Camp, came to Greenville to recruit new members. He was to deliver a speech at the Washington County Courthouse. The Percys learned of this in advance and deliberated about how to respond. "Evidently some of our own people were Klansmen," Will Percy recalled. "Our best citizens, those who thought for the common good, met in father's office and agreed almost unanimously that the Colonel should be answered and by father."[15]

On the night of March 1, 1922, the Washington County Courthouse filled with citizens who had come to hear Colonel Camp's speech and LeRoy Percy's response. Camp began, and in his speech, he described the impending dangers to American-born Anglo-Saxons, claiming that the only "100 per cent American organization today is the Knights of the Ku Klux Klan." He declared that "aliens are seeking to shift the foundations of government from the hands of the Anglo-Saxon" and argued that since Catholics and immigrant workers were organized, it stood to reason that white, Christian, patriotic Americans should be organized. There were some nods and grunts of approval in the audience.[16]

LeRoy Percy—by this time sixty-one years old, gray-haired, and bespectacled—took the podium confident he knew the priorities and prejudices of his people better than anyone else. He began his long rebuttal with a defense of the first Klan as a desperate measure in a time when the South needed vigilante justice. It was a war-torn region in need of protection, he said, lest radical Republicans and Negroes take control over every office in the former Confederacy. But now, "after the need for it has gone, with the white man in control of every department of government, of the courts, judges and juries, the machinery of the Ku Klux Klan is dragged from its grave and revamped for profit." Percy then turned to his main concern: the lack of labor in the region, largely due to "the steady trend of the black man away from the South." While this trend could not be stopped, he argued, the Ku Klux Klan was surely expediting the process to the detriment of all who lived and worked in the South. The principles of the Klan were not all bad, he explained, but the tactics and the effects of it were devastating. Percy essentially agreed with their "stand for Christianity, for the protection of womanhood, and white supremacy," but he asked, "In the name of God, do they need to be masked to do that?" Their practice of intimidation, their reliance on secrecy and violence, and their essential lawlessness had the effect of driving away black labor and tearing communities apart. The audience greeted Percy's speech with a standing ovation, and a Greenville deputy, who happened to be an Irish Catholic, escorted out the Klansman. After they left, those who remained passed a resolution condemning the Ku Klux Klan.[17]

In the days and months after the speech, LeRoy Percy involved himself in correspondence with local and national leaders, journalists, and friends and began to take his message across the country. He received hundreds of letters from supporters, both black and white, across Mississippi and the nation who had read reprints of his speech in the *Greenville Democrat, Houston Chronicle, Vicksburg Herald, New Orleans Times-Picayune*, and *New York World*.[18] The bulk of his incoming mail praised him for his manliness, patriotism, and leadership.[19] Although the majority of the letters were from white readers, Percy also received several letters from African American lawyers, professors, and school principals. F. S. Armstrong, a black attorney in Washington, D.C., wrote to Percy: "My love for Mississippi is unbounded and when I hear the voice of men of your type, representing the best of white manhood of our state, I am genuinely proud." His letter echoed the sentiment of a large number of letters from African Americans that "the old bugbear of social equality, which you know we do not seek, ought to be tossed to the things forgotten." These black leaders had a great deal at stake in Booker T. Washington's vision for the industrial and agricultural education of blacks with the support and leadership from whites like Percy.[20]

Percy continued his correspondence and politicking through the fall of 1922 and the spring of 1923 and prepared for the county and state elections of that summer—elections in which a Klansman and an anti-Klan supporter would contend for nearly every office. He established, along with fifty of Greenville's "best citizens," an organized group to oppose the Klan called the "Protestant Committee of Fifty Opposed to the Ku Klux Klan." On April 23, 1923, LeRoy Percy delivered a two-hour diatribe at the People's Theatre in Greenville in which he paid particular attention to local context and specific Klan activity in Washington County. Percy named all the local Klansmen that he knew of and responded to personal attacks on him made by the local Klan, namely that he was "the Big Cheese" and was a member of the "PPP"— or "Parker, Pope, and Percy." He argued against religious bigotry and for "the religion of our community," which "finds its expression in love, helpful service, man to man. ... The kind of religion that made you know as you walked down the streets of Greenville, that behind every house—you might not know whose house it was, whether it was Jew, Protestant, or Catholic— but behind every house was a friend." He pointed out the grave danger of the Delta's labor situation and noted that blacks were like sheep and Klansmen were like wolves: "This feeling of restlessness, of uneasiness, which the white people of this community feel is intensified 100 fold when it is passed on to the brother in black." In the end, the sacrifices made by soldiers in the First World War, the American ideals of democracy and freedom, and the "blessings of civilization and free government" were too good to let them be trampled by the Ku Klux Klan.[21]

During the spring of 1923, Will Percy was sick in bed with the flu. He traveled to Palm Beach, Florida, for six weeks in March and April to rest, but when he returned to Greenville, the town was tense after LeRoy Percy's People's Theatre speech. A few nights before his thirty-eighth birthday, Will Percy was in the parlor of the Percy home playing the piano when a rain-soaked, unshaven man knocked at the door and asked for LeRoy Percy. LeRoy came to the foyer, and the man explained that he and his sister were stranded, that his car had broken down outside of town, and that he needed a ride to the nearest mechanic. LeRoy went to put on a coat and call for his car, and in the meantime, a group of his friends arrived to play cards, one of whom was the county sheriff. The stranger disappeared into the darkness, and a neighbor told the Percys that he left with another man who was parked across the street. It turned out that the stranger was a member of the local Ku Klux Klan and wanted LeRoy Percy dead. The next morning, Will Percy walked into the office of the leader of the local Klan and said, "I want to let you know one thing: if anything happens to my father or to any of our friends you will be killed. We won't hunt for the guilty party. So far as we are concerned the guilty party will be you."[22]

Percy feared for his father's life. He wrote to a friend: "We are in the midst of an awful Ku-Klux fight here. The little community is torn wide open, friends have been severed and it's gotten to the part where everyone goes armed and expects trouble." Responding to an editor seeking new poems, Percy wrote: "Our fight against the Klan here has grown intolerably bitter, even dangerous, and my father is the center of it. Until our local elections are over in August, I shan't have much heart for things literary." Though Will Percy was not leading the fight, he felt a degree of solidarity with his father that disrupted some of his own ambitions.[23]

In the elections of that summer, the Percy candidates won all the major offices except the office of sheriff, in which there was a runoff. In many ways, this was the most important office because, as Will Percy later recalled, if the Klan "could have the law-enforcement machinery under their control, they could then flout the law and perpetuate such outrages as appealed to them." The Percys threw all their support behind George B. Alexander, "a powerful, square bearded, Kentucky aristocrat. ... He was Father's favorite hunting companion and friend." In his memoir, Percy dramatized the night of the election runoff as one of the most important in the town's history: "The whole population was in the street, milling, apprehensive, silent." When the vote counting began, LeRoy Percy retired to his house to play bridge while others waited for the results. After several hours, a man emerged from the election office and yelled, "'We've won, we've won! Alexander's elected! God damn the Klan!'" A mob of people gathered at the Percy mansion. People seemed in the mood to celebrate, so LeRoy ordered his servants to bring out four kegs of whiskey and invited everyone to stay. "There were few inhibitions and no social distinctions," Will Percy recalled. "A banker's wife hobnobbed with the hot-tamale man, a lawyer's careened with a bootlegger. ... The little town had come through, righteousness had prevailed, we had fought the good fight and for once had won. Everybody was affectionate with everybody else, all men were equal, and all were brothers-in-arms."[24]

For the Percy family, this was more than a local victory; it was a vindication of their class interests and view of racial hierarchy. They opposed the Klan because they thought it was hateful, intolerant, and crass. But they fought against the Klan, they risked considerable time and money and personal safety, because the Klan threatened the foundations of their way of life. It threatened the cultural authority of the planter class; it threatened the stability of labor in the Delta; and it threatened paternalism as a structure of race relations. To have opposed the Klan was to protect and maintain these things that ordered the Percy's Delta world.

From the perspective of Mississippi's black population, white supremacy was just as intact after the Klan fight as it had been before it. Neither the Percys nor the Klansmen ever questioned that. Many black people in Greenville did, though—some of whom, perhaps, missed word of the party at the Percy house because they were home getting rest, preparing to catch an early-morning train.

11. ON GOD, SIN, AND THE MEDITERRANEAN

> If men would but forget what not
> To do, and fix their wills and uttermost minds
> On what to do and do it—they'd breed the world
> With loveliness and power beyond all guessing!
> —WILLIAM ALEXANDER PERCY, "Enzio's Kingdom"

"I'm now regarded as a citizen of Capri," Will Percy proclaimed to his parents from Italy in August 1922. Shortly after his father had delivered his anti-Klan speech at the Washington County courthouse, Percy left for the summer. In Greenville, his father remained embroiled in the Ku Klux battle and his legal work, and his mother had recently returned from the Glen Springs sanitarium in Watkins, New York, where she was treated for nervous exhaustion during late 1921 and early 1922. As Percy was writing about his citizenship in Capri, the local discussion in Greenville was about citizenship, too: who was in and who was out, what kind of citizenship—if any—Catholics and Italians and African Americans were capable of. Will Percy was invested in this problem. But while in the Mediterranean, he experienced and enjoyed communities that had wholly different views about morality, art, and sex than either the Klan or the anti-Klan factions in Mississippi. Being a "citizen of Capri" was a different kind of belonging.[1]

Percy traveled to Capri in particular for several reasons. The island was widely known in the early twentieth century as a welcome community for international painters, sculptors, composers, and poets who wanted a peaceful and beautiful place to work. It was also widely known in some circles for having a thriving queer community. In what has been called the first gay travel guide, a contemporary French writer explained that it was common knowledge among Europeans that homosexuality "flourishes abundantly" in Italy, but that Capri was the epicenter of the queer world. "The Isle of Capri is a sodomic capital in miniature, the Mecca of inversion," he wrote, "a Geneva or Moscow of the future internationalism of homosexuality." The author noted that what he called "The Third Sex" would find many like-minded guests on Capri. He expressed surprise at travelers who did not know this. "I know a young couple who, quite unwisely, went there on their honeymoon," he joked. "A deplorable inspiration!"[2]

Will Percy obviously did not write to his parents about the sex scene on Capri, though he did tell them that it was a place populated by fashionable, forward-thinking men and that he was one of them. "The men wear white flannel trousers, no coat (even to meals)," he wrote, "a shirt with the collar turned in or open at the throat, or if you are very chic an undershirt in place of a shirt, white sneakers without socks, and no hat." He told them he, too, had begun to roll up his pants to show his ankles, and he had let his hair grow long as well: "My unbound curls and bare ankles twinkle with the best of them. Everybody knows everybody else at least by sight."[3]

Percy told his parents that when he was not working on his poetry, he spent his time with other artists—though he did not mention them by name. "I've been walking and tea-ing afternoons with two French journalists and a Dante-esque Italian," he wrote. "Through an elderly and homely English-man I've met some of the English residents and a most charming American artist who has lept into fame with two pictures." In addition to making new friendships, he said, his main occupations were to enjoy Capri's beauty and to work on his writing. By mid-August he had finished a full draft of a long new poem called "Enzio's Kingdom," and he was working on some shorter pieces as well. He described the island as a "heavenly place" to write poetry, "so full of color and sunshine, with such width of sapphire green-mottled sea all around." It gave him the peace of mind he needed to write. After two months, he decided to stay longer. "I'll remain right here," he wrote, "which is as nice a place as there is in the world."[4]

The writing Percy did in Capri reflects this context of open-mindedness, natural beauty, and male camaraderie. The poems in *Enzio's Kingdom* give voice to Percy's enduring quarrel with religion, which he wished would be more focused on God than on sin, more expansive with regard to love, and less anxious about control. The lyrical poems attempt to capture moments of sublime beauty, and many of them portray men in moments of solidarity amid the indescribable: watching a sunset, listening to falling leaves, walking through a quiet rain shower. The poems speak to moments of peace that always dissolve, fragments of meaning that never cohere. They are expressions of a poet who found meaning in human relationships, natural beauty, and what he believed to be universal human goodness. But taken as a whole, the poems are also infused with an inherent melancholy about the fleeting nature of human connection, the inability to fully experience the sublime, and humanity's enormous capacity for evil.

Like *Sappho in Levkas* and *In April Once*, the title piece in *Enzio's Kingdom* is a long poem whose dramatic focus centers on an ethical question. Where "Sappho In Levkas" is about the relationship between sexual pleasure and spiritual love, and "In April Once" is about pagan joy coexisting with duty and responsibility, "Enzio's Kingdom" is about the meaning of personal freedom. In the poem, Enzio, the historical son of the Holy Roman Emperor Frederick II (1194–1250), learns that his father has died and reflects on his father's life in an extended monologue. Scholarship written about "Enzio's Kingdom" generally interprets Enzio's reflections as biography: Enzio, who is imprisoned and alone, is Will Percy, and Frederick II, who was a warrior and a leader, is LeRoy Percy. This interpretation grows out of the common belief that Will Percy hated himself for not being as "manly" as his father, whom he worshipped. This reading of Percy also echoes the broader Freudian interpretation of male homosexuality as stemming in part out of repressed rage toward one's overbearing father. Lewis Baker declares that "Enzio's Kingdom" is clearly about LeRoy and Will Percy because "in the main story line, the son is decidedly inferior to the father," and this reflects "a dimming of Will's hope that he might after all prove fit to succeed his father as a leader." Similarly, Richard King interprets the poem as evidence that "for all the positive influence of his father, Will Percy was in some fundamental way unmanned by him." There are several more examples of this interpretation, all of which seem to shed more light on a late twentieth-century expectation among historians—that a gay man would naturally have been "inferior to" and "unmanned by" his father—than the poem itself.[5]

The poem is not an autobiographical account of Will Percy and his father. Percy told a friend that such a reading would be tempting because some of Frederick's qualities—his steadfastness, his strength, his courage—"remind me so strongly of my father." But as with all his long poems, Percy envisioned "Enzio's Kingdom" as "a contemporary poem," a meditation on "a poignant human problem that vexed me." The problem that the poem engages is not conflict between father and son—in fact, there is almost no conflict between father and son in the poem, but rather a remarkable depth of mutual love and admiration. The "human problem" in the poem is the possibility that both father and son could live in a world without religion as moral authority—and more specifically, whether mankind was capable of having true freedom of thought and action in what the poem describes as "this religious and oppressive world." The overpowering force in the poem is not Frederick but the church, against which Enzio and Frederick fight and lose. This conflict, Percy explained, was reflective of the broader themes in which his poetry was always interested: "man and God, man and love, and man in the trap of fate."[6]

As Enzio tells the story of his father's life, it becomes quite clear that Percy did not intend Frederick to represent LeRoy Percy. As a historic figure, Frederick II was a critic of the papacy and a religious doubter. He was a charismatic if sometimes unpredictable leader, and his court was known for its ethnic diversity and open-mindedness.[7] In the poem, Percy imagines Frederick's conflict with the church as a sexual one. Much of the poem is a recounting of one of Frederick's monologues, in which he asks: "How am I judged here, now, / By this religious and oppressive world?" He answers his own question by saying that the church has paid no attention to the good he has done, "All I have wrought for justice and for peace, / for beauty's burgeoning and joy's flower," but rather has focused exclusively on his sexual behavior. "I am not chaste, and so I spoil for hell!" he mocks.

> These priests that never do the deed, but dream of it
> Till their minds are porous—foetid—maggot's meat—
> They grieve for me, who feed the monster I
> Am caged in decently, I hope.

In contrast to the expectations of the priests, Frederick takes pleasure in "our sweet bodies" and the fact that he does not enjoy them "half-heartedly, / betwixt a dream and a sleep, the sanctioned way."[8]

The problem for Frederick, then, was that the church controlled the contours of moral authority in his world. It did so by focusing on sin rather than on virtue. "Oh, all this cry of 'sin,' these acts forbidden, / Ruffle my gorge!" he laments.

> With hortatives and childish talk of sin
> They so have staled the cleanly natural air
> That life stinks like a sick-room. Bah! Their "sin."

What once was beautiful—the redeeming, empowering love of Christ—was now merely an instrument of power:

> I see the thing that calls itself
> Christ's Church a noble detriment, a dream
> Once valid, but in the dawning old and evil.

One need look no further, he says, than the blood that has "blistered" the earth as a result of religious wars, to learn that what is at stake is not love but power.[9]

Significantly, Frederick does not stop at this critique but also offers an alternative vision for moral authority. He speaks of how he has read and understood religious texts but felt that the truth in them is unnamable, that "still the ultimate word's not written." He explains:

> When I have made my tablet of the laws
> To guide the flight of my young Enzios,
> "Thou shalt not" shall be missing from its rubric.
> Perhaps two words will make its decalogue:
> "Courage: Unselfishness." These two suffice.

This focus on virtue rather than vice would allow poets and philosophers, "the flashing-eyed minority, / the Enzio's of the world," to pursue truth without fear of recrimination.

> Think, think, O Gods, what freedom could mean here,
> Freedom to think and be and to pursue
> The sovereign hope a stormy heart may spring!

This freedom, though, must be fused with the ethical responsibility not to harm others. Because for any act, Frederick warns, "There is no taint save its own consequence." Personal freedom, combined with moral seriousness and concern for the common good, could "breed the world / With loveliness and power beyond all guessing!"[10]

Frederick gives voice to a vision that is at its core a liberal, secular rendering of social relations: people should be free to think and act as they choose so long as their actions do not harm others; in return for this privilege of freedom, one has the responsibility to serve others with courage and selflessness; and finally, religious dogma should not order human society but rather the bigger, more capacious truths beyond dogma: love, empathy, and sacrifice. Far from being a poem about a son's inferiority to his father, "Enzio's Kingdom" depicts a son admiringly recounting what he sees as his father's noble vision for a free, open society.

The poem's ending, however, is not a hopeful one. Enzio and Frederick, along with Frederick's army, attack the military forces of the papacy in hopes of reigning in a new era of freedom and peace under Frederick. The pope's army overpowers them, Frederick is killed in battle, and Enzio is imprisoned. It is from prison that Enzio tells his story, and his story grieves the inability of freedom to flourish in a world dominated by religious authority. "There is no certain thing I can lay hold on," Enzio explains, "And say, 'This, this is good! This will I worship!' / Except my father." Enzio believed in his father because he brought idealism and action together—he believed deeply in his ideals and was also prepared to die for them. Enzio shared his father's idealistic vision, and laments:

> It seems now nothing else in life was worth
> The seeing. What the crop is of his sowing
> I am not seer enough to speculate:
> I only know the grain was golden and
> The earth is culpable if there's no harvest.

There was nobility in Frederick's life, Enzio says, and now that he is dead, all that is left are his ideals. They are not the ideals that govern the world, but, the poem concludes, "we have much to dream on."[11]

Like "Sappho in Levkas" and "In April Once," "Enzio's Kingdom" is a poem in which Percy worked through the themes that animated his moral imagination. It is not a poem about LeRoy Percy; it is difficult to imagine him, for example, proclaiming the sensual goodness of "our sweet bodies" and celebrating the poetic vision of his son. Rather, it is a poem in which Percy dramatized his own ideas about God, sin, and morality through the characters of Frederick and Enzio, who share the same perspective and suffer for it. The poem's melancholy timbre is not borne of a dominated son but of a moral vision that can gain no traction in the world. "Enzio's Kingdom" suggests that within the minds and bodies of people there are wellsprings of meaning; it gestures toward the "loveliness and power" of which humans are capable; it finds courage and unselfishness where the priests insist there is vice and heresy. In the end, though, the priests win. Frederick and Enzio are silenced, and Enzio is left to conclude, from prison, that the good lay not in the outcome but in the fight.

Percy said that he liked to write outside when he was in Italy, and one can imagine him writing "Enzio's Kingdom" in that context, "with such width of sapphire green-mottled sea all around." Surely it was a stark contrast to what he had left behind in Mississippi, where the Ku Klux Klan was at the same moment promising to monitor the Delta in order to maintain moral standards and what they called a Christian way of life. The Klan represented only the most extreme and explicit manifestation of the kind of coercive moral authority Percy always wrote about in his poetry: the power to control behavior; the power to silence independent thought in the name of morality;

the power to transform the mysteries of God into a set of cultural values. It was not the Christian message that posed this problem; it was the Christian people and the Christian churches. "The churches wouldn't recognize religion," Percy wrote, "if they met it in the middle of the big road."[12]

Indeed, Percy wrote more about God in *Enzio's Kingdom* than in his earlier volumes. One poem, "His Peace," was so admired by the Episcopal church that church officials set it to music and put it in their hymnal, where it remains today. The short poem is about Jesus's disciples, who were "contented, peaceful fishermen" before they met Christ and came to know "the peace of God that filled their hearts / Brim-full, and broke them too." This presence of God in their hearts brought not only peace but also the promise of suffering and martyrdom. John died homeless in Patmos, Peter "head-down, was crucified." The poem ends ambiguously:

> The peace of God, it is no peace,
> But strife closed in the sod.
> Yet, brothers, pray for but one thing,
> The marvelous peace of God.

When the Episcopalians asked Percy's permission to set the poem to music, they also asked if they could remove the last stanza. Percy answered no because he felt the meaning of the poem lay in the tension within the final four lines. What remains is probably the least exhortative hymn in the Episcopal hymnal.[13]

Percy returned to Mississippi in October 1922 with a journal full of poems and a body rested for the Klan fight that continued to rage in Greenville. He also carried with him memories of the Mediterranean that he did not share with his parents. We do not know what those memories were beyond the brief glimpses he offered in his letters home and in his poetry, but we can safely assume that Percy developed a well-crafted silence with his family. While at home, he protected himself by not talking specifically about the themes he explored in his poetry or about the details of his relationships. He portrayed a degree of the pressure he felt from this intentional duplicity in his poem "Safe Secrets." One imagines Percy writing this poem not on a patio in Capri, but in the library of the house on Percy Street.

> I will carry terrible things to the grave with me:
>   So much must never be told.
> My eyes will be ready for sleep and my heart for dust
>   With all the secrets they hold.

The piteous things alive in my memory
  Will be safe in that soundless dwelling:
In the clean loam, in the dark where the dumb roots rust
  I can sleep without fear of telling.[14]

Percy finished the revisions for *Enzio's Kingdom* by the spring of 1924. After he mailed the final version to the press, he went to New York to meet up with Huger Jervey and Gerstle Mack. Jervey was now dean of the law school at Columbia, and Mack was an architect and theatre designer who would also soon begin working on a biography of the French painter Paul Cézanne.[15] From New York, the three of them left for a three-month vacation. They began in Italy, sailed through the Mediterranean and the Greek Isles, and ended in Paris. Their highbrow expectations for their trip were temporarily interrupted on the Atlantic. From aboard the ship, Percy wrote to his mother: "Last night was the usual ship concert at which a lady of mature years and quantities of blondined hair screamed selections from the opera in a voice so strong and harsh and flat that the mermaids must have had tooth-aches for miles around."[16]

A more refined artistic community awaited them in Taormina, Italy, where they arrived in early June. Like Capri, Taormina was a gathering spot for queer men in the early twentieth century. The Sicilian town was renowned for two reasons: first, for its breathtaking beauty, with its panoramic views of the Mediterranean and Mount Aetna; and second, for the work of its most famous resident, Baron Wilhelm von Gloeden, the pioneering photographer who was known for his photographs of nude Italian youths. Von Gloeden attempted to capture chaste yet eroticized scenes in which one or several young men posed among ancient ruins or nature scenes surrounded by suggestive imagery, such as blooming flowers and climbing vines. He and others viewed his work not as pornographic but as conveying the purity and beauty of the male body. "W. v. Gloeden has taken it upon himself to animate the landscape of this magnificent, history-laden island with naked human figures," wrote a contemporary admirer, "according to the Hellenic ideal of beauty that left its characteristic mark upon it for all time." Many of von Gloeden's admirers interpreted his work along these pederastic lines: here was an erotic rendering of the body that was not vulgar but delicate, not crass but refined, even ethereal. Indeed, much like Percy's poetry, von Gloeden's classical themes protected him from charges of indecency; that is, many viewers saw his work not as homoerotic at all but as aesthetic evocations of classical beauty. Some of his less sexually charged photographs were widely

Caino, *by Baron Wilhelm von Gloeden, 1902 (Courtesy of Wikimedia Commons)*

known as postcards, and his admirers included not only men such as Percy, Jervey, and Mack but also J. P. Morgan, Alexander Graham Bell, and King Edward VII of England.[17]

As in Capri, Percy's correspondence home captures his love of Taormina's physical beauty but says little of the kinds of people there. "It certainly is one of the most heavenly spots in all creation," Percy wrote to his mother, "and I wanted to stay there the rest of the summer." But Percy, Jervey, and Mack traveled on to Athens, Greece, and from there traveled through Delphi, Crete, Lesbos, Constantinople, Vienna, and Budapest before ending up in Paris. Percy wrote home describing their itinerary and his affection for southern Europe, but as usual he did not write to his parents about the deeper meanings and pleasures these places offered to him.[18]

A more compelling portrait of this trip comes in Percy's memoir, in which he wrote not only about where he went but also about what these moments meant. In *Lanterns on the Levee*, Percy wrote two evocative vignettes about his time in Greece and Turkey. In the first vignette, Percy recounted that he was on a walk alone when he encountered a "satyr on the slopes of Parnassus." In Greek mythology, a satyr is often figured as an oversexualized man, and perhaps Percy also had in mind one of the many photographs by Wilhelm von Gloeden of young men with titles like "Sicilian Satyr" or "Sicilian Faun."[19] But in this instance, the satyr was a "brown boy. . . . hardly half as tall as the goatherd's crook he carried." His hair was uncombed, he was wearing a goatherd's skirt and tunic, and he had a knife in his belt. Percy described the boy as antique and primitive and himself as a god drinking in the splendor of the "high lost world" of a Greek dusk. The boy stared at Percy "as though I were a mortal," and he asked to see Percy's watch. To emphasize the primal nature of the boy and the timelessness of the moment, Percy recounted that "he shook it and put it to his ear, but of course did not look at the time." The boy turned to one of his goats and from his throat "issued animal sounds, half cluck, half gutteral bleat," and the boy and the goat "danced together. The full moon and I saw them dance together." After this act of natural connectedness, the boy ran to Percy and took him by the hand. For a moment the two "walked in silence, hand in hand," but suddenly the boy looked at Percy and "smiled once—but it was like a gale of laughter—and was gone. And the night seemed suddenly bleak." The language of this encounter suggests but does not name mystical possibility in Greece. The scene is a delicate rendering of an encounter marked by purity and innocence: it was outside of time; it did not need human language to render communication possible; it suggested an innate equality between two people otherwise separated by age, language, class, and background. Percy surrounded the moment with silence and sunset and celebrated the possibility of connection between two humans even as he mourned its impermanence.[20]

Innocent and primitive love also animates the second vignette, this one set in the Anatolian headland of Turkey. In his first draft of this piece, Percy named Jervey and "our friendly Turkish ship-mates" in the story, but he removed these details from the final draft.[21] In this instance, Percy, Jervey, and the Turkish men were having a picnic overlooking the sea. The imagery of the passage is among the most colorful and positive in the entire autobiography. The sea and the sun were laughing, the sapphire water glistened below the clouds, the men "seemed suspended magically" as they were bathed with "palest pink and lavender in the ecstatic light." "Except that it was live with rushing air," Percy wrote, "it would have seemed a fortunate bright dream. We lay on the ground in the penciled shadow, each in his own burnished reverie." As they lay looking out toward the distant horizon, they began to hear what sounded like singing in the water below them. They crawled to the edge of the cliff and peered over, and in the water, "a young man, white and naked, with a mop of gold hair, was swimming beneath us, and as he swam he sang." In the silence, the young man was unaware of the onlookers and swam along playfully, "brimming with some hale antique happiness not ours to know." But, like the encounter with the satyr, the moment was brief. The swimmer disappeared from sight as "the dazzle hid him from us, but we still heard his voice." In this instance, Percy again emphasized the timeless beauty of the native, him being possessed of an untouchable and momentary happiness. Though the voyeuristic pleasure was fleeting, Percy had companions. Percy used the image of the naked man to indicate that in their watching, he, Jervey, and the Turks experienced this ecstasy together. Percy depicted a sexually charged moment of human connection and mutual understanding that he wanted his readers to know about. In an era when men rarely if ever wrote public, autobiographical accounts of their own erotic experiences, this passage was risky and revealing. It speaks not only of a moment of deep pleasure during his Mediterranean trip of 1924 but also of his desire to make known what he felt and experienced in his life.[22]

It would be remiss at this point not to point out how Percy's considerable racial and economic privilege made these particular experiences of sexual freedom possible. His wealth allowed him to travel around the world, and that wealth was created in large part by black slaves and sharecroppers. His vision of equality—the camaraderie he felt with Jervey and the others, the sense of oneness he felt with the young goatherd—not only did not include African Americans; it also depended on them. Furthermore, his experience as a white American admiring the "primitivism" of dark-skinned people abroad was not unique. In the late nineteenth and early twentieth centuries, many affluent Americans gazed longingly at non-Western, nonwhite people with the implicit belief that they possessed singular wellsprings of joy and freedom. From their position of racial and economic superiority, which they were not willing to forego, they were able to believe that "primitive" people were both especially free and especially unfit for the privileges of empire. It is suggestive that Percy positioned himself and his friends on a cliff, looking down at the Turkish swimmer.[23]

When Percy arrived home in October 1924, he was greeted with bad news. Both of his parents, now in their mid-sixties, were in poor health; they had spent the late summer in Asheville, North Carolina, LeRoy recovering from a drop in blood pressure and Camille from chronic fatigue. In addition, *Enzio's Kingdom*—which Percy felt was his finest work to date—had received very little critical attention, and those who did review it were not enthusiastic. "His sense of form is crude and he overwrites," wrote Herbert Gorman in the *The Bookman*. "He is indubitably surcharged with poetry which pours out of him, but the receptacles wherein he catches the divine substance are only too often broken pieces."[24] No one wrote about the ideas in Percy's poetry; no one engaged the themes Percy most wanted them to engage. He wrote to a friend: "Enzio was as flat a failure as I've ever known."[25]

Percy had spent almost twenty years writing poetry that had seemed to him quite good. His poetry, he said, was borne out of what he called "long brooding on one idea, or set of ideas." He brooded upon the possibility of meaning in the modern world—upon the struggle for some kind of faith, for fulfilling human relationships, for an authentic experience of the good and the beautiful. What he wrote, he said, was "essentially myself."[26] As such, Percy's career as a poet should be viewed as an experiment in self-expression in a limiting environment: here was an only child of a prominent family in a small town who felt a great deal of admiration and loyalty toward his parents. Through his experiences in the South and elsewhere, he came to believe that love between men was not only legitimate but also beautiful, and that life's meanings were not found in religious dogma but in love, beauty, and responsibility to other people. These were themes he could not write about fully without recrimination from his family and community. So he wrote in such a way that expressed his fundamental ideas while also protecting himself from charges of indecency. He wrote in such a way that invited and allowed multiple interpretations. He used female narrators, classical settings, and aestheticized expressions of desire as a way of speaking out and covering up at the same time. His poetry was inspirational to a few who understood, and it was tolerated—if sometimes suspiciously—by those who did not.

When read biographically, Percy's poetry becomes a window onto his innermost thoughts. When read in the context of homoerotic literary history, it becomes historically significant. But when read in the context of mainstream poetry in this period, Percy was decidedly a minor figure. Though he achieved some stature as a poet whose books were reviewed nationally, his work lacked the emotive power and stylistic virtuosity of the canonical poets of his day—writers such as T. S. Eliot, William Carlos Williams, and Langston Hughes, among others. Perhaps this was because he was a part-time poet; perhaps he was too autobiographical; perhaps, as critics pointed out, his penchant for antiquated language and long, dramatic forms doomed him to a limited readership. At the end of the day, the significance of Percy's work lies not so much in its literary achievement as its personal honesty and its use of a coded, historically specific homoerotic idiom.

The publication of *Enzio's Kingdom* marked a turning point in Percy's life in which he transitioned away from writing poetry. Though he would publish several more short lyrics, he focused his energies on caring for his aging parents and taking a more active role in Greenville's civic life. He settled, unenthusiastically but with steadfastness, into leadership roles on the YMCA board and in the Rotary Club. He chaired a fund-raising effort to build a town swimming pool and gym. When a Greenville woman wrote to him with a question about the town's Levee Board, his response indicated both his sense of commitment to his community and his exasperation with it. "The truth is," he replied, "I care about the Levee Board only because every citizen should care about it. I do not follow its doings and am not interested in its personnel." Despite his lack of interest, he would soon be on the board; and when the levee broke a few years later, he would be at the center of the flood-relief efforts.[27]

A more intriguing kind of service presented itself to Percy in the spring of 1925. The president of the Yale University Press wrote Percy to ask if he would consider being the editor of the Yale Series of Younger Poets, a role in which he would judge manuscripts of young American poets under the age of thirty.[28] Percy was to choose the best of several dozen submissions each year, and his choice would be published by the Yale Press. The Yale Series of Younger Poets was one of the most prestigious prizes in poetry, and over the next eighty years (it continues to this day), it would publish many of America's best poets. Percy saw this as an opportunity to interact with younger artists and perhaps have a hand in shaping the trends in American poetry. He accepted the offer, and for the next seven years, his literary life would be spent not writing but editing. He did not like reading the piles of bad poetry—"I must confess I get little joy out of editing," he later admitted to a friend. "Most of the manuscripts I receive are terrible."[29] But he did find meaning in encouraging younger writers. The significance of this episode lies not in the books Yale published (indeed, most have long been forgotten) but in the pedagogic role Percy moved into—a role he would relish the rest of his life, most notably with the writers Walker Percy and Shelby Foote and the artist Leon Koury.

It is telling that Percy's first action as editor was to contact two young poets, Countee Cullen and Lindley Williams Hubbell, who wrote homoerotic poetry.[30] Countee Cullen, who would become one of the leading African American poets of his generation, never responded to Percy's inquiry. Lindley Hubbell, though, responded enthusiastically, saying the publication of his poems would be "nearer my heart than anything else life could give me."[31] Percy worked closely with Hubbell for nearly two years on his volume, which Yale published in 1927 and which contained several poems written in the pederastic tradition. Poems such as "Epitaph for a Chaste Youth," "Poet to Poet," and "The Sealed Mouth to the Baffled," for example, delicately depict the male body, romantic friendship between men, and the gift of a selfless teacher. Perhaps most tellingly, Hubbell borrowed a line from Percy's poem "Mr. W. H. to the Poet" for the book's dedication page: "For W. A. P.," it reads, "There's nothing shines but took its light from you."[32]

Hubbell and Percy's relationship is significant for two reasons. First, Percy clearly came to view himself as a mentor to Hubbell, and Hubbell used a line from one of Percy's most explicitly pederastic poems to describe his appreciation. The contours of their relationship—developed over a shared love of poetry, with Percy advising and encouraging the younger poet, and a mutual interest in aestheticized homoerotic expression—fits in with a larger pattern in Percy's life. From his own teachers, like Judge Griffin and Huger Jervey, to those who looked up to him, like Malcolm Vaughan, Raymond Ganger, and Lindley Hubbell, the teacher-student relationship between men was centrally important to Percy. These relationships may not have been sexual (though some likely were), but they were all erotic. The shared experience of knowledge passing from an older to a younger man was, as Diotima explained in the *Symposium*, a kind of reproduction, a way of achieving immortality. Percy took this seriously. Throughout his life, he developed emotionally intimate relationships with men, both as a student and as a teacher. And particularly in his own role as a teacher, he encouraged younger artists whose work was explicitly homoerotic.[33]

A second reason Percy and Hubbell's relationship is significant is that, apart from their initial exchange, no evidence about it survives. With the other poets in the series, Percy's papers include extensive correspondence, draft manuscripts, and publishing contracts. But with Hubbell, there is none of this. This highlights an important and unfortunate dynamic of Percy's archive: often very little evidence exists about the relationships that meant the most to him. Whether Percy himself destroyed such letters or—more likely—his estate did after his death, their absence speaks to the significant pressure to keep the Percy name distinct from any kind of gender or sexual queerness. This conspicuous absence tells us something about the culture of the South, which accommodated queerness as long as it was private and quiet, and it also speaks to the obvious need that someone felt to destroy or withhold evidence.[34]

Percy's ideas about pederasty and pedagogy meshed with his broader ideas about individual morality and personal freedom. That is, he believed erotic expression between men was not immoral, but the freedom to make that expression should be paired with a responsibility to act ethically toward others. Percy had a high degree of moral seriousness, and this played out in his correspondence with these younger poets. He wrote extensive, personal letters to each of them urging confidence and continued work. His letter to a poet named Mary Edgar Comstock reflects this common sentiment in his rejection letters: "Do not be discouraged by this rejection," he wrote. "Critics are exceedingly fallible and you know much more truly the imperishable stuff that is in you than any of us can ever know." After the critical reception of *Enzio's Kingdom*, it seems possible that Percy was speaking to himself as well as to Comstock.[35]

Several poets did not appreciate Percy's unsolicited responses. "Have you no mind of your own?" wrote one. "I think, Mr. Percy, that you are too stupid to recognize my colossal genius."[36] In another instance, Percy told a poet named Edmond Kowalewski that he could not publish his manuscript, but that he was "particularly anxious, however, to tell you how highly I think of your work." Percy went into detail about the singular virtues of Kowalewski's poetry and also offered a few suggestions, and he concluded by reiterating his encouragement: "It is a beautiful manuscript and one the reading of which gave me keen joy."[37] Percy felt conflicted about writing such letters, as he confessed to his editor the next day: "I feel as if I had just come through a massacre of the Innocents, myself the Herod!"[38] But Kowalewski did not buy it. "Might you not have been sensitive enough to have returned my treasure without the needlessly twitted reply?" he wrote to Percy. "Who asks for your appraisal? I have never heard of you." In a long, breathless rant, he told Percy what he thought of him and the publishing industry, concluding: "Out of a fullness of the heart let me tell you to go to hell!"[39]

Percy sent the letter to his contacts at the Yale Press "as an example of the woes of Ye Editor," but he asked them to please return it because "it is too precious to lose."[40] He also wrote to Kowalewski offering to help him find a publisher for his manuscript, which, he reiterated, was very good and should be published.[41] Kowalewski responded: "Your answer perplexes me. I thought I had calculated my letter so carefully that it would not inspire any reply." Perhaps, he wrote, "you are not the person I was thinking of." He then went on, over several pages, to explain his frustration in a way that struck a chord with Percy. He said that his anger came not from his unpublished poetry but from the recent death of his mother and from "the modern world," which "takes the elements of natural music out of life." The life of an observant and sensitive person, Kowalewski wrote, "must end either in madness or spiritual death. I move about from dawn to darkness in a round of existence that has no meaning for me, and at night I should be glad never to wake again." He concluded: "Why? Why? Do you know, Sir—It is horrible to be alive when one is really dead."[42]

Percy responded that he did indeed know what that was like. Unfortunately, his letter does not survive, but we know from Kowalewski's next long reply that Percy had written to him and said that, yes, he knew what it was like to feel dead inside, and he suggested that writing could be therapeutic for Kowalewski. He also said that he was planning a trip north over the winter and perhaps could stop in Philadelphia, where Kowalewski lived, and they could talk. Kowalewski responded: "What a curious person you must be! Why are you not like the others? Why do you not run off and hate me?" He told Percy that he could come to Philadelphia if he liked, but the truth was he did not want to live any longer. He wrote of "the uselessness of saying anything," but also of "the uselessness of saying nothing." All life was useless, he said, and his only ambition was to walk out into a street of speeding cars: "I shall stalk headlong into their toppling hell, and give up my blood and bone as grist for the wheels."[43] After receiving this letter, Percy set himself to trying to divert Kowalewski's inward gaze by finding him a job. He contacted the Yale Press, the American Bookseller's Association, and *Publisher's Weekly* and recommended Kowalewski for a job. We do not know what happened to Kowalewski, but we do know that he did not kill himself, because his manuscript, *Deaf Walls*, was published seven years later in Philadelphia.[44]

This is not to imply that Percy saved Kowalewski's life. It does illustrate, however, an important aspect of Percy's personality: he cared deeply about acting ethically toward other people. His strength was in relating to other people as individuals. Committee work bored him; he had no faith in broad political change; he never felt compelled to openly challenge the status quo. Rather, he was most drawn to self-sacrifice when it involved another person's emotional needs. He explained on several occasions that this ideal animated his writing, that "if I have a philosophy of life it may be found in my volumes of poetry."[45] Those volumes, as we have seen, suggest that empathy and self-sacrifice were the necessary correlates to personal freedom. Kowalewski's story and others like it suggest that Percy took this ideal seriously.

In addition to reading manuscripts and practicing law, Percy also managed to travel for a good deal of 1925. In February he went to New York to visit Huger Jervey, Gerstle Mack, and Janet Dana Longcope. While there, he also delivered a reading of poems from *Enzio's Kingdom*, which was well received. "This is the wildest yet! I haven't one sense left," he wrote to his mother. "The poet's dinner was a scream, but I did very well—something of a hit in a small way—and the audience laughed wildly at the mild jokes I unexpectedly—to myself—pulled."[46] After New York, he spent a month in Greenville before spending the summer in Sewanee, where he and Jervey finalized the purchase of Brinkwood, a vacation home that would serve as a sanctuary for the two men and many guests over the next fifteen years. "It's impressive to spend one's summer with a dean," Janet Longcope wrote to Percy. "And a law dean at that. 'My cousin, a poet, who's living with a dean' will add eclat (influence of x-word puzzle) to my conversation throughout the season."[47]

Percy planned a more elaborate vacation for the following summer, during which he spent almost four months in Florence, Italy. Like Capri and Taormina, Florence was not an arbitrary destination.[48] Florence offered the aesthetic and historical appeal of those towns but, also like Taormina, had a famous resident: Norman Douglas. Douglas, who lived from 1868 to 1952, was an English writer and expatriate who had fled England in 1916 after a homosexual scandal. He was most famous for his novel *South Wind* (1917), which celebrated the Mediterranean as an emotionally and sexually uninhibited place, though he also wrote travel books, memoirs, and essays throughout his life. For his dominant personality—which was often mean, vindictive, and selfish as well as witty, flamboyant, and urbane—and his frankness about his sexual tastes, he was a visible figure in Italy's queer subculture. Douglas had little interest in aestheticizing and valorizing gay desire; for him, the physical enjoyment of sex needed no explaining, only enjoyment. "Why prolong life save to prolong pleasure?" he wrote. "What ecstasy, of all of them, is more fervid than that of young lovers locked in voluptuous embracement, beside which every other joy of earth sinks to the consequence of a trifle?" He was one for whom pederasty was not merely an intellectual concept, and he made no effort to hide his preference for Italian teenagers. "He was quite literally *paiderastes*, a lover of boys," a friend explained, "and it is falsifying his whole existence to ignore it."[49]

Percy met Douglas in Florence in the summer of 1926. He told a friend a few months later that he had spent his vacation with "that extraordinary, almost mythical creature, Norman Douglas."[50] The two became quite close, as evidenced by the one letter that survives between them—which, significantly, is not in Percy's papers but in Douglas's. The letter, from Percy to Douglas, was written a decade after they met and captures Percy's fondness for Douglas. Percy addressed Douglas familiarly—"Dear Uncle Norman," it began—and apologized for not writing more frequently. He explained: "I should have, because I owe you thanks for so many things—my fountain, your boy's book, the much trouble you went to, your letters—and I've thought of you such a lot." None of those letters survive, nor do we know what "trouble" Douglas went to for Percy. Douglas's "boy's book" is also not extant, but it was perhaps a book of reflections, photographs, or stories. Perhaps it was a book of pictures by Wilhelm von Gloeden, whom Douglas was known to admire. Percy concluded his letter: "Wish you were with me. Thank you for so much. I am always, affectionately, your Will Percy."[51]

Though there is much we do not know about Percy and Douglas's relationship, it is clear that they shared a high degree of intimacy and similar homoerotic tastes. They may have also shared similar experiences of sex scandal—Douglas in England in 1916 and Percy in Sewanee in 1919. Another piece of evidence that survives speaks to their relationship, as well as to Percy's experience of Florence in 1926. Douglas was at the time writing a book about natural history in Greek literature, and he asked Percy to write a foreword to the American edition. Instead of introducing the book itself, Percy wrote a vignette about meeting Norman Douglas in Florence in 1926. There are also two other characters in Percy's story: Pino Orioli and Reggie Turner. Orioli (1884–1942) was a bookseller in Florence and Douglas's best friend and housemate (their friends called them "Pinorman" because they were always together). Orioli was charming, generous, and animated, and he bragged that he could give a man an erection just by looking at him.[52] Reggie Turner (1869–1938) was an English novelist who was widely respected in queer circles because he was one of Oscar Wilde's few friends who stood by him during and after his sodomy scandal in 1895.[53] All three men, Douglas, Orioli, and Turner, were lively conversationalists and lovers of art, travel, and men. Orioli and Turner asked Percy to change their names in his fore-

Norman Douglas in Florence, 1935 (Photograph by Carl Van Vechten;
courtesy of Wikimedia Commons)

word to Douglas's book; Orioli had already been through one court battle for
publishing an "indecent" book and did not want to take any chances.[54]

Percy's foreword to *Birds and Beasts of the Greek Anthology* is a campy
account of Norman Douglas and his circle in Florence. Percy described
being at a café with Turner and Orioli waiting for Douglas, who would
only eat at "smaller, almost peasant, places where he was sure to meet no
English and American tourists," according to one friend.[55] Percy portrayed
Douglas's arrival as a sexually charged, almost regal event: "Norman Douglas appeared. ... A person, a personage had entered, one whom Frans Hals
would have walked miles to paint: the untidy room was galvanized, something robustious and electric accelerated the tempo of the waiters, stiffened
the patrons into expectancy." When he entered the room, his booming voice
ushered forth a greeting that "seemed an adequate climax." Two days later,
Percy wrote, he met Douglas on a side street as Percy was headed to see the
Giottos at Santa Maria Novella. When Percy asked if he would care to join
him, Douglas declined, commenting with tenderness: "Two years ago. ...

It's the most famous and convenient place in Florence for lover's meetings." Percy went alone but almost tripped over a step in the church, he remembered, as he was "thinking of other things."[56]

Percy's foreword draws from the era's homoerotic idiom to describe a group of queer friends without labeling their identity or behavior in explicit terms. His juxtaposition of aesthetic beauty and homoerotic expression, his discussion of colors in the landscape, museums, and artwork—all enjoyed in the context of male "friendship" and "companionship"—serve as markers of queer desire and practice.[57] In the next vignette, Percy and Orioli ("Berto") were walking along the Arno River in Florence at dusk, discussing Douglas. "Norman is amazing," Orioli observed. "With him the end of a love affair is never the end of a friendship. The charming friends of his earlier years come back to him from all over Italy, in fact from all over Europe, for advice or merely to be shone on by his vitality. Of course you've recognized his terrific sunshine."[58] Natural beauty, friendship, and vitality—these were things that Percy wanted to convey about Florence and about the men he met there. And possibly because he had similar relationships while in Italy, he portrayed Douglas's relationships as uplifting and well regarded.

Percy's final vignette further illustrates this blend of sensuality, beauty, and friendship that he found in Florence. Percy, Douglas, and Reggie Turner ("Carey") were having lunch with one another when Percy mentioned that he spent his morning marveling at the Botticellis in the Uffizi gallery. "Isn't that sweet, Carey?" quipped Douglas. "Think, there are still persons who look at the Botticellis. I haven't seen one for twenty years." Douglas admonished Percy for being such a dilettante and suggested that if he wanted to see some truly beautiful works, he should take the bus to Volterra to see the Etruscan art, which was "worth all your Michelangelos and da Vincis and Botticellis put together." To Douglas, Volterra had an additional benefit: "the charming boys there are all lightly powdered with alabaster dust, even their eyelashes. Exquisite! Like Pierrots!"[59] For many in this community, artistic beauty was inseparable from sexual desire, and sexual desire often found its object in Italian teenagers. Just as Douglas associated Etruscan art with its alabaster-dusted attendants, for Will Percy the Mediterranean, artistic expression, and male companionship were intertwined.[60] It was likely this dynamic that he was thinking of when, a few years later, he was asked to describe his favorite place: "The part of the world I love best is the Mediterranean. This to me is indeed the most beautiful spot in the universe."[61]

Percy returned to Mississippi in late September 1926 and took up his editorial work. "I am just back from Europe and feel peppy enough to tackle any number of manuscripts, so send them on," he wrote the Yale Press.[62] It was then that he recommended that the press publish Lindley Hubbell's volume, about which, Percy wrote, "I have no mental reservation whatever." He did complain about the other volumes, though. "Isn't bad verse dreadful?" he wrote. "I am feeling quite wan from my diet of the past week, and shall joyfully turn to Bacchae or Housman to restore my faith in poetry."[63]

As he read and wrote in his book-lined library in the Percy house, the Mississippi River flowed quietly outside, less than a mile away and behind the levee. A functional levee was a luxury Percy had never taken for granted, but one he would soon have to learn to live without.

12. THE FLOOD AND AFTER

I learned from it due humility as to my own indispensability and due wonder
at that amazing alloy of the hellish and the divine which we call man.
—WILLIAM ALEXANDER PERCY, *Lanterns on the Levee*

Early 1927 found Will Percy writing a letter to his friend Witter Bynner. Bynner was a poet who lived in Santa Fe, New Mexico, and who counted among his friends artists such as D. H. Lawrence, Ansel Adams, Igor Stravinsky, and W. H. Auden, among others. He was a part of the circle of intellectuals who made Santa Fe and Taos home to a culture of experimentation—with drugs, with sexual expression, with art. Percy and Bynner had been friends since at least 1914, though only two letters between them have surfaced, both in Bynner's papers. Bynner lived openly in a monogamous homosexual relationship with his partner, Robert Hunt, for thirty-four years and was outspoken about his racial egalitarianism and his advocacy of women's suffrage and gay artists. He traveled to China and Japan and translated Chinese poetry. Percy wrote to Bynner that the reading he had done recently "fires me up to go to China. If I go next summer will you give me a line to a Chinese gentleman or two? May I expect wisdom or peace or romance ... ? I'm prepared to receive a lot. I'm very needy."[1]

In addition to planning his trip to Asia, which he would take later in the year, Percy was also writing. In fact, he wrote in his memoir, in April 1927 he was in "a writer's tantrum."[2] He was trying to finish a poem called "Three April Nocturnes." The poem provides a compelling snapshot of Percy writing in Mississippi in 1927, perhaps thinking of his recent trip to Florence, perhaps of a more recent episode. It begins with a reminiscence:

This night of air like warm finger-tips touching
Sleepily my cheek or asleep in my shoulder's hollow,
I remember the kisses they gave me in tenderness or passion,
Never in love, the ones they could spare me, forgetful,

210

And I am thankful for each, regretting nothing,
Only wishing they lay on my mouth again
To-night when the moist buds are uncrinkling in starlight.[3]

Like many of Percy's poems, "Three April Nocturnes" celebrates sexual passion; though one notable difference is that here, sex is disconnected from love. "They" are not named, they are "forgetful," and they brought pleasure without regret. This is an instance in Percy's writing that depicts physical passion enjoyed merely for the pleasures of the body. The narrator is not troubled by this but rather takes pleasure in the memory and wishes for more.

It was raining outside as Percy worked on this poem, and it had been raining for weeks. The river was beginning to swell, as was its habit every spring. But this rain seemed to keep coming. Another Greenville writer, the diarist Henry Waring Ball, was in his home writing as well. His observations of Greenville life in his diary during March and April gave voice to his range of anxieties, foremost among which was the rain: "pouring almost incessantly for 24 hours"; "Rain almost all night"; "I believe the filth of theatres and pictures, dress, 'music,' is due largely to Jew dominance"; "Violent storm almost all night"; "Rain last night, of course"; "We have heavy showers and torrential downpours almost every day and night"; "Nell and I to church, Red hot sermon on the evils of the theatre and moving pictures and women's immodest dress"; "The worst Good Friday I ever saw. A night of incessant storm—wind, lightning, thunder and torrents of rain"; "I have never seen it look so appalling. I am very anxious."[4]

On the night of April 21, the levee broke. When it did, a torrent of water washed over the Mississippi Delta that eventually covered ten counties in water five to twenty feet deep. Over 100,000 people fled their homes. Within days, Greenville's population doubled as black and white refugees poured into town. Cow and mule and horse corpses floated past houses and schools. The deep brown and foaming water cut Greenville off from the rest of the world: train tracks were underwater, roads were underwater, cars were underwater; to dock a boat at the landing in Greenville risked further damage to the levee. The mayor called the Percy house and suggested that Will Percy's experience with the Red Cross in Belgium made him the ideal candidate in town to head the disaster relief. LeRoy Percy got on the phone to New Orleans and Washington and New York to arrange for loans and contributions to the relief effort. Camille Percy ordered servants to carry sofas and record players and books upstairs. Will Percy walked through the rising water to the opera house, which would become headquarters for his relief effort.[5]

The Mississippi River, with its regular overflows and unpredictable temper, was a constant threat to life in the Delta. In the spring of each year, when the snow thaws in the West and the Midwest, the volume of the river increases. For thousands of years, this has led to regular floods in the Delta, which is why the soil is so fertile; the topsoil has continually been replenished and is rich with minerals. After the Civil War, when Delta pioneers like Colonel William Alexander Percy aimed to make the Delta more inhabitable, a primary concern was to strengthen the levees. The federal government was largely uninterested in this, and a major priority for Delta planters was to lobby for federal dollars to build levees. People like LeRoy Percy made it their lifework to build, protect, and sustain the levee system. The wealth of the Delta depended on preventing massive floods that would wipe out a season's cotton crop. But the floods inevitably came, and locals counted time in "flood years"—1858, 1862, 1867, 1882, 1884, 1890, 1897, 1903, 1912, 1913, and 1922.[6]

The experience of these floods was always different for black people than it was for white people. At stake for whites were economic stability and a way of life. For blacks, the threat was more physical: many lived just below the levee, and most did not have cars, telephones, or access to boats. If people died during a flood, they were more likely to be black than white. Furthermore, the weeks before, during, and after a flood required extraordinary amounts of labor: plugging leaks with sandbags, unloading relief boats, rebuilding broken sections of the levee. This labor was expected to be performed by black people. LeRoy Percy felt this was the natural order of things, and he took pleasure in it. "Nothing could be more interesting, so far as a racial study goes," he explained to a friend, "than to see five or six thousand free Negroes working on a weak point [on a levee] under ten or twelve white men, without the slightest friction and of course without any legal right to call upon them for work, and yet the work is done not out of any feeling of patriotism but out of a traditional obedience to the white man."[7] One of Greenville's black citizens, Addie Oliver, remembered such a scene differently. Black workers were treated "just like dogs, I'll tell you. They were treated like dogs."[8]

After the overflow of April 21, Will Percy set to work on the most immediate problems: securing housing and food for the 8,000 refugees that crowded what remained of the levee; commandeering boats; making contact with the state and federal government and the Red Cross; finding a way to bury dead

Greenville, Mississippi, during the flood of 1927 (Courtesy of the Mississippi Department of Archives and History, Jackson, Mississippi)

bodies; and creating a way for steamers and barges to dock at Greenville. He persuaded the governor to call in the National Guard, and within a few days, the Red Cross arrived as well. The most pressing problem, though, was the mass of hungry, cold, uprooted refugees. To feed them, a massive centralized kitchen would have to be established; to house them, thousands of tents and blankets would have to be delivered. The weather was unseasonably cold, and those living on the levee were exposed. The refugees who were scattered about town living on rooftops and in attics and second stories of houses could not stay where they were for long.[9]

Percy's first thought was of the region's white citizens. He ordered all white women, children, and elderly men to board the steamer *Control* on Monday morning, April 25, four days after the levee broke. Nearly 500 of them did so in a scene of "desperate confusion" in which people pushed and shoved themselves aboard the steamer that would take them out of town. Some women, such as Camille Percy, refused to leave.[10] Of the black refugee population, Percy came to the same conclusion: they must be evacuated. They were cold and hungry, and conditions on the levee made disease and malnutrition immanent. He thought of their lives after he thought of the lives of whites, and he thought of them because he did not believe they could think for themselves. "Of course," he wrote, "none of us was influenced by what the Negroes themselves wanted: they had no capacity to plan for their own welfare; planning for them was another of our burdens."[11] His thought was about how to provide what they needed most: to be warm and to eat. He arranged for the Red Cross to build a temporary camp in Vicksburg where black refugees could more suitably be fed and housed. A group of furious planters approached Percy and explained to him that if he sent the blacks out of the Delta, they would never return. They fumed that he would be doing his region a grave and long-term injustice. Percy told these men that they were only thinking of money, and, he later wrote, that he "would not be bullied by a few blockhead planters into doing something I knew to be wrong." The steamers *Wabash* and *Kappa* were at the dock waiting to take the black population to Vicksburg.[12]

LeRoy Percy found his son on the levee and asked what his plans were for the black refugees. He told him. LeRoy said it was a "grave decision," one that would be wise for him not to make alone. Percy agreed and said he had discussed it with his committee members, and they had all come to the same conclusion. LeRoy suggested that he canvass them again. "Although nothing new had happened to cause them to change their minds," Percy wrote, "I promised father I would call them for a last consultation." After a few hours, he gathered his committee to confirm their plans. They had all changed their minds. "I was astounded and horrified," Percy wrote, "when each and every one of them gave it as his considered judgment that the Negroes should remain and that we could provide for their needs where they were. I argued for two hours but could not budge them." Eventually, Percy walked down to the levee and told the waiting captains that they should go to Vicksburg without passengers. He claimed to have learned later—though it seems likely he knew at the time—that his father had met with each of the committee members and persuaded them to change their minds. It was humiliating, and an explicit manifestation of LeRoy Percy's lack of trust in his son.[13]

The black population on the levee became agitated. Life in tents (which eventually arrived) was not pleasant. They were expected to unload the steamers that docked at the levee, perform the manual labor to fix the levee, and do anything else asked of them by the white leadership. By early May, though, three weeks after the flood began, national black newspapers began to report on the conditions on the levee. The reports were not positive. A black minister in Greenville wrote to President Calvin Coolidge that blacks on the levee were "being made to work under the gun, [whites] just bossing the colored men with big guns buckled to them. ... All of this mean and brutish treatment of the colored people is nothing but downright slavery."[14] The *Chicago Defender* reported that Will Percy and the Red Cross were withholding supplies and food from any black families that did not have a male head of household, and that Percy spent most of his time on the golf course at the Greenville Country Club. He was not playing golf (because the course was underwater), but a wealth of evidence suggests that exploitation, undernourishment, and systematic abuse took place under Percy's watch.[15]

For his part, Percy acknowledged that unjust coercion existed, but he felt himself powerless to control other white people. He wanted to act ethically, but he also had to rely on others to get things done. He wrote to a friend that it was true: many whites in Greenville "were guilty of acts which profoundly and justly made the Negroes fear them."[16] However, he felt that the situation forced him to be authoritarian, and that "if I had to be a despot I was very anxious to be a beneficent one."[17] The biggest problem, according to Percy, was not the white people. It was black recalcitrance, an attitude stemming from the fact that black people could read—and when they read, they read the *Chicago Defender*. He believed in his own rightness; he believed that Greenville's blacks should trust him. When they did not, he took it personally.

In June the water rose another six feet. Greenvillians black and white lost whatever idealism they had. Many black refugees began to refuse to unload the boats or work on the levees for no wages for men carrying guns. "The guns are the problem," one black leader said. "All the white folks carry guns."[18] Many of those living on the levee waded back to their homes. Percy met with his committee to figure out how to persuade the black community that they must work. One member suggested they get the local police to round up work crews. Percy refused. Members of the committee began to resign. Finally, feeling he had no other option, Percy agreed to allow police to go into black neighborhoods. When they did, blacks resisted. Within two hours, a white policeman shot and killed a black man.[19]

The black population during the flood was more than double the white population. Rumors began to circulate that there would be an uprising. Percy's black informant told him that the black population blamed Percy for the killing. He was already seething that the blacks who should have been in Vicksburg were in Greenville and now in a frenzy. He decided this was his problem to fix.

Percy called a citywide meeting at a prominent black church and demanded there be no whites present but himself. He arrived at the church, and black Greenvillians trickled in until the church was full. "It was the surliest, most hostile group I've ever faced," Percy wrote. A black preacher rose and said, "I will read from the scripture." Then they sang, their voices sounding to Percy like "a pounding barbaric chant of menace." After the hymn, the preacher turned to Percy, who mounted the pulpit and looked out into the crowd. "A good Negro has been killed," he began,

> by a white policeman. Every white man in town regrets this from
> his heart and is ashamed. The policeman is in jail and will be tried.
> I look into your faces and see anger and hatred. You think I am the
> murderer. The murderer should be punished. I will tell you who he is.
> ... We white people could have left you to shift for yourselves. Instead
> we stayed with you and worked for you, day and night. During all this
> time you Negroes did nothing, nothing for yourselves or for us. You
> were asked to do only one thing, a little thing. The Red Cross asked
> you to unload the food it was giving you, the food without which you
> would have starved. And you refused. Because of your sinful, shame-
> ful laziness, because you refused to work in your own behalf unless
> you were paid, one of your race has been killed. ... The murderer
> is you! Your hands are dripping with blood. Look into each other's
> faces and see the shame and the fear God has set on them. Down on
> your knees, murderers, and beg your God not to punish you as you
> deserve.

Percy recalled, with some ambivalence, that they all got down and prayed, but when he then called for volunteers to unload the boat, only four men stood up—"a friend of mine, a one-armed man, and two preachers who had been slaves on the Percy Place and were too old to lift a bucket."[20]

Percy's outrage, and yet his admittance that his outrage was ineffective, suggests something of his feelings during the spring and summer of 1927. His leadership had been thwarted by his father, and the result of his father's connivance was that the black population in town wanted to rise up against him. Rather than respect for the "beneficent" despot, they had rage; rather than controlling the race relations in the Delta, Percy had allowed disaster. The floodwaters had washed away the edifice of politeness and revealed the coercive power of white planters, as well as the limits of that power in the face of black refusal to capitulate. The racial tensions of Greenville rose to the surface, and Percy was the target of the fury of the black population. That he lashed out at them with such unfairness was in some measure an expression of the frustration he felt at having been usurped by his father. And that he wrote that his best efforts resulted in the conversion of a one-armed man and a few preachers seems an implicit confession that his was not the constitution of a planter businessman. He had the rage, but not the effectiveness in strong-arming others to do his will.

Nor was he effective in confronting his father. His father had manipulated him, and Percy did not stand up to him. In his own account of the flood, he praised him: "Father, though he was not a member of the committee, was the brains and the faith back of everything, the strong rock on which we leaned and in whose shade we renewed our strength." Instead of expressing his resentment, or allowing that his father had deceived him, he excused him: "He was a natural gambler," Percy wrote. "He bet on warm weather and tents." This seems to have been characteristic of the uneasy alliance LeRoy and Will Percy forged throughout their lives: they would live together, work together, and speak well of one another; they would publicly admire one another's strengths and downplay their weaknesses. But they would not be emotionally intimate, nor would they ever trust one another entirely.[21]

In August 1927 Percy resigned as chairman of the relief efforts. The flood of the previous four months had been the greatest natural disaster to that point in American history. Over 16 million acres of land flooded, and nearly 200,000 homes were underwater; $100 million worth of cotton was destroyed. As many as 500 people died, most of them black.[22] Less than a year after the flood, Congress passed a $300 million bill that for the first time gave Washington responsibility for managing the Mississippi River—a development that significantly increased the power and scope of the federal government.[23] This was an outcome LeRoy Percy had long fought for. The bill and its reconfiguration of emergency management and the levee system made the 1927 flood the last major Mississippi River disaster until Hurricane Katrina in 2005.

Will Percy's leadership during the flood was both a success and a failure. Particularly during the chaotic and uncertain early days of the flood, his efforts to achieve some measure of stability were effective. Coordinating food and housing for 8,000 refugees was an extraordinary task, and Percy's prior experience with the Red Cross gave him a measure of competency that made him a viable leader. On the other hand, Percy did not see past his own predispositions. He resented the possibility that blacks did not trust him, and he failed to understand their perspective—or rather, he failed to imagine that they had a perspective worth understanding. Insofar as he did not personally abuse black laborers, he also failed to prevent others from doing so. Perhaps most painfully for him, he was not able to accomplish what he felt was ethical: the evacuation of the black refugees from the levee. He was not able to veto his father, and the result was a painful confrontation that revealed his own lack of authority as well as his father's basic lack of trust in and support for his son. In Percy's moment to lead the rigidly hierarchical society of the Delta, he failed to secure his own place on top of the hierarchy.

Percy's success or failure as a leader during the flood had nothing to do with sexuality. In his best-selling book, *Rising Tide: The Great Mississippi Flood of 1927 and How It Changed America* (1997), John Barry characterizes Percy as a self-loathing, evasive poet who worshipped his father and felt deeply inferior to him. Barry quotes homoerotic lines from Percy's poetry and concludes that "such desires had to torture him" and "always Will hated this part of himself."[24] He explains that Percy's sexuality was due to his lack of self-control and the effects of European travel: "Europe had awakened in him something he found hypnotizing and frightening."[25] Barry describes Percy as "less of a man in every way" than his father, and when faced with the challenge of leadership, he simply was not strong enough. "He could not tolerate criticism," he writes, "he could not tolerate public failure; he could not tolerate being treated as irrelevant; he could not tolerate the truth."[26] The implicit message of Barry's portrayal is that Percy embodied all the worst stereotypes of gay men: he was cowardly, he lacked self-control, he was effete, he was dominated by his father, and he was incapable of leadership. He was unable to overcome his lack of manhood in order to do the right thing. "In the sultriness of the Delta," Barry reminds us, "sex represented everything."[27]

Rising Tide has sold millions of copies and provides the standard account of the 1927 flood, and since its publication, it also has been the most widely read account of Will Percy's life. On the flood and its broader political ramifications, it is an excellent book; Barry is a compelling storyteller and his book an illuminating history of the Mississippi River and its significance to American life. It justly deserves its wide readership. Unfortunately, though, Barry uses the character of Will Percy to create sensationalized conflict in the narrative in such a way that makes a spectacle of Percy's sexuality and, in doing so, reinforces the problematic notion that queer men are ill equipped for the hard realities of leadership. In contrast, Percy's shortcomings as leader during the flood—and they were considerable—should be explained with more specificity: his racial prejudice limited his ability to serve black people, his leadership strengths did not lie in organizing groups of people, and his complex relationship with his father prevented him from insisting that the refugees be evacuated. Furthermore, the task he faced was enormous and unprecedented. It is a rich, nuanced story, but it is not the one Barry tells about a "slight, frail," and "boyish" Percy whose tenure as a leader logically ended by his "escaping Greenville, escaping the criticism, escaping the struggle, escaping."[28]

PERCY LEFT GREENVILLE in September 1927 feeling that he had made an honest effort at an impossible task. He felt like he had no perspective and needed calm. "Nothing has so completely disoriented and jazzed me up since the war as those four and a half months," he wrote to his friend Charlotte Gailor, who lived in Sewanee and would become one of his closest friends during the last fifteen years of his life. "I probably didn't do it well, but at least I didn't spare myself and I still have an out-of-socket feeling. No poetry in sight."[29] He traveled across the country and stopped in New Mexico, presumably to see Witter Bynner. He then met Huger Jervey in San Francisco, where they deliberated on whether to go to China in addition to Japan.[30]

They settled on going only to Japan, where they arrived in late September. Only one letter survives from this trip—a letter from Percy to Gailor—which is illuminating both about what Percy did and how he processed what he saw. Percy and Jervey went to Mount Fuji, Nikko, and the Kyoto district, and along the way they bought ornamental trees, silk scarves, kimonos, and "a coolie coat" to send home. They also went to Tokyo ("Tokyo I would avoid as I would the plague—it is the most god-awful repellant city in the world"), where they stayed at the Imperial Hotel, which he said "would do for a mausoleum, but as a hostelry it gives me the willies." On the whole, he seemed to enjoy the trip (except for Tokyo); it was the Japanese people he could not understand.[31]

Percy's impressions of Japanese people reflect his broader inability to allow his liberal moral imagination to translate into a liberal racial imagination. He held fast to a fixed hierarchy of racial categories in which Anglo-Saxons were at the top, followed by what he called the yellow, red, and brown races of the world. This put him squarely in the mainstream of American racial thought in the early twentieth century, and his feelings about the Japanese echo his and other Americans' belief that other races could be beautiful, sensuous, and admirable, but they could not be equals. During the debate leading up to the Japanese Exclusion Act of 1924 (which barred Japanese immigrants from coming to America), Percy had written to a friend: "It seems to me the question is truly an oriental one and distinguished from a Japanese one. I am becoming daily more convinced that a law excluding the brown and yellow races is a right and necessary step for our highest national development."[32]

In Japan in 1927, Percy could admire what he felt to be exotic qualities of Japanese people with the reassurance that their fundamental inequality was written into law in the United States. But he found even their exotic qualities difficult to comprehend. He confessed to Gailor: "All my impressions of this country are colored with strangeness to the point that I can never surrender myself to its beauty and always feeling a vague disquiet not far from hostility." Percy wanted release into the primitive, into the exotic—like what he had experienced in Greece and Turkey—but there seemed to him some fundamental, insuperable difference between himself and the Japanese. "They are so polite, so quietly gay," he wrote, "they have such grace and style that I feel ashamed of myself for not loving them, but I don't. They are remote, impersonal, and so ugly." This physical attraction seemed to be a key missing component, a component that Percy allowed was mutual. He explained to Gailor that he was sitting with a local in the countryside outside of Nikko when he asked the local why all the people were staring at him. "They think you are so ugly," he said, "all blue eyes and white hair are ugly."[33]

Whether Percy had found the Japanese quaint and beautiful or ugly and impersonal, one thing remained the same: they were different. This belief in fundamental racial difference allowed him to make grand pronouncements on the Japanese, and his doing so was a way of articulating what he felt to be his own cultural and racial superiority. Such beliefs, which he shared with the majority of white Americans, lent legitimacy to national policies aimed at excluding Japanese immigration and barring Japanese Americans from obtaining citizenship. This is obviously not to hold Percy responsible for widespread American prejudice and its attendant policies; it is to place his prejudice in the context of a historical moment in which Americans created antidemocratic, exclusionary policies that grew out of belief in fixed racial hierarchies. Percy's travels afforded him leisure and rest, and his encounters reassured him of his racial superiority.

In December 1927 Percy brought his belief in white racial supremacy home with him to Mississippi, where the river had returned to normal levels and the town was coated in silt. He walked into his home and found sixteen new manuscripts to be judged and his two parents in declining health.[34] Camille and LeRoy Percy would soon leave for Florida for several weeks to recuperate in the salt air, and Percy told Janet Longcope that he feared the worst for his mother. He also wrote that he would like to see Longcope when he traveled north in February.[35]

Percy went to New York in February almost every year during the 1920s and early 1930s.[36] Such a pattern invites an explanation, since of all months in New York, February may be the least pleasant. We may never know with full certainty why Percy went each February, but one speculation is that he went to attend the Masquerade and Civic Ball put on each year in February by the Hamilton Lodge. This yearly event, George Chauncey has explained, was New York City's largest and most famous gathering of homosexuals in the 1920s and 1930s. It was an officially sanctioned, well-attended drag ball in Harlem. By the late 1920s, it had acquired the name "the Faggots Ball," and (depending on the year) between 1,000 and 7,000 people took part in or witnessed the spectacle that one newspaper described as "effeminate men, sissies, 'wolves,' 'ferries' [sic], 'faggots,' the third sex, 'ladies of the night,' and male prostitutes ... for a grand jamboree of dancing, love making, display, rivalry, drinking and advertisement." Middle- and upper-class whites often bought tickets to sit in the gallery and watch, and many participated— though most of the drag queens were black.[37]

In February 1928, 5,000 people attended the Hamilton Lodge Ball, including three undercover investigators. The investigators' report stated that at the ball were "5,000 people, colored and white, men attired in women's clothes, and vice versa. The affair, we were informed, was a 'Fag/Masquerade Ball.' This is an annual affair where the white and colored fairies assemble together with their friends, this being attended also by a certain respectable element who go here to see the sights."[38] With the Hamilton Lodge Ball's widespread notoriety and large attendance, it is not hard to imagine Huger Jervey—who boasted that he always encouraged young people to "bc wild as sin and lesbians as well as coquettes"—in this crowd.[39] When Percy went to New York, he stayed with Jervey. The two likely attended the Hamilton Lodge Balls, either as spectators or participants. They may also have visited Harlem's many cabarets designed for white patrons, like the Cotton Club or the Elks Café. As Chad Heap has shown, "slumming" was very much in vogue in the 1920s, and queer men and women often made a more public display of their sexual attitudes while in Harlem. The presumed "primitivism" of black life—what one guidebook called the "happy-go-lucky and joyous spirit supposed to be inherent in the Negro soul"—was an allure that drew curious and adventurous whites to Harlem by the thousands.[40]

Percy's long-standing admiration for what he believed to be the primitive vitality of colored people and his equally long-standing belief in white supremacy suggest a complicated set of intellectual equivocations. In addition, this engages the question of Percy's attitude toward interracial sex. There is some anecdotal evidence that suggests Percy had sexual affairs with black men. John Barry cites six interviews with black Greenvillians who said that rumors abounded about Will Percy's liaisons with his chauffeurs. William Armstrong Percy also interviewed one of the same people, Millie Commodore, who said the same thing.[41] Furthermore, in *Lanterns on the Levee*, Will Percy dedicated an entire chapter to a discussion of his servant, Ford Atkins, whom he described as "my only tie with Pan and the satyrs and all earth creatures who smile sunshine and ask no questions and understand." One day, Percy wrote, Atkins walked into the bathroom where Percy was showering, looked at his naked body, and said, "You ain't nothing but a little old fat man." Percy claimed to have fired him for this but also to have paid for his tuition at a mechanics' school in Chicago—though Atkins called regularly and returned often.[42]

Percy might have had black lovers, and these relationships might have been mutually affectionate. Percy might also have used his power and wealth to compel sexual affection by bestowing favors on those who would have sex with him—much like many planters had long done in the South with black women. Indeed, it may have been the unequal power relationship that attracted him to young black men. Millie Commodore opted for this interpretation: "At that point down there it was very prevalent with the richer class of people. They had their boys working for them. Treated them royal. … It was a way to get ahead. It was hard to refuse [men like Mr. Percy] if they picked you out because, at least, it was a living and education or something."[43] It is also possible that Percy's black servants offered sex in order to get what they wanted from him. John Barry believes this to be the case: "The rumors said that blacks had a power over Will. That his chauffeurs, young black men, showed their power to him." In his book, Barry cites one man's recollection of Percy's chauffeur "Honey" playing pool in a black bar while Percy hid in the car outside. When he was done with his game, Honey said "I got to take my who' home" and left.[44] This evidence suggests that not only did Percy develop cross-racial relationships but also that his black servants pressed the situation to their full advantage.

The problem lies not in the possibility that Percy had interracial sex but in uncovering the evidence—a more general difficulty in studying the history of sexuality.[45] We simply cannot know what happened behind closed doors, nor should we insist on having evidence before we believe that queer sex was possible (just as we do not insist on having evidence for heterosexual acts). Rather than trying to prove or disprove any particular sexual act, we can only try to understand the significance of race and sexuality to Percy. This much we know: Percy viewed blacks as emotionally and sexually free, and he depicted their bodies in erotic and admiring ways. He also wholly believed in white supremacy and social segregation. If he had sex with black servants, those relationships should be thought of in terms of power: Percy had money and status and resources, and his black partners would have had something to gain from finding his favor. Insofar as Percy ever had mutually affectionate relationships with black men, he never conceived of them as equals—or if he did, he never spoke out against the social order that ensured they remain unequal. Whether there was sex, or sex and love, or no sex at all, the subject points to recurring themes in Percy's story: his views about sexual freedom always coexisted with his racial prejudice. Yet his views about sexual freedom also involved racial fantasy—such as his eroticized depictions of South Pacific, Mediterranean, and black American men. These were incongruities he lived with, if at times uneasily.

Or they may not have been incongruities to him. The Greek tradition of pederasty valued asymmetrical pairings—such as one between an older man and a younger man, or a wealthy man and an untrained youth. Recall Percy's poem "Sappho in Levkas," in which the older Sappho describes how the shepherd Phaon "looked to me for praise," and how their relationship increased his "maturing loveliness."[46] Percy may well have seen a sexual relationship with a servant as a kind of uplift, a way of empowering someone beneath him. He may have seen such relationships as a kind of beneficence, a beneficence from which he also derived sexual pleasure. Percy lived in a society in which white planters routinely thought this way about black female mistresses. He also lived in a society in which open, long-term, mutually affectionate homosexual relationships were not the norm. What may seem like hypocrisy to some may have seemed like benevolence to him. At the end of the day, we can never know with certainty; we can only consider the possibilities.

Whatever the nature of Percy's relationship with his black servants, it would have been Ford Atkins who picked Percy up at the train station when Percy returned from New York in March 1928. It would have been him who carried Percy's bags, unloaded the car, and disappeared to the servant's quarters when Percy sat down with his parents to tell them about his trip. What he told them we do not know, but surely one topic of conversation was health. Camille Percy survived a serious heart attack sometime in early 1928,

The Patriot *statue, Percy family plot, Greenville cemetery. After LeRoy Percy's death in 1929, Will Percy commissioned the sculptor Malvina Hoffman to build this in honor of his father. (Photograph by the author)*

and she would spend the summer through early 1929 in Pass Christian, Mississippi, for its salt air.[47] Will Percy's health was fragile as well. He was suffering from congestion and stomach pain and had recently had an X-ray. The doctors recommended rest and mountain air, and when his parents went to Pass Christian, he returned to New Mexico. He spent the late summer and fall there, at one point taking a brief trip to the Grand Canyon.[48]

Camille Percy continued her slow decline in health, and as she did, so did her husband. All their lives, the couple had been consistent figures in Greenville society, with Camille lauded for her lavish parties and immaculate garden and LeRoy renowned for his civic advocacy and thriving business pursuits. They had also been consistent figures in Will Percy's life. The delicate silences that must have created tension in their relationship also allowed them loyalty, devotion, and tenderness. They not only tolerated one other but also loved one another. Though Will Percy never fully trusted his father, he admired him; though Percy did not fully confide in his mother, he loved her and was grateful for her love. He sensed their ambivalence toward him and also accepted their love. Perhaps the ambivalence of both parents and son deepened their attachment to one another, necessitated a different and more intense kind of loyalty.

Camille Percy died on October 15, 1929, and LeRoy Percy followed soon after on Christmas Eve. "Father was the only great person I ever knew and he would not have been great without my mother," Percy recalled. "Without them my life seemed superfluous." At a cost of almost $30,000, Percy hired the sculptor Malvina Hoffman to create a bronze statue of a knight for LeRoy Percy's grave. He then went to New York to see Huger Jervey, Gerstle Mack, and Janet Longcope, and when he returned, the emptiness of his house must have seemed vast. It was an emptiness that did not last long.[49]

13. UNCLE WILL

Suddenly my house was filled with youth, and suddenly I found myself,
unprepared, with the responsibility of directing young lives.
—WILLIAM ALEXANDER PERCY, *Lanterns on the Levee*

In July 1929, Will Percy's cousin LeRoy Pratt Percy committed suicide in the attic of his Birmingham mansion. He was a successful lawyer who loved his wife, Mattie Sue, and his three young sons, Walker, Roy, and Phinizy. He was a hunter and a sportsman, and he traveled often with his Uncle LeRoy, the senator, to hunt in places like Alaska and Wyoming and French Lick, Indiana. They brought trophy elk and deer and antelope busts home and hung them on the walls. Despite his successful professional and family life, though, LeRoy Pratt Percy dealt constantly with what he called "the Crouching Beast." His depression rarely lifted. He drank more than his friends. A neighbor recalled at least one instance in the 1920s when he drove by and saw LeRoy tending his rose garden with white bandages wrapped around his wrists. His son Walker, thirteen when his father died, would grow up to write novels about the loneliness and despair created by life in the modern world. As a grown man one day in 1979, fifty years after his father's suicide, Walker Percy was sitting alone in his office during a year of teaching at Louisiana State University. A student wandered in to talk to him. Percy, caught off guard, looked up at the student and said, "I guess the central mystery of my life will always be why my father killed himself. Come here, have a seat."[1]

That Walker Percy did not meet the same end as his father is remarkable in itself—crippling depression was a recurring predisposition in the Percy family line, and suicides punctuated the family's history. But that Walker Percy invited this student in to talk with him, that he worked to understand himself and his world through creativity, was in large part due to the fact that Will Percy, after the death of his cousin, adopted the three boys and became a father to them. "It was the most important thing that ever happened to me," Walker Percy said. "I never would have been a writer without his influence. I've never met anybody like him."[2]

The Percys of Birmingham were a New South family. After the Civil War, the sons of William Alexander Percy, the Gray Eagle, had responded to new opportunities. Walker, the youngest, moved to Birmingham in 1886 and began to practice law. Within two years, he married Mary Pratt Debardelaben, the daughter of the town's richest industrialist. Within another year, he represented his father-in-law's corporate conglomerate, Tennessee Coal, Iron and Railroad—which would eventually merge with J. P. Morgan's vast enterprise, U.S. Steel. The Percys became a prominent family in Birmingham. Walker became a state senator and the president of the Birmingham Country Club. He made a great deal of money. He and his wife often had other couples over to play ping-pong and cards in their sprawling home, which has been described as "a turreted Gothic monster of a place."[3]

The young couple had their first son, LeRoy Pratt, a year after their marriage. LeRoy grew up in Birmingham, went to Princeton and then on to Harvard Law School, and did a year of postgraduate study at the University of Heidelberg in Germany. He was two years younger than Will Percy, who called him his "favorite cousin." LeRoy returned home in the fall of 1914 and joined his father's law firm, and a year later he married Mattie Sue Phinizy, whom he had met at a resort in Arkansas while on vacation. They wasted no time: just short of nine months after their elegant wedding in Athens, Georgia, Mattie Sue gave birth to their first son, whom they named after his grandfather Walker. Everything seemed fair and bright for the Percy family in 1916—financial security, political and social power, and a new life in their midst.[4]

Just six months after the birth of his grandson, however, the elder Walker Percy shot himself through the heart with a twelve-gauge shotgun. The coroner ruled the death a suicide. The public figure—successful, well traveled, loyal to his community—was haunted by private demons. His death hovered over his son LeRoy, who would perform an almost identical act thirteen years later.

Walker Percy was too young to remember his grandfather, and what he learned about his death had to be learned from intuition. He grew up amidst a heavy silence. But like most children, his focus was not on uncovering family tragedy. His memories were of a happy childhood, riding the Birmingham streetcars with his brothers and sneaking into movies. He remembered his father sipping bourbon whiskey out of a barrel in the basement during Prohibition. He remembered the gothic mansion—his grandfather's house into which his father moved them after his death—with its angled walls and dark rooms; it was "spooky," he said, "like the Munsters' house on TV."

Walker remembered then moving to a home on the country-club golf course, which would forever color his view of the South. His South was not one of plantations and cotton fields but of suburbs and sand traps.[5]

Mattie Sue Percy was a doting mother to her children—she had two more sons, Roy in 1917 and Phinizy in 1921—and a popular Birmingham socialite. She was a sure hand at tennis, a good athlete, and widely thought to be one of the most attractive women in town. She was also delicate. She worried about her husband's instability. She worried when her sons arrived home late on their bicycles. For all her devotedness and kindness, she was distant. Her sons remembered her with fondness but they spoke of her with a sense of detachment. They loved their parents, but their father's unpredictability and their mother's distance did not go unnoticed. Years later, Roy Percy put it succinctly: "It just wasn't a happy family."[6]

After the death of her husband in the summer of 1929, Mattie Sue moved the boys to Athens, Georgia, where they lived in their grandmother's spacious house on Milledge Avenue, one of the town's two main streets. They enrolled in school and tried to feel at home in a new town, but they felt somewhat restricted. Though their grandmother clearly loved them, she was strict and, like her daughter, detached. Phinizy Percy's primary memory of Athens was that they were not allowed to use scissors on Sunday. But in the summer of 1930, everything changed for them.[7]

Will Percy was on his way to Europe in the summer of 1930 when he stopped in Athens to visit Mattie Sue and her boys. He warmed to them at once, and they to him. "I liked him the first time I saw him," Phinizy recalled about Will Percy. "He was a very handsome fellow, and very gentle. I immediately took to him. There was no way not to like him." Walker remembered being thirteen years old and already having a well-developed and fabled notion of his Mississippi cousin: the son of a U.S. senator, a war hero, a poet, a man who had traveled around the world. At that moment and forever after, Walker remembered him as "a personage, a presence" who exuded "exoticness" and "radiated that mysterious quality we call charm."[8] Will Percy suggested they all come live with him in Greenville, and they accepted.

Percy had not allowed his home to stay empty for long. He was at a point in his life when he was free to indulge his every whim to travel and to write—he was forty-five years old and had just inherited a great deal of money and land. (His checking account balance in early 1930 was almost $180,000—worth about $2.3 million in 2010 dollars.)[9] He could have split his time between Florence, New York, and Santa Fe. He could have moved to Taormina and begun a new book of poems. He did not have to take in Mattie Sue's family, but he seemed to have wanted to. He needed his family around, it seems, and to have responsibility. Phinizy would later recall: "If he saw anything that approached a duty, he would reach out and grab it."[10]

The three boys could not believe their good fortune. The home they moved to in the summer of 1930 was a new and foreign world. The house on Percy Street had been renovated in the late 1920s and now had a stuccoed off-white exterior, a massive front edifice, and a tennis court in the back. The house had rooms with odd angles, secret hiding places, and stained-glass windows. In the attic, World War I–era Springfield rifles, cartridge holders, helmets, and memorabilia overflowed from trunks and boxes; Phinizy once found an aluminum leg up there. The upstairs of the house was set up as a series of suites, almost like apartments, in which people came to stay for a night or a week or several years. There was an elevator and a book-lined library and an army of servants. Indica azaleas and lilacs and roses with names like Talisman, Dainty Bess, Malmaisons, and Maman Cochets grew in the yard. Percy had filled the house with art from all over the world—a bronze statue of Lorenzo de Medici, a marble statue of Venus, Moroccan rugs, Japanese paintings, and Persian vases. "It was a window through which you could see the world," family friend Shelby Foote remembered. "No, it was even more than that—it was as if some of that other world had been brought into this little town."[11]

More exciting than the house itself were the people there. Odd people, foreign people, black people—the kinds of people Walker and his brothers had never seen before except as servants or characters in books. The boys were shocked to find that Will Percy had black friends. "I remember one black guy who was more or less off the street," Walker Percy recalled. "He'd walk up and down the street at night and talk to people." Once, a traveling black musician came to the house and came inside and played the blues on his harmonica all afternoon.[12]

The black poet Langston Hughes stayed at Percy's home several times in the early 1930s.[13] During one visit, Percy went to the all-black African Methodist Episcopal Church to introduce Hughes before he gave a poetry reading. Hughes remembered that he "introduced me most graciously" to the multiracial audience and was surprised to hear Percy describe him as something of an equal, as "my fellow poet." This was particularly uplifting to Hughes, who had recently been in Nashville where the poet Allen Tate cancelled a party when he found out Hughes would be there. Meeting Hughes at a party, Tate explained, would be like consorting socially with his cook.[14] That Percy not only interacted with Hughes in public but also allowed him to sleep under his roof was thought by many white Greenvillians to be disgraceful. They called Percy a "nigger-lover" and a "mixer" and were outraged at his gestures of equality.[15]

Percy's Greenville home was a gathering place for artists and intellectuals. The Percy boys remembered it as being in a constant swirl of activity. "It was almost like living in a hotel," Phinizy Percy remembered. There were men who had fallen on hard times and were living upstairs, and "when we lived there, there were two or three other people who were also friends of his who were also living there. Then there were always guests popping in and out."[16] These guests were often world-famous writers, artists, and intellectuals, many of them queer men. William Faulkner came for tennis in the summer wearing white flannel pants and no shoes and left stumbling drunk. The poet and Lincoln biographer Carl Sandburg got drunk on whiskey and played country songs on his guitar. ("Everybody got tired of listening," Roy Percy remembered. "He kept playin'. It seemed like he wouldn't stop.") The psychiatrist Harry Stack Sullivan stationed himself in the pantry with a pitcher of vodka martinis and watched life in the Percy house in both directions—the life of the white guests in the front and the life of the black servants in the back kitchen. The poet Vachel Lindsay got drunk and recited one of his poems, loudly, off the Percy porch in the middle of the night, just months before he committed suicide by drinking Lysol.[17]

Amidst this remarkable and serendipitous atmosphere, Will Percy was mysterious to his young cousins. Despite the constant flow of guests, despite the regular affection shown him by his friends, melancholy increasingly pervaded his disposition. Walker Percy later remembered his eyes as "piercing gray-blue and strangely light. … They were beautiful and terrible eyes, eyes to be careful around. Yet now, when I try to remember them, I cannot see them otherwise than as shadowed by sadness." Will Percy would pace the sidewalk at night with his hands in his pockets, back and forth in front of the house. He would take walks alone on the levee. He had his chauffeur, Ford, take him for long drives in the countryside. He played his grand piano for hours in the evenings, with passion that sometimes silenced his audience; one hearer recalled that he was good enough to have been a concert pianist. He stood in his garden frowning down at his irises and azaleas. He closed himself in his library and wrote translations of the French poet Verlaine. Phinizy, who shared a suite with Percy upstairs, would often hear him awake in the middle of the night, vomiting into the toilet.[18]

Percy's life had changed a great deal after the death of his parents. They had provided a center for him, a mostly constant presence that shaped

*Will Percy, likely at Brinkwood, early 1930s (Courtesy of the
William Alexander Percy Library, Greenville, Mississippi)*

Greenville and his life there. They were stable and predictable, and knowing
they were home gave Percy comfort. In addition to losing his parents, Percy's
own health declined markedly: he had high blood pressure, a sensitive stomach, and a weak immune system. He often fell sick and remained in bed for
weeks at a time. His body seemed older than that of a forty-five-year-old,
and increasingly, his outlook came to reflect his physical state. He talked
more about the decline in American values, the lack of courage among corrupt politicians, the lack of concern for virtues like integrity and honor in
American culture. He wrote to one of the contributors to the Yale Series of

Younger Poets in 1930: "Your problem is saving your soul in a typical mediocre American environment." He explained that this was difficult enough; but worse, there were no guarantees: "Sometimes when we fight hard enough for our own integrity, beautiful things sprout out of us, maybe deeds or thoughts or poems. What difference does it make."[19]

Percy also had a fiery temper. One of his favorite diversions was to sit in his living room and listen to classical music. He had a collection of 78-rpm records—Brahms, Beethoven, Wagner, Bach—that he played on a Capehart record player, which was less than reliable. The size of a piece of furniture, the automatic Capehart would play ten records in a row. Percy would lay on the couch all afternoon listening to music. "He had this great love which I'd never seen before," Walker Percy remembered, "which was unusual and is even now to see somebody who actually gets a high delight, great joy out of listening to music."[20] The record player, though, sometimes jammed, and Percy would get up and curse it, kick it, fly into a rage. "He would break records," Walker said, "throw records around."[21]

In one instance, Roy, Phinizy, and their new friend Shelby Foote were playing with tennis balls in Percy's dining room when one of the balls became lodged in the chandelier. Phinizy got up on the table and tried to get the ball out, and in doing so he pulled the chandelier out of the ceiling and fell crashing to the floor. The three boys walked downtown to Percy's law office and told him what happened.

"Uh, Uncle Will," Roy said, "that chandelier in the library, I'm afraid it got broken."

"What do you mean 'it got broken,'" Percy asked. The boys were silent. "Goddammit!" he fumed. "People who don't know how to take care of good property shouldn't be allowed around it!"

Foote explained that they were all "scared to death of him." "He had a capacity for great anger," Foote said. "You mustn't think Mr. Will was all sweetness and light. He could get as mad as anyone I've ever known in my life. ... I don't know exactly what we thought he was going to do, but his anger was a fearsome thing to be around."[22]

As the Percy boys and their mother became settled in Will Percy's lively household in 1931 and 1932, some of the townsfolk began to speculate that Mattie Sue and Will Percy might marry. Some Greenvillians insisted that Percy had fallen in love with Mattie Sue, and she with him.[23] The two played tennis and bridge together, and Mattie Sue seemed to have a sense of belonging in Percy's house. When the writer David Cohn was in town and considering a move to Greenville, she told him, "Oh Dave, Greenville is the most peaceful place on the earth." Just then, they heard two gunshots outside the window. "Oh Dave," Mattie Sue said, "I take it back."[24] But Roy and Walker, doubtless still dealing with grief, fought a lot during the family's first year in Greenville, and this took a toll on Mattie Sue's nerves. One time she yelled at her two older sons: "If you don't stop your fighting you will kill me!"[25] Walker Percy would later say that during her years in Greenville, his mother "was not well."[26]

On the morning of Easter Saturday in April 1932, Mattie Sue asked her youngest son, Phinizy, to go for a car ride with her. The two got in her Buick coupe and left the house. Mattie Sue said nothing and seemed distracted and irritable. She would not tell Phinizy where they were going. They headed north out of town toward the country. Mattie Sue turned down a dirt road and sped toward Metcalf, Mississippi. As they drove onto a wooden bridge, the Buick spun out of control and plunged off the bridge and twenty feet down into a river. As the car sank into the water, Phinizy looked for a means of escape. His mother grabbed his wrist and would not let go. Phinizy, seeing that a rear window was open, tried to pull his mother toward it. She would not move, and her grip tightened around his wrist. She remained seated in the driver's seat. Desperately, Phinizy wrenched himself free and swam out of the rear window and to the bank. Hoping to turn around and see that his mother had followed him, all he saw instead were ripples in the brown muddy water.[27]

Passersby comforted the wet child and went for help. Others arrived and eventually pulled Mattie Sue from the water. An ambulance arrived and medics tried to revive her, but she was dead. By sheer coincidence, Walker and Roy drove by with a friend and saw the crowd of people. Curious, they went toward the scene. Will Percy had arrived by this time and intercepted the boys on the road. "You shouldn't be here," he said. But Walker and LeRoy had seen their mother. His eyes filling with tears, Walker stumbled away saying, "It's my mother, my mother . . ."[28]

At home, Will Percy comforted the three boys. He told them that he loved them, and that he would adopt them and provide for them. He arranged to hold the funeral services at the house and for Mattie Sue to be buried at the Greenville cemetery in the Percy family plot. The next day, Easter Sunday, the pastor from the Presbyterian church presided over the funeral and they buried her. Percy filed a petition for adoption.[29]

Phinizy was traumatized. He often woke at night screaming with terror. He had vivid nightmares about the meaning of time and the beginning and end of life.[30] Will Percy moved him into his room, and when Phinizy woke at night Percy would talk to him. He would ask him how he felt, encourage him to talk if he wanted to. When Phinizy did not want to talk, or could not go back to sleep, Percy would read to him from the Greek myths. Phinizy became deeply and emotionally attached to him. "I trusted him completely," he said. "His only thought was comforting me and getting me back to sleep." For the rest of his life, Phinizy carried this trauma with him, and even as a grown man he would be moved to tears at the mention of his mother. At the mention of Will Percy, he would speak in superlatives and become acrid at the slightest challenge to his character. "It's trite to say he was like Christ," Phinizy said, "but he certainly was more like Christ than anybody I've ever known or heard of."[31]

That summer of 1932, Percy arranged for Walker and Roy to take a trip out west while he took Phinizy to Washington, D.C., and Baltimore. The older boys went with Percy's secretary, Mitchell Finch, to the Grand Canyon, San Francisco, and New Mexico. While they were in Washington, Percy took Phinizy around the city and spent time talking with him about his mother.[32] He also took Phinizy to the Phipps Clinic at the Johns Hopkins Hospital in Baltimore to speak with a psychiatrist. In July he and Phinizy took a train out west and met Roy and Walker at Jackson Hole, Wyoming. They stayed there for two weeks, taking trips into Yellowstone National Park, riding horses, and even playing softball. (One has a hard time imagining Percy participating in this; perhaps he was the coach.) After Wyoming, the group of four took a train to Sewanee, Tennessee, and spent the rest of the summer at Brinkwood, hiking in the nearby coves and reading aloud to each other at night.[33]

Will Percy's commitment to his three adopted sons was remarkable. They entered his life at a time when he was prepared to spend his time traveling around the world, living off of his inheritance and income, writing poetry and tending his garden. After the death of his parents, he was free to structure his household as he chose, free to live outside of the expectations of his family; after a lifetime of deep love as well as ambivalence toward his parents, he was free of them. Walker Percy explained that late in life, he realized what Percy had done for him: for a man who "felt more at home in Taormina than in Jackson" to have forsaken his own freedoms in order to raise three young boys "amounted to giving up the freedom of bachelorhood and taking on the burden of parenthood without the consolations of marriage." The three boys idolized their new father figure. "He was to me a fixed point in a confusing world. ... He was the most extraordinary man I have ever known," Walker wrote. "I owe him a debt which cannot be paid."[34]

For his part, Percy approached parenting carefully. He felt responsible for the physical as well as the spiritual well-being of his three new sons. He wrote in his memoir about what he felt was the solemn burden of advising them "in a world that was changing and that seemed to me on the threshold of chaos." The greatest threat, he felt, was to their spirits. Life in the twentieth century, as he saw it, offered very few meaningful attachments: the promises of consumer goods or professional success were empty; science offered explanation but not comfort; religion seemed only to produce hypocrites and crooks, and rather than access to truth, it offered merely "bribes" for good behavior. He worried that Walker, Roy, and Phinizy would "drift through the world, aimless, unemployed, with no certainties in their heart to give them anchorage or peace." "It is a sober thing," he wrote, "when they come to you so lost and ask the way. I am always afraid for them and afraid of myself."[35]

Percy directed them to the Christian gospels and to Greek literature, and he told them that the search for love and beauty and God was itself the way to peace. Avoid the fear of hell, he said, but "meditate on Jesus"; avoid seeking rewards now or later, or even forgiveness. "To seek outlet for our emotions, our intellect, our spiritual cravings," he told them, "to blossom and fruit with our whole nature, to keep its unity and proportion, of such is our occupation." Percy's advice echoed the themes he had been writing about all his life in his poetry: that the profoundest reality is to experience the Divine in beauty and experience; that humans need freedom of thought and action in order to achieve this; that this freedom demands a concomitant ethic of service and a concern for the well-being of others. Religious dogma was not necessary to access truth, he said, though figures like Christ and Buddha, as well as Socrates and Marcus Aurelius, served to point the way. "He was more than a teacher," Walker later wrote of Will Percy. "It was usually in relation to him, whether with him or against him, that I defined myself."[36]

Percy's ethic of service manifested itself in his commitment to his three sons. Though he disliked practicing law, Percy continued to work in order to pay for the boys' education. During these years, his health problems increased, and practicing law did not help his congenitally high blood pressure. He worked out a deal with his partner, Hazelwood Farish, by which he did not have to work in the summertime; each summer he would spend with the boys at Brinkwood, or he would park them at Brinkwood under the care of one of their aunts and travel. Janet Longcope knew what he had sacrificed in order to be a good father figure to the Percy boys, and she admired him for it. "Your courage, Will, which is both fine and steadfast," she wrote to him, "the tenderness of your human understanding—your sympathy which

Roy Percy, Shelby Foote, and Walker Percy in Will Percy's garden, Greenville, Mississippi, early 1930s (Courtesy of the William Alexander Percy Library, Greenville, Mississippi)

transcends your own loneliness—the wit and wisdom for which you have wrestled life and pain—the pure flame of truth you guard as a knight—your exquisite awareness of beauty. These you give to those who love you."[37]

Percy wrote no more poetry after he adopted the boys, though he continued to read and maintain strong opinions. Shelby Foote and Walker Percy, in particular, loved to engage him on literary matters because he had such firm convictions on what was "good" and what was "bad" art. The two began to track with current artistic trends and would try and persuade Percy of the virtues of modern forms. One afternoon, they were sitting on the porch together in Greenville, and Foote played a record of Bing Crosby and Kay Star singing "If I Could Be with You (One Hour Tonight)."

"Now Mr. Will, you have to listen to this," Foote said.

They sat and listened to the song. The chorus, in part, went:

> If I could be with you one hour tonight,
> If I was free to do the things I might,
> I'm telling you true, I'd be anything but blue,
> If I could be with you.

Walker and Shelby waited in anticipation to see if Percy would approve. "Did you like it?" Shelby asked.

"She sounds like a whore," Percy replied.[38]

On another occasion, Percy and the boys were at Brinkwood, and Foote brought to Percy John Crowe Ransom's famous modernist poem "Bells for John Whiteside's Daughter." In it, Ransom describes ironic melancholy outside a funeral for a young girl by showing an image of several geese on the lawn:

> The lazy geese, like a snow cloud
> Dripping their snow on the green grass,
> Tricking and stopping, sleepy and proud,
> Who cried in goose, Alas.

Foote waited for his judgment. At last, all Percy said was, "That's not the way geese act."[39]

When Walker was a junior in high school, he entered a poetry contest for which Percy was appointed judge. Though the poems were submitted anonymously, Percy picked Walker's as the winner. The poem was a sentimental and romanticized depiction of a group of black slaves working in a cotton field. It read, in part:

> By plough-shares rude your fields were tilled
> 'Neath azure summer skies
> When happy slaves the warm air filled
> With drowsy lullabies.

Walker, proud of himself, went to his adoptive father and told him that the winning poem was his. Percy said: "You needn't be happy about it because it was the worst bunch of poems I've ever had occasion to judge."[40]

Will Percy was enamored of the classics, but he was also not close-minded with regard to modern literature. Shelby Foote, for example, mentioned on several occasions that it was Percy who recommended the three modernist books that changed his life: James Joyce's *Ulysses*, Thomas Mann's *The Magic Mountain*, and Marcel Proust's *Remembrance of Things Past*. Percy told him that these were the three most important novels of the century. To the young Foote, Percy seemed almost foreign, so unpredictable were his views and opinions in the context of a homogenous South. "Will Percy had a culture that was alien to me and to that country," he recalled. "He had been almost everywhere and seen almost everything." And what was more, Percy wanted to share what he had seen, what he knew, with younger people. "He was a very good teacher," Foote said. "It was by example. Here was a man who was a world traveler, who was widely read, who knew about the cultured forms of life on other continents, who had experienced the company of some of the fine writers of our time, and he would talk about it in a way that made you not only know the reality of it, but also appreciate the beauty of present day literature and past. I've heard Mr. Will talk about Keats, for example, in a way that made you wish the conversation would hurry up and get over so you could go home and read some Keats."[41]

Walker Percy, too, highlighted this quality in Will Percy. To have lived in his house for twelve years, he said, was to be "informed in the deepest sense of the word. What was to be listened to, dwelled on, pondered over for the next thirty years was of course the man himself, the unique human being, and when I say unique I mean it in its most literal sense: he was one of a kind: I never met anyone remotely like him." Percy would sit with Walker in his living room and point out moments in a symphony or read aloud from Shakespeare. "I had a great teacher," Walker wrote. "The teacher points and says *Look*; the response is *Yes, I see*."[42]

Indeed, throughout the 1930s, Will Percy transitioned from artist to patron and teacher of the arts. He opened his home to writers and artists who needed an environment to create their art; David Cohn, for example, wrote his memoir, *God Shakes Creation*, while he lived at Percy's house for two years. Percy invited Hodding Carter to move to Greenville to start a more liberal newspaper, which he did and for which he eventually won the Pulitzer Prize during the civil rights movement. Shelby Foote once was suspended from Greenville High School, and Percy told him to stay in his library for a week and read. Percy oversaw the formation of the Delta Art Association (funded by the New Deal's Federal Arts Project), which he hoped would be a beacon of creativity in a society that evinced no "joy in living." Percy encouraged the artists to create with joy, and he encouraged nonartists to think of living as art; in one speech, he suggested that "all of our jobs are petty jobs but how we do them, whether we put loyalty and courage above all, makes the difference between being God-like and beast-like."[43] Likewise, he explained to Walker Percy that sincerity and courage were the most important values. "My whole theory of life," he wrote to his son, "is that glory and accomplishment are of far less importance than the creation of character and the individual good life. What the world thinks of any one person is largely a matter of chance, but what we are in the eyes of ourselves and of the high Gods is a matter largely of our own making."[44]

Will Percy's commitment to younger artists was, to him, deeper than civic activism. He was committed to the idea of pedagogical relationships as spiritually and artistically nourishing. His relationship with Leon Koury, a gay man who would become a widely renowned sculptor, demonstrates this. Koury was the son of Lebanese immigrants who moved to Greenville in the 1920s to open a grocery store. They lived in the black section of Greenville and served a working-class clientele from their store across town from where Percy lived. In the early 1930s, a teenaged Koury, who spent most of his time skipping school and reading Nietzsche and Schopenhauer, wrote to Percy to tell him he admired a poem he had published. Percy's secretary forwarded Koury's letter to Percy, who was in Europe at the time. Percy wrote from France to thank Koury and to ask him to stop by his house when he returned home. Koury worked up the courage to go to Percy's house, and when he did, Percy read some of Koury's poems and told him they were not very good, but the sketches on the back of the poems were. "I'll tell you what to do," Percy told Koury, "forget the writing right now, and bring me some drawings."[45]

Koury brought Percy some drawings, and Percy encouraged him to keep practicing and also invited him to come around and listen to music with him. "The first symphony I ever heard was in Will's parlor," Koury remembered, "in his study—and I remember it was Pathetique—Tchaikovsky. I was in a daze for weeks after that, just in a daze. This was something that I felt I had heard thousands of years before and it had come back to my ears. *I knew it*! It was saying something to me." Percy opened up a world of art and culture to Koury. As with Walker Percy, Leon Koury felt that Percy did not *teach* him so much as lead him to see something that was already inside of him. Koury described Percy's influence on him as leading him "into realizing that there was so much more to acquire. ... This wasn't a conscious—it wasn't deliberate—he didn't go about this in any kind of way. It was just during our visits. ... It was just *there*, but he didn't realize that to me it was like a miner being in a mine and finding a gold nugget after struggling so long—and not knowing what I was looking for, you know." During one such visit, Koury played around with some modeling clay, and Percy noticed his work. Shortly thereafter, fifty pounds of clay appeared on Koury's doorstep across town, and his sculpting career began.[46]

Percy took Koury to New York and introduced him to his friend Malvina Hoffman. Within a few years, Koury showed his sculpture at the National Art Exhibit, the World's Fair, and the Whitney Museum in New York, as well as at galleries in Los Angeles. Though he lived in New York during the 1950s, he returned to Greenville in 1960 and lived there until his death in 1993.[47] An art historian once asked Koury to write about his career as a sculptor, and

Leon Koury in his studio (Photograph courtesy of William N. Beckwith)

Koury responded: "When I am asked for personal history, I can think of only one man who found a spark and tried to fan it into a flame, my friend and patron William Alexander Percy. As I write his name I am again in the quiet of his peaceful study, talking of many things. But always the last question seemed to be: What is demanded of a human being?" Koury explained that often while he worked, the ghost of Will Percy intruded into his thoughts, reminding him of "the dignity of the little actor called man." What Percy taught him was not how to sculpt; it was how to be, how to express himself as an artist. Because of Percy, he wrote, "I understood that it is never what you say in art that is important, but how much of you is speaking."[48]

It is worth noting that Koury reproduced this ethic in his own relationships with younger artists in Greenville, many of whom went on to garner international acclaim. Robert Marcius, a jewelry, furniture, and interior-accessory designer, remembered of Koury: "He was a mystic thinker. He made you figure out what you wanted by leading you inward. He always said, 'Don't run from something; always run to something.' He gave me massive amounts of time. It would be impossible to calculate how much time he spent helping me." William Beckwith, a sculptor and mentee of Koury, said: "He consistently urged a bunch of searching, young bohemians to read the Harvard Classics and many of them did. Leon wanted to expose his young friends to the same quality of art that Will Percy had exposed to him." And Allen Frame, a queer photographer, spoke of the lineage he had inherited in Greenville. Koury, he said, was "a very wise and interesting gay man who always had offbeat people hanging around him. He had been a protégé of the gay Mississippi poet William Alexander Percy." Koury, like Percy, took seriously the charge to identify talent and "fan it into a flame."[49]

DESPITE WILL PERCY'S civic idealism and his considerable efforts in these years to help his community, he evinced a mounting sadness and sometimes irascibility that coincided with poor health. He felt overworked, and his blood pressure was consistently high. Both Shelby Foote and Walker Percy remembered how regularly Percy took sick and remained in bed. He would emerge "padding around in fuzzy slippers" and his favorite purple kimono he had brought back from Japan, irritable and tired.[50] A student once went to his law office to interview Percy, expecting to find him elbow deep in work, but when she arrived at 9:30 AM, Percy's partner laughed and said she would be lucky to catch him there. "He usually comes in between 10:30 and 12," he said. When she said she would come back at 10:30, he replied: "But sometimes he doesn't come in at all."[51]

Though doggedly devoted to his three sons, he also tired of them. Percy wrote to his friend Charlotte Gailor of his irritation at the timing of Phinizy's Easter break from school: "Of all others [this weekend] is Phin's Easter vacation and in desperation I am having him spend it in New Orleans with Bob and myself. That means I cannot see the pageant."[52] To Gerstle Mack, Percy wrote: "The Percy boys are interesting little animals." And another time, he complained: "God, Christmas was awful as usual."[53] Because they offered excellent educations, but likely also in an attempt to preserve some peace of mind, Percy enrolled Roy and Phinizy in boarding schools for high school—Roy at Episcopal in Virginia and Phinizy at McCallie in Tennessee. Walker later wrote to Shelby Foote that rereading Will Percy's letters from the 1930s "makes you see how much fell in on him in such a short time, death of parents in 1929, the Depression, mother's death, having to lawyer, bad health. … It's amazing he carried on despite all. It's also surprising how much he traveled even after we arrived. Apparently he would call in an aunt to take charge, Aunt Ellen—'a pleasant totally inefficient woman'—or park us in Sewanee—and take off—to Tahiti, Samoa, Rio."[54]

Indeed, Percy continued to travel throughout the 1930s. In the case of Samoa, there was something there he had read about that he needed to see for himself.

14. SAMOA, SHARECROPPING, AND RACE

We are destroying every race lacking our pigmentation. The white plague.
—WILLIAM ALEXANDER PERCY, "The White Plague"

On June 24, 1936, Will Percy boarded the SS *Monterrey* in Los Angeles to sail just under 4,000 miles to Samoa. He had traveled to Polynesia before in 1931, and his fascination with the South Seas resembled those of a number of American and European intellectuals and artists before him. The French painter Paul Gauguin abandoned his wife and five children to live in Tahiti and paint. The novelists Herman Melville, Somerset Maugham, and D. H. Lawrence, among others, traveled there to find inspiration for their fictions. The American anthropologists Ruth Benedict and Margaret Mead did fieldwork in the South Seas that led to seminal publications in the field of social anthropology. They were all looking for something the "civilized world" did not offer—a different ethic, exotic climes, primitive experience. Percy wrote about his own hopes to Norman Douglas: "I am going to Samoa at the end of June for a month's respite among people who are stupid & lazy & wise, & I hope beautiful. Wish you were with me."[1]

Percy's trip from Los Angeles to the South Pacific would have taken almost a month, with a stop in Honolulu along the way. Arriving in the main port in the Samoan Islands—Pago Pago on the island of Tutuila—one would find sheer cliffs that ringed the one-time crater of a volcano. Though travelers like Percy went looking for contact with primitive peoples and premodern civilizations, Samoa had by 1936 been in contact with the West for almost 200 years. French explorers arrived on Samoa in the mid-eighteenth century and were met with violent resistance from the natives. British missionaries went to Samoa in the 1830s, and the German navy invaded Samoa in 1889—leading to a conflict with the United States, which had laid claim to parts of the islands. The 1899 Tripartite Convention divided Samoa in half—the eastern half for the Germans and the western half for the Americans. The American navy built a coaling station in the bay of Pago Pago and established a regular presence. Samoans fought and died for the United States during World

War I. In 1925, when Margaret Mead arrived in Pago Pago to do her field-work, she was disturbed to find a smokestack and radio towers rising from the beautiful volcanic crater. She found the native ceremonies "depressing" because, during tribal dances, the natives carried black American umbrel-las and wore tunics made of "various hideous striped American stuffs." The scene was "ludicrous," she said; "the brightest costumes melt into a back-ground of endless umbrellas." By 1939 American marines outnumbered the indigenous population of the island.[2]

Arriving in 1936, Percy would have been met with much the same scene: American sailors in the shops and bars; local women and men stripped to the waist carrying fruit to the market and wearing a combination of grass skirts and American clothes; islanders and Americans alike crowding the narrow streets of the small harbor town. In July it would have been hot but breezy, with occasional brief rain showers. A central bus route ran through the center of the island—the buses old and rattling, the roads unpaved and rocky. The villages along the bus route, Mead had noted, did "not present a typical picture of the original culture," for they were "very much influenced by American goods and American visitors."[3] But if one was willing to travel by walking path or by boat, a more remote village could be found that was less marked by commerce and missionary.

In order to understand why Percy went to Samoa and the significance of his time there, his trip should be placed in a broader context—specifically, the emerging conversation among anthropologists about the relationship between moral values and culture. Margaret Mead's controversial and best-selling book, *Coming of Age in Samoa* (1928), posited in part that Samoan sexual norms were less repressive than those in America, and that young Samoan women passed through adolescence with little turmoil, enjoying casual sex with both sexes, free from the pressures of romantic love. For Mead, who advocated free love and unrestrained enjoyment of the body, Samoan culture suggested an alternative to American sexual ethics.[4] Ruth Benedict famously argued that moral values were relative and contingent upon cultural patterns in her book *Patterns of Culture* (1934), which grew out of her research in the South Seas. These two arguments—foundational ideas regarding cultural relativism and sexual liberation—predictably upset many Americans when they appeared. It is almost certain Will Percy read these books, best sellers that they were and wide reader that he was, and his trip to Samoa in 1936 led him to reaffirm their ideas about culture and sexual-ity—as well as the long-standing romantic conception of the Pacific Islands as pristinely primitive in their disconnect from civilization. Percy's relativist views on sex and culture stood alongside his conviction of the fundamental difference between races and what he felt was the spiritual superiority yet intellectual inferiority of nonwhite people across the world. The vexed question with regard to Will Percy and race is this: how did he become a cultural relativist, a sexual liberationist, and a white supremacist?[5]

When Percy was in Samoa in the summer of 1936, he interacted with the natives and took notes on their sexual behavior, moral attitudes, and religious practices. Drawing from these observations, he wrote an essay entitled "The White Plague," which discoursed upon the relationship between race, culture, and moral values. He addressed the essay to an American audience and wanted to publish it in a magazine; he never did, but he did include it in the first draft of *Lanterns on the Levee*. (The chapter, though, was never published because his publisher insisted he take it out.)[6] Studying indigenous sexual practices while on vacation was not customary for American tourists, but Percy was something of a steamboat anthropologist—he saw his travels not merely as leisure and relaxation but also as a way of gathering information to inform his opinions and perspectives. In this case, his trip to Samoa and his subsequent writings shed light on his convoluted perspective on racial difference, spiritual wholeness, and moral authority.

Percy noticed that, to Samoans, sex was merely corporeal. Samoans saw bodies as bodies and intercourse as a physical act, and they did not attach rigid moral values to sexual behavior. "Copulation is esteemed a bodily function," Percy wrote of Samoans. "You indulge as the need asserts itself." He admired the casual way Samoans treated sex. Unlike American culture, which Percy felt was overbearing in its regulation of sexual values—with emphasis on chastity, heterosexuality, and reticence—Samoan culture had a more balanced view of sex: "It is pleasant but not important, certainly not a matter of special consideration." Samoans, Percy found, had no attachment to the idea of romantic love with its pressures to possess and control; rather, their relationships seemed less possessive, less bound up with jealousy and envy. Samoans placed little value on privacy, and Percy was surprised to find that they made love even when sleeping in a large room "with eight or ten of the family snoring obliviously." Unlike many Westerners, who described this kind of sexual behavior as "savage" and "heathen," Percy found it refreshing. Samoans, he said, were "a people gracious, superbly healthy, handsome & happy."[7]

It seems likely that Percy's views on Samoan sexuality were somewhat predetermined, for these writings closely echoed Mead's findings in *Coming of Age in Samoa*. She, too, wrote of the "general casualness of the whole society" and their "free and easy experimentation" with sex.[8] In her appendix, she tracked the sexual practices of Samoan adolescent girls, and her data suggested that the large majority of girls had experienced both heterosexual and homosexual relations during adolescence.[9] She noted the absence of romantic love or pressures toward chastity and concluded that, as a result, "sex was a natural, pleasurable thing."[10] It was American culture, she felt, that was odd. Unlike Samoans, Americans were almost entirely disconnected from the processes of birth, sex, and death—the most fundamental experiences in human life. Consequently, American culture very often produced frigid and repressed individuals, whereas Samoan culture produced a broader spectrum of "normal" people: "homosexuality," Mead wrote, "statistically unusual forms of heterosexual activity, are neither banned nor institutionalized. The wider range which these practices give prevents the development of obsessions of guilt which are so frequent a cause of maladjustment among us. . . . This acceptance of a wider range as 'normal' provides a cultural atmosphere in which frigidity and psychic impotence do not occur."[11]

Mead and Percy both felt that this sexual freedom was an outgrowth of an expansive cultural attitude toward personal morality. Mead's fieldwork led her to distrust the homogeneity of American values and to advocate for a culture more tolerant of diversity. She wrote in 1935: "If we are to achieve a richer culture, rich in contrasting values, we must recognize the whole gamut of human potentialities, and so weave a less arbitrary social fabric."[12] Likewise, when Percy went to Samoa, he wrote about and admired how Samoan culture, unlike American culture, created a profound sense of personal freedom among its denizens. For example, he felt Samoans had no discontent that led them to envy and to steal. "Individual ownership is almost nonexistent," Percy noted, admiring how it was entirely appropriate to walk into one's neighbor's house and take what you needed. That the Samoans did not covet was related to the ways their culture was cohesive and ritualized. They had a shared identity, a shared system of meaning that they did not challenge. "Their native way of life, their ceremonials, their culture," Percy wrote, was "stylized and beautiful and completely adequate to their needs." In many ways, Percy read into the Samoan culture an absence of the features of American life—its Christian sexual ethics, its capitalist possessiveness, its spiritual emptiness—that he disliked.[13]

These features, though, were encroaching on Samoan life (and had been for many decades by the time Percy arrived). The main topic of debate in Samoa while Percy was there was whether English or Samoan was to be taught in schools. Percy dreaded the spread of English with especial disgust.

Samoan "is a singularly sensitive and poetic language which lends itself perfectly to the elaborate ritualistic speeches of their talking chiefs, so exquisite in compliment, so gracious and flowery, so silly if translated." The beauty of ritual, the meanings embedded in ceremonies, even the pathos of small observations in day-to-day life, Percy felt, were connected to the native language. "Substitute English as the language of the people & their whole culture falls: you make of them merely imitation white men." Speaking to what he presumed would be his American audience, he continued: "They are now proud, self-respecting, with no sense of inferiority, but when they shall have become imitation white men, the whole world will have no need of them; they will lose their pride, their self-respect, their charm, their integrity. Yet that is what your government with the best of intentions is now engaged in doing. Let it continue a few years and the disintegration will be complete. It will be too late to change."

Percy associated racial characteristics with spiritual and emotional ones, and the nonwhite characteristics—charm, sensitivity, simplicity—were decidedly better. Openness, honesty, and freedom were characteristics that flourished outside of white culture, which he viewed as stultifying and repressive. He associated modernity with white people and saw the process of globalization as making "imitation white men." The expansion of Western culture across the globe had deleterious effects on the last remaining authentic cultures. "We will destroy them," Percy wrote, "as we are destroying every race lacking our pigmentation. The white plague."[14]

Percy's idealization of Samoan culture grew out of his feeling that American life was structured in a way that did not allow for free expression, for alternatives to the status quo. American life, he felt, was regulated by a curious combination of Puritan morality and insatiable consumerism. On the other hand, "simple" cultures like Samoa's were free of these pressures. The problem, it seemed to Percy, was that dark-skinned people across the globe possessed neither the will nor the prescience to resist flashy American goods; they did not know that with the goods comes the morality, and with the morality comes repression. "They want to be destroyed," Percy wrote. "Our good gifts are so patent, our evil ones so hidden, even to ourselves." The Samoans lauded the arrival of crates of iceboxes, radios, record players, mattresses, and especially bicycles and automobiles; these products made their lives easier and more comfortable. But the islanders took these things, Percy wrote, "never suspecting that taking these they must take too our weariness, our restlessness, our unhappy hearts." In contrast to the rooted, ritualized traditional culture of the Samoans, American consumer culture would lead to dislocation and discontent. "We are the nomads of the world," Percy explained, "without home fires, wandering by stars not fixed, whose passion is to force the older & younger tribes of the race to join our tumultuous and futile pilgrimage." In forcing "primitive" cultures like the Samoans to join them, Americans would give them objects but take their souls: unwitting islanders receive "things, amusing things, miraculous things," but as a consequence, they lose "the one thing for the lack of which we sob ourselves to sleep—sweet, sweet content."[15]

Percy associated whiteness with modernity, and modernity with discontent. In turn, he associated nonwhite people with spiritual fullness and premodern cultural forms. The contrast is striking and could be read as a typical anthropological fallacy: primitive cultures possess authenticity that modern cultures lack. This view would suggest that for Percy, the South Seas were a fantasy space onto which he scripted his own desires—a useful space, one that was sufficiently far away for him to write about with disconnect from his Mississippi world. To a degree, this is true. However, in a significant move, Percy spent the second half of the essay applying the knowledge he gained from "studying" the Samoans to the race relations in the American South. The result is a vexed, ambivalent discourse on race in which several patterns emerge. First, Percy perceived a fundamental difference between blacks and whites that he grounded in scientific racism; this difference was evolutionary, not immutable—blacks could "catch up" with whites because both groups were human, "brothers." But the difference was so vast that equality was not likely in the near future. Second, Percy described the sharecroppers on his plantation in much the same manner as the islanders of Samoa—content, eroticized, charming—with one important distinction: the damage had been done to the blacks in the South, their souls corrupted by American values and American history. Finally, Percy's application of his Samoan anthropology to Mississippi emphasized the evils of capitalism and its attendant morality as the fundamental cause of the "White Plague." More than merely a place about which to fantasize, Samoa also provided data that Percy used to grapple with the "Negro problem" in America.

The American race problem, Percy wrote, was fundamentally a problem of two alien cultures living side by side at different stages of development. Where an earlier phase of development—the primitive stage in which the Samoans still operated—was preferable in many ways, modernity had done its damage to American black culture. "Our evil to [the Negro] is not immanent as to the Samoans, but accomplished," Percy explained. "Forced into an alien culture, among a different, more intellectual people, told to become like a white man the Negro has lost his pride, his self-respect, his dignity as a human being; he is losing his remnants of native content, of native happiness." The tragedy, according to Percy, was not that blacks had contaminated white culture or were disruptive to the good life in the South, but precisely the opposite: in being told to act white, they had lost their blackness. "He makes at best a second-rate white man," Percy wrote of the Negro. "He could have made something far more precious in the eyes of any god, a first-rate Negro."[16]

Percy blamed much of this development on northern capitalists and philanthropists. He felt that northern liberals regarded African Americans "sentimentally, as a white man with black skin." This, Percy believed, was not true at the present "stage of development."[17] Percy felt that the findings regarding "genes & Mendelian laws & inherited characteristics" proved that whites and blacks were fundamentally different at present, and to regard them as otherwise was an illusion. This illusion dominated postemancipation race relations in the United States, and though the South "knew the northern throng was ridiculous & cruel, in practice it accepted" this illusion. The result was that blacks were allowed only a limited freedom—the freedom to act and think like white people. Given this harsh and prescribed reality, "slavery would have been a far more comfortable and self-respecting status for the negro than his present so-called freedom, north or south." Rather than living uncomfortably in a white man's world, rather than having to live in freedom yet having no real freedom, the black man would have been better to remain in slavery, where "his position, his caste as it were, would have been fixed, unequivocal, he could have developed his own way of life, his own culture, uninterfered with so far as his inner life was concerned by the white culture around him."[18]

Much of Percy's description of race relations followed a traditional narrative among white southerners: blacks were not fit for citizenship at emancipation; their simple, childlike nature was suited for slavery and benevolent white guidance; they were incapable of full civic and economic participation in American society. But two parts of Percy's perspective stood apart from this familiar story. First, he explained that the reason slavery needed to be abolished was that slave owners were not strong enough to avoid hubris, and they never made good on their avowed responsibility to treat slaves with "wisdom, kindliness, honesty." Percy implied that slave owners were not strong enough because the burden of benevolence was simply too great. The tragedy was that a strong, virtuous aristocracy was overburdened by this responsibility and collapsed. This was probably their due, Percy allowed, because the system had a fundamental flaw: southerners had "no right to own another human being."[19]

A second peculiar feature of Percy's version of southern history was his interest in the "inner life" of black people. The main thrust of his "white plague" theory was that white culture destroyed the inner life of black people, which was beautiful, even sublime. This inner life could only be sustained when separate from white culture. Slavery allowed, in Percy's mind, for this necessary separation of the races. This separation would "have afforded a better chance for [the black man] to develop as a human being, to achieve his own happiness, than we are now permitting him." Since slavery, American culture has demanded the "impossible" of the former slave: "he is to act, think & feel like a white man, but not to be a white man." The American problem was infinitely more complicated than the Samoan problem, he wrote, because "the Samoan still has his own well-established good way of life. ... The Samoan has an isolated country of his own." The vital inner life could only be sustained in a faraway place; the black soul and spirit, fragile and beautiful and corruptible, could not withstand the pressures of assimilation.[20]

White Americans, for their part, only made this situation worse. Northern idealists "drummed into [the Negro's] receptive ear" constant talk about rights and privileges with no corresponding talk about duties and responsibilities. Meanwhile, Percy wrote, the only thing the southerner said was: "'keep your place, nigger.'" Percy saw no practicable solution to the race problem in America. The only glimmer of hope was if both blacks and whites had a "change of heart." The black man needed to develop "a pride in himself as a negro," and whites needed to allow him that pride, "moreover, encourage him in it." The greatest crime since Reconstruction, Percy explained, had been committed by white southerners, but no one ever spoke of it: "Since slavery, we have been unwilling to grant to the negro the one thing without which no human soul can grow, self-respect." "How tragic," Percy lamented, "how profoundly moving the plight of the charming & child-like people!"[21]

Racial inequality, to Percy, essentially meant difference, sometimes an inferior difference and sometimes a superior difference. Percy's views on race worked to idealize black people while also not challenging the status quo; his ambivalence was borne out of his considerable wealth and privilege but also a sense of dislocation within the system that so privileged him. Black people, he felt, were not as intellectual, not as fit for political and economic participation, not as well suited for leadership as white people. But that was because they had largely remained outside of the historical process that had created the "white" world. In turn, white people were not as spiritual, not as charming or funny or able to live in the present as black people—this being a result of their participation in history. "Three apples plus two grapes do not equal five bananas," Percy explained. "White qualities & Negro qualities do not equal each other. That, however, does not prove that what the Vendor of Fruits gave the Negro is less sweet or less nourishing—to me, at any rate, it has always seemed more luscious, with sunshine for sap."[22]

To the extent that his views were grounded in his belief that Western sexual mores were oppressive, and to the extent that he believed the Christian ethics that governed "white society" were also repressive, Percy's figuration of blacks as better for being outside of history was an expression of his dissatisfaction with modern American culture. In addition, in titling his essay "The White Plague" and in conflating modernity with whiteness and discontent, Percy expressed a historical critique of capitalist America—granted, a critique filled with wishful thinking about the pleasantness of the past and of premodern societies. Percy's nostalgia, his irreconcilable proclamations about equality, and his simultaneous longing for and condescension toward black people represent the tormented engagement of a white southerner trying to reconcile white supremacy and cultural relativism.

PERCY RETURNED to California in the fall of 1936, and from there he took a train back to Mississippi. While on the train and after arriving home, he continued to write about race, and he eventually included much of this work in his autobiography. His writings about race in America mirror those that he produced while on a steamship coming home from Samoa. As in "The White Plague," race in *Lanterns on the Levee* emerges as a central tension within Percy's worldview. He addressed the topic with boastful confidence at moments, utter humility at others; his views look like blatant racism at moments, at others tender, even intimate regard for black individuals. Attempts to categorize Percy's racial views run up against his own contradictory claims, his ambivalent feelings, his movement between idealism and white supremacy.

One thing Mississippi had that Samoa did not was poor white people. As we have seen, Percy loathed them. Recall his father's bitter and unsuccessful fight against James K. Vardaman and his "redneck" followers—the Percys had a long-standing and unwavering view of themselves as a superior class of white people. Will Percy, though, took this a step further and portrayed blacks, too, as superior to poor white people. The poor whites of the present, he felt, were bigoted, close-minded, violent, angry, stupid people. "I can forgive them as the Lord God forgives," Percy said, "but admire them, trust them, love them—never." His white supremacy included the supremacy of the white aristocracy over blacks, but also the supremacy of both the white aristocracy and blacks over poor whites.[23]

"I often conclude that the only Southerners worth talking about are the darkies," Percy wrote. Blacks, to Percy, were well mannered, inefficient, charming, lovable, and spiritual. They had no sense of their own past, nor did they care or worry about the future. They had an "obliterating genius for living in the present." In contrast to the Negro, who neither remembered nor planned, "the white man does little else: to him the present is the one great unreality." Percy positioned blacks as impervious to historical change, but he also positioned them outside of the marketplace. Indeed, in every instance a black character is working or in a place of work in *Lanterns on the Levee*, he or she fails, makes a mistake, or breaks something. "None of them feels that work per se is good," Percy explained, only a means to "idleness," which white people called "leisure." Whites, on the other hand, felt that work was good and idleness must be evil since it was pleasant. "I leave it to the wise," Percy wrote, "to say which is the more fruitful philosophy."[24]

Percy admitted that though he wrote about race as if he had "an innate and miraculous understanding" of blacks, "the sober fact is we understand one another not at all." "The barrier is of glass," he wrote of the divide between white and black; "you can't see it, you only strike it." He wrote that even the views of race about which white southerners were "certain" usually turned out not to be true. Race was an enigma, and just as one began to feel understanding, one ran into a wall of glass.[25]

Despite these gestures toward his own finitude, Percy still essentialized the "peculiarly Negroid" characteristics he perceived in black people. Two of the central weaknesses of blacks in the South were violence and thievery. But Percy portrayed them not so much as flaws as idiosyncrasies. "Negroes are as charming before as after a crime," he explained. "The gentle, devoted creature who is your baby's nurse can carve her boy-friend from ear to ear at midnight and by seven A.M. will be changing the baby's diaper while she sings 'Hear the Lambs a-calling.'" As such, white society did not treat black-on-black crimes seriously. For a knifing, for example, a white man would be charged with intent to kill, while a black man would be charged with assault. Lawyers like himself were at their wit's end "trying to deal justly with crimes committed by simple and affectionate people whose criminal acts do not seem to convert them into criminal characters."[26] Percy's writings about black vices suggest he did not view them as full moral agents. They were simply incapable of containing certain primal urges—another example of why they were not fit, and would not soon be fit, for white society. In another sense, Percy's anecdotes about black vice imply what he felt was their frustration at white values being imposed upon them; the "white plague" had corrupted their primitive morals, which were well-suited for island life but not for urban-industrial society.

Percy's views on race were halting, ambivalent, and often contradictory. But central to his thinking was a firm sense that black and white people were fundamentally different and ought to remain separate. They had played different roles in history, and white history—which Percy associated with repressive ethics, America, and consumerism—was not headed in a healthy direction. Fundamentalist morality, religious close-mindedness, rampant selfishness, and consequently unrest, discontent, and oppression were the result of that history. Black history, on the other hand, was removed from this, and Percy therefore wrote of "blackness" as essentially otherworldly: charming, at peace, sexually and emotionally free, unconcerned with productivity and advancement.

However, since American slaves were emancipated and "forced" to live in modern America, forced to join history, their charm and beauty had been corrupted. They were now murdering, thieving, and lying—though they could not be held responsible for those things. Charm remained, inefficiency and carelessness and naïveté remained, but these qualities would do them little good in the white man's world. Eventually, these qualities would be turned into vices because there would be no one to appreciate them. "It is not pleasant to make these bald and bitter statements," Percy wrote. "I make them because they are true and because I am afraid for the Negro. Only the truth can help him, and that can help him little unless he helps himself."[27]

And here was the truth, according to Percy: "I would say to the Negro: before demanding to be a white man socially and politically, learn to be a white man morally and intellectually—and to the white man: the black man is our brother, a younger brother, not adult, not disciplined, but tragic, pitiful, and lovable; act as his brother and be patient."[28]

PERCY HAD an elaborate articulation of white supremacy, but it was white supremacy nonetheless—a fact that was clearer to the sharecroppers on his plantation than to anyone. As Percy was discoursing upon race in the abstract, about 400 tenant farmers were growing cotton on Trail Lake, the 3,000-acre cotton plantation he inherited from his father. Percy was not an enterprising planter like his father and made no efforts to expand the business or acquire new land. His friend Hodding Carter later wrote: "He didn't know a thing about farming. In the springtime, instead of commenting on the weather or the condition of the land, he'd stand in a field and say that he liked the aroma of the freshly ploughed earth. When a manager or tenant pointed out a rich stand of cotton, Will would stray off to the cabin yard to look at the flowers he encouraged the tenant wives to plant."[29] As soon as Will Percy's adopted son LeRoy turned twenty-one—literally the day he returned from his post-college European vacation—Percy called him and the plantation managers into his office and said, "As of noon today, I no longer have any business connection with Tralake Planting Company.... My son LeRoy is boss and you are going to have to deal with him, and that's the end of that."[30]

Though Percy did not have any inclination toward farming or business, he did have an attachment to the family plantation (and its income). He felt a duty to retain the plantation upon his father's death, and when the institution of southern sharecropping came under attack in the 1930s, Percy came to its defense. That he did was somewhat anachronistic, since sharecropping was soon to be obsolete. Throughout the 1930s, writers, journalists, sociologists, intellectuals, and agricultural reformers together decried sharecropping as unjust, inhumane, inefficient, and backward.[31] Those who studied sharecropping in the thirties reported that these southern cotton farmers were mired in cycles of poverty that led to malnutrition, disease, illiteracy, substandard housing, lack of opportunity, and inescapable patterns of debt. Furthermore, government-based agriculture programs and trends within cotton production itself led to the redundancy of sharecroppers as cotton production became mechanized and moved westward. The 1930s were a watershed in the history of southern agriculture and the social makeup of the South; it was during this decade that the foundations for cotton monoculture, worked primarily by black laborers, crumbled. A central consequence of this agricultural shift was a demographic and economic reorganization of the South. The movement of many blacks out of the region, the diversification of the southern economy, the growth of urban centers, and the flowering of industry all worked to fundamentally reshape southern society. The Cotton Belt became the Sun Belt.[32]

The consensus among American intellectuals in the 1930s was that the South was unusually backward—primarily due to its race relations and labor arrangements. Of the states in the South, Mississippi became the chief example of these problems.[33] One study in the *American Mercury*, entitled "The Worst American State," compiled 106 tables representing various indicators

*Will Percy at Trail Lake Plantation, late 1930s (Courtesy of the Mississippi
Department of Archives and History, Jackson, Mississippi)*

of "progress and civilization" in each state, including per capita income, literacy rates, school enrollment, magazine circulation, death rates, medical
facilities, crime rates, government outlay for public services, and other fac-
tors.[34] In every category, Mississippi was at or near the bottom of the list.
Mississippians had the lowest spendable income, attended school the fewest days of the year, received the fewest newspapers, experienced the most
maternal deaths in childbirth, committed the most lynchings, and were sec-

ond only to South Carolina in the number of deaths from pellagra.[35] The rate of illiteracy in the United States was 4.3 percent, and in Mississippi it was 13.1 percent; the average annual teacher salary in the United States was $1,364, and in Mississippi it was $545; 29.5 percent of American farmers were tenants in 1931, while 68.3 percent of Mississippi's farmers were tenants.[36] These facts and others led the authors to conclude: "The Cotton Belt ... is the least advanced part of the United States, and of all the Cotton States Mississippi is the most unfortunate. ... [I]t seems to be without a serious rival to the lamentable preeminence of the Worst American State."[37]

And if Mississippi was the worst American state, the Mississippi Delta was the worst section of Mississippi. The Delta was, in Rupert Vance's words, "cotton obsessed, Negro obsessed, and flood ridden, it is the deepest South, the heart of Dixie." "Nowhere," he wrote, "are antebellum conditions so nearly preserved as in the Yazoo Delta."[38] In 1930 three out of four Delta residents were black, and nine out of ten blacks were tenant farmers.[39] Plantations were large and prosperous, and Delta land was the richest in the state, producing a crop value per acre of $42.96, compared to $15.60 for the rest of Mississippi.[40] Although the average Delta plantation in 1934 earned over $8,000 a year, the average tenant farmer's net cash income was just over $100.[41] Delta tenant farmers were on the whole malnourished, unsatisfied, desperately poor producers of a fickle crop that brought wealth to some and poverty to most involved with it. The Mississippi Delta, with its rich soil and wealthy planters such as the Percys, delivered a meager standard of living to its labor force. Many would have agreed with Buck Sims, an evicted tenant farmer, who concluded about white people: "Not for you to have nothin', that's what they really want."[42] There was little food, little cash, and little hope of things changing for sharecroppers in the Mississippi Delta in the 1930s.[43]

Percy's plantation, Trail Lake, largely bears this out. Trail Lake was a sprawling cotton plantation fifteen miles south of Leland, Mississippi, and five miles east of the Mississippi River. The majority of its acreage was cultivated in cotton, though corn, alfalfa, and vegetable gardens also grew in pockets. The rest of the land was uncleared hardwood stands of oak, cypress, gum, and pecan trees. Paved roads and drainage ditches crossed the plantation, and the fields were dotted with small green tenant houses. There was no "big house." LeRoy Percy had acquired the land in patches over time and never lived on it; there was no avenue of oaks, nor a vista of the distant river's banks; it was a plantation geared for production rather than leisure. There was a muddy slough that wandered onto the plantation, grew shallow and calm toward the middle of the property, and sat still and brown and lifeless save for hovering mosquitoes and gnats. This was Trail Lake, the namesake of the plantation and the habitation of mud-colored catfish occasionally pulled out by giddy plantation children and old men. But the dominant visual feature of Trail Lake, particularly if approached in late summer, would have been acres and acres of waist-high cotton, growing thick and green out of the dark earth. Scattered throughout the stands of cotton would be men and women, all of them black, wielding hoes and working to prevent the Johnson grass and crabgrass from choking out their livelihood. It would be hot and quiet save for the occasional rumbling past of the manager's truck.

Fortunately, abundant evidence is extant about the lives of Trail Lake sharecroppers. A sociologist, Raymond McClinton, lived on the plantation during 1936 and made a detailed study of it.[44] The plantation was 3,255.5 acres and was operated as a corporation called the Tralake Planting Company. The plantation was run by two managers, one of whom, McClinton noted, "tries to reason with his tenants and to develop in them a sense of responsibility and pride." The other manager "is more stern and forceful," and if his tenants disobey or antagonize him, "he will resort to force and violence." Both managers rarely consulted with Will Percy for day-to-day decisions. But Percy did set the policies of the plantation, hold conferences with the managers, sign all the checks, and visit Trail Lake a few times a year. McClinton felt that Percy "has a high sense of honesty, and being economically secure, he attempts to see that the tenants are given good treatment and honest settlements." The plantation also had a company store with $10,000 worth of stock, a gin, a blacksmith shop, a tool shop, a school, and three churches. A branch of a railroad called the Black Dog maintained a dilapidated but often-used depot there.[45]

The cotton on Trail Lake was grown solely by tenants. There were 150 tenant families totaling almost 600 people (nearly 200 of whom were children). The sharecroppers provided their labor and one-half of their fertilizer and received housing, land, fuel, tools, work stock, feed for the stock, seed, one-half of their fertilizer, and one-half of their cotton. The majority of the tenant families lived in homes in which only their immediate family resided, but twenty-five of the families resided with people other than immediate family—adopted children, grandchildren, in-laws, cousins, and nonrelatives who moved in and became a part of the economic household. Eighteen families had female heads who shouldered the responsibility of providing for the family and who secured the "furnish" from the company and made the settlements at the end of the year. But the majority of the families were composed of a husband, a wife, and almost always children.[46]

After the credit used during the year was subtracted from the sale of the Trail Lake tenants' cotton, their actual cash income averaged $378.66, which was above the Delta average. The year 1936 was better than average for the Great Depression, with cotton fetching an average of 12.33 cents a pound, and every tenant family on Trail Lake had cash in their pockets after the settlement. But that cash did not last long. Tenant farmers on Trail Lake did not save their money when they made it but spent it quickly and extravagantly. After settlement in 1936, celebrations began, and "the tenants attend[ed] the social gatherings in their nicest clothes of the latest styles." Tenants drove to town and bought new kid- and patent-leather shoes, new suits, and silk dresses; they went to the movies, to circuses, and to fairs, and some even traveled to Chicago, St. Louis, and Memphis. But the greatest desire among tenants was to purchase a car: after harvesting season, new- and used-car salesmen brought their cars to Trail Lake, and those who could afford cars bought them. There were thirty-six tenant-owned automobiles in 1936, and many of them were unlicensed and only used on the plantation; several of the families that did not have cows, hogs, or chickens did own cars, and they kept them in meticulous order. Some cash-laden tenants went to town and came home with radios, record players, iceboxes, and sewing machines. This consumerism suggests something of the widely held belief among black Mississippians that long-term economic opportunity was not available to them—cash, so rare in the cotton South, provided a momentary and pleasurable release from an otherwise grim situation.[47]

For the rest of the year, when cash was not on hand and credit at the store came in limited installments, tenant life was demanding and monotonous. Cultivation of cotton was arduous work, and time during the day not spent on cotton and corn was spent tending gardens, performing wage labor, and tending to livestock. Tenants lived in well-constructed and well-maintained homes that had wood stoves, fireplaces, water pumps, front porches, and screened windows and doors, although "some of [the tenants] cut holes in the doors and windows to throw out water and to let the cats enter the house." The homes averaged three rooms and five windows, and tenants tended to spend most of their time outside the houses, either working or resting on the porch. The screens and the clean water, combined with clean outhouses and readily available medical care, led to a low rate of disease on Trail Lake.

Malaria was almost nonexistent, and there was only one case of pellagra in 1936.[48]

Tenants spent their leisure in many different ways. Of the 150 families, 136 had gardens, many of which were flower gardens as well as vegetable gardens. Percy held a contest among the tenants for the best garden each year, and many of the tenants put a good deal of effort into their gardens. On days off, tenants went into nearby towns, watched local professional baseball games, and often traveled to see relatives. The most popular gathering spot for men on Saturday nights was the plantation store, where tenants would get together and drink bootleg whiskey, dance, and throw crap games until the sheriff came. And the sheriff often did come and disperse the tenants, some of whom, McClinton noted, "roam the turnpikes shouting and talking until day break." At home, many tenants read, and some debated current events. About 35 percent of the tenants regularly received local and state papers, farm journals, or religious or fraternal magazines. Several of the tenants took northern Negro papers such as the *Chicago Defender* and the *Pittsburgh Courier*, which were doubtless shared with others. They sat on their porch swings, told stories and read aloud, and chewed tobacco. A highlight of the year was Christmastime, when Percy would buy a Christmas tree and throw a Christmas party at which he gave out presents and drinks.[49]

Percy described one such visit in *Lanterns on the Levee*. On this occasion, Ford Atkins drove Percy out to Trail Lake. As they drove up to the crowd of farmers, Percy heard one of them ask, "Whose car is dat?," and another answered, "Dat's us car." Percy was not quite sure what to make of that, but he concluded sarcastically (and in retrospect): "how sweet it was to have the relation between landlord and tenant so close and affectionate that to them my car was their car. Warm inside, I passed through the crowd, glowing and bowing, the lord of manor among his faithful retainers."

Percy mentioned to Atkins on the way home how funny it was for the man to have mentioned that.

"Funnier than you think," Atkins said. Percy asked him to explain.

"He meant that's the car *you* has bought with *us* money. They all knew what he meant, but you didn't and they knew you didn't. They wuz laughing to theyselves."

Percy asked his managers a few days later if this was true, and they, laughing, said yes. "I laughed too," Percy recounted, "but not inside."[50]

That Percy included this story at all suggests a degree of open-mindedness on his part, an ironic stance toward his own authority and benevolence. But it also points to a recurring theme that Percy used to portray the "tragedy" of race relations in the South: black people did not trust white people. Percy, "glowing and bowing, the lord of the manor," portrayed himself as the most trustable white man in a society of untrustworthy whites—and the blacks did not trust even him. This was the tragedy: blacks were losing "their negro quality, care-free and foolish and innocent," in trying to participate in the white man's world; but they were also not acquiring the necessary characteristics to participate in that world because they did not trust those who could help them. "I want with all my heart to help him," Percy wrote. But that which Percy offered would "help him little unless he helps himself."[51]

The tenants, though, were trying to make the most of a bad situation that held little promise of improving. "Trusting" Percy very likely did not seem like it would change much about their situation. They did not accept his paternalism as simple and unwitting members of an inferior race; they accepted it with cunning and self-interest. It was nice to have free drinks at Christmas and screens on the doors and windows, and Trail Lake was a better place to live than many Delta plantations. They were active participants in their relationship with Percy; they demanded better conditions and often complained about various aspects of plantation life. They made their voices heard, although, as McClinton noted, "the landlord usually justifies their position by pointing out that there is no other enterprise in the capitalist system that will take a pauper and extend him several hundred dollars credit with no security except the promise of a crop if it is made." What negotiating leverage they lacked in their relationship with the landlord they attempted to make up for by creating lives for themselves within the limits of plantation life. They traveled, they bought cars, they chewed tobacco and listened to the radio, they read about the outside world, and on some Saturday nights, they got drunk and danced and gambled until morning.[52]

As they did, Percy was in his house in Greenville writing about them. He wrote about them, about his family, about the people and places that made up his world. He quit practicing law in 1937 and became a full-time father, gardener, traveler, and autobiographer. He began to have heart problems and chronic fatigue in addition to his high blood pressure and weak immune system. His declining health led to increasing bouts with depression and a sense of his own mortality. This mental state colored the pages of his final piece of writing, *Lanterns on the Levee: Recollections of a Planter's Son*, which would appear less than a year before his death.

15. THE AUTOBIOGRAPHER

I will indulge a heart beginning to be fretful by repeating to it the stories
it knows and loves of my own country and my own people.
—WILLIAM ALEXANDER PERCY, *Lanterns on the Levee*

In the spring of 1937, Percy was thinking about his flowers. The camellias were already in bloom, and so were the tulips and redbuds and azaleas. He was thinking about a summer trip to Sewanee, where he and Leon Koury, Tommy Shields, and Huger Jervey were to spend June and July. He was thinking about his body, which was not well. "For a month I have been sick," he wrote to Charlotte Gailor, "and I am still on a diet and puny."[1] He was also thinking about his life and whether he had a story to tell. He had begun drafting short autobiographical pieces—first a reminiscence of his college years at Sewanee, then essays on Samoa and race relations in the South. Now he wanted to fill in the rest. Telling his own story, though, proved to be a delicate act. He initially invited his readers to consider what was in the story as well as what was not. The first draft contained a dedication that he later removed:

> To Huger and Rufus,
> Bob, Tommy, and a few
> who have understanding heart and
> understanding head, who will read these lines
> and between them.[2]

Percy wrote his autobiography in an era when he could expect public recrimination and possibly censorship if he were to write fully about his life experience. He was writing a book that he knew his aunts and cousins and neighbors and business partners would read; he was also writing a book he knew Norman Douglas and Huger Jervey and Witter Bynner would read. His readership included a broad range of people, and he spoke to them in different ways. When he explained that he wanted to write the stories "of my own country and my own people," he was speaking about the whole of his experience, not just the South.[3] What emerged was a book in which a love of the South and a love of family stand alongside a celebration of Greek sexuality and a coded narration of sexual awakening. It is a book in which white supremacy and class prejudice stand alongside a refutation of other cultural values—namely religious fundamentalism, philistinism, and rigid sexual ethics—of the South he so loved. Percy's racist descriptions of black people stand alongside eroticized depictions of Ford Atkins. The book is one of contrasts, of deliberate omissions and careful inclusions. Percy likely felt that the omissions were necessary to protect himself and others; for example, Harold Bruff, Huger Jervey, Lindley Hubbell, Tommy Shields, and Leon Koury—several of the most important people in his life—appear only briefly. *Lanterns on the Levee* is remarkable for what Percy left out, and also for how much he said.

The tone of *Lanterns on the Levee* is elegiac and even mournful in parts. In other moments, it is funny, whimsical, and affirming. In many ways, the book reflects the period of Percy's life during which he wrote it. He had lived a full life, traveled across the world, held meaningful relationships, and had success as a poet and a mentor and a father. By the late 1930s, though, he held all this in his memory, but he also lived daily with sickness, a degree of financial uncertainty, and concern for his sons and the world they would live in. As he did during the lead-up to the First World War, he watched closely the events in Europe and worried about democracy. He wrote his autobiography over several years during which, in more ways than one, he was poised on the brink of the unknown. The book he wrote resonates both with these anxieties and with warmth; it resonates with a sense of foreboding as well as a celebration of life's fullness.

Shortly after his return from Sewanee in the late summer of 1937—a trip for which no evidence remains except a few snapshots of him and an unidentified man—he arranged to retire from his law practice and write full time. In early 1938, Percy sent Alfred A. Knopf four chapters he had written, and Knopf sent them out for reader's reports. One of the readers was Harold Strauss, who would become the primary editor for the project. Strauss wrote to Knopf about the "magnificent prose" and the way Percy came across as "a salty, unique individual, with strong notions but a great deal of warmth and kindliness." He noted that Percy was depressive and did not seem to want to "reveal a good deal about himself and his personal life." Their main task was "simply a matter of putting our wits together on how to handle Mr. Percy."[4]

Strauss met with a group of other readers to discuss the manuscript. Afterward, he told Knopf that they had agreed that the autobiography was

Will Percy and an unidentified friend, 1937, Sewanee, Tennessee (Courtesy of the archives, Jessie Ball duPont Library, University of the South, Sewanee, Tennessee)

excellent and should be published. "The big question," though, was "who is Percy, and why should he write an autobiography?" But Strauss felt he had a good sense of who Percy was and how he could pitch the project to the sales department in order to get "a really big advance sale." Strauss's explanation of "who" Percy was gives a good indication of the shaping of the reception of *Lanterns on the Levee*:

> I could of course give the answer myself: I could say Percy is a well-known Southerner, a lawyer who cares nothing for the law, but whose passions are life, poetry and war. I could say that his father was a senator from Mississippi and that Percy is the friend of almost every person of prominence in the South, and of many in the North. He is an aristocrat, and I could say that the reason that made him write and

we publish his autobiography is that it presents, through one man's struggles, a noble vision of a simple, satisfying, but fast-vanishing way of life—the way of the Southern aristocrat. This book transmutes to non-fiction the appeal of southern historical novels.

Even before the book was written, then, Percy's publisher had a marketing strategy for Percy's life story. The past, the South, the aristocracy—these were the features of Percy's life that made his story saleable. The particular South that Strauss had in mind—"simple, satisfying, but fast vanishing"— was an ideal type that was a proven seller, the 1930s having seen images of the South commodified and sold in record numbers. From *Gone With the Wind* to *So Red the Rose*, the opulent South of the distant past sold.[5]

Percy, during this time, had to get out of Mississippi. The latter half of the 1930s, when he was writing his autobiography, saw him in Samoa, Sewanee, New York, Arizona, New Mexico, Florida, Baltimore, and Brazil. As he traveled, he wrote about his life. At the El Tovar Hotel in the Grand Canyon, he cut out cigarettes, walked four miles a day, and wrote a chapter on sharecropping.[6] He wrote seven chapters at Fort Walton Beach, he told Charlotte Gailor, while "icicles hang from my ears." In writing his own story, though, he continually felt that it would have no appeal. "I can understand how anyone could write this stuff," Percy wrote to Gailor, "but I can't understand why anyone should read it—and they won't."[7] He had intimated the same feeling to Harold Strauss. Strauss replied: "You misapprehend entirely the degree of interest that your autobiography will arouse. As publishers we feel that it is so strong and honest and genuine as well as so beautifully written, that it cannot fail to attract wide attention."[8]

In addition to Percy's strengths as a writer, Strauss knew that he, as the book's editor, could shape its marketing in order for it to attract such attention. In his memo to Knopf, Strauss explained that while he believed he knew "who" Percy was, he nevertheless did not have the fame to introduce Percy to the world on a dust-jacket blurb. "I want it to have the stamp of authority," he explained. "I can make people … say it for me." He listed several literary figures, such as Carl Sandburg, Jonathan Daniels, Gerstle Mack, and Dorothy Thompson. "I want to make this book much talked about before it is ever published. … I want to see if I can make this promotion behave like an avalanche, gathering mass as it goes." The celebrities need not read the manuscript itself, he wrote, so long as they could write a 200-word blurb entitled "William Percy and what he stands for in the South."[9]

As Percy sent in new chapters of the book, Strauss encouraged him to give a "fuller portraiture" of life in the South and concentrate less on his abstract and philosophical musings. Strauss wrote to Knopf that the advent of World War II in 1939 had sent Percy "into an acute (although not morbid but philosophical) depression." The charm and narrative drive of his earlier chapters had given way to fatalistic ruminations and abstractions, chapters "concerned with death, religion, philosophy, etc., and they are the products of Percy's mental depression, and everything that an autobiography should not be." "This is the old trouble I have had with Percy," Strauss concluded. "I am sure that he will see the light, as he has before. What he needs now is to emerge from his mental depression."[10]

When Percy sent in a final draft in the summer of 1940, Strauss was elated. "It is a magnificent book, both distinguished and saleable," Strauss wrote to Knopf. "The static, essay-like material that once slowed up the book is now mostly gone." The only remaining problem was the chapter Percy had written on Samoa, which was "out of place" entirely in a book about the South. Strauss felt that it should certainly be eliminated, and after that the book would have "tremendous possibilities."[11]

After Percy submitted his draft, he continued to work on his revisions. He was increasingly worried about world affairs, feeling useless as war raged on in Europe. He tried to join the American army in some capacity. He went to New York in November and had lunch with Assistant Secretary of State Adolf Berle; but because of Percy's age and poor health, they had no place for him. He contacted the Canadian army and received the same response.[12] While in New York, he discovered that Lindley Hubbell was on the verge of a nervous breakdown, so Percy "shipped him off to Puerto Rico." He wrote to Charlotte Gailor: "I'm getting right fed up with neurotics."[13] It seemed to him as though the world was making people go mad, including his friends. He could only help on a small scale by helping the people he loved. But on a large scale, he was not needed. "Being on the outside," he explained to Sinclair Lewis's son Wells, "inactive, inefficient and unneeded in this sort of world is enough to drive one completely nuts."[14]

Strauss and Knopf went to work preparing the book for publication. They had a designer come up with a dust jacket they felt was perfectly suited for a book about the South. The cover had a picture of a stately and columned white mansion with a smaller quarters just off to the side. Lit by a sunset over the Mississippi River, live oaks and Spanish moss graced the mansion's grounds. Lanterns burned faintly in the distance along a levee and the river. When they sent the book to Percy, he wrote to Charlotte Gailor and begged her to come up with a different sketch—perhaps a silhouette of a levee guard figure walking along a levee with a lantern. Anything but this, he said: "I think the book itself is pretty good looking, but the cover struck me as horrible and in the most ghastly magnolia tradition as conceived by a Yankee."[15] The magnolia tradition, though, was a big seller. Knopf took out a large ad in the *New York Times* that asked readers in bold letters: "Is the Old South Really Gone with the Wind?" No, the ad promised, it lives on in *Lanterns on the Levee*, written by a man who "is the Old South, living and incarnate."[16]

The book that Percy wrote, which came out in March 1941, was a bit more complicated than merely an evocation of the Old South. Percy's rendering of his own life story did, however, offer enough folksy reminiscence of his family history in Mississippi to please readers looking for such things. His descriptions of his black nursemaid, Nain, his black childhood playmates, and his Confederate kin, for example, were enough to justify many readers' understanding of the book as a nostalgic paean to the South. (Walker Percy aptly described this type of reader, who "comes bearing down at full charge, waving *Lanterns on the Levee* like a battle flag. 'He is right! The Old South was right!'")[17] And these reminiscences were not disingenuous; Percy did love the South, and he was proud of his family name and his ancestors' considerable role in southern history. His writings on race likely did not unsettle his many white readers who lived in the Jim Crow South. Those who wanted to find in *Lanterns on the Levee* a vindication of what they called "the southern way of life" could do so. But they would have to ignore some things.

As we have already seen, *Lanterns on the Levee* offers a coded narration of Percy's sexual awakening in Sewanee, an affirming description of Greek "bisexuality," and homoerotic descriptions of men. Percy portrays himself as queer in terms of gender: he is small, effeminate, and artistic, but he is also resolute, sacrificial, and a fighter. He portrays other southerners as at times small-minded, mean-spirited, and pathetic in their devotion to the South. "You will find in any southern town," he jokes, "a statue in memory of the Confederate dead, erected by the Daughters of something or other, and made, the townsfolk will respectfully tell you, in Italy." These statues always have at the top "a little man with a big hat holding a gun."[18] It is easy to imagine Percy at a café in Florence describing such statues to an incredulous Norman Douglas, or in a Manhattan apartment laughing with Huger Jervey and Malvina Hoffman. Such moments in Percy's memoir speak to his ironic distance from the South yet also of his intimate knowledge of it.

Indeed, any understanding of *Lanterns on the Levee* must seek a reading of the book that includes the whole tapestry of Percy's meanings and attachments. His love of the South and his immersion in its culture stand alongside his rejection of many of its central values. It is a story of a person very much grounded in the *local*—the local history of a small town, a family, a region. It is also a story of a person very much influenced by ideas and people and experiences across the world. The places and peoples Percy experienced in his life—their cultures, their values, their attitudes—resonate in the pages of his writing. It is a story that is at once melancholic and deeply hopeful. Percy opens the book promising to tell the story of "a heart beginning to be fretful" and a world "crashing to bits." He ends it on a different note: "I have seen the goodness of men and the beauty of things. I have no regrets. I am not contrite. I am grateful."[19]

The final chapters of the book serve as Percy's most deliberate expression of the themes and memories he most treasured. Among the most expressive chapters of *Lanterns on the Levee* is "Jackdaw in the Garden." In this chapter, Percy assumes the role of a jackdaw, which is a type of crow that is noted for its quiet watchfulness. He describes a bench that Tommy Shields made for him and imagines himself sitting on it, a jackdaw looking out onto his garden. His garden, he implies, is a metaphor for his own struggle to flourish in a difficult environment. "The major moral afforded by a garden," Percy writes, "comes from watching the fight for sunlight waged by those unhappy things rooted against their will in the shade."[20] The lilacs, for example, would prefer another climate, farther north: "They will exist if I take enough pains with them, but they are not happy and the meagerness of their bloom betrays their incurable nostalgia. The heart too has its climate, without which it is a mere pumping-station."[21] Percy portrays the aridity of Mississippi, the dryness of life, and his own efforts to reach for sunlight in spite of his rootedness in local soil. His shade plants "thrust emaciated feelers, gangling and scant of leaf, toward a spot of light. To escape the deeper shadow they twist themselves into ungainliness. Branches die so that the remnant whole may survive. They are bleached as by a sickroom." In the same way, such was life in Mississippi: "Standing at the post-office corner I recognize my poor sunless plants in the passers-by, sickly, out of shape, ugly with strain, who still search for a sunlight vital to their needs and never found, or found and lost."[22] The climate in Mississippi was not the climate for Will Percy's heart.

However, it was his climate, the one in which he endured throughout his life. He loved it, he hated it, he missed it when he was gone—it was his home. He could neither change that nor ask for sympathy. When he looks at the native plants, he realizes that, like him, "they don't need coddling: they are so glad of life they fight for it. After all, strength is one of the primary colors." It is resilience, he feels, occasional flourishes of beauty, that characterize their existence, and his own.

Having set up this guiding metaphor, Percy describes another reward of a garden. "It's a closed and quiet place, the best sort of Ivory Tower," he tells us. "It's a starting point for thoughts and backward looks and questionings. ... You sit there and think of the trip you have made, fifty-five years of trip, and you wonder what it totals up to."[23] As such, he sets out to reminisce about his own life, its meaning, its occasional triumphs, and its constant struggle. Percy decides that rather than chronicle the sadness and the failures, he will write about the treasures in his heart. In a book otherwise marked by ambivalence, vacillation between restlessness and humor, foreboding and nostalgia, he attempts in this section to record instances that represent his fullest experiences: "what was mine to possess utterly and sovereignly, without counterclaim ... the jackdaw pickings of my curious and secret heart." "Now is the time," he writes, "to spread my treasure out." For the remainder of the chapter, Percy tells of what, when he looks like a jackdaw into his own heart, he finds of value.

Percy's reminiscences have several repeating themes. Moments of love between two people, moments of understanding, and moments of self-fulfillment take place across the world—in Mississippi, Spain, Greece, Turkey, Capri, Taormina, and France and on sea vessels approaching Bora Bora and Rio de Janeiro. In each instance, Percy casts himself with another man or a group of men. Percy's expression of his homoerotic desire, his portrayal of those he was able to "love and understand," is carefully yet lovingly crafted. This was Percy's struggle, and likely the struggle of many with queer desire in the South: how to both express this love honestly and articulate it in a way that would not end in public humiliation. Such was the dilemma throughout his life. The struggle, Percy writes, "has all been good and worth the tears. I see it as a dream I long to hold, but not to relive. I hear voices unbelievably soft (whose are they, was it in Rio or Barcelona or the islands? No matter) that murmur: 'Don't go, don't leave me, I love you,' and I smile, knowing I will hear them no more and grateful for their music." In a series of vignettes, he lays his treasure out "for the mere delight of recalling."[24]

Percy's first portrayal is of Tommy Shields. He is a "real gardener," Percy writes. "Tom in April always has the air of the Lord God after he did it in seven days." After Percy asserts that "half a century is a long time, specially in a world as lovely as ours, as starred with brave and pitiful people with honey at their hearts and on their lips," his first memory is of Shields: "I'll think of

Tom in the hot summer evenings watering his roses and dousing the screaming children as they tip up behind him." He then tells of walking through a
garden, "slowly with one you love and understand (as understanding goes
between us mortals)." As Percy and his companion, who is not named, stand
in awe of the beauty around them, Percy's companion says, "'[A]nd some
people say there is no God.'" As with all of Percy's writing about intimate
relationships, he portrays this love as spiritual. Mutuality, communication,
connectedness—these things call forth the presence of God, or at least the
possibility of God's presence.[25]

Another of Percy's vignettes takes place on the deck of a ship approaching
Rio de Janeiro on a moonlit night. It is dark and silent, otherworldly: "Our
ship receded from reality, became a tiny world abandoned to itself." Though
ostensibly headed for Brazil, in this imagining the ship becomes both place-
less and without destination, for "despite the appeasing pathos of the moon,
it seemed a lonely world, forgotten and adrift, pursuing some mysterious
course that might not count a port." Percy is watching the crew, an exoti-
cised, all-male, working-class group of men from Portugal, Samoa, Finland,
America, and Greece. In this detached but sexually charged setting, the men
take on an ethereal beauty: "I watched them moving like somnambulists, the
wind whipping their hair, the moonlight turning their bodies slender and
unsubstantial, daubing their cheek-bones and shoulders, the arch of their
chests or their buttocks with pallor, and a stillness was on them. They came
on deck from the hatches in a sudden glory of light. ... They came in all
manner of garbs, in work clothes or stripped to the waist; mostly they came
alone and kept to themselves." The men sit on the deck in silence as the
wind muffles the occasional song or comment. Though the men are beautiful, Percy ascribes to them prescience of human limitation and the reality
of pain. As they stand shrouded in moonlight, they gaze into the unending
ocean. Percy suggests that they may have been thinking of many things, but
likely they "were thinking each of the same thing. ... The patience of loneliness and the tranquility of unescapable pain were on their faces like grave
beauty. I thought of a lost chart and an unknown port, and I too looked to
the sea." The sea, the distant horizon, the endless night—these things suggest unlimited possibility. Unlimited possibility, like the destination of a
ship bound for nowhere, was not a reality in Percy's world. But in another
moment of reclamation, Percy offers hope. As he and the sailors gaze out into
the expanse, the night watchman clangs his bell to sound the hour and yells
to the captain, "in a voice piercingly young and full of hope, 'The lights are
bright, sir!'"[26]

This note, accommodating of both the pain and the pathos of being alive, is the one on which Percy ends the book. The final chapter takes place in the Greenville cemetery. "I come here not infrequently," Percy writes, "because it is restful and comforting. I am with my own people." He describes the peace of the cemetery with its death and cedar trees and mockingbirds, who "append arpeggios and cadenzas to pitiful unreassuring funeral sermons." He describes the graves of the people he had loved: his mother, father, and younger brother; his aunts and uncles and grandparents; his teachers and friends and lovers. To his family plot, he writes, "I should like to bring from that far corner where the poor sleep well one brown-eyed lad who sleeps along there, for he had loved me and gaspingly had told me so while death was choking him." He writes of his enemies and the people he had hated, and, he says, "I find myself smiling. ... I know their stories, but not their hearts." Standing in the cemetery, which reduces all people alike to piles of dust, "Understanding breaks over my heart and I know that the wickedness and the failures of men are nothing and their valor and pathos and effort everything."[27]

Of his own life—"one tiny life with darkness before and after, and it at best a riddle and a wonder"—he declares that he had searched for God and for beauty and for decency, and in the end, his search had been a tarnished one. He had loved himself too much, he admits, and had come up short as a citizen, a teacher, a lawyer, and a poet. It had not been in success that his search had meaning, but in sincerity. He imagines himself on the other side of death, stumbling toward God along with the rest of humankind. When he arrives at the foot of God, God asks him, "Who are you?" Percy ends his story with his answer: "The pilgrim I know should be able to straighten his shoulders, to stand his tallest, and to answer defiantly, 'I am your son.'"[28]

PEOPLE FLOCKED to the stores to buy *Lanterns on the Levee*. By the end of the year, the book had sold over 20,000 copies. Alfred Knopf wrote to tell Percy that a first book of any kind almost never sold that well.[29] Within a month of its issuance, Percy received almost 300 pieces of fan mail—all of which he responded to.[30] Percy was excited and surprised by the success of his autobiography. "I am amazed that people down here seem to like the book so much," he wrote self-deprecatingly to Knopf, "and frankly I am puzzled when I try to analyze what makes them like it."[31]

Lanterns on the Levee drew a range of responses from readers. The most common portrayal of the book was glowing praise for its portrayal of what one reviewer called "the distinctive quality of southern civilization."[32] Will

Percy had accurately articulated "the viewpoint of a Mississippian," readers felt, and "his life has exemplified perfectly the southern aristocratic tradition at its best."[33] The South was "personified by Mr. Percy," according to another reviewer, and in his book, "the traditions of the Old South lend grace to the new aristocracy."[34] Another writer gushed forth the images that made Percy's book so uniquely southern: "From such memories as when cotton was king; darkies singing in the moonlight on the levee; and the arrival of a steamboat on the Mississippi, the author has presented a moving account of his life in the Delta region."[35] In the book itself, there are no "darkies" singing on the levees; and Percy had very little to say about the time when cotton was king. In many ways, it seems as though readers read the book through the lens of the dust jacket—it was about mansions and slaves, live oaks and dusky southern evenings. And these were just the northern reviews.

In the South, reviews were yet more effusive. In Knoxville, the reviewer wrote that *Lanterns on the Levee* should "make every southerner proud," while the *Nashville Banner* declared that the book will "click with Southerners as readily as fried chicken and apple dumpling."[36] The review in the *Dallas Morning Herald* was entitled "Charming Tale of Old South Is Well Told" and promised readers the book was "definitely, graciously Southern, deep Southern."[37] The piece in the *Richmond Times-Dispatch* began: "Here at long but happy last is a real book about the South by a real Southerner."[38]

Percy, who did not think of himself as a very typical southerner, was amused by this. That the book had become a best seller, largely on its appeal as a quintessentially "southern" book, vexed him. He was surprised by the reviews, most of which seemed to misunderstand him, he believed, and "mostly want to make me appear as a professional southerner or professional aristocrat."[39] It seemed to Percy that readers, both in the South and elsewhere, wanted a book that embodied "the South." He received letters from Oregon and California, China and Honolulu, and even from a descendent of Harriet Beecher Stowe, thanking him for writing so evocatively about the South. This all seemed "very queer," Percy wrote to Knopf. "Apparently Southerners think it speaks the truth for them. I'm still quite confused."[40]

Local Mississippi newspapers, which carried reviews by writers who knew Will Percy, were more nuanced. In the *Jackson Daily News*, the reporter who covered LeRoy Percy's 1910–11 senate campaign and who had met Will Percy in the fall of 1910 in the Percy home, reviewed *Lanterns on the Levee*. He used the occasion to retell the story of meeting Will Percy, "shy, tender, timid … effeminate," so many years ago. He recounted how Mississippians tended to think of him as a "sissy," and how even his father thought him "the queerest chicken." In a regular trope among Mississippians who knew Will Percy and felt compelled to protect him, the reviewer spent much of the review defending Percy's manhood. He recounted Will Percy's many battles—World War I, the Ku Klux Klan, the 1927 flood—as evidence of his valor. Each of his paragraphs began with a litany of gendered praise: "You can hardly call a man a sissy who . . ." "There was not much that is sissy in the heart of the lad who . . ." "No sissy was a chap, who . . ." "Not much of a sissy . . ." "Far from being a sissy . . ." In Mississippi, on the local level, Will Percy was a more complex figure; rather than merely a symbol of the Old South, he was a man who needed some explaining.[41] The reviews of *Lanterns on the Levee* in Mississippi suggest the contours of the open secret of Percy's sexuality. Mississippians knew he was a "sissy"—and they knew what that meant—but Percy's status as an aristocrat, war hero, and flood fighter protected him to a degree. His effeminacy and queerness was offset by his strong, practical civic contributions. The structure of the *Jackson Daily News* review—written to prove Percy's manhood while calling attention to his queerness—is a compelling illustration of the ways Mississippians accommodated and spoke about homosexuality.

Lanterns on the Levee was not universally praised. The *Journal of Negro Education* pointed out the conceits and condescension in Percy's view of race: "Negroes," wrote the reviewer, "now that they are trying to live like free men, have lost their fine qualities and alas are doomed."[42] Writing in *The Nation*, Charles Curtis Munz read the book as evidence that the South was "the nation's intellectual problem No. 1," and he characterized Percy's view of race as, "Struggle on, Black Brother, be obedient, tip your hat to your betters, and in a thousand years or so maybe you will be as good and as smart as I am now, and then possibly you can have the vote and a berth in the Pullman car." This was obviously, Munz concluded, "hollow nonsense."[43] Percy wrote to Knopf about the "pretty magnificent ... blast of *The Nation*" and suggested that the next advertisement for the book "should show on one side the excoriations and on the other the hyperboles of some of the Southern papers. It's very amusing."[44]

Percy's enjoyment of—and consternation with—his book's reception was compromised by the fact that Tommy Shields lay dying in the spring of 1941. Percy spent hours of every day that spring at his bedside. Percy told a friend that Shields's illness "depressed me" greatly and that often he did not feel up to charting the progress of *Lanterns*.[45] He apologized to Charlotte Gailor, saying: "I haven't had the heart to write. Tommy Shields is in the hospital fatally and hopelessly ill with a brain tumor. He is terribly pitiful to see, though suf-

Will Percy in author publicity photograph for Lanterns on the Levee,
*ca. 1941 (Courtesy of the Mississippi Department of Archives and
History, Jackson, Mississippi)*

fering less pain than might have been expected. As I can think of little except
his condition and the war, I'm not able to work up much pep. ... I can't be
away from the hospital even for a day."[46] When Shields had a lucid moment,
he would cry out for Percy. One friend remembered that Percy often did not
leave his bedside for days at a time during Shields's last six weeks. When
asked why he spent so much time at the hospital despite Tommy's comatose
condition, he replied, "Tommy needs me." When Shields finally died, Percy
had him buried in the family plot at the Greenville cemetery.[47]

Tommy Shields is likely to remain something of a mystery in Percy's story
because there is almost no evidence about him. The fragments that survive
suggest that for over twenty-five years, Percy and Shields were extraordinarily close. They traveled together and shared in one another's suffering,

and Shields lived in Percy's house for at least one year, if not more. Their remains lie close to one another in the Greenville cemetery. But how they spoke to each another, the structure and significance of their relationship, its meanings and pleasures, we will never fully know. Like so much of Percy's story, the historical record remains silent.

Percy spent the rest of his days in the spring of 1941 tending his garden, in which the pear trees and redbuds were in full bloom, and reading volumes of mail. For two weeks in February, he went to Charleston to take care of Huger Jervey, who was sick.[48] He wrote to Charlotte Gailor that "my garden is a wreck," and he was constantly demanding that she visit and help him make decisions. ("Now to the point," he chided her. "If you don't come by here, you are a perfect what-not. I am in desperate need of expert advice.")[49] She came for a visit and consulted with him about his wrecked camellias, jonquils, and tulips. He tried to urge her to come again to help with another problem: "Mr. Knopf is coming by for the weekend and I don't know what in the world to do with him."[50]

Despite brief trips to New York and to Lee, Massachusetts, for the Berkshire Music Festival, Percy spent most of the summer and fall at Brinkwood. One evening, Percy and his son Walker went to dinner at Charlotte Gailor's house, where there would be a group of young people who all wanted to meet Percy. The dinner party included talk about books and politics, the war, and the amazing success of *Lanterns on the Levee*. Percy loved to talk to young people, and at some point a "sculptor-poet" asked him a question; as Percy was responding, he could not get any words to come out of his mouth. He tried to speak but could not remember words. He tried again, and a stream of mumbled phrases came out. He was terrified; he grabbed Walker's arm and insisted he take him home. Walker, who had just finished medical school, recognized this condition as aphasia, in which a series of strokes in the brain damage speech patterns and memory. The next morning, a doctor came to Brinkwood, and he determined that Percy's blood pressure was a frightening 280 over 150.[51]

Walker and Will Percy boarded a train and traveled to Johns Hopkins Hospital in Baltimore to see a specialist. The doctors told him he had the oldest-looking body of anyone they had ever seen at his age. He was suffering from malignant hypertension and acute exhaustion—conditions that had been developing intensely for the past five years but gradually over his entire adulthood. He wrote to Charlotte Gailor and apologized for leaving abruptly with no explanation, but "imagine not being able to talk!" He had been deeply troubled by the experience. The doctors could do nothing for him and advised rest and quiet.[52]

Percy returned to Greenville, where he kept to bed. He emerged only occasionally to visit with people. He sometimes looked at Phinizy, befuddled, not able to remember his name. He wrote to Charlotte Gailor that he felt "like hell" and that "the world is falling to pieces in the middle of a headache."[53] His sons remembered him emerging from his room on December 7, 1941, to express his delight at the United States' entry into the war. Roy Percy recalled that "he was gung-ho and raring to go, ready to go again."[54]

In January 1942 Percy entered the hospital with intestinal hemorrhaging. He lay in bed for two weeks at King's Daughters Hospital before dying in his sleep on January 21, 1942. The next day, the funeral was held at his home. His sons had difficulty finding a pastor in Greenville who would perform a funeral for a nonbeliever. A Catholic priest finally agreed to do so. He delivered a funeral oration that lasted forty-five seconds, and he never took his overcoat off.[55]

ON THE DAY of Percy's funeral, the Greenville city hall and courthouse closed, and flags in the city flew at half-mast. Tommy Shields's brother Arnold was one of Percy's pallbearers, and they buried him in the cemetery next to his parents, not far from his grandparents, his little brother, and Tommy Shields. Percy's three sons were distraught. Phinizy later recalled: "I felt cut adrift. The anchor was gone. . . . I couldn't believe it." Even forty years later, he said in an interview that "every time I think about it it's extremely painful."[56]

In his life, Will Percy was to his family and his neighbors a loving and kindhearted, if mysterious, person. In his death, these same people replaced the mystery—the queerness, the effeminacy, the foreignness—with a more sanctioned memory: Percy represented the best of the South, the best of the old aristocracy, the best of Greenville. They did not want the things about which they spoke privately to be part of his heritage. The local paper's obituary cataloged his virtues and his talents and called attention to his service to his people. "It was as a civic leader and a humanitarian," it read, "that Mr. Percy will longest be remembered by those who knew him best." The paper's editor, Hodding Carter, described his heartbreak over Percy's death: "I loved Will Percy for every reason that any of our numbered legion could have had: for the greatness of his spirit, the goodness of his heart, the courage that shone in his eyes and spurred his frail body, the honesty, the tenderness, the full catalogue of virtues that made him one of God's few saints."[57]

Roy, Walker, and Phinizy inherited Will Percy's wealth—he left them about a million dollars, as well as the Percy home, the Percy plantation, and Brinkwood—and an unspoken responsibility to preserve his memory. Roy Percy lived in the Percy home for a few years after Will Percy's death but sold the house when it became too expensive to maintain. When he did, the three brothers divided up Percy's belongings—his library, his art, his furniture—and moved his many boxes of letters, diaries, and personal papers to a building on the Percy plantation, where they sat untouched for almost forty years. The house passed through several owners until 1969, when it was demolished. Its last owner had been the Greenville Church of Christ, which held worship services in the living room.[58] All that remains today of Will Percy's house is a portion of the brick wall that once surrounded the garden. The rest of the lot has been developed into an apartment complex, a rent-subsidized housing project intended to assist low-income families, which in Greenville are primarily African American.

EPILOGUE

On Sex, History, and Trespassing

Sewanee, Tennessee, 2005

All biography is trespassing. To tell a life story requires breaking into a person's innermost thoughts, into their diary, into the secret spaces of their past.

All biography is also autobiography. The story one tells about someone else's life is shaped by one's own predilections and preferences.

These two thoughts strike me most explicitly as I think of myself standing, uninvited, in Will Percy's attic during the winter of 2005.

At the time, I was doing the research for this book, and I took a trip to the archives at the University of the South in Sewanee, Tennessee. An academic history conference happened to be meeting at Sewanee at the same time, and the conference organizers offered a guided tour of Brinkwood. I went on the tour. The property sits on a cliff overlooking a valley studded with pine trees and pin oaks. We toured the gardens, looked out across the long vista, talked about Brinkwood's many visitors. When the group prepared to leave, I explained to the leader I was going to hang back and take some pictures.

I felt strangely mesmerized by the place. To occupy the same space as historical figures whose mail you have read is intoxicating. Furthermore, Percy was, and to some degree remains, a mystery to me. What did his voice sound like? What sorts of conversations did he have at Brinkwood? Did he bring lovers here? Did he find peace?

I decided to sit on the porch. To sit where he sat, to see what he saw—these are certainly the imaginative ambitions of the biographer. The door of the screen porch was open, so I walked in and sat on the rocking chair overlooking the long lawn that led to the cliffs. I sat and tried to imagine what it was like for Percy to see what I was seeing. But I was conscious of myself as a subject—a legal subject, if nothing else, committing an illegal act. My misdeeds were getting in the way of my imaginative project.

So I decided to try the door. I was already trespassing. Perhaps breaking and entering would transform mild self-consciousness into real historical

Brinkwood, Percy's house in Sewanee, Tennessee (Photograph by the author)

imagination. I tried the door from the porch, and it was locked. I breathed a sigh of relief. I had never broken into anyone's house before, living or dead.

I walked back into the garden, took a few more pictures. There was a breeze coming up from the valley, and the air was thin and dry. As I began to walk away, I saw another door by the driveway. When I tried it, the door opened and led into the kitchen, which had been renovated—it had linoleum floors and a microwave. But walking through the house, it was clear that much of it had not been changed. The walls were plastered. The light switches were buttons on the wall. The floors were wide and worn and warped. There was a chandelier in the dining room hanging from the ceiling with no light bulbs, only candleholders. I walked through the house, filtering each room in the present into the past of my imagination. A large stone fireplace connected the living room with the master bedroom, and I imagined Huger Jervey building a fire; I imagined an eighteen-year-old Leon Koury lying on the couch, bored; Will Percy was in an armchair reading and smoking a cigarette.

The imagination, though, is less than reliable. I needed letters. What if there was a trunk in the attic? I headed upstairs. Of course, I told myself as I walked up the stairs, I couldn't just steal the letters if there were any; but I could surely make friends with the property owner later and work my way back into the attic, knowing what I'd find. The second floor was cramped.

The walls angled with the roof. The attic turned out to be bare—no trunks, no letters. Only studs and insulation and plywood and, beyond that, shingles and the air outside.

In retrospect, I see myself standing in Percy's attic in that moment, and I find it both ridiculous and sublime. The ridiculous part, of course, is that I had no business being in someone else's attic. (I have since met the property owner and confessed my trespass. She graciously forgave me and invited me back to Brinkwood.) And I had no good reason to suspect that, sixty years and three owners later, Brinkwood's attic would contain a trunk full of letters. On the other hand, this instance was a physical manifestation of the trespass that is writing biography: I had broken into the man's home, made my way into his attic—I had entered the space of his life. My body occupied the same place as his once had. In writing this book, I have tried to enter his world in my imagination, tried to understand and recreate his motivations and his feelings and his beliefs. This is nothing if not trespassing, and the story is one of my own making, not his.

Nonetheless, throughout this book, I have tried to tell a story that can be documented with verifiable, archival evidence. Where I have made conjecture and interpretations, I have done so in a way I believe is fair to the evidence. But there is good reason to think that the evidence in the archive tells us only part of Percy's story. This is true of all history, of course—letters are thrown away, diaries get lost, records of whole lives lay silent and dusty in boxes in attics and basements. Only a fraction of historical evidence about any subject is preserved in archives. The stories we tell about the past are always incomplete.

But Percy's archive is even less complete than it should be. In the late 1970s, when the executor of Percy's estate—Percy's adopted son Roy, in consultation with his brothers Walker and Phinizy—donated the Percy Papers to the state archives, he took a good deal out. Phinizy told an interviewer that Roy "was going to do some screening" before they donated the papers. "I kept about as much as I gave," Roy told another interviewer later.[1] It is left to our imaginations to guess his reasons for doing this or the nature of the evidence that may or may not still be in a box, or a safe, in Greenville.[2]

Knowing as we do that there is missing evidence, we can only speculate about what the family removed and the significance of this for Percy's story.[3] My feeling is that Percy's heirs removed materials that seemed to threaten their view of him as a loving father and role model. Percy was to them a paragon of self-sacrifice and kindness—he took them in when he did not have to; he worried about them and counseled them and provided for them.

In Phinizy's case, he was a constant and loving presence in his hour of need. "He was like Christ," Phinizy said. "He was the most extraordinary man I have ever known," Walker said. They wanted to protect him. They wanted a particular kind of story to be told about him.[4]

We do not know what is missing from Percy's archives, but there is a pattern to the gaps in the record. Some of the most important people in Percy's life are almost completely absent from Percy's papers: Huger Jervey, Sinkler Manning, Lindley Hubbell, Tommy Shields, Norman Douglas, Harry Stack Sullivan, Witter Bynner, Leon Koury, and Gerstle Mack. (Most of what I have written about these men in this book comes out of evidence in other archives and in secondary sources.)[5] Percy was, of course, a prolific correspondent, and he also kept his letters. There are thousands of letters in his papers—from Janet Dana Longcope, from editors and clients and readers and friends. Harold Bruff's letters suggested that he kept his intimate correspondence. But the absence of substantial evidence from these men, most of whom self-identified as queer, is striking. It suggests that the story the handlers of Percy's estate had in mind when they gave his papers to the world need not include sex. It suggests that "loving father" and "homosexual" was an incongruity his family could not reconcile. One could not be a role model and a gay man, a war hero and a gay man, a Percy and a gay man. So they vetted the papers to ensure his story fit their hopes for his official memory.

But did they have a point? Shouldn't someone's private life remain private? Shouldn't we not be so concerned about what happened behind closed doors? Isn't that too much of a trespass?

I would argue that the answer to each of these questions is no. The purpose of biography is to find out what was important to historical people, to listen to them, to look around both the public and private spaces of their lives, to learn about their quarrels with the world—and to explain them within their context. Will Percy's quarrels had a great deal to do with sexual desire and its relationship to morality, pleasure, God, beauty, and art, among other things. Throughout his poetry, his correspondence, and his prose, we see him consistently asking the same questions: What does it mean to live a virtuous life? What is good and beautiful? What is the relationship between God and man? And in all these things, where do earthly pleasures—the pleasures of the body, the ecstasy of sex and romantic love—fit in? Sex to Percy was not merely a private matter; it was one about which he wrote publicly. It was an ethical matter, a social matter, and a historical matter.

As such, Percy's life story suggests a few broader conclusions and speculations. First, Percy's story lends credence to the recent efforts of historians to reveal and explain the ways queer men in early twentieth-century America were not merely closeted, self-loathing, lonely people. George Chauncey in particular has called into question what he calls the myths of isolation, invisibility, and internalization, whereby gay men could neither meet nor recognize one another, and whereby they internalized social prejudices against homosexuality. In contrast, he finds queer networks, subcultures, meeting places, and cultural expressions in an era that was also hostile toward queer sexuality.[6] In much the same way, Percy's life suggests that he was not a closeted gay man who was alone in Mississippi and who was, in Richard King's words, "unable to express openly his essential sexual desires."[7] Rather, he had many queer friends and relationships. He had ways of recognizing and communicating with other queer folks, and they with him. Without minimizing the real difficulties he faced, the considerable pressures he was under, we should consider the ways he worked against the prevailing attitudes of his day.

Second, Percy's biography provides the beginnings of a history of the queer subculture in Mississippi in the first half of the twentieth century. There is much work left to be done—a biography can only explain so much—but Percy's story suggests that much of what John Howard found for the middle decades of the twentieth century also holds true for its early decades: there was a queer subculture in the South in which queer southerners noticed one another, kept in touch with one another, and created space in which to meet, pair off, have sex, and share religion, conversation, consolation, frustration, and comfort. In Percy's case, evidence suggests that his relationships may have crossed social lines of race and class. It seems that many people in Greenville, Mississippi, knew about this—a regime Howard rightly describes as "quiet accommodation." Uncovering this history continues the work of debunking the myth that Donna Jo Smith describes as "particularly southern *and* queer ... that it's harder to be queer in the South than in the rest of the nation."[8]

Third, there has been a tendency among those who have written about Percy to focus on his sadness, his melancholy. On the one hand, this approach is supported by solid facts. Percy experienced a lot of sadness. He had the sadness of a sensitive and reflective person who looked curiously onto the world and tried to find meaning in it. He had the sadness of a person for whom tragedy came at regular intervals: he lost his brother at age seventeen; his lover at twenty-six; his Uncle Walker and friend Sinkler Manning at thirty; his mother, father, and cousin LeRoy at forty-four; Mattie Sue Percy at forty-six; and Tommy Shields at fifty-five. Percy's sexuality was a source of deep pleasure and meaningful relationships to him, but he also lived among people in whose minds and values and laws homosexuality was a punishable offense, a crime against nature. He worked against this grain, but it was not easy.

On the other hand, though, I think this focus on Percy's melancholy reflects two things. First, it reflects the prominence of *Lanterns on the Levee* as evidence for Percy's life story. Percy's memoir has a decidedly more elegiac and somber tone than his correspondence throughout his life. Most people read *Lanterns on the Levee* and not his letters, and this reading emphasizes his perspective during the last years of his life, when he was depressive and physically sick. Second, this focus reflects the presumption that Percy *must* have been sad because he was a gay man living in the South. The dominant metaphor in the literature is that of a trap: Percy was trapped in Mississippi, trapped in his body, trapped in his family home and under the weight of his family name. John Barry speaks of the desires that "had to torture him," and Bertram Wyatt-Brown describes Percy as "sexually sequestered and vulnerable."[9] I hope I have shown throughout this book, in contrast, that Percy lived neither in a trap nor a torture chamber. He made the most of the cultural resources available to him in vindicating and acting on his desires, and in doing so, he experienced a constellation of emotions that included joy and sorrow, certitude and ambivalence, ecstasy and deep unrest. If there is a theme that emerges throughout the whole of his life, it is more likely resilience than melancholy. Percy made this case himself in a letter to a reader. "I think liveliness does not decrease with the years," he wrote in 1930, "but somehow we become inoculated to it and learn to endure the dark and the solitude with an incredible sort of dignity. On the whole it seems to me whatever gods put on the play should feel very proud of the actors."[10]

Percy had a liberal moral imagination that challenged his own culture's values and called for compassion and sympathy for all people. But his liberal moral imagination never translated into a liberal political imagination. He was not an activist, he did not advocate broad-scale political change, and he did not believe the state had a responsibility for increasing social well-being or lessening inequality. He believed social change was the provenance of "good men," of philanthropists and aristocrats who had the courage and honor to lead, especially on the local level. He felt the South's race problem could be fixed by good manners and more decency—though he was not optimistic. He did not believe black and white people could live alongside one another as social equals. His views on personal liberation coexisted with his belief in a society in which everyone—black people, poor people, elite people—had a *place*. He never correlated, as many southerners later would, the struggle for racial and sexual equality as political issues.

In this particular trespass into Percy's life, in this story as I see it, the ending does not resolve. The story has no clear moral. Percy's white supremacy stood alongside his emancipatory views about sex, his class prejudice stood alongside his cultural relativism, his conservatism stood alongside his strong hope that the world would change. The last word in Percy's story should be an unfinished one, a hopeful one, one that expresses both ambivalence and promise—and it should be his.

In 1940, two years before Percy died, a young southern writer named John Seymour Erwin read *Lanterns on the Levee*, and afterward he sent Percy a manuscript of a gay-themed novel he was writing. Erwin asked Percy what he felt southerners would think if he published it. Percy read the novel and wrote to the young author, telling him that it was a lovely story, courageous and insightful. But it would also bring Erwin pain and alienation, Percy said, if he were to publish it. Percy wrote: "Due to the subject treated, and to the subsequent repercussions upon your family (in a small community) it is just not for today. Perhaps some years hence all the inhibited will become less so and the world will develop a policy of live and let live (although I doubt this, and don't count on it)." Of his own autobiography, *Lanterns on the Levee*, Percy explained to Erwin that he had left much of his life story out. "I have, perhaps, left as much unsaid as I have said," Percy told him. "But so much must necessarily die with us that cries out to be heard."[11]

ACKNOWLEDGMENTS

To borrow a phrase from Will Percy, it has taken a lot of other people's love, goodwill, money, time, and energy to make something out of me that doesn't look like the Good Lord slapped it together absentmindedly. So it goes with this book. It is a singular pleasure to put in writing what I feel about the people and institutions that have helped me.

This book was made possible by financial support from the Rice University History Department; the Rice University Humanities Research Center; the Andrew W. Mellon Foundation; the National Endowment for the Humanities; the Gordon Gray Fund at Harvard University; the Expository Writing Program at Harvard University; the Arthur Schlesinger Library at the Radcliffe Institute for Advanced Study; the Deep South Regional Humanities Center at Tulane University (now the New Orleans Gulf South Center); the Center for the Study of the American South at the University of North Carolina at Chapel Hill; and the University of Florida College of Liberal Arts and Sciences and History Department. I would like to thank the staff at the University of North Carolina Press, especially my editors Chuck Grench and Jay Mazzocchi.

Like most poor souls who grow up to be writers, I have had so many wonderful teachers. Ricks Carson and Stan Gillespie taught me to love books. Natasha Trethewey taught me to love words and to respect their power. When I was an undergraduate at Auburn, Joseph Kicklighter, Donna Bohanon, Wayne Flint, and Ed Harrell taught me history and inspired me with their commitment to their craft. Ward Allen taught me to be slow to form judgments and quick to turn to the *Oxford English Dictionary*. David Carter started out as my teacher and has become a lifelong friend, confidant, and co-conspirator. Somewhere along the way he picked up an immoderate helping of human kindness, and I cannot imagine him other than to see his nodding head, his affirming smile.

John Boles is the best adviser a graduate student could ever ask for. He is patient, available, and generous, and this project would have never seen completion were it not for his constant support. At Rice, I was also fortunate to study with Thomas Haskell, Allen Matusow, Ussama Makdisi, Kerry Ward, and Ira Gruber, all of whom challenged me to become a more reflective historian. Chandler Davidson was and remains a model of scholarly generosity. Alex Lichtenstein was an early and persistent advocate; he read many drafts of this project and has always supported me. A year-long Andrew W. Mellon research seminar led by Caroline Levander led me to think about history, literature, and culture from an interdisciplinary perspective. Ann Ziker, Molly Robey, Liz Fenton, Greg Eow, Randal Hall, Scott Marler, Connie Sehat, Luke Harlow, and Meg Olsen were excellent readers, friends, and colleagues. I owe special thanks to Gale Kenny for her many and insightful readings of early drafts of this book. David L. Davis is a singularly compassionate soul, and I am happy that our paths merged for a too-brief season. Anne Chao is a gracious and generous friend, and I would not have made it through graduate school without her.

In Cambridge, Nancy Sommers was welcoming and beneficent, and she gave me a wonderful opportunity to teach Harvard undergraduates and still have time to write. Tom Jehn, Karen Heath, Gordon Harvey, Jane Rosenzweig, Pat Bellanca, and Suzanne Lane were excellent people to work with on the vexing problem of how to teach writing. Denny Kinlaw unearthed some obscure sources for me that were crucial for the book. Also, I was lucky to come across a group of sassy and mischievous friends, whom I miss dearly: Jill Constantino, Michael Baran, Jim Herron, Rachel Meyer, Ken Urban, David Haglund, Marlon Kuzmick, Steve Sutherland, and Salvatore Scibona made my life in Cambridge really lovely.

The Center for the Study of the American South at the University of North Carolina at Chapel Hill granted me a year-long fellowship to revise this book. This time was critical for me in my thinking and writing about Percy, and I am especially grateful for the generous support of Harry Watson and Joe Flora. The center also happens to employ and attract the nicest bunch of people one is liable to run across; Jacqueline Hall, Bill Ferris, Fitz Brundage, Ayse Erginer, Dave Shaw, Hodding Carter III, Tim West, Fred Hobson, and Barb Call all made my time in Chapel Hill rich, productive, and fun. To Dan Cable, Jonathan Shectman, Amos Fodchuck, Mike Harris, and Kevin Holt: what can I say? Neither in the past have I experienced, nor in the future shall I expect, a more complete meeting of the minds.

The University of Florida provided an ideal atmosphere in which to finish this book. I am grateful to have received a Faculty Enhancement Grant and research leave during 2010 to revise this manuscript. The history department chairs Joe Spillane and Ida Altman have been understanding, supportive, and generous. Bill Link has been a sage mentor, and Louise Newman is always available with frank, humane advice and encouragement. My colleagues in the history department, as well as the Center for Women's Studies and Gender Research, have welcomed me and eased my transition to Gainesville. It was one of the great good fortunes of my life to have moved in down the street from Beverly and Jon Sensbach. Bev is the most prolific distributor of goodwill I have ever met; Jon has provided the rarest and most delightful kind of friendship: one where we can sit and listen to music and feel no need to talk.

Over the course of researching this book, I have become indebted to librarians and archivists across the country. I would like to thank the staffs of the Harry Ransom Center at the University of Texas; the Hill Memorial Library at Louisiana State University; the Williams Library at the University of Mississippi; the New Orleans Public Library; the University of Illinois Archives; the University of California at Los Angeles Special Collections; the South Caroliniana Library at the University of South Carolina; the Albert and Shirley Small Special Collections at the University of Virginia; the Brooklyn Historical Society; the New York Public Library; the Beinecke Rare Books Collection and the Manuscripts and Archives at Yale University; the Houghton Library and the Law School Library at Harvard University; and the Wilson Library at the University of North Carolina at Chapel Hill. Special thanks to Charlie Blanks and Kay Clanton at the William Alexander Percy Memorial Library; Clinton Bagley at the Mississippi Department of Archives and History; Esther Crawford at Fondren Library at Rice University; and Annie Armour at the Jessie Ball duPont Library at the University of the South.

For reading and commenting on earlier drafts of this book, I would like to thank (in addition to those listed above, many of whom gave helpful feedback at various points) Fred Hobson, Richard King, Nancy Cott, Walter Johnson, Susan O'Donovan, William J. Harris, Katherine Mellon Charron, Jay Wise, Andrew Alvarez, Rebecca Wise, Clay Holland, Harry Thomas, Pat Roach, Deborah Cohn, and Matthew Pratt Guterl. To Bertram Wyatt-Brown, who read the entire manuscript, advised me about research in Mississippi, and made himself generously available for conversation during these last years, I owe especial thanks. For taking time out to talk to me about Will Percy and Greenville, I am grateful to the late Shelby Foote, as well as to Robert Coles, Fred England, Hugh McCormick, Eugene Ham, Jerry Hafter, Robert Marcius, Kate Betterton, Mary Lee Johansen, Lewis Baker, John Barry, Jay Tolson, McKay Jenkins, and Kenneth Holditch.

There are a great many people who may or may not have read parts of this book but who have influenced me, taught me in some way to see the world with the unworn parts of my eye. Sarah Kozinn, Wesley White, Josh Youssef, the late Jay Kaplan, Andrew Colvin, J. Wes Yoder, Sally Pickren, Grimes Williams, Billy Snowden, Frank Brown, and J. B. Ward are strange and wonderful people whom I have been lucky to know. Eleanor Seigler has been my constant friend since the eighth grade, and the world is a better place because she's in it. And the one good thing to come from my ill-fated and decidedly comical career as a cowboy was my friendship with Seth Hagen, who introduced me to a whole new world of music, ideas, and conversation at a critical juncture in my life.

Two people deserve special thanks. Coming to know John Howard has been one of the great rewards of writing this book. His reputation as one of the most humane, expansive, and generous people in this profession is richly deserved. His trenchant criticism and kind encouragement have deeply informed this project. Likewise, David Sehat read every word of this draft at some point and is always available when I call him for advice, gossip, procrastination, tall tales, and his recalcitrant opinions. I daresay I haven't made many important decisions in the past near decade without his advice.

For financial support, love, and occasional child care while I researched, I would like to thank Randy Wolfe, Sally Wolfe, Anna Louise Wolfe, Rebecca Wise, and John Wise. To John Wise, my father, thank you for always wanting the best for me and always supporting me.

My mother, Laura Wise, passed away just as I was beginning this project. Her life was beautiful and filled with music, and it ended way too soon. Though I can't call her, which is what I really want to do, I can remember her. That she will never read this book, nor meet my children, are facts I'd prefer not to have to live with; to have known her at all, to have received so much of her good love, are memories I could not live without.

To Henry, Spencer, and Maggie: you are the earth's most delightful creatures. Lucky me, to get to be around you every day, to watch your beautiful lives. You make me want to laugh and dance around the kitchen. And finally, this book has been informed by the creative spirit, critical questions, and generous conversation of Alston Wise, my best friend and my companion. This project has taken us through four states, several dastardly apartments, and more than a little uncertainty, and the thread of continuity has been your strong presence, your daily kindnesses, your eyes full of love.

NOTES

Abbreviations

AKP   Alfred A. Knopf Papers, Harry Ransom Humanities Center, University
of Texas at Austin

CGP   Charlotte Gailor Papers, Jessie Ball duPont Library, University of
the South, Sewanee, Tenn.

JDLP   Janet Dana Longcope Papers, Hill Memorial Library, Louisiana
State University, Baton Rouge, La.

MDAH   Mississippi Department of Archives and History, Jackson, Miss.

WAPAF   William Alexander Percy Alumni File, Jessie Ball duPont Library,
University of the South, Sewanee, Tenn.

WAPD   William Alexander Percy Diary, William Alexander Percy Papers,
Mississippi Department of Archives and History, Jackson, Miss.

WAPP   William Alexander Percy Papers, Mississippi Department of Archives and
History, Jackson, Miss.

Introduction

1. WAPD, December 5, 1910, WAPP. For background information on William Alexander Percy and his family's history, see Bertram Wyatt-Brown, *The House of Percy: Honor, Melancholy, and Imagination in a Southern Family* (New York: Oxford University Press, 1992); Jay Tolson, *Pilgrim in the Ruins: A Life of Walker Percy* (New York: Simon and Schuster, 1994); Lewis Baker, *The Percys of Mississippi: Politics and Literature in the New South* (Baton Rouge: Louisiana State University Press, 1984); Patrick H. Samway, *Walker Percy: A Life* (New York: Farrar, Straus and Giroux, 1997); John Barry, *Rising Tide: The Great Mississippi Flood of 1927 and How It Changed America* (New York: Touchstone, 1997), esp. parts 2, 6, and 9; Richard King, *A Southern Renaissance: The Cultural Awakening of the American South, 1930–1955* (New York: Oxford University Press, 1980), chap. 4; Fred C. Hobson, *Tell about the South: The Southern Rage to Explain* (Baton Rouge: Louisiana State University Press, 1983), chap. 4; McKay Jenkins, *The South in Black and White: Race, Sex, and Literature in the 1940s* (Chapel Hill: University of North Carolina Press, 1999), chap. 3; Scott Romine, *Narrative Forms of Southern Community* (Baton Rouge: Louisiana State University Press, 1999), chap. 3; and James W. Silver, *Running Scared: Silver in Mississippi* (Jackson: University Press of Mississippi, 1984), appendix H.

2. For context on Harvard during Percy and Bruff's time there, see especially Douglas Shand-Tucci, *The Crimson Letter: Harvard, Homosexuality, and the Shaping of American Culture* (New York: St. Martin's Press, 2003); Kim Townsend, *Manhood at Harvard: William James and Others* (New York: W. W. Norton, 1996); and John T. Bethell, *Harvard Observed: An Illustrated History of the University in the Twentieth Century* (Cambridge: Harvard University Press, 1998).

3. William Alexander Percy, *Lanterns on the Levee: Recollections of a Planter's Son* (New York: Alfred A. Knopf, 1941), 122. Scholars have shed a great deal of light on the ways in which queer men and women narrated their own life stories in eras during which censorship or legal recrimination were likely if they wrote openly about sexual desire and practice. Sources that have influenced my interpretation of *Lanterns on the Levee* include Paul Robinson, *Gay Lives: Homosexual Autobiography from John Addington Symonds to Paul Monette* (Chicago: University of Chicago Press, 1999); Oliver Buckton, *Secret Selves: Confession and Same-Sex Desire in Victorian Autobiography* (Chapel Hill: University of North Carolina Press, 1998); James T. Sears, *Growing up Gay in the South: Race, Gender, and Journeys of the Spirit* (Binghamton, N.Y.: The Haworth Press, 1991); and Carlos L. Dews and Carolyn Leste Law, eds., *Out in the South* (Philadelphia: Temple University Press, 2001). Other queer southern autobiographies include Kevin Sessums, *Mississippi Sissy* (New York: Picador, 2008); and Ben Duncan, *The Same Language*, edited and with an afterword by John Howard (Tuscaloosa: University of Alabama Press, 2005). For scholarship specifically on *Lanterns on the Levee*, see Jennifer Jensen Wallach, *"Closer to the Truth than Any Fact": Memoir, Memory, and Jim Crow* (Athens: University of Georgia Press, 2008), chap. 4; King, *A Southern Renaissance*, chap. 4; Hobson, *Tell about the South*, chap. 4; Jenkins, *The South in Black and White*, chap. 3; Romine, *Narrative Forms of Southern Community*, chap. 3; William L. Andrews, "In Search of a Common Identity: The Self and the South in Four Mississippi Autobiographies," *Southern Review* 24 (Winter 1988): 47–64; Edward J. Dupuy, "The Dispossessed Garden of William Alexander Percy," *Southern Quarterly* 29 (Winter 1991): 31–41; James E. Rock, "The Art of *Lanterns on the Levee*," *Southern Review* 12 (1976): 814–23; and Carolyn Holdsworth, "The Gorgon's Head and the Mirror: Fact versus Metaphor in *Lanterns on the Levee*," *Southern Literary Journal* 14 (Fall 1981): 36–45.

4. Harold Bruff 1905 Alumni File and Edward Kirkham 1905 Alumni File, Yale University Manuscripts and Archives, New Haven, Conn.; Percy, *Lanterns*, 122–23.

5. WAPD, October 18, 1910, WAPP; Harold Bruff to William Alexander Percy, September 8, 1910, WAPP. The phrase "de profundis" possibly refers to Oscar Wilde's famous letter to his former lover Alfred Douglas. Wilde wrote the letter, which he entitled "De Profundis," while in jail after having been convicted of sodomy in 1895, and the letter was later published and became widely read as a treatise on love between men. See Oscar Wilde, *De Profundis and Other Writings* (New York: Penguin, 1974); Richard Ellmann, *Oscar Wilde* (New York: Vintage, 1988), 510–34; and Neil McKenna, *The Secret Life of Oscar Wilde* (New York: Basic Books, 2005), 420–28.

6. Percy, *Lanterns*, 135 and 130.

7. We do not know for certain if Percy attended this meeting on December 5, 1910. But we do know he did occasionally attend meetings of the Washington County Historical Society and that his actions from 6:00 P.M. to 11:00 P.M. of that day are not documented. Regardless of whether he was actually there or not, the story is an ideal type; it was a version of a story Percy heard many times in his life. To place him in the audience on this night, literally or figuratively, is to hear history as he heard it.

8. This account is based on Sam Worthington, "Ante-Bellum Slave-Holding Aristocracy of Washington County," in *Memoirs of Henry Tillinghast Ireys: Papers of the Washington County Historical Society, 1910–1915*, ed. William D. McCain and Charlotte Capers (Jackson: Mississippi Department of Archives and History, 1954), 350–65 (quotes on 350). On white southern nostalgia, see Tara McPherson, *Reconstructing Dixie: Race, Gender, and Nostalgia in the Imagined South* (Durham, N.C.: Duke University Press, 2003); James C. Cobb, *Away Down South: A History of Southern Identity* (Oxford: Oxford University Press, 2005), esp. chaps. 3 and 4; David W. Blight, *Race and Reunion: The Civil War in American Memory* (Cambridge, Mass.: Harvard University Press, 2001); Michael Kammen, *Mystic Chords of Memory: The Transformation of Tradition in American Culture* (New York: Vintage, 1993), esp. part 2; Paul M. Gaston, *The New South Creed: A Study in Southern Mythmaking* (Montgomery, Ala.: NewSouth Books, 2002); Gaines M. Foster, *Ghosts of the Confederacy: Defeat, the Lost Cause, and the Emergence of the New South, 1865–1913* (Oxford: Oxford University Press, 1988); Charles Reagan Wilson, *Baptized in Blood: The Religion of the Lost Cause, 1865–1920* (Athens: University of Georgia Press, 1983); and David Anderson, "Down Memory Lane: Nostalgia for the Old South in Post–Civil War Plantation Reminiscences," *Journal of Southern History* 71, no. 1 (February 2005): 105–36.

9. Worthington, "Ante-Bellum Slave-Holding Aristocracy of Washington County," 350–55 (quote on 351).

10. Ibid., 351–56 (quotes on 356 and 351).

11. Ibid., 364–65.

12. Percy, *Lanterns*, 244. The literature on manhood and masculinity is vast and growing, but for starters, see E. Anthony Rotundo, *American Manhood: Transformations in Masculinity from the Revolution to the Modern Era* (New York: Basic Books, 1993); Michael Kimmel, *Manhood in America: A Cultural History* (New York: Free Press, 1996); Gail Bederman, *Manliness and Civilization: A Cultural History of Gender and Race in the United States, 1880–1917* (Chicago: University of Chicago Press, 1995); David D. Gilmore, *Manhood in the Making: Cultural Concepts of Masculinity* (New Haven: Yale University Press, 1991). On southern manhood and masculinity, see Craig T. Friend, ed., *Southern Manhood: Perspectives on Masculinity in the Old South* (Athens: University of Georgia Press, 2004); Friend, ed., *Southern Masculinity: Perspectives on Manhood in the South since Reconstruction* (Athens: University of Georgia Press, 2008); Lorri Glover, *Southern Sons: Becoming Men in the New Nation* (Baltimore: Johns Hopkins University Press, 2007); Ted Ownby, *Subduing Satan: Religion, Recreation, and Manhood in the Rural South, 1865–1920* (Chapel Hill: University of North Carolina

Press, 1993); Trent Watts, ed., *White Masculinity in the Recent South* (Baton Rouge: Louisiana State University Press, 2008); Angela M. Hornsby-Gutting, "Manning the Region: New Approaches to Gender in the South," *Journal of Southern History* 75, no. 3 (August 2009): 663–76; and Riché Richardson, *Black Masculinity and the U.S. South: From Uncle Tom to Gangsta* (Athens: University of Georgia Press, 2007).

13. Any historical account of the Mississippi Delta must begin with James C. Cobb, *The Most Southern Place on Earth: The Mississippi Delta and the Roots of Regional Identity* (New York: Oxford University Press, 1992). See also Robert L. Brandfon, *Cotton Kingdom of the New South: A History of the Yazoo Mississippi Delta from Reconstruction to the Twentieth Century* (Cambridge, Mass.: Harvard University Press, 1967); John C. Willis, *Forgotten Time: The Yazoo-Mississippi Delta after the Civil War* (Charlottesville: University of Virginia Press, 2001); William J. Harris, *Deep Souths: Delta, Piedmont, and Sea Island Society in the Age of Segregation* (Baltimore: Johns Hopkins University Press, 2001); John Hebron Moore, *The Emergence of the Cotton Kingdom in the Old Southwest: Mississippi, 1770–1860* (Baton Rouge: Louisiana State University Press, 1988); Vernon Lane Wharton, *The Negro in Mississippi, 1865–1890* (Chapel Hill: University of North Carolina Press, 1947); Richard Aubrey McLemore, ed., *A History of Mississippi*, 2 vols. (Hattiesburg, Miss.: University and College Press of Mississippi, 1973); Neil McMillan, *Dark Journey: Black Mississippians in the Age of Jim Crow* (Urbana: University of Illinois Press, 1989); John M. Giggie, *After Redemption: Jim Crow and the Transformation of African American Religion in the Delta, 1875–1915* (New York: Oxford University Press, 2008); Nancy Bercaw, *Gendered Freedoms: Race, Rights, and the Politics of Household in the Delta, 1861–1875* (Gainesville, Fla.: University Press of Florida, 2003); Albert D. Kirwan, *Revolt of the Rednecks: Mississippi Politics, 1876–1925* (Gloucester, Mass.: P. Smith, 1951); John Dollard, *Caste and Class in a Southern Town* (New York: Doubleday, 1949); and Hortense Powdermaker, *After Freedom: A Cultural Study in the Deep South* (New York: Viking, 1939).

14. "Will Percy's Book," *Jackson Daily News*, n.d.; clipping in AKP. On the existence of "open secrets" and the lack of rigid sexual categories in Mississippi, John Howard has remarked about a later period: "In Protestant evangelical Mississippi, religious principles guided understandings of the queer as more a range of sinful but forgivable behaviors than an identity or way of being. Conceptions of sexuality and gender nonconformity did not comport easily to dyads of homosexual versus heterosexual." He notes that "Mississippians could live with homosexuality, like other unpleasantries, as long as it went unremarked." See John Howard, *Men Like That: A Southern Queer History* (Chicago: University of Chicago Press, 1999), 261–62. Eve Kosofsky Sedgwick theorizes about the "open secret" in *Epistemology of the Closet* (Berkeley: University of California Press, 1990), esp. chaps. 1 and 2; Leslie J. Reagan also provides useful insight into the concept in *When Abortion Was a Crime: Women, Medicine, and the Law in the United States, 1867–1973* (Berkeley: University of California Press, 1997), chap. 1.

For examples of depictions of queers in southern newspapers during this period, see Lisa Duggan, *Sapphic Slashers: Sex, Violence, and American Modernity* (Durham, N.C.:

Duke University Press, 2000); Duggan, "The Trials of Alice Mitchell: Sensationalism, Sexology, and the Lesbian Subject in Turn-of-the-Century America," *Signs* 18, no. 4 (Summer 1993): 791–814; Lisa J. Lindquist, "Images of Alice: Gender, Deviancy, and a Love Murder in Memphis," *Journal of the History of Sexuality* 6, no. 1 (July 1995): 30–61; and John Howard, "The Talk of the County: Revisiting Accusation, Murder, and Mississippi, 1895," in *Queer Studies: An Interdisciplinary Reader*, ed. Robert J. Corber and Stephen Valocchi (Malden, Mass.: Blackwell, 2003), 142–58.

15. WAPD, October 17, 1910, WAPP.

16. Percy, *Lanterns*, 94.

17. Ibid., 282 and 20.

18. Cobb, *The Most Southern Place on Earth*; George Chauncey, *Gay New York: Gender, Urban Culture, and the Making of the Gay Male World, 1890–1940* (New York: Basic Books, 1994).

19. WAPD, December 5, 1910, WAPP.

20. WAPD, December 5, 6, and 8, 1910, WAPP.

21. WAPD, December 11, 1910, WAPP; "Apologized for Suicide," *New York Times*, October 13, 1911, 3.

22. "Driven by Disease to Give up Girl He Loved, Kills Self," *New York Daily World*, October 13, 1911; "Young Lawyer Commits Suicide," *Connecticut Courant*, October 16, 1911; "Belmont Guest Self-Slain," *New York Morning Sun*, October 13, 1911; "Apologized for Suicide," *New York Times*; "H. Bruff, of Brooklyn, Ends His Life," *Brooklyn Times*, October 13, 1911, 14. I include Bruff's story here wary of John Howard's compelling warning to scholars against reproducing what he calls "homosexual suicide mythology," whereby homosexuality leads logically to suicide (or in other cases, homicide). Doing so, he argues, reinforces the social perception of "homosexuality as deadly dangerous." I retell Bruff's story not to portray his suicide as inevitable but to illustrate an important turning point in Percy's life—a tragedy he responded to, in part, by turning to poetry. See Howard, *Men Like That* (quotes on xvi and 229).

23. William Alexander Percy to Carrie Stern, January 7, 1919, WAPP.

24. On queer communities in Percy's era, see Chauncey, *Gay New York*; Matt Cook, *London and the Culture of Homosexuality, 1885–1914* (Cambridge: Cambridge University Press, 2008); Kevin J. Mumford, *Interzones: Black/White Sex Districts in Chicago and New York in the Early Twentieth Century* (New York: Columbia University Press, 1997); Chad Heap, *Slumming: Sexual and Racial Encounters in American Nightlife, 1885–1940* (Chicago: University of Chicago Press, 2010); Marc Stein, *City of Sisterly and Brotherly Loves: Lesbian and Gay Philadelphia, 1945–1972* (Chicago: University of Chicago Press, 2000); John D'Emilio, *Sexual Politics, Sexual Communities: The Making of a Homosexual Minority in the United States, 1940–1970* (Chicago: University of Chicago Press, 1998); and William A. Peniston, *Pederasts and Others: Urban Culture and Sexual Identity in Nineteenth-Century Paris* (New York: Routledge, 2004). On the homoerotic idiom that Percy drew from and wrote in, see especially Scott Bravmann, *Queer Fictions of the Past: History, Culture, and Difference* (Cambridge: Cambridge University Press, 1997),

particularly chap. 4; Jim Elledge, ed., *Masquerade: Queer Poetry in America to the End of World War II* (Bloomington: Indiana University Press, 2004); Timothy D'Arch Smith, *Love in Earnest: Some Notes on the Lives and Writings of English "Uranian" Poets from 1880–1930* (London: Routledge and Kegan Paul, 1970); and Linda Dowling, *Hellenism and Homosexuality in Victorian Oxford* (Ithaca: Cornell University Press, 1994).

25. On the development of sexual identities and cultural understandings of sexuality in the late nineteenth and early twentieth centuries, see Michel Foucault, *The History of Sexuality*, vol. 1, *An Introduction*, trans. Robert Hurley (1978; repr. New York: Vintage Books, 1990); Sedgwick, *Epistemology of the Closet*; John D'Emilio and Estelle B. Freedman, *Intimate Matters: A History of Sexuality in America*, 2nd ed. (Chicago: University of Chicago Press, 1997), esp. part 3; Jonathan Ned Katz, *The Invention of Heterosexuality* (New York: Dutton, 1995); Katz, *Love Stories: Sex between Men before Homosexuality* (Chicago: University of Chicago Press, 2001); Duggan, *Sapphic Slashers*; Duggan, "The Trials of Alice Mitchell"; Chauncey, *Gay New York*; Chauncey, "Christian Brotherhood or Sexual Perversion? Homosexual Identities and the Construction of Sexual Boundaries in the World War I Era," *Journal of Social History* 19, no. 2 (Winter 1985): 189–211; Chauncey, "From Sexual Inversion to Homosexuality: Medicine and the Changing Conception of Female Deviance," *Salmagundi* 58–59 (Fall 1982–Winter 1983): 114–46; John D'Emilio, "Capitalism and Gay Identity," in *Powers of Desire: The Politics of Sexuality*, ed. Ann Snitow, Christine Stansell, and Sharon Thompson (New York: Monthly Review Press, 1983); Sharon R. Ullman, *Sex Seen: The Emergence of Modern Sexuality in America* (Berkeley: University of California Press, 1997); Siobhan B. Somerville, *Queering the Color Line: Race and the Invention of Homosexuality in American Culture* (Durham, N.C.: Duke University Press, 2000); Julian B. Carter, *The Heart of Whiteness: Normal Sexuality and Race in American Culture, 1880–1940* (Durham, N.C.: Duke University Press, 2007); Lillian Faderman, *Odd Girls and Twilight Lovers: A History of Lesbian Life in Twentieth-Century America* (New York: Columbia University Press, 1991); David Halperin, *How to Do the History of Homosexuality* (Chicago: University of Chicago Press, 2002); and Kevin White, *The First Sexual Revolution: The Emergence of Male Heterosexuality in Modern America* (New York: New York University Press, 1992).

26. Ellis quoted in D'Emilio and Freedman, *Intimate Matters*, 225–26. Though Ellis wrote this particular phrase in 1933, he had been writing throughout his life about the diversity of human sexual behaviors and attitudes. See especially Havelock Ellis, *Studies in the Psychology of Sex, Volume 2: Sexual Inversion* (Philadelphia: F. A. Davis Company, 1901); Ellis, *Studies in the Psychology of Sex, Volume 6: Sex in Relation to Society* (Philadelphia: F. A. Davis Company, 1910); and Ellis, *Man and Woman: A Study of Secondary and Tertiary Sexual Characters* (Boston: Houghton Mifflin, 1929).

27. See, for example, Wilde, *De Profundis*; John Addington Symonds, *A Problem in Greek Ethics, Being an Inquiry into the Phenomenon of Sexual Inversion; Addressed Especially to Medical Psychologists and Jurists* (London: The Areopagitiga Society, 1908); Edward Carpenter, *The Intermediate Sex: A Study of Some Transitional Types of Men and Women* (New York: Kennerley, 1912); Margaret Mead, *Coming of Age in Samoa: A*

Psychological Study of Primitive Youth for Western Civilization. (1928; repr. New York: Harper, 2001); Willy, *The Third Sex*, trans. and with an introduction and notes by Lawrence R. Schehr (Urbana: University of Illinois Press, 2007); Sigmund Freud, *Three Contributions to the Theory of Sex*, trans. A. A. Brill (1905; repr. New York: Dover Books, 2001); and Radclyffe Hall, *The Well of Loneliness* (London: Jonathan Cape, 1928).

28. Donald H. Mader, "The Greek Mirror: The Uranians and Their Use of Greece," in *Same-Sex Desire and Love in Greco-Roman Antiquity and in the Classical Tradition of the West*, ed. Beert C. Verstraete and Vernon Provencal (Binghamton, N.Y.: Harrington Park Press, 2005), 388.

29. Quoted in Chauncey, *Gay New York*, 179.

30. Many scholars have argued that the emergence of "homosexuality" and "heterosexuality" as fixed categories of sexual and social identity was detrimental to a more fluid regime under which a broader range of expressions, identities, and behaviors could be accommodated. These scholars have rightly warned against a triumphalist narrative of a history of sexuality in which society moves naturally toward more open and inclusive structures of understanding and experience, and they have pointed out the ways sexual regulation, representation, and even desire and behavior are contingent upon historically specific structures of power, space, and discourse. To point out that Percy celebrated and benefited from an emerging sense of solidarity with other queer men and women is not to say that the emergence of "homosexuality"—particularly with its Freudian emphasis on childhood trauma and repression during Percy's lifetime— was an unmitigated social good. It is to say, however, that Percy wanted to meet and communicate with other queer men and women, and the increasing visibility of queer subcultures and literary networks allowed him to do so. See especially Foucault, *The History of Sexuality*; Sedgwick, *Epistemology of the Closet*; Katz, *The Invention of Heterosexuality*; and D'Emilio, *Sexual Politics, Sexual Communities*.

An ironic and unintended outcome of this queer network of affiliation was the later Cold War persecution of gay men and lesbians as "cosmopolitans" whose sexual identities and communities compromised their national allegiance. For more on the association of communism and homosexuality, see especially David K. Johnson, *The Lavender Scare: The Cold War Persecution of Gays and Lesbians in the Federal Government* (Chicago: University of Chicago Press, 2004); and Michael S. Sherry, *Gay Artists in Modern American Culture: An Imagined Conspiracy* (Chapel Hill: University of North Carolina Press, 2007).

31. Notable exceptions to this include Duggan, *Sapphic Slashers*; Duggan, "The Trials of Alice Mitchell"; Lindquist, "Images of Alice"; John Howard, "The Talk of the County"; John Howard, ed., *Carryin' On in the Lesbian and Gay South* (New York: New York University Press, 1997), chaps. 2–6. For scholarship on queer sexuality in the more recent South, see Howard, *Men Like That*; Howard, *Carryin' On in the Lesbian and Gay South*, chaps. 7–15; James T. Sears, *Rebels, Rubyfruit, and Rhinestones: Queering Space in the Stonewall South* (Piscataway, N.J.: Rutgers University Press, 2001); Sears, *Lonely Hunters: An Oral History of Lesbian and Gay Southern Life, 1948–1968* (Boulder, Colo.:

Westview Press, 1997); E. Patrick Johnson, *Sweet Tea: Black Gay Men of the South* (Chapel Hill: University of North Carolina Press, 2008); Gary Richards, *Lovers and Beloveds: Sexual Otherness in Southern Fiction* (Baton Rouge: Louisiana State University Press, 2005); and Michael Bibler, *Cotton's Queer Relations: Same-Sex Intimacy and the Literature of the Southern Plantation, 1936–1968* (Charlottesville, Va.: University of Virginia Press, 2009).

32. Jenkins, *The South in Black and White*, 103; Wyatt-Brown, *House of Percy*, 205; King, *A Southern Renaissance*, 97. Others have discussed Percy's sexuality in more positive terms, most notably William Armstrong Percy in "William Alexander Percy: His Homosexuality and Why It Matters," in *Carryin' On in the Gay and Lesbian South*, ed. John Howard, 75–92. My treatment of Will Percy picks up on several of the themes in William Armstrong Percy's 1997 essay. For a fuller discussion, see chap. 12. See also Donald Mader, "The Greek Mirror"; and Kieran Quinlan, "From William Alexander Percy to Walker Percy: Progress or Regress?," *European Contributions to American Studies* 65 (2006): 143–54.

33. For works dealing with the concept of place, see Doreen Massey, *Space, Place, and Gender* (Minneapolis: University of Minnesota Press, 1994); Louis D. Rubin and Robert Jacobs, eds., *The Southern Renascence: The Literature of the Modern South* (Baltimore: Johns Hopkins University Press, 1953); Louis D. Rubin, *The Faraway Country: Writers of the Modern South* (Seattle: University of Washington Press, 1963); Richard Gray, *Southern Aberrations: Writers of the American South and the Problems of Regionalism* (Baton Rouge: Louisiana State University Press, 2000); Martyn Bone, *The Postsouthern Sense of Place in Contemporary Fiction* (Baton Rouge: Louisiana State University Press, 2005); and Michael O'Brien, *Placing the South* (Jackson: University Press of Mississippi, 2007).

Some readers will take issue with using the term "sexual liberationist" to describe Percy, since in the late twentieth century, sexual liberation became associated with a set of political goals that Percy never shared. Percy was not a sexual liberationist in this activist context; rather, he, like many others in the early twentieth century, came to question (and in some cases, reject) the sexual values of American culture and to live outside of them. I use this term in its most basic sense: he believed that people should be free to do what they wanted with their own bodies, so long as their decisions did not harm other people. Those looking for a late twentieth-century "coming out" in Percy's story—with a concomitant public declaration of gay identity, a move from country to city, and an activist, emancipatory political orientation—will not find such a narrative. Rather, this book tries to uncover the idiom available to, and to some degree created by, Percy in order to understand his historical experience.

Chapter 1

1. Mikko Saikku, *This Delta, This Land: An Environmental History of the Yazoo-Mississippi Floodplain* (Athens: University of Georgia Press, 2005), 79 and 40.

2. Ira Berlin, *Generations of Captivity: A History of African American Slaves* (Cam-

bridge, Mass.: Harvard University Press, 2003), 274. On the emergence of the cotton South, see especially Berlin, *Many Thousands Gone: The First Two Centuries of Slavery in North America* (Cambridge: Harvard University Press, 1998); Adam Rothman, *Slave Country: American Expansion and the Origins of the Deep South* (Cambridge: Harvard University Press, 2007); and John Hebron Moore, *The Emergence of the Cotton Kingdom in the Old Southwest: Mississippi, 1770–1860* (Baton Rouge: Louisiana State University Press, 1988).

3. Berlin, *Generations of Captivity*, 161.

4. Valerie Lambert, *Choctaw Nation: A Story of American Indian Resurgence* (Lincoln: University of Nebraska Press, 2007), 39.

5. William Alexander Percy, *Lanterns on the Levee: Recollections of a Planter's Son* (New York: Alfred A. Knopf, 1941), 273.

6. James C. Cobb, *The Most Southern Place on Earth: The Mississippi Delta and the Roots of Regional Identity* (New York: Oxford University Press, 1992), 8.

7. On slave culture, see especially Eugene Genovese, *Roll, Jordan, Roll: The World the Slaves Made* (New York: Pantheon Books, 1974); John W. Blassingame, *The Slave Community: Plantation Life in the American South*, revised and enlarged edition (New York: Oxford University Press, 1979); and John B. Boles, *Black Southerners, 1619–1869* (Lexington, Ky.: The University Press of Kentucky, 1984).

8. Sam Worthington, "Ante-Bellum Slave-Holding Aristocracy of Washington County," in *Memoirs of Henry Tillinghast Ireys: Papers of the Washington County Historical Society, 1910–1915*, ed. William D. McCain and Charlotte Capers (Jackson: Mississippi Department of Archives and History, 1954), 356. On slave resistance, see especially Anthony E. Kaye, *Joining Places: Slave Neighborhoods in the Old South* (Chapel Hill: University of North Carolina Press, 2009).

9. Bertram Wyatt-Brown, *The House of Percy: Honor, Melancholy, and Imagination in a Southern Family* (New York: Oxford University Press, 1994), 175.

10. See, for example, William Alexander Percy to Janet Dana Longcope, n.d., 1915, JDLP.

11. Lewis Baker, *The Percys of Mississippi: Politics and Literature in the New South* (Baton Rouge: Louisiana State University Press, 1983), 3–4; Wyatt-Brown, *House of Percy*, 25–41.

12. Wyatt-Brown, *House of Percy*, 65 and 75.

13. Quoted in Baker, *The Percys of Mississippi*, 4.

14. Percy, *Lanterns*, 271.

15. Wyatt-Brown, *House of Percy*, 65.

16. William W. Stowe, *Going Abroad: European Travel in Nineteenth-Century American Culture* (Princeton: Princeton University Press, 1994), 19. See also Steven M. Stowe, *Intimacy and Power in the Old South: Ritual in the Lives of the Planters* (Baltimore: Johns Hopkins University Press, 1987); Daniel Kilbride, "Travel, Ritual, and National Identity: Planters on the European Tour, 1820–1860," *Journal of Southern History* 69 (August 2003): 549–84; Kilbride, *An American Aristocracy: Southern Planters in Ante-*

bellum Philadelphia (Columbia, S.C.: University of South Carolina Press, 2006), chap. 6; Jeremy Black, *Italy and the Grand Tour* (New Haven: Yale University Press, 2003); Michael O'Brien, *Rethinking the South: Essays in Intellectual History* (Athens: University of Georgia Press, 1988), esp. chap. 4, "Italy and the Southern Romantics."

17. Michael O'Brien, *Conjectures of Order: Intellectual Life and the American South, 1810–1860* (Chapel Hill: University of North Carolina Press, 2004), esp. vol. 1, chap. 3, "European Attachments." See also Elizabeth Fox-Genovese and Eugene Genovese, *The Mind of the Master Class: History and Faith in the Southern Slaveholders' Worldview* (Cambridge: Cambridge University Press, 2005), esp. parts 2 and 3.

18. Percy, *Lanterns*, 273.

19. Cobb, *The Most Southern Place on Earth*, 8.

20. These figures come from David Brion Davis, *Inhuman Bondage: The Rise and Fall of Slavery in the New World* (New York: Oxford University Press, 2008), 197–98. On the demographics of the slave South, see also Robert William Fogel, *Without Consent or Contract: The Rise and Fall of American Slavery* (New York: W. W. Norton, 1994), chap. 5; and Peter Kolchin, *American Slavery, 1619–1877* (New York: Hill & Wang, 2003), chaps. 4–6.

21. Cobb, *The Most Southern Place on Earth*, 12.

22. W. W. Stone, "Some Post-War Recollections," in *Memoirs of Henry Tillinghast Ireys*, ed. McCain and Capers, 257.

23. Worthington, "Ante-Bellum Slave-Holding Aristocracy of Washington County," 359.

24. Cobb, *The Most Southern Place on Earth*, 30–32; Bern Keating, *A History of Washington County, Mississippi* (Greenville, Miss.: Greenville Junior Auxiliary, 1976), 32.

25. Cobb, *The Most Southern Place on Earth*, 32; Robert Lowry and William H. McCardle, *A History of Mississippi* (Spartanburg, S.C.: The Reprint Company, Publishers, 1978 [repr.]), 342.

26. Keating, *A History of Washington County, Mississippi*, 34.

27. Baker, *The Percys of Mississippi*, 5–7; Wyatt-Brown, *The House of Percy*, 175.

28. Percy, *Lanterns*, 9–10. On women in the South during the Civil War era, see especially Drew Gilpin Faust, *Mothers of Invention: Slaveholding Women of the Antebellum South* (Chapel Hill: University of North Carolina Press, 1996); Catherine Clinton, *The Plantation Mistress: Woman's World in the Old South* (New York: Pantheon, 1984); Elizabeth Fox-Genovese, *Within the Plantation Household: Black and White Women of the Old South* (Chapel Hill: University of North Carolina Press, 1988); Anne Firor Scott, *The Southern Lady: From Pedestal to Politics, 1830–1930*, 25th anniversary ed. (Charlottesville: University of Virginia Press, 1995); and Laura F. Edwards, *Scarlett Doesn't Live Here Anymore: Southern Women in the Civil War Era* (Urbana: University of Illinois Press, 2004).

29. Stone, "Some Post-War Recollections," 275; Katherine Branton and Alice Wade, *Early Records of Mississippi: Issaquena and Washington Counties*, vol. 1 (Leland, Miss.: K. Branton, 1982), 99. On the fluidity of race relations in Mississippi during this period,

see especially Vernon Lane Wharton, *The Negro in Mississippi, 1865–1890* (Chapel Hill: University of North Carolina Press, 1947).

30. Quoted in J. S. McNeilly, "Climax and Collapse of Reconstruction in Mississippi, 1874–1876," *Publications of the Mississippi Historical Society* 12 (1912): 378.

31. Ibid.; Baker, *Percys of Mississippi*, 10.

32. Percy, *Lanterns*, 274.

33. Baker, *Percys of Mississippi*, 10.

34. One perspective of this story Will Percy would have never heard was that of a black Mississippian who wrote a letter to John Marshall Stone. His was the voice of not a few of the state's majority black population. "Infamous Scoundrel!" the note began. "You Democratic devil; you unjust cowardly dog. . . . The southern people are a Whisky-drinking, tobacco-chewing, Constant-spitting, Negro-hating, Negro-killing, red-handed, ignorant uneducated, uncivilized set of devils. . . . I will soon come to Jackson to kick your ass. You thief." Not having quite said his share, the man wrote Governor Stone again a year later: "You good for nothing nasty, stinking, Southern Son of a Solid South. . . . All the Southern people are Barbarians, a Whisky drinking, Tobacco-chewing, Constant-Spitting, nasty, dirty, Corn Bread eating, molasses-licking, Fat-back swallowing, Negro hating, Negro-killing, negro-women ravishing, lousy set. . . . Your wife is a nasty *wench*." Both letters are in Bradley G. Bond, ed. *Mississippi: A Documentary History* (Jackson: University Press of Mississippi, 2003), 143–45. Italics in original.

35. On Reconstruction in Mississippi, see Eric Foner, *Reconstruction: America's Unfinished Revolution, 1862–1877* (New York: Harper & Row, 1988); Wharton, *The Negro in Mississippi*; and Nancy Bercaw, *Gendered Freedoms: Race, Rights, and the Politics of Household in the Delta, 1861–1875* (Gainesville, Fla.: University Press of Florida, 2003).

36. Nicholas Lemann, *Redemption: The Last Battle of the Civil War* (New York: Farrar, Straus and Giroux, 2006), 154 (voting statistics) and 132 (quote).

37. Percy, *Lanterns*, 73–74.

38. On the codification of this version of Reconstruction, see especially John David Smith, *An Old Creed for a New South: Proslavery Ideology and Historiography, 1865–1918* (Carbondale: Southern Illinois University Press, 1985); and Laura F. Edwards, "Southern History as U.S. History," *Journal of Southern History* 75, no. 3 (August 2009): 533–64. For the sources themselves, see especially William Archibald Dunning, *Essays on the Civil War and Reconstruction and Related Topics* (New York: The Macmillan Company, 1898); and on Mississippi, see James Wilford Garner, *Reconstruction in Mississippi* (New York: The Macmillan Company, 1901).

39. Mary V. Duval, *History of Mississippi and Civil Government: Compiled and Arranged for the Use of the Public Schools of Mississippi* (Louisville, Ky.: Courier-Journal Job Printing Company, 1892), 220.

40. On the historiography of Reconstruction, see John B. Boles, ed., *A Companion to the American South* (Malden, Mass.: Blackwell Publishing, 2004), esp. chaps. 16–18.

41. Quoted in Cobb, *The Most Southern Place on Earth*, 59.

42. On the late nineteenth-century cotton South, see Gavin Wright, *Old South, New*

South: Revolutions in the Southern Economy since the Civil War (Baton Rouge: Louisiana State University Press, 1996); Roger L. Ransom and Richard Sutch, One Kind of Freedom: The Economic Consequences of Emancipation, 2nd ed. (Cambridge: Cambridge University Press, 2001); C. Vann Woodward, Origins of the New South, 1877–1913, 2nd ed. (Baton Rouge: Louisiana State University Press, 1971), esp. chaps. 7 and 11; and Edward L. Ayers, The Promise of the New South: Life after Reconstruction, 15th anniversary ed. (New York: Oxford University Press, 2007), esp. chaps. 8 and 9.

43. Journal of the Sixty-First Annual Council of the Diocese of Mississippi (Natchez, Miss: Church News and Job Print, 1888), 23–24.

44. Wyatt-Brown, House of Percy, 177; Percy, Lanterns, 8.

45. Henry Waring Ball Diary, February 3, 1911, MDAH.

46. Ibid., July 22, 1904, MDAH.

47. On the history of romantic friendship in the nineteenth century, see Jonathan Ned Katz, Love Stories: Sex between Men before Homosexuality (Chicago: University of Chicago Press, 2003), esp. part 1; Graham Robb, Strangers: Homosexual Love in the Nineteenth Century (New York: W. W. Norton, 2005); Carol Smith-Rosenberg, Disorderly Conduct: Visions of Gender in Victorian America (New York: Oxford University Press, 1986), esp. part 1; and Donald Yacovone, "'Surpassing the Love of Women': Victorian Manhood and the Language of Fraternal Love," in A Shared Experience: Men, Women, and the History of Gender, ed. Laura McCall and Donald Yacovone (New York: New York University Press, 1998), 195–221.

48. Yacovone, "'Surpassing the Love of Women,'" 196.

49. On other stories of sexual deviance or gender queerness circulating in the South in the late nineteenth century, see Lisa J. Lindquist, "Images of Alice: Gender, Deviancy, and a Love Murder in Memphis," Journal of the History of Sexuality 6, no. 1 (July 1995): 30–61; John Howard, "The Talk of the County: Revisiting Accusation, Murder, and Mississippi, 1895," in Queer Studies: An Interdisciplinary Reader, ed. Robert J. Corber and Stephen Valocchi (Malden, Mass.: Blackwell, 2003), 142–58; Lisa Duggan, Sapphic Slashers: Sex, Violence, and American Modernity (Durham, N.C.: Duke University Press, 2000); Duggan, "The Trials of Alice Mitchell: Sensationalism, Sexology, and the Lesbian Subject in Turn-of-the-Century America," Signs 18, no. 4 (Summer 1993): 791–814.

50. Stone, "Some Post-War Recollections," 251.

51. Percy, Lanterns, 37.

52. Ibid., 38.

53. Henry Waring Ball Diary, January 2, 1905, MDAH.

54. Percy, Lanterns, 142.

55. Jay Tolson, Pilgrim in the Ruins: A Life of Walker Percy (New York: Simon and Schuster, 1992), 59; Wyatt-Brown, House of Percy, 193.

Chapter 2

1. *Greenville Times*, May 16, 1885, MDAH.

2. Two letters from Percy's childhood survive and are reprinted in Hester Sharbrough Ware, "A Study of the Life and Works of William Alexander Percy" (M.A. thesis, Mississippi State University, 1950), 13–14. Though they do not contain substantial information of thematic value, they may provide some insight into Percy's childhood personality, so I reprint them here using the original punctuation, spelling, and presentation. Percy was seven years old when he wrote the first letter to his Aunt Leila Bourges, who was away with Percy's mother and his baby brother, LeRoy Percy Jr.:

> Greenville, Miss.
> Will Alexander Percy
> February 3 1893
> Dear Tante I miss you so much I want you to come home will you let me know
> LeRoy is all-right and Mama Give my love to unkel Jack How do you like the place
> Good-by I hope you will right soon
> A kiss for all   o o

Percy wrote the second letter, also to Leila Bourges, when he was eight:

> Greenville, Miss.
> Jan. 1, 1894
> Dear Tante
> I will just write a few lines to tell you I appreachate your kindness of sending me
> the lovely gold studs and little hatchet. Did you have a merry Xmas. We did but we
> had a great excightment. I will tell you about it. We were all shoting Roman Candles and on takeing they from a great pile Uncle Walker who was shooting one off
> at the time let a spark drop on the pile and set it on fire. They went every where
> Aunt Pratt who was standing near the steps flew up like a chicken with her head
> cut off. A when she got to the [top] she sat down and watched them go into Manners rooms. I am writeing this letter on New Years night so I wish you a happy
> New Year. The fire whistel blew for about a 1//2 and our at 12 oclock to show that a
> new year was born. Ed and Wewe took dinner here today as it was New Year.
>
> I must stop now but by the way Wewe says how did the cake [come] out and I
> say what did Uncle Jack give you for Christmas?
>
> Good By
> I am your nephue Will Percy

3. William Alexander Percy, *Lanterns on the Levee: Recollections of a Planter's Son* (New York: Alfred A. Knopf, 1941), 26. The most perceptive analysis of Percy's writing about race, and particularly about Percy's descriptions of black freedom and other-worldliness in *Lanterns on the Levee*, is McKay Jenkins, *The South in Black and White:*

Race, Sex, and Literature in the 1940s (Chapel Hill: University of North Carolina Press, 1999), chap. 3.

4. See Susan Tucker, "The Black Domestic in the South: Her Legacy as Mother and Mother Surrogate," in *Southern Women*, ed. Caroline Matheny Dillman (New York: Hemisphere Publishing Company, 1988), 93–102; David M. Katzman, *Seven Days a Week: Women and Domestic Service in Industrializing America* (New York: Oxford University Press, 1978), esp. chap. 5; Joan Wylie Hall, "'White Mamma . . . Black Mammy': Replacing the Absent Mother in the Works of Ruth McEnery Stuart," in *Southern Mothers: Fact and Fictions in Southern Women's Writing*, ed. Nagueyalti Warren and Sally Wolff (Baton Rouge: Louisiana State University Press, 1999).

5. Percy, *Lanterns*, 26.

6. Ibid., 27.

7. Ibid.

8. Ibid., 46–49 and 287. On race relations in Mississippi in the 1890s, see especially Neil McMillan, *Dark Journey: Black Mississippians in the Age of Jim Crow* (Urbana: University of Illinois Press, 1989).

9. Percy, *Lanterns*, 48–49.

10. Ibid., 49.

11. Ibid., 54–55.

12. Ibid., 56–57.

13. Ibid., 57–58.

14. Ibid., 126 and 128.

15. Ibid., 65–68.

16. Ibid., 69.

17. WAPD, November 16, 1910, WAPP.

18. See, for example, LeRoy Percy to William Alexander Percy, April 28, 1908, WAPP.

19. Lewis Baker Interview with Brodie S. Crump, Hill Memorial Library, Louisiana State University, Baton Rouge, La.

20. Percy, *Lanterns*, 76–77.

21. Both quotes in Michael Kimmell, *Manhood in America: A Cultural History* (New York: The Free Press, 1996), 121. On the "crisis of masculinity" (some historians prefer to call it "an obsession with masculinity") during this period, see especially Gail Bederman, *Manliness and Civilization: A Cultural History of Gender and Race in the United States, 1880–1917* (Chicago: University of Chicago Press, 1995); and E. Anthony Rotundo, *American Manhood: Transformations in Masculinity from the Revolution to the Modern Era* (New York: Basic Books, 1993), esp. chap. 10.

22. See, for example, "Address by Senator LeRoy Percy, Greenville Miss., March 18, 1922," WAPP.

23. Quoted in Bederman, *Manliness and Civilization*, 193.

24. See George Chauncey, *Gay New York: Gender, Urban Culture, and the Making of the Gay Male World, 1890–1940* (New York: Basic Books, 1994); Kevin J. Mumford, *Interzones: Black/White Sex Districts in Chicago and New York in the Early Twentieth Cen-*

tury (New York: Columbia University Press, 1997); and Chad Heap, *Slumming: Sexual and Racial Encounters in American Nightlife, 1885–1940* (Chicago: University of Chicago Press, 2010).

25. Chauncey, *Gay New York*, 56.

26. Percy, *Lanterns*, 126, 161, 169, 173, 92.

27. Ibid., 126 and 347.

28. Lewis Baker Interview with Brodie S. Crump, Hill Memorial Library, Louisiana State University, Baton Rouge, La.; Sally Bolding, *The Cyclops Window: A View Into Southern Life* (Pensacola Beach, Fla.: LeveePressTwo, 2003), 85.

29. Percy, *Lanterns*, 76–78.

30. Ibid., 76–79.

31. Ibid., 81–83.

32. Ibid., 83–86.

33. Ibid., 89.

34. William Alexander Percy to Janet Dana Longcope, n.d., JDLP.

Chapter 3

1. LeRoy Percy to B. L. Wiggins, June 30, 1900, WAPP.

2. Arthur Benjamin Chitty Jr., *Reconstruction at Sewanee* (Sewanee, Tenn.: The University Press, 1954), 183n34.

3. Moultrie Guerry, *Men Who Made Sewanee* (Sewanee, Tenn.: The University Press, 1932), ix and xi.

4. Quoted in Woody Register, "Remembering Ninety-Nine Iron: A Historical Perspective on the Legendary Football Team That Won Five Games in Six Days," in *Sewanee Perspectives: On the History of the University of the South*, ed. Gerald L. Smith and Samuel R. Williamson (Sewanee, Tenn.: The University Press, 2008), 352. The mania for football during these years was extraordinary, perhaps especially so at Sewanee, which had a dominant team. An acquaintance of Percy's during his time at Sewanee captured this atmosphere in a letter home. Charles Manning (Sinkler Manning's cousin) wrote to his father in 1904: "Papa, I hope you will let me go to Nashville Thanksgiving to see the Vanderbilt-Sewanee game. This is the game of the year, everybody from the 'V.C.' and his family down to the cooks going up to see it. Not more than 25 or 30 people will be left on the mountain." Charles Manning to William Sinkler Manning, November 16, 1904, William Sinkler Manning Papers, South Caroliniana Library, University of South Carolina, Columbia, S.C. Underlining in original.

5. Chitty, *Reconstruction at Sewanee*, 180. On "intellectual manhood," see especially Lorri Glover, *Southern Sons: Becoming Men in the New Nation* (Baltimore: Johns Hopkins University Press, 2007), esp. part 2; and Timothy J. Williams, "Intellectual Manhood: Becoming Men of the Republic at a Southern University, 1795–1861" (Ph.D. diss., University of North Carolina, 2010).

6. T. J. Jackson Lears, *No Place of Grace: Antimodernism and the Transformation of*

American Culture, 1880–1920 (Chicago: University of Chicago Press, 1981); Lears, *Rebirth of a Nation: The Making of Modern America, 1877–1920* (New York: Harper, 2009); Linda Dowling, *Hellenism and Homosexuality in Victorian Oxford* (Ithaca: Cornell University Press, 1994).

7. On Hellenism in the nineteenth century, see especially Richard Jenkyns, *The Victorians and Ancient Greece* (Cambridge, Mass.: Harvard University Press, 1980); Frank M. Turner, *The Greek Heritage in Victorian Britain* (New Haven: Yale University Press, 1984); Michael O'Brien, *Conjectures of Order: Intellectual Life and the American South, 1810–1860* (Chapel Hill: University of North Carolina Press, 2004), esp. vol. 1, chap. 3; Elizabeth Fox-Genovese and Eugene Genovese, *The Mind of the Master Class: History and Faith in the Southern Slaveholders' Worldview* (Cambridge: Cambridge University Press, 2005), esp. parts 2 and 3; and Suzanne L. Marchand, *Down from Olympus: Archaeology and Philhellenism in Germany, 1750–1970* (Princeton: Princeton University Press, 2003).

8. Dowling, *Hellenism and Homosexuality*, 26; Wilde quoted in Richard Ellman, *Oscar Wilde* (New York: Alfred A. Knopf, 1988), 463.

9. On nineteenth-century developments regarding male homosexuality, see David M. Halperin, *One Hundred Years of Homosexuality, and Other Essays on Greek Love* (New York: Routledge, 1990); Scott Bravmann, *Queer Fictions of the Past: History, Culture, and Difference* (Cambridge: Cambridge University Press, 1997); Jonathan Ned Katz, *Love Stories: Sex between Men before Homosexuality* (Chicago: University of Chicago Press, 2001); Jeffrey Weeks, *Coming Out: Homosexual Politics in Britain from the Nineteenth Century to the Present* (London: Quartet Books, 1977); Matt Cook, *London and the Culture of Homosexuality, 1885–1914* (Cambridge: Cambridge University Press, 2003); William A. Peniston, *Pederasts and Others: Urban Culture and Sexual Identity in Nineteenth-Century Paris* (New York: The Haworth Press, 2004); and Graham Robb, *Strangers: Homosexual Love in the Nineteenth Century* (New York: W. W. Norton, 2005).

10. Plato, *Symposium and Phaedrus*, trans. Tom Griffith with an introduction by R. B. Rutherford (New York: Alfred A. Knopf, 2000), 55, 63, 64.

11. Symonds quoted in Phyllis Grosskurth, *John Addington Symonds: A Biography* (London: Longmans, Green, and Company, 1964), 270; Wilde quoted in Ellman, *Oscar Wilde*, 298; Cook, *London and the Culture of Homosexuality*, 126–27.

12. William Porcher DuBose, *Turning Points in My Life* (New York: Longmans, Green, & Co., 1912), 4–5.

13. William Alexander Percy, *Lanterns on the Levee: Recollections of a Planter's Son* (New York: Alfred A. Knopf, 1941), 92–93.

14. "Matriculation Book," September 18, 1868, through June 24, 1913, University Archives, University of the South, Sewanee, Tenn.

15. Percy, *Lanterns*, 95–96.

16. Byrne R. S. Fone, "This Other Eden: Arcadia and the Homosexual Imagination,"

in *Literary Visions of Homosexuality*, ed. Stuart Kellogg (New York: The Haworth Press, 1983), 13.

17. Percy, *Lanterns*, 93.

18. Interview with Marymor Sanborn Cravens, February 18, 2005, Sewanee, Tenn.

19. Cynthia Sanborn Diary, May 22, 1929, in author's possession. The author would like to thank Pamela Tyler for pointing out this source.

20. Percy, *Lanterns*, 95.

21. Ibid., 94–95.

22. William Alexander Percy to Carrie Stern, January 7, 1919, WAPP.

23. "Mrs. Manning Gave Six Sons to Army," *New York Times*, December 1, 1918, 10.

24. Percy, *Lanterns*, 95–99.

25. Ibid., 100–103.

26. Ibid., 101, 79, 95.

27. William Alexander Percy, *In April Once* (New Haven: Yale University Press, 1920), 132–34.

28. On Percy's comments about "Sappho in Levkas," see, for example, William Alexander Percy to DuBose Heyward, 3 July 1923, WAPP. "Sappho in Levkas" has been read as evidence of Will Percy's homoeroticism also in William Armstrong Percy, "William Alexander Percy: His Homosexuality and Why It Matters," in *Carryin' On in the Gay and Lesbian South*, ed. John Howard (New York: New York University Press, 1997), 75–92; and John Barry, *Rising Tide: The Great Mississippi Flood of 1927 and How It Changed America* (New York: Touchstone, 1997), 296–97.

29. William Alexander Percy to Elizabeth Monroe, January 29, 1932, WAPP.

30. Roark Bradford, "Foreword," in William Alexander Percy, *The Collected Poems of William Alexander Percy* (New York: Alfred A. Knopf, 1943), 5.

31. All quotes from Percy, *Sappho in Levkas, and Other Poems* (New Haven: Yale University Press, 1915), 2–18.

32. Fone, "This Other Eden," 13.

33. Percy, *Lanterns*, 103.

Chapter 4

1. LeRoy Percy to William Alexander Percy, August 14, 1902, WAPP.

2. William Alexander Percy, *Lanterns on the Levee: Recollections of a Planter's Son* (New York: Alfred A. Knopf, 1941), 105. For LeRoy Percy's hunting trips with Teddy Roosevelt, see Minor Ferris Buchanan, *Holt Collier: His Life, His Roosevelt Hunts, and the Origin of the Teddy Bear* (Jackson, Miss.: Centennial Press, 2002).

3. Percy, *Lanterns*, 105; William Alexander Percy to Camille Percy, September 29, 1904, WAPP.

4. William A. Peniston, *Pederasts and Others: Urban Culture and Sexual Identity in Nineteenth-Century Paris* (Binghamton, N.Y.: Harrington Park Press, 2004); Vernon A.

Rosario II, "Pointy Penises, Fashion Crimes, and Hysterical Mollies: The Pederasts' Inversions," in *Homosexuality in Modern France*, ed. Jeffrey Merrick and Bryant T. Ragan Jr. (New York: Oxford University Press, 1996), 146–76.

5. William Alexander Percy to Camille Percy, September 15, 1907, WAPP. In this letter, though written in 1907, Percy is describing his 1904 apartment to his mother.

6. Percy, *Lanterns*, 106.

7. Ibid.

8. William Alexander Percy to Camille Percy, September 29, 1904, WAPP.

9. Ibid.

10. William Alexander Percy to Camille Percy, October 6, 1904, WAPP.

11. Percy, *Lanterns*, 107.

12. Ibid.

13. William Alexander Percy to Camille Percy, September 29, 1904, WAPP; Percy, *Lanterns*, 106.

14. William Alexander Percy to Camille Percy, December 22, 1904, WAPP; William Alexander Percy to Camille Percy, September 29, 1904, WAPP. On Natalie Clifford Barney, see especially Suzanne Rodriguez, *Wild Heart: A Life: Natalie Clifford Barney and the Decadence of Literary Paris* (New York: Harper Perennial, 2003); and Natalie C. Barney, *Adventures of the Mind: The Memoirs of Natalie Clifford Barney*, trans. John S. Gatton (New York: New York University Press, 1993). When Percy and Harold Bruff traveled to Paris in 1907, they stayed at 22 Rue Jacob; Natalie Clifford Barney's famous and controversial Left Bank salon—with its "Temple of Friendship" in the courtyard and its regular "Sappho Parties"—was located at 20 Rue Jacob, though she did not move there until 1909. Nonetheless, this reiterates Percy's proximity to radical sexual politics throughout his life. See William Alexander Percy to Camille Percy, September 15, 1907, WAPP.

15. Percy, *Lanterns*, 110–11.

16. Francis Haskell and Nicholas Penny, *Taste and the Antique: The Lure of Classical Sculpture* (New Haven: Yale University Press, 1981), 321–23; Mary Beard and John Henderson, *Classical Art: From Greece to Rome* (Oxford: Oxford University Press, 2001), 128.

17. Percy, *Lanterns*, 111. The preeminent theorist of the biological manifestation of sex in the human body is Anne Fausto-Sterling, who offers a compelling critique of rigid categories such as "male" and "female" in human societies. She also discusses hermaphroditism in a way that sheds light on Percy's connection of hermaphroditic sculptures with queer sexuality. "Hermaphrodites have unruly bodies," Fausto-Sterling writes, "inasmuch as hermaphrodites literally embody both sexes, they challenge traditional beliefs about sexual difference: they possess the irritating ability to live sometimes as one sex and sometimes the other, and they raise the specter of homosexuality." See Anne Fausto-Sterling, "The Five Sexes: Why Male and Female Are Not Enough," *The Sciences* (March/April 1993): 24. See also Fausto-Sterling, *Myths of Gender: Biological Theories about Women and Men*, rev. ed. (New York: Basic Books, 1992); Fausto-Sterling, *Sexing the Body: Gender Politics and the Construction of Sexuality* (New York: Basic

Books, 2000); and Thomas Laquer, *Making Sex: Body and Gender from the Greeks to Freud* (Cambridge, Mass.: Harvard University Press, 1992).

18. William Alexander Percy, *In April Once* (New Haven: Yale University Press, 1920), 132–33. Percy's interpretation of the ancient Greeks was part truth, part stereotype, and part myth. Historians have shown that "homoerotic Hellenism" was useful for nineteenth- and early twentieth-century homosexual men, though their interpretation was often selective and presentist. My concern with Percy is less with the veracity of his interpretation than the use to which he put it in forming his beliefs about history, art, and sexuality. See Scott Bravmann, *Queer Fictions of the Past: History, Culture, and Difference* (Cambridge: Cambridge University Press, 1997); David Halperin, *One Hundred Years of Homosexuality, and Other Essays on Greek Love* (New York: Routledge, 1990); K. J. Dover, *Greek Homosexuality* (Cambridge, Mass.: Harvard University Press, 1978); Linda Dowling, *Hellenism and Homosexuality in Victorian Oxford* (Ithaca: Cornell University Press, 1994); James N. Davidson, *The Greeks and Greek Love: A Radical Reappraisal of Homosexuality in Ancient Greece* (London: Phoenix, 2008).

19. William Alexander Percy, *The Collected Poems of William Alexander Percy* (New York: Alfred A. Knopf, 1942), 209; William Alexander Percy to Evelyn Rivers, September 26, 1922, WAPP. When "A Canticle" was published in the August 1922 issue of *Scribner's*, a man from Wilmore, Kentucky, wrote to the editor of the magazine and said, "The men's Bible class of the Methodist church here wish to enter a protest against this." The editor sent the note to Percy, who responded that the protest gave him "amusement and real pleasure." See W. B. Hughes to Charles Scribner's Sons, September 2, 1922, WAPP; and William Alexander Percy to Robert Bridges, September 26, 1922, WAPP.

20. First Symonds quote in Phyllis Grosskurth, *John Addington Symonds: A Biography* (London: Longmans, Green, and Company, 1964), 272; second Symonds quote in Herbert M. Schueller and Robert L. Peters, eds., *The Letters of John Addington Symonds* (Detroit: Wayne State University Press, 1969), 459.

21. Percy, *Lanterns*, 110.

22. William Alexander Percy to LeRoy Percy, n.d., 1905, WAPP.

23. William Alexander Percy to Camille Percy, November 15, 16, and 17, 1904, WAPP.

24. William Alexander Percy to LeRoy Percy, March 30, 1905, WAPP.

25. John Addington Symonds, *Sketches in Italy* (Leipzig: Bernhard Tauchnitz, 1883), 13.

26. William Alexander Percy to Camille Percy, April 10, 1905, WAPP.

27. Robert Aldrich, *The Seduction of the Mediterranean: Writing, Art, and Homosexual Fantasy* (New York: Routledge, 1993), x.

28. Ibid., 169. See also Willy, *The Third Sex*, trans. and with an introduction and notes by Lawrence R. Schehr (Urbana: University of Illinois Press, 2007), esp. chaps. 1 and 4.

29. John Addington Symonds, *Sketches in Italy and Greece* (London: Smith, Elder, & Co., 1879), 274–75.

30. Percy, *Lanterns*, 321.

31. Ibid., 315, 320–21.

32. Several scholars (including myself, in earlier drafts of this book) have overemphasized the connection between Percy's melancholy and unrequited sexual desire and feelings of alienation in the American South. While containing some truth—one should not underestimate the general homophobic orientation of southern (and American, and European) culture during Percy's lifetime—this is too narrow a view in consideration of the full spectrum of intellectual, spiritual, cultural, and sexual questions with which he wrestled. Insofar as possible, these aspects of his life should be considered together. See Richard King, *A Southern Renaissance: The Cultural Awakening of the American South, 1930–1955* (New York: Oxford University Press, 1980), 95–98; Bertram Wyatt-Brown, *House of Percy: Honor, Melancholy, and Imagination in a Southern Family* (New York: Oxford: University Press, 1994), 195–97; McKay Jenkins, *The South in Black and White: Race, Sex, and Literature in the 1940s* (Chapel Hill: University of North Carolina Press, 1999), 103; John Barry, *Rising Tide: The Great Mississippi Flood of 1927 and How It Changed America* (New York: Touchstone, 1997), 293–302; Benjamin E. Wise, "The Cosmopolitanism of William Alexander Percy," in *Southern Masculinity: Perspectives on Manhood in the South since Reconstruction*, ed. Craig T. Friend (Athens: University of Georgia Press, 2009), 129–49.

33. Percy, *Lanterns*, 112.

34. William Alexander Percy to Camille Percy, January 17, 1905, WAPP.

35. William Alexander Percy to Camille Percy, April 19, 1905, WAPP.

36. William Alexander Percy to Camille Percy, n.d., WAPP.

37. William Alexander Percy to Camille Percy, January 9, 1905, WAPP.

38. William Alexander Percy to Camille Percy, January 28, 1905, WAPP.

39. William Alexander Percy to Camille Percy, February 4, 5, 6, and 7, 1905, WAPP.

40. Ibid.

41. Ibid.

42. Ibid.

43. William Alexander Percy to LeRoy Percy, March 30 (no year), WAPP.

44. William Alexander Percy to Camille Percy, April 10, 1905, WAPP.

45. Ibid.

46. William Alexander Percy to Camille Percy, April 19, 1905, WAPP.

47. Percy, *Lanterns on the Levee*, 111.

48. Ibid., 112.

Chapter 5

1. John Maxtone-Graham, *Crossing and Cruising: From the Golden Era of Ocean Liners to the Luxury Cruise Ships of Today* (New York: Charles Scribner's Sons, 1992), 30.

2. See http://www.ellisisland.org/search/shipManifest.asp?MID=06832220420159 684096&LNM=MAR&PLNM=MAR&SYR=1905&EYR=1905&last_kind=1&town_

kind=0&ship_kind=0&SHIP=SAINT+PAUL&RF=104&SHP=SAINT+PAUL&
pID=102407070505& (September 9, 2008).

3. William Alexander Percy, *Lanterns on the Levee: Recollections of a Planter's Son*
(New York: Alfred A. Knopf, 1941), 113, 126, 114.

4. Donald C. King, *Theatres of Boston: A Stage and Screen History* (Jefferson, N.C.:
Macfarland & Company, 2008); Tobie Stein, *Boston's Colonial Theatre: Celebrating a
Century of Theatrical Vision* (Boston: Colonial Theatre, 2000).

5. *Official Register of Harvard University* 3, no. 8 (March 31, 1906): 14–15. Harvard Law
School Archives, Cambridge, Mass.

6. Harold Bruff 1905 Alumni File, Yale University Manuscripts and Archives, New
Haven, Conn.

7. "An Education in Firearms," *New York Times*, August 6, 1893, 2; "Sea Coast Rapid-
Fire Guns," *New York Times*, March 12, 1898, 2; Henry W. B. Howard, ed., *The Eagle
and Brooklyn* (Brooklyn: Brooklyn Daily Eagle, 1893), 1038, Brooklyn Historical Society,
Brooklyn, N.Y.

8. *Official Register of Harvard University*, 39.

9. Percy, *Lanterns*, 116 and 122; *Official Register of Harvard University*, 6.

10. William Alexander Percy to Camille Percy, 4 November 1907, WAPP; Kristin
Hogansen, "Cosmopolitan Domesticity: Importing the American Dream, 1865–1920,"
American Historical Review 107, no. 1 (February 2002): 55–83.

11. William Alexander Percy to Camille Percy, February 13, 1906, WAPP.

12. Percy, *Lanterns*, 120.

13. William Alexander Percy to Camille Percy, February 13, 1906, WAPP.

14. William Alexander Percy to Camille Percy, n.d., Sunday, WAPP.

15. Percy, *Lanterns*, 121.

16. Quoted in John T. Bethell, *Harvard Observed: An Illustrated History of the University in the Twentieth Century* (Cambridge, Mass.: Harvard University Press, 1998), 55.

17. Quoted in Kim Townsend, *Manhood at Harvard: William James and Others* (New
York: W. W. Norton, 1996), 16.

18. Bethell, *Harvard Observed*, 29 and 15.

19. Theodore Roosevelt, "The College Man," reprinted in Donald Wilhelm, *Theodore
Roosevelt as an Undergraduate* (Boston: J. W. Luce, 1910), 78–90.

20. William Alexander Percy to LeRoy Percy, n.d., WAPP.

21. Roosevelt quoted in Sarah Watts, *Rough Rider in the White House: Theodore
Roosevelt and the Politics of Desire* (Chicago: University of Chicago Press, 2003), 6–8.

22. Douglas Shand-Tucci, *The Crimson Letter: Harvard, Homosexuality, and the
Shaping of American Culture* (New York: St. Martin's Press, 2003).

23. Ibid., 102.

24. Havelock Ellis, *Studies in the Psychology of Sex*, vol. 2, *Sexual Inversion*, 2nd ed.
(Philadelphia: F. A. Davis Company, 1908), 240–42.

25. William Alexander Percy to Camille Percy, June 27, 1908, WAPP.

26. William Alexander Percy to Camille Percy, n.d., WAPP.

27. Percy, *Lanterns*, 127.

28. William Alexander Percy to Camille Percy, April 30, 1906.

29. Charles Francis Adams, "Reflex Light from Africa," *The Century Magazine* 72, no. 1 (May 1906): 106–7.

30. William Alexander Percy to Camille Percy, April 30, 1906, WAPP.

31. William Alexander Percy to Camille Percy, March 26, 1906; April 30, 1906; and n.d.; all in WAPP.

32. William Alexander Percy to Camille Percy, January 14, 1906, WAPP.

33. William Alexander Percy to Camille Percy, February 13, 1906, WAPP.

34. William Alexander Percy to Camille Percy, April 30, 1906, WAPP.

35. William Alexander Percy to Camille Percy, n.d., WAPP.

36. William Alexander Percy to Camille Percy, May 14, 1906; n.d.; June 11, 1906; and June 28, 1906; all in WAPP.

37. William Alexander Percy to Carrie Stern, January 7, 1919, WAPP.

38. Shand-Tucci, *The Crimson Letter*, 108.

39. George Chauncey, *Gay New York: Gender, Urban Culture, and the Making of the Gay Male World, 1890–1940* (New York: Basic Books, 1994), 35, 41, 138. On "Slumming," see also Chad Heap, *Slumming: Sexual and Racial Encounters in American Nightlife, 1885–1940* (Chicago: University of Chicago Press, 2009).

40. William Alexander Percy to Camille Percy, November 18, 1906, WAPP.

41. "Gay men quickly spread the word about which restaurants and cafeterias would let them gather without guarding their behavior," Chauncey writes. "Several Childs cafeterias and restaurants located in heavily gay neighborhoods became known among gay men as meeting places." Chauncey, *Gay New York*, 166.

42. William Alexander Percy to Camille Percy, November 18, 1906, WAPP.

43. Ibid.

44. William Alexander Percy to Carrie Stern, January 7, 1919, WAPP. On Manning's later family life, see William Sinkler Manning Jr. to William Sinkler Manning, October 30, 1912, William Sinkler Manning Papers, South Caroliniana Library, University of South Carolina, Columbia, S.C.; and "Major Manning Honored," *New York Times*, April 18, 1919, 12.

45. William Alexander Percy to Camille Percy, n.d., WAPP.

46. William Alexander Percy to Camille Percy, November 18, 1906, and n.d.; both in WAPP.

47. Percy, *Lanterns*, 122.

48. William Alexander Percy to Carrie Stern, April 21, 1907, WAPP.

49. Percy, *Lanterns*, 131.

50. William Alexander Percy, *The Collected Poems of William Alexander Percy* (New York: Alfred A. Knopf, 1943), 241.

51. William Alexander Percy to Camille Percy, January 3, 1907, WAPP.

52. *New York Times*, August 12, 1911, 4; *New York Times*, October 1, 1910, 13.

53. Harold Bruff to William Alexander Percy, July 1, 1907, WAPP.

54. William Alexander Percy to Camille Percy, August 11, 1907, WAPP.

55. William Alexander Percy to Camille Percy, August 21, 1907, WAPP.

56. William Alexander Percy to Camille Percy, September 1, 1907, WAPP.

57. Ibid.

58. William Alexander Percy to Camille Percy, August 26, 1907, WAPP.

59. William Alexander Percy to LeRoy Percy, November 9, 1907, WAPP.

60. William Alexander Percy to Camille Percy, n.d., WAPP.

61. Percy, *Lanterns*, 123.

62. William Alexander Percy to Camille Percy, n.d., WAPP.

63. William Alexander Percy to Camille Percy, December 21, 1907, WAPP.

64. William Alexander Percy to Camille Percy, April 6, 1908, WAPP.

65. Ibid.

66. William Alexander Percy to Camille Percy, May 25, 1908, WAPP.

67. Quoted in Townsend, *Manhood at Harvard*, 24.

68. William Alexander Percy to Camille Percy, July 2, 1908, WAPP.

69. Harold Bruff to William Alexander Percy, August 29, 1908, WAPP.

70. Ibid.

71. Ibid.

Chapter 6

1. William Alexander Percy, *Lanterns on the Levee: Recollections of a Planter's Son* (New York: Alfred A. Knopf, 1941), 122.

2. Lynching data in Neil R. McMillen, *Dark Journey: Black Mississippians in the Age of Jim Crow* (Urbana: University of Illinois Press, 1989), 232. In 1903 a black man accused of attacking a white woman in Greenville was lynched before a mob crowd downtown. "Everything was very orderly," one local observer wrote in his diary. "There was not a shot, but much laughing and hilarious excitement. . . . It was quite a gala occasion, and as soon as the corpse was cut down, all the crowd betook themselves to the park to see a game of baseball." See James C. Cobb, *The Most Southern Place on Earth: The Mississippi Delta and the Roots of Regional Identity* (New York: Oxford University Press, 1992), 113.

3. David Delaney, *Race, Place, and the Law, 1836–1948* (Austin: University of Texas Press, 1998), 99.

4. Percy, *Lanterns*, 21.

5. Ibid., 20.

6. "Privilege Tax License," n.d., WAPP; Percy, *Lanterns*, 125–26.

7. Percy, *Lanterns*, 270, 57, 126.

8. William Alexander Percy, "The Fifth Autumn," undated manuscript, WAPP.

9. Percy, *Lanterns*, 78 and 130.

10. William Alexander Percy, *In April Once* (New Haven: Yale University Press, 1920), 120.

11. Percy, *Lanterns*, 126.

12. Harold Bruff to William Alexander Percy, November 24 (no year), WAPP.

13. Ibid. Underlining in original.

14. Sewanee Class of 1909 to William Alexander Percy, April 7, 1909, WAPP.

15. WAPD, October 15, 1910, WAPP.

16. Percy's return from Europe can be accessed at http://www.ellisisland.org/search/passRecord.asp?MID=06832220420159684096&FNM=WILLIAM&LNM=PERCY&PLNM=PERCY&bSYR=1885&bEYR=1885&first_kind=1&last_kind=0&TOWN=null&SHIP=null&RF=4&pID=101687031114 (March 4, 2010); Bruff's record can be accessed at http://www.ellisisland.org/search/passRecord.asp?MID=06832220420159684096&FNM=HAROLD&LNM=BRUFF&PLNM=BRUFF&bSYR=1884&bEYR=1884&first_kind=1&last_kind=0&TOWN=null&SHIP=null&RF=2&pID=101718020205 (March 4, 2010).

17. Quoted in Stephen Cresswell, *Rednecks, Redeemers, and Race: Mississippi after Reconstruction, 1877–1917* (Jackson: University Press of Mississippi, 2006), 197.

18. Quoted in William F. Holmes, *The White Chief: James Kimble Vardaman* (Baton Rouge: Louisiana State University Press, 1970), 109.

19. Percy, *Lanterns*, 143–44. On Mississippi political history as it relates to Percy and Vardaman, see Cresswell, *Rednecks, Redeemers, and Race*, chap. 11; Holmes, *The White Chief*, chaps. 7–10; Nannie Pitts McLemore, "The Progressive Era," in *A History of Mississippi*, vol. 2, ed. Richard Aubrey McLemore (Jackson: University and College Press of Mississippi, 1973), chap. 23; Lewis Baker, *The Percys of Mississippi: Politics and Literature in the New South* (Baton Rouge: Louisiana State University Press, 1983), chap. 3; Bertram Wyatt-Brown, *The House of Percy: Honor, Melancholy, and Imagination in a Southern Family* (New York: Oxford University Press, 1994), chap. 9; Albert D. Kirwan, *Revolt of the Rednecks: Mississippi Politics, 1876–1925* (Lexington: University Press of Kentucky, 1951), chaps. 11–18; and Cobb, *The Most Southern Place on Earth*, 144–50.

20. V. O. Key, *Southern Politics in State and Nation* (New York: Alfred A. Knopf, 1949); George Brown Tindall, *The Emergence of the New South, 1913–1945* (Baton Rouge: Louisiana State University Press, 1967), esp. chaps. 5 and 6; C. Vann Woodward, *The Origins of the New South, 1877–1913* (Baton Rouge: Louisiana State University Press, 1951), esp. chap. 4; Joel Williamson, *The Crucible of Race: Black-White Relations in the American South since Emancipation* (New York: Oxford University Press, 1984), esp. parts 1 and 2. I use the term "populist" here to indicate the grassroots appeal of someone like Vardaman, not as a reference to the Populist movement of the 1890s.

21. Barbara Fields, "Ideology and Race in American History," in *Region, Race, and Reconstruction: Essays in Honor of C. Vann Woodward*, ed. J. Morgan Kousser and James M. McPherson (New York: Oxford University Press, 1982), 157.

22. See, for example, Stephen Kantrowitz, *Ben Tillman and the Reconstruction of*

White Supremacy (Chapel Hill: University of North Carolina Press, 2000); C. Vann Woodward, *Tom Watson: Agrarian Rebel* (New York: The Macmillan Company, 1938); Dan Carter, *The Politics of Rage: George Wallace, the Origins of the New Conservatism, and the Transformation of American Politics* (Baton Rouge: Louisiana State University Press, 1995); and T. Harry Williams, *Huey Long* (New York: Alfred A. Knopf, 1969).

23. Wyatt-Brown, *House of Percy*, 178–79.

24. Holmes, *The White Chief*, 15–32; quote on 39.

25. See, for example, C. Vann Woodward, *The Strange Career of Jim Crow* (New York: Oxford University Press, 1955), esp. chap. 3.

26. Holmes, *The White Chief*, 198.

27. Ibid., 96–97; Cresswell, *Rednecks, Redeemers, and Race*, 190–93; Kirwan, *Revolt of the Rednecks*, chap. 11; and William F. Holmes, "William Alexander Percy and the Bourbon Era in Mississippi Politics," *Mississippi Quarterly* 26 (Winter 1972–73): 71–87.

28. Percy, *Lanterns*, 143–44.

29. Ibid., 144; Holmes, *The White Chief*, 201.

30. Holmes, *The White Chief*, 206–8.

31. Ibid., 212.

32. Percy, *Lanterns*, 146; Holmes, *The White Chief*, 214–15, 227.

33. Quoted in Wyatt-Brown, *House of Percy*, 182. Harry Hotspur (Sir Henry Percy) was the Earl of Northumberland in the fourteenth century and a major character in Shakespeare's *Henry IV*.

34. Harold Bruff to William Alexander Percy, January 1, 1910, WAPP.

35. Harold Bruff to William Alexander Percy, "Wednesday," n.d., WAPP.

36. WAPD, "Sunday November 29 or so," WAPP.

37. George Creel, "What Are You Going to Do about It? The Carnival of Corruption in Mississippi," *Cosmopolitan* 2 (November 1911): 725–35.

38. Holmes, *The White Chief*, 209 and 226.

39. A. Wigfall Green, *The Man Bilbo* (Baton Rouge: Louisiana State University Press, 1963), 37.

40. Percy, *Lanterns*, 147.

41. Holmes, *The White Chief*, 234–36.

42. WAPD, November 1, 1910, WAPP.

43. Quoted in Holmes, *The White Chief*, 236.

44. Lewis Baker interview with Brodie S. Crump, Hill Memorial Library, Louisiana State University, Baton Rouge, La.

45. Percy, *Lanterns*, 149.

46. Ibid., 73–74.

47. Ibid., 149.

48. Quoted in Wyatt-Brown, *House of Percy*, 187; Holmes, *The White Chief*, 238.

49. Quoted in Green, *The Man Bilbo*, 39.

50. Holmes, *The White Chief*, 253; Green, *The Man Bilbo*, 40–41.

51. Green, *The Man Bilbo*, 39.

52. Holmes, *The White Chief*, 240–41.

53. Percy, *Lanterns*, 149–50.

54. Holmes, *The White Chief*, 241; Wyatt-Brown, *House of Percy*, 189.

55. Percy, *Lanterns*, 151.

56. Quoted in Baker, *The Percys of Mississippi*, 51.

57. Holmes, *The White Chief*, 244–45.

58. Harold Bruff to William Alexander Percy, n.d., WAPP.

59. Harold Bruff to William Alexander Percy, "Thursday," n.d., WAPP.

60. Harold Bruff to William Alexander Percy, "Wednesday," n.d., WAPP. On Wilde and "De Profundis," see Richard Ellman, *Oscar Wilde* (New York: Alfred A. Knopf, 1988), 513–16; Neil McKenna, *The Secret Life of Oscar Wilde* (New York: Basic Books, 2005), 420–28; and Oscar Wilde, *De Profundis*, with an introduction by Jacques Barzun (New York: Vintage Books, 1964).

61. Harold Bruff to William Alexander Percy, "Thursday," n.d., WAPP.

62. "Obituary Notes," *New York Times*, October 1, 1910, 13.

63. *Brooklyn Times*, October 13, 1911, 14, Brooklyn Historical Society.

64. WAPD, October 15, 1910, WAPP.

65. Ibid., November 16 and October 15, 1910.

66. Ibid., October 17, 1910.

67. Ibid., October 28, 1910.

68. Ibid., November 6, 1910.

69. Ibid.

70. Ibid.

71. Ibid., October 18, 1910.

72. Ibid., October 24, 1910.

73. Ibid., October 28, 1910.

74. While in Washington, D.C., Camille Percy gave a talk to the "D.C. Ladies Club" that reveals something of her own perspective on race relations. She said: "The Negro Question, which seems such a paramount issue up here, has long ago been settled to our satisfaction in the South. The Negro must pay a poll tax two years in advance of voting, and that practically eliminates him from the political question." Undated clipping in WAPP.

75. WAPD, November 7, 8, 9, 10, 16, and "Sunday November 29 or so," 1910, WAPP.

76. Ibid., November 19 and 29, 1910, WAPP.

77. Ibid., December 1, 1910, WAPP.

78. Ibid., December 5, 1910, WAPP.

79. Ibid., December 8, 1910, WAPP.

80. Ibid., December 11, 1910, WAPP.

81. Ibid.

82. Holmes, *The White Chief*, 250–51.

83. Quoted in ibid., 253.

84. Percy, *Lanterns*, 151.

85. Wyatt-Brown, *House of Percy*, 190.

86. Quoted in Cobb, *The Most Southern Place on Earth*, 147.

87. Quoted in ibid., 146–47.

88. Percy, *Lanterns*, 153.

89. Harold Bruff to William Alexander Percy, August 4, 1911, WAPP.

90. Harold Bruff to William Alexander Percy, August 14–15, 1911, WAPP.

91. Percy, *Lanterns*, 154.

92. WAPD, October 15, 1910, WAPP.

93. Percy, *Lanterns*, 143 and 154.

94. Wyatt-Brown, *House of Percy*, 13, 35–38, and 248–54.

95. William Alexander Percy, *Sappho in Levkas, and Other Poems* (New Haven: Yale University Press, 1915), 66–67.

Chapter 7

1. Bertram Wyatt-Brown, *The House of Percy: Honor, Melancholy, and Imagination in a Southern Family* (New York: Oxford University Press, 1994), 344–45.

2. William Bryk, "The Father of the Four Hundred," *New York Sun*, August 9, 2005, http://www.nysun.com/article/18321. Robert Wiebe writes: "Even elite families who pretended to scorn the most brazen displays allowed themselves to be numbered by Ward McAllister, prime minister of high society: the Four Hundred officially quantified social quality." Robert Wiebe, *The Search for Order, 1877–1920* (New York: Hill and Wang, 1967), 41.

3. David Traxel, *Crusader Nation: The United States in Peace and the Great War, 1898–1920* (New York: Vintage Books, 2006), 48–52, quote on 50. See also Christine Stansell, *American Moderns: Bohemian New York and the Creation of a New Century* (New York: Metropolitan Books, 2000); Robert A. Rosenstone, *Romantic Revolutionary: A Biography of John Reed* (Cambridge: Harvard University Press, 1990); and Anne Douglas, *Terrible Honesty: Mongrel Manhattan in the 1920s* (New York: Farrar, Straus and Giroux, 1995).

4. Janet Percy Dana to William Alexander Percy, June 28, 1911, WAPP.

5. William Alexander Percy to Janet Percy Dana, n.d., JDLP.

6. William Alexander Percy, *Sappho in Levkas, and Other Poems* (New Haven: Yale University Press, 1915), 44.

7. Ibid., 73–74.

8. Ibid., 28.

9. Ibid., 1.

10. See Janet Percy Dana to William Alexander Percy, April 15, 1913; Janet Percy Dana to William Alexander Percy, July 29, 1913; and Janet Percy Dana to William Alexander Percy, February 3, 1914; all in WAPP.

11. Janet Percy Dana to William Alexander Percy, February 3, 1914, WAPP.

12. Janet Percy Dana to William Alexander Percy, November 22, 1913, WAPP.

13. Ibid.

14. Janet Percy Dana to William Alexander Percy, April 9, 1914, WAPP.

15. William Alexander Percy to Janet Percy Dana, "Saturday," n.d., JDLP.

16. William Alexander Percy to Janet Percy Dana, May 4 (no year), JDLP.

17. Janet Percy Dana to William Alexander Percy, June 10, 1914, WAPP. Underlining in original.

18. William Alexander Percy, *Lanterns on the Levee: Recollections of a Planter's Son* (New York: Alfred A. Knopf, 1941), 157.

19. William Alexander Percy to Carrie Stern, July 3, 1914, WAPP.

20. William Alexander Percy to Janet Percy Dana, July 24, 1914, JDLP.

21. Modris Eksteins, *Rites of Spring: The Great War and the Birth of the Modern Age* (Toronto: Lester & Orpen Dennys Ltd., 1989), 202.

22. See especially Paul Fussell, *The Great War and Modern Memory* (New York: Oxford University Press, 1975); Eksteins, *Rites of Spring*; David M. Kennedy, *Over Here: The First World War and American Society* (New York: Oxford University Press, 1980); and Jay Winter, *Sites of Memory, Sites of Mourning: The Great War in European Cultural History* (Cambridge: Cambridge University Press, 1998).

23. Quoted in Hew Strachan, *The First World War* (New York: Viking, 2004), xvi.

24. William Alexander Percy to Janet Percy Dana, n.d., 1914, JDLP.

25. Janet Percy Dana to William Alexander Percy, October 11, 1914, WAPP.

26. William Alexander Percy to Janet Percy Dana, n.d., 1914, JDLP.

27. William Alexander Percy to Janet Percy Dana, January 7, 1915, JDLP.

28. Janet Percy Dana to William Alexander Percy, December 30, 1914, WAPP.

29. Greenville, Miss., *City Directory*, vol. 6, 1927–28, 229.

30. Interview with Mrs. Louise E. Crump of Greenville, Mississippi, July 23, 1963, quoted in Carol Malone, "William Alexander Percy: Knight to His People, Ishmael to Himself, and Poet to the World" (M.A. thesis, University of Mississippi, 1964), 44. William Armstrong Percy remembers his mother calling Tommy Shields Will Percy's "boyfriend" in William Armstrong Percy, "William Alexander Percy: His Homosexuality and Why It Matters," in *Carryin' On in the Lesbian and Gay South*, ed. John Howard (New York: New York University Press, 1997), 85.

31. William Alexander Percy to Janet Percy Dana, "Saturday," n.d., 1915, JDLP.

32. Janet Percy Dana to William Alexander Percy, February 28, 1915, WAPP.

33. Janet Percy Dana to William Alexander Percy, February 14, 1915, WAPP.

34. William Alexander Percy to Janet Percy Dana, n.d., JDLP.

35. William Alexander Percy to Janet Percy Dana, "Sunday," n.d., JDLP.

36. William Alexander Percy to Janet Percy Dana, "Tuesday," n.d., JDLP.

37. William Alexander Percy to Janet Percy Dana, n.d., 1915, JDLP.

38. William Alexander Percy to Janet Percy Dana, n.d., 1915, JDLP.

39. John Howard, *Men Like That: A Southern Queer History* (Chicago: University of Chicago Press, 1999), xiii. See also James T. Sears, *Rebels, Rubyfruit and Rhinestones: Queering Space in the Stonewall South* (Piscataway, N.J.: Rutgers University Press, 2001);

Sears, *Lonely Hunters: An Oral History of Lesbian and Gay Southern Life, 1948–1968* (Boulder, Colo.: Westview Press, 1997); and E. Patrick Johnson, *Sweet Tea: Black Gay Men of the South* (Chapel Hill: University of North Carolina Press, 2008).

40. William Alexander Percy to Janet Percy Dana, April 9, 1915, JDLP.

41. William Alexander Percy to Janet Percy Dana, n.d., 1915, JDLP.

42. William Alexander Percy to Janet Percy Dana, n.d., 1915, JDLP.

43. William Alexander Percy to Janet Percy Dana, April 9, 1915, JDLP.

44. William Alexander Percy to Janet Percy Dana, May 4 (no year), JDLP.

45. William Alexander Percy to Witter Bynner, "Sunday," n.d., Witter Bynner Papers, Houghton Library, BMS 1891.28, Harvard University. Though this letter is undated, in it Percy tells Bynner, "I'm twenty-nine," which dates it sometime in late 1914 or early 1915.

46. William Alexander Percy to Janet Percy Dana, "Friday Night," 1915, JDLP.

47. William Alexander Percy to Janet Percy Dana, n.d., JDLP.

48. William Alexander Percy to Janet Percy Dana, n.d., JDLP.

49. Janet Percy Dana to William Alexander Percy, June 23, 1915, WAPP. Italics mine.

50. Janet Percy Dana to William Alexander Percy, June 9, 1915, WAPP.

51. William Alexander Percy to Janet Percy Dana, n.d., 1915, JDLP.

52. William Alexander Percy to Janet Percy Dana, May 28, 1915, JDLP.

53. William Alexander Percy to Janet Percy Dana, n.d., 1915, JDLP.

54. Ibid.

55. Janet Percy Dana to William Alexander Percy, June 9, 1915, WAPP.

56. Janet Percy Dana to William Alexander Percy, June 23, 1915, WAPP. Italics mine.

57. William Alexander Percy to Carrie Stern, July 11, 1915, WAPP.

58. William Alexander Percy to Janet Percy Dana, n.d., JDLP.

59. Janet Percy Dana to William Alexander Percy, August 22, 1915, WAPP.

60. William Alexander Percy to Janet Percy Dana, "Wednesday Night," JDLP.

61. William Stanley Braithwaite, "A Poet Comes out of Mississippi," *Boston Transcript*, January 22, 1916; clipping in WAPP.

62. "Classic Measures," *New York Evening Post*, January 10, 1916; "Poems Full of Promise," *Hartford Times*, January 8, 1916; clippings in WAPP.

63. *Glasgow Herald*, n.d., included as a clipping in Yale University Press to William Alexander Percy, September 22, 1916, WAPP.

64. Harriet Monroe, "A Misguided Poet," *Poetry: A Magazine of Verse* 10, no. 4 (July 1917): 49 and 51.

65. O. W. Firkins, "Tale-Tellers and Lyrists," *Nation* 102, no. 2656 (May 25, 1916): 566.

66. William Alexander Percy to Janet Percy Dana, "Sunday," n.d., JDLP.

67. S. T. Clover to William Alexander Percy, July 16, 1917, WAPP.

68. William Alexander Percy to S. T. Clover, July 12, 1917, WAPP.

69. Percy, *Sappho in Levkas*, 10, 44, 66.

70. William Alexander Percy to Janet Percy Dana, "Tuesday," n.d., JDLP.

71. Janet Percy Dana to William Alexander Percy, September 14, 1915, WAPP. Parentheses in original.

72. Janet Percy Dana to William Alexander Percy, September 22, 1915, WAPP. Italics mine.

73. Janet Percy Dana to William Alexander Percy, October 5, 1915, WAPP. Underlining in original.

74. William Alexander Percy to Janet Percy Dana, "Saturday," n.d., JDLP.

75. William Alexander Percy to Janet Percy Dana, "Sunday," n.d., JDLP.

76. Janet Percy Dana to William Alexander Percy, November 2, 1915, WAPP.

77. Janet Percy Dana to William Alexander Percy, November 22, 1915, WAPP.

78. Janet Dana Longcope to William Alexander Percy, December 8, 1915, WAPP.

79. William Alexander Percy to Carrie Stern, February 16, 1916, WAPP.

80. William Alexander Percy, *In April Once* (New Haven: Yale University Press, 1920), 70.

81. Ibid., 70–71.

82. Ibid., 71–72.

83. Ibid., 72.

84. Ibid., 72–73.

Chapter 8

1. Stéphane Audion-Rouzeau, "Combat," in *A Companion to the First World War*, ed. John Horne (Oxford: Wiley-Blackwell, 2010), 184. See also Joanna Bourke, *An Intimate History of Killing: Face-to-Face Killing in Twentieth-Century Warfare* (New York: Basic Books, 1999).

2. A. J. P. Taylor, *The First World War: An Illustrated History* (New York and London: Penguin, 1966), 123.

3. See, for example, Michael C. C. Adams, *The Great Adventure: Male Desire and the Coming of World War I* (Bloomington, Ind.: University of Indiana Press, 1990), 88; Kristen Hoganson, *Fighting for American Manhood: How Gender Politics Provoked the Spanish-American and Philippine-American Wars* (New Haven: Yale University Press, 2000); Sarah Watts, *Rough Rider in the White House: Theodore Roosevelt and the Politics of Desire* (Chicago: University of Chicago Press, 2006).

4. Quoted in David Kennedy, *Over Here: The First World War and American Society* (New York: Oxford University Press, 1980), 184.

5. William Alexander Percy to Janet Percy Dana, n.d., 1915, JDLP.

6. David Burner, *Herbert Hoover: A Public Life* (New York: Alfred A. Knopf, 1979), 74–75.

7. George H. Nash, *The Life of Herbert Hoover: The Humanitarian, 1914–1917* (New York and London: W. W. Norton & Company, 1988), ix.

8. William Alexander Percy to Janet Dana Longcope, "Sunday," n.d., September 1916, JDLP.

9. William Alexander Percy, *Lanterns on the Levee: Recollections of a Planter's Son* (New York: Alfred A. Knopf, 1941), 160–61.

10. Quoted in Burner, *Herbert Hoover*, 80.

11. William Alexander Percy to Carrie Stern, March 2, 1917, WAPP.

12. Percy, *Lanterns*, 162–63.

13. Ibid., 163 and 166.

14. William Alexander Percy to Janet Dana Longcope, n.d., JDLP.

15. William Groom Leftwich to G. J. Leftwich, October 21, 1917; G. J. Leftwich to Le-Roy Percy, October 25, 1917; both in WAPP.

16. D. W. Houston to LeRoy Percy, July 10, 1917, WAPP.

17. William Alexander Percy to Janet Dana Longcope, n.d., 1917, JDLP.

18. Percy, *Lanterns*, 169.

19. William Alexander Percy to Janet Dana Longcope, n.d., 1917, JDLP. Parenthetical question mark in original.

20. Passport, William Alexander Percy, March 24, 1917, WAPP; Percy, *Lanterns*, 172–73.

21. Percy, *Lanterns*, 173.

22. Ibid., 176.

23. Army Special Orders, November 15, 1917, WAPP; William Alexander Percy, *In April Once* (New Haven: Yale University Press, 1920), 118; Lewis Baker, *The Percys of Mississippi: Politics and Literature in the New South* (Baton Rouge: Louisiana State University Press, 1983), 82.

24. Percy, *Lanterns*, 184. On Gerstle Mack, see "Gerstle Mack, 88, Author, Biographer and Historian," *New York Times*, February 17, 1983, D-23. In addition, Gerstle Mack wrote a book on Spanish architecture in the late 1920s, and he sent a draft of the book to Percy for his criticism and comments. See "Modern Architecture Research Materials: Notes and thoughts. Begins with an extract from a letter to W.A.P," Gerstle Mack Papers, University of California, Berkeley, Calif.; and Gerstle Mack, *Architectural Details of Southern Spain* (New York: W. Helburn, Inc., 1928).

25. Percy, *Lanterns*, 185–89.

26. Ibid.

27. Janet Dana Longcope to William Alexander Percy, March 2, 1918, WAPP.

28. Janet Dana Longcope to William Alexander Percy, May 11, 1918, WAPP.

29. Percy, *Lanterns*, 192–93.

30. Ibid.

31. Ibid., 196–97.

32. Janet Dana Longcope to William Alexander Percy, September 7, 1918, WAPP.

33. Percy, *Lanterns*, 200. For a much different history of black soldiers in World War I, see especially Chad L. Williams, *Torchbearers of Democracy: African American Soldiers in the World War I Era* (Chapel Hill: University of North Carolina Press, 2010); Adriane Lentz-Smith, *Freedom Struggles: African Americans and World War I* (Cambridge, Mass.: Harvard University Press, 2009); Gail Buckley, *American Patriots: The Story of Blacks in the Military from the Revolution to Desert Storm* (New York: Random House, 2001), chap. 6; Bernard C. Nalty, *Strength for the Fight: A History of Black Ameri-*

cans in the Military (New York: The Free Press, 1986), chap. 8; and Robert B. Edgerton, *Hidden Heroism: Black Soldiers in America's Wars* (Boulder, Colo.: Westview Press, 2001), chap. 3.

34. LeRoy Percy to William Alexander Percy, June 18, 1918, WAPP.

35. Hew Strachan, *The First World War* (New York: Viking, 2003), 298.

36. Quotes in ibid., 311 and 316.

37. William Alexander Percy to Billy Wynn, August 16, 1918, WAPP.

38. William Alexander Percy to Camille Percy, September 13, 1918, WAPP.

39. Percy, *Lanterns*, 215.

40. Ibid., 216.

41. William Alexander Percy to Camille Percy, September 25, 1918; reprinted in Percy, *Lanterns*, 201.

42. William Alexander Percy to LeRoy Percy, October 4, 1918, WAPP.

43. Ibid.

44. Ibid.

45. Ibid.

46. Hew Strachan, ed., *The Oxford Illustrated History of the First World War* (New York: Oxford University Press, 1998), 251. See also Taylor, *The First World War*, 233–36.

47. William Alexander Percy to Camille Percy, November 4, 1918; reprinted in Percy, *Lanterns*, 209.

48. William Alexander Percy to Camille Percy, November 11, 1918; reprinted in Percy, *Lanterns*, 213.

49. William Alexander Percy to LeRoy Percy, November 15, 1918, WAPP.

50. Paris Central Headquarters, Army of France to William Alexander Percy, January 25, 1919; Certificate from King Albert of Belgium, May 16, 1919; United States War Department to William Alexander Percy, April 30, 1919; all in WAPP.

51. William P. Jackson to Camille Percy, January 5, 1919; William P. Jackson to William Alexander Percy, May 10, 1919; both in WAPP.

52. "William Sinkler Manning," *New York Times*, January 5, 1919, 30.

53. Percy, *Lanterns*, 94.

54. William Alexander Percy to Carrie Stern, January 7, 1919, WAPP.

55. William Alexander Percy to Carrie Stern, January 31, 1919, WAPP.

56. William Alexander Percy to Camille Percy, February 2, 1919, WAPP.

57. Percy, *Lanterns*, 223.

58. Ibid.

Chapter 9

1. *Delta Democrat-Times*, April 18, 1919; clipping in WAPP.

2. Janet Dana Longcope to William Alexander Percy, July 4, 1919, WAPP.

3. William Alexander Percy to Carrie Stern, n.d., 1919, WAPP.

4. Arthur Chitty to Louise LaCoss, September 11, 1959, WAPAF.

5. Ben Wasson to Arthur Chitty, February 6, 1960, WAPAF.

6. Sewanee Board of Trustees to William Alexander Percy, June 15, 1920, WAPP.

7. John Howard, "The Talk of the County: Revisiting Accusation, Murder, and Mississippi, 1895," in *Where These Memories Grow: History, Memory, and Southern Identity*, ed. W. Fitzhugh Brundage (Chapel Hill: University of North Carolina Press, 2000), 200–202.

A common medical treatment for those with same-sex desire in this period was hypnosis. The well-known psychiatrist Richard von Krafft-Ebing recorded his treatment for men with what he called "Onanism," or "disgraceful inclinations toward men." Once he hypnotized his patient, he would suggest to him:

1. I abhor onanism, because it makes me sick and miserable.
2. I no longer have inclinations toward men; for love of men is against religion, nature, and law.
3. I feel an inclination toward women; for woman is lovely and desirable, and created for man.

Quoted in Jonathan Ned Katz, *The Invention of Heterosexuality* (Chicago: University of Chicago Press, 2007), 24–25. For more on medical treatment during this period, see Estelle B. Freedman, "'Uncontrolled Desires': The Response to the Sexual Psychopath, 1920–1960," *Journal of American History* 74, no. 1 (June 1987): 83–106.

8. William Alexander Percy to Major McKellar, May 4, 1922, WAPP.

9. Huger Jervey to William Alexander Percy, January 12, 1920, WAPP.

10. WAPD, November 6, 1910, WAPP.

11. On Percy's nostalgia, see Benjamin E. Wise, "On Naïve and Sentimental Poetry: Nostalgia, Sex, and the Souths of William Alexander Percy," *Southern Cultures* 14, no. 1 (Spring 2008): 54–79.

12. Jean Starobinski, "The Idea of Nostalgia," *Diogenes* 54 (Summer 1966): 81–103; Christopher Lasch, *The True and Only Heaven: Progress and Its Critics* (New York: W. W. Norton & Company, 1991), 82; Svetlana Boym, *The Future of Nostalgia* (New York: Basic Books, 2001), xiii; Susan J. Matt, "You Can't Go Home Again: Homesickness and Nostalgia in U.S. History," *Journal of American History* 94, no. 2 (September 2007): 469–97.

13. Faulkner quoted in Carvel Collins, ed., *William Faulkner: Early Prose and Poetry* (New York: Atlantic Monthly Press, 1962), 71–72; and Jay Tolson, *Pilgrim in the Ruins: A Life of Walker Percy* (New York: Simon and Schuster, 1992), 77.

14. Quoted in Collins, *William Faulkner*, 72.

15. Friedrich von Schiller, *Naïve and Sentimental Poetry and On the Sublime: Two Essays*, trans. Julius A. Elias (New York: F. Unger Publication Company, 1966), 102.

16. On Hellenism in the nineteenth century, see especially Richard Jenkyns, *The Victorians and Ancient Greece* (Cambridge, Mass.: Harvard University Press, 1980);

Frank M. Turner, *The Greek Heritage in Victorian Britain* (New Haven: Yale University Press, 1984); and Linda Dowling, *Hellenism and Homosexuality in Victorian Oxford* (Ithaca: Cornell University Press, 1994).

17. William Alexander Percy to Ellery Sedgwick, December 10, 1921, WAPP; William Alexander Percy, *Lanterns on the Levee: Recollections of a Planter's Son* (New York: Alfred A. Knopf, 1941), 111.

18. George Chauncey, *Gay New York: Gender, Urban Culture, and the Making of the Gay Male World, 1890–1940* (New York: Basic Books, 1994); John Howard, *Men Like That: A Southern Queer History* (Chicago: University of Chicago Press, 1999); E. Patrick Johnson, *Sweet Tea: Black Gay Men of the South* (Chapel Hill: University of North Carolina Press, 2009).

19. William Alexander Percy, *In April Once* (New Haven: Yale University Press, 1920), 80; William Alexander Percy to William Stanley Braithwaite, March 13 (no year), William Stanley Braithwaite Papers, Houghton Library, Harvard University, Cambridge, Mass. On nineteenth-century views of Will Hughes, see, for example, Oscar Wilde, "The Portrait of Mr. W. H.," in Oscar Wilde, *Complete Short Fiction*, ed. and with an introduction by Ian Small (New York: Penguin Books, 1994), 47–80.

20. Wilde and Pater quoted in Denis Donoghue, *Walter Pater: Lover of Strange Souls* (New York: Alfred A. Knopf, 1995), 80 and 52; Paul Fussell, *The Great War and Modern Memory* (New York: Oxford University Press, 2000 [repr.]), 282.

21. William Alexander Percy to Medora Hambough, April 13, 1929, WAPP; Percy, *In April Once*, 49.

22. Quotes from Percy, *In April Once*, 19, 41, 33, 56, 57, 58.

23. Edward M. Slocum, *Men and Boys: An Anthology*, reprint with an appreciation by Timothy D'Arch Smith and introduction by Donald H. Mader (New York: Coltsfoot Press, 1978), lv, 81, and xxiii.

24. Percy, *In April Once*, 100.

25. Ibid., 110–16.

26. *New York Times*, October 31, 1922, 14; William Alexander Percy to Charles Puckett, November 9, 1922; see also reviews in *Boston Evening Transcript*, January 22, 1916; and *Hartford Times* (Connecticut), January 8, 1916; all in WAPP. For more on Lindley Hubbell, see chap. 11.

27. Raymond W. Ganger to William Alexander Percy, November 12, 1921, WAPP.

28. John Gill to William Alexander Percy, May 6, 1921; Stuart P. Sherman to L. C. Painter, March 2, 1921; L. C. Painter to William Alexander Percy, April 9, 1921; all in WAPP.

29. Kathleen Tankersly Young to William Alexander Percy, January 20, 1930; Elizabeth C. Road to William Alexander Percy, December 1, 1921; Reginald Turner to William Alexander Percy, November 8, 1922; all in WAPP. On "Grecian beauty," see also Eudora Sellner to William Alexander Percy, October 15, 1922, WAPP. On Reginald Turner, see Stanley Weintraub, *Reggie: A Portrait of Reginald Turner* (New York: George

Braziller, 1965). Percy writes about Turner in his foreword to Norman Douglas, *Birds and Beasts of the Greek Anthology* (New York: J. Cape and H. Smith, 1929). For more on Turner, see chapter 11.

30. Malcolm Vaughan to William Alexander Percy, May 5, 1921, WAPP.

31. Percy, *Lanterns*, 131–32.

32. Richard King, *A Southern Renaissance: The Cultural Awakening of the American South, 1930–1955* (New York: Oxford University Press, 1980), 96; Bertram Wyatt-Brown, *The House of Percy: Honor, Melancholy, and Imagination in a Southern Family* (New York: Oxford University Press, 1994), 223.

33. David L. Cohn, *The Mississippi Delta and the World: The Memoirs of David L. Cohn*, ed. James C. Cobb (Baton Rouge: Louisiana State University Press, 1995), 162–65.

34. Percy, *Lanterns*, 132. Italics mine.

35. LeRoy Percy to William Alexander Percy, July 30, 1920, WAPP.

36. DuBose Heyward to William Alexander Percy, July 3, 1923, WAPP; William Alexander Percy to DuBose Heyward, July 14, 1923, WAPP.

37. DuBose Heyward to William Alexander Percy, July 3, 1923, WAPP; William Alexander Percy to DuBose Heyward, July 14, 1923, WAPP.

38. William Alexander Percy to W. S. Lewis, March 16, 1921, WAPP. See also Allen Tate to William Alexander Percy, September 28, 1922; William Alexander Percy to Allen Tate, July 23, 1923, WAPP.

39. Thomas H. Lipscomb to William Alexander Percy, February 6, 1922, WAPP; William Alexander Percy to Thomas H. Lipscomb, March 27, 1922, WAPP.

40. W. B. Hughes to Charles Scribner's Sons, September 2, 1922; William Alexander Percy to Robert Bridges, September 26, 1922; William Alexander Percy to Evelyn Rivers, September 26, 1922; all in WAPP.

41. William Alexander Percy to DuBose Heyward, July 14, 1923, WAPP; William Alexander Percy to J. R. Moreland, December 9, 1921, WAPP.

Chapter 10

1. Evidence suggests that the Mississippi Delta was statistically less violent than the rest of Mississippi, though historians have rightly pointed out that this was small consolation to the black population. "Less violent" was still violent. There were sixty-six recorded lynchings between 1900 and 1930 in the Delta, or an average of one every five and a half months. See James C. Cobb, *The Most Southern Place on Earth: The Mississippi Delta and the Roots of Regional Identity* (New York: Oxford University Press, 1992), 114–15; and Neil McMillen, *Dark Journey: Black Mississippians in the Age of Jim Crow* (Urbana: University of Illinois Press, 1989), 227.

2. See, for example, Lewis Baker interview with Brodie S. Crump, Hill Memorial Library, Louisiana State University, Baton Rouge, La.; Millie Commodore, a black woman from Greenville, spoke of Will Percy's concern for local blacks in an interview

cited in William Armstrong Percy, "William Alexander Percy: His Homosexuality and Why It Matters," in *Carryin' On in the Gay and Lesbian South*, ed. John Howard (New York: New York University Press, 1997), 75–92.

3. The *New Republic* never published this letter. Percy included it in William Alexander Percy, *Lanterns on the Levee: Recollections of a Planter's Son* (New York: Alfred A. Knopf, 1941): 226–29.

4. Ibid., 284.

5. LeRoy Percy, "A Southern View of Negro Education," *The Outlook* (August 3, 1907): 732. On Chinese immigration, see James W. Loewen, *The Mississippi Chinese: Between Black and White* (Cambridge, Mass.: Harvard University Press, 1969).

6. On Italian immigration, see Bertram Wyatt-Brown, "LeRoy Percy and Sunnyside: Planter Mentality and Italian Peonage in the Mississippi Delta," in *Shadows over Sunnyside: An Arkansas Plantation in Transition, 1830–1945*, ed. Jeannie M. Whayne (Fayetteville: University of Arkansas Press, 1993), 77–94; Bertram Wyatt-Brown, *The House of Percy: Honor, Melancholy, and Imagination in a Southern Family* (New York: Oxford University Press, 1994), 188–89; and Cobb, *The Most Southern Place on Earth*, 109–12.

7. McMillen, *Dark Journey*, 259.

8. Cobb, *The Most Southern Place on Earth*, 115.

9. Quoted in ibid., 98. Cobb makes a similar observation about northbound blacks on the Illinois Central in ibid., 115. Another salient point is that despite the massive outmigration of blacks from Mississippi, there was also a considerable amount of migration within the state, so much so that the Delta's black population was relatively stable in this period and even grew in the 1920s. Though the population numbers were stable, it was not a static population; for this reason, Neil McMillan describes the Delta as a "staging area" for moving North, a region blacks moved through on their way out of Mississippi. See McMillen, *Dark Journey*, 268–69.

10. On the first Ku Klux Klan, see David M. Chalmers, *Hooded Americanism: The First Century of the Ku Klux Klan, 1865–1965* (New York: Doubleday & Company, 1965), 1–22; Wyn Craig Wade, *The Fiery Cross: The Ku Klux Klan in America* (New York: Simon and Schuster, 1987), 9–116; and William Loren Katz, *The Invisible Empire: The Ku Klux Klan Impact on History* (Washington, D.C.: Open Hand Publishing, 1986): 7–59.

11. Immigration and Catholic statistics from Robert Moates Miller, "The Ku Klux Klan," in *Change and Continuity in Twentieth-Century America: The 1920s*, ed. John Braeman and others (Columbus: Ohio State University Press, 1968), 226 and 221; DuBois quoted in Mark Robert Schneider, *"We Return Fighting": The Civil Rights Movement in the Jazz Age* (Boston: Northeastern University Press, 2002), 13.

12. Quoted in Mark C. Carnes, *Secret Ritual and Manhood in Victorian America* (New Haven: Yale University Press, 1989), 1; 30 million figure from Miller, "The Ku Klux Klan," 243.

13. Nancy MacLean, *Behind the Mask of Chivalry: The Making of the Second Ku Klux Klan* (New York: Oxford University Press, 1994), xi. Recent scholarship has argued that

the 1920s Klan was not a fringe group of extremist xenophobes and racists but a popular movement composed of a broad cross section of American Protestants concerned with declining morality, changing gender norms, massive immigration, the growth of Catholicism, and changing race relations. See MacLean, *Behind the Mask of Chivalry*; Leonard J. Moore, "Historical Interpretations of the 1920s Klan: The Traditional View and the Populist Revision," *Journal of Social History* 24 (Winter 1990): 341–57; Michael Kazin, "The Grass Roots Right: New Histories of U.S. Conservatism in the Twentieth Century," *American Historical Review* 97 (February 1992): 136–55; and Leonard J. Moore, *Citizen Klansmen: The Ku Klux Klan in Indiana, 1921–1928* (Chapel Hill: University of North Carolina Press, 1991).

14. All printed in the *Leland Enterprise*, March 18, 1921, WAPP.

15. Percy, *Lanterns*, 232.

16. "Address by Senator LeRoy Percy, Greenville Miss., March 18 [*sic*], 1922," WAPP.

17. Ibid.

18. See *Greenville Democrat*, March 4, 1922; *Houston Chronicle*, March 19 and 23, 1922; *Vicksburg Herald*, March 4, 1922; *New Orleans Times-Picayune*, March 6, 1922; and *New York World*, March 26, 1922, all in WAPP.

19. See, for example, the letter dated March 13, 1922, to LeRoy Percy in which the writer, whose name is not legible, congratulated Percy on his "manly, patriotic defense of your fellow citizens"; Louis U. Babin to LeRoy Percy, March 15, 1922, in which Babin praised Percy's speech as "the most manly that I have ever read"; and W. L. Evans to LeRoy Percy, March 3, 1922, in which Evans thanked Percy for his "eloquent and able defense of true American ideals and principles"; all in WAPP.

20. Perry W. Howard to LeRoy Percy, March 27, 1922, WAPP. See also Wallace A. Battle of the Okolona Industrial School to LeRoy Percy, March 4, 1922, in which Battle expressed "the praise and congratulations of 13,000,000 Negroes in the United States. . . . If white people knew how much colored people respected them, how much they feared them, how much they honored them and how much they loved them, there would be no problem between the Negro and the white people in the United States"; J. M. Williamson of the Industrial Agricultural College for Negroes to LeRoy Percy, March 7, 1922, the letterhead of which stated, "Civilization begins on the farm. Farming is a divine occupation. The Negroes should remain on the farm as less competition, better health, and more happiness on the farm [*sic*]. This school teaches the ideas and principles that will cement the feeling between the two races and show the Negroes why the South is his home and why the white people are their friends"; James V. Mitchell to LeRoy Percy, March 28, 1922, in which Mitchell praised Percy's speech as "the bravest deed recorded in favor of a southern white man"; and Rev. Norman Bell to LeRoy Percy, March 6, 1922, who noted that "this is an evidence that we have some great white friends in the South that will stand by the colored people. All we want Senator Percy here in the South is good schools, justice in the courts, and treated as human beings [*sic*]"; all in WAPP.

21. "Address of Hon. LeRoy Percy, Delivered at Peoples Theatre, Greenville, Mississippi, April 23, 1923: Under Auspices of the Protestant Committee of Fifty Opposed to the Ku Klux Klan," WAPP.

22. LeRoy Percy to Ray Toombs, May 13, 1923, reprinted in the *Greenville Democrat*, May 14, 1923, WAPP; William Alexander Percy to Elliot Cage, May 21, 1923, WAPP; Percy, *Lanterns*, 235–36.

23. William Alexander Percy to Elliott Cage, May 21, 1923, WAPP; William Alexander Percy to Wilson Follett, May 23, 1923, WAPP.

24. Percy, *Lanterns*, 237–39.

Chapter 11

1. William Alexander Percy to Camille Percy, August 25, 1922, WAPP. On Camille Percy's time in Glen Springs, see William Alexander Percy to Lucy R. Hawkins, September 3, 1921, WAPP; and T. C. Catchings to Camille Percy, June 2, 1922, WAPP.

2. Willy, *The Third Sex*, trans. and with an introduction and notes by Lawrence R. Schehr (Urbana: University of Illinois Press, 2007), 25.

3. William Alexander Percy to Camille Percy, August 15 (no year), and August 25, 1922; both in WAPP.

4. William Alexander Percy to Camille Percy, August 8, 1922; August 15 (no year); and August 25, 1922; all in WAPP.

5. Lewis Baker, *The Percys of Mississippi: Politics and Literature in the New South* (Baton Rouge: Louisiana State University Press, 1983), 126; Richard King, *A Southern Renaissance: The Cultural Awakening of the American South, 1930–1955* (New York: Oxford University Press, 1980), 97. See also Bertram Wyatt-Brown, *The House of Percy: Honor, Melancholy, and Imagination in a Southern Family* (New York: Oxford University Press, 1994), 206; Billups P. Spalding, "William Alexander Percy: His Philosophy of Life as Reflected in His Poetry" (M.A. thesis, University of Georgia, 1957), 142–62; and Mary Campbell Stewart, "William Alexander Percy: The Poet and His Delta Country" (Ph.D. diss., University of Maryland, 1995), 128–57.

6. William Alexander Percy to John Chapman, July 3, 1930, WAPP; William Alexander Percy, *The Collected Poems of William Alexander Percy* (New York: Alfred A. Knopf, 1943), 315.

7. On Frederick the Second, see T. L. Kington, *History of Frederick the Second, Emperor of the Romans* (Cambridge and London: Macmillan, 1862), which was likely the biography of Frederick the Second that Percy read. See also Donald H. Mader, "The Greek Mirror: The Uranians and Their Use of Greece," in *Same-Sex Desire and Love in Greco-Roman Antiquity and in the Classical Tradition of the West*, ed. Beert C. Verstraete and Vernon Provencal (Binghamton, N.Y.: Harrington Park Press, 2005), 394–96.

8. Percy, *Collected Poems*, 315–16.

9. Ibid., 314–15.

10. Ibid., 314, 312, 315.

11. Ibid., 342.

12. William Alexander Percy, *Lanterns on the Levee: Recollections of a Planter's Son* (New York: Alfred A. Knopf, 1941), 81. For a penetrating analysis of the concept of "coercive moral authority" throughout American history, see David Sehat, *The Myth of American Religious Freedom* (New York: Oxford University Press, 2011).

13. Percy, *Collected Poems*, 212; William Alexander Percy to A. T. Molligen, September 21, 1938, quoted in Spalding, "William Alexander Percy," 101; *The Hymnal of the Protestant Episcopal Church in the United States of America* (New York: Church Pension Fund, 1940), no. 437.

14. William Alexander Percy, "Safe Secrets," *The Fugitive* 1, no. 4 (December 1922): 119.

15. "Gerstle Mack, 88, Author, Biographer and Historian," *New York Times*, February 17, 1983, D-23. The only extant evidence about Gerstle Mack in Percy's papers are a letter Mack wrote to LeRoy Percy from Greece on July 3, 1924, and a letter from an art dealer in New York to Percy saying, "G. Mack of 681 Madison Ave" had ordered Percy a Persian blue pottery jar. See H. Kahn Monif to William Alexander Percy, February 6, 1926, WAPP. Walker Percy once mentioned he had "over 100 letters" written between 1918 and 1941 from Will Percy to Gerstle Mack, but every effort to uncover them has been unsuccessful. See Jay Tolson, ed., *The Correspondence of Shelby Foote and Walker Percy* (New York: W. W. Norton, 1997), 265. See also "Modern Architecture Research Materials: Notes and thoughts. Begins with an extract from a letter to W.A.P.," Gerstle Mack Papers, University of California, Berkeley, Calif.; and Gerstle Mack, *Architectural Details of Southern Spain* (New York: W. Helburn, Inc., 1928).

For more on Percy's archive, see the epilogue of this book. See also Estelle B. Freedman, "'The Burning of Letters Continues': Elusive Identities and the Historical Construction of Sexuality," *Journal of Women's History* 9, no. 4 (Winter 1998): 181–200.

16. William Alexander Percy to Camille Percy, "Tuesday," n.d., WAPP.

17. Ulrich Pohlmann, *Wilhelm von Gloeden: Taormina* (New York: teNeues Publishing Company, 1998), 10 and 21. The executor of von Gloeden's estate was not so fortunate as to be thought in possession of classical nudes; Pancrazio Bucini was charged with selling pornographic material in 1933, and though he was eventually acquitted, thousands of von Gloeden's prints and negatives were destroyed by fascist Italy's police in the 1930s. See ibid., 24.

18. William Alexander Percy to Camille Percy, June 16 and 17 (no year), WAPP; William Alexander Percy to LeRoy Percy, June 27, 1924, WAPP. For the rest of the itinerary, see Gerstle Mack to LeRoy Percy, July 3, 1924, WAPP; and William Alexander Percy to Camille Percy, July 22, 1924, WAPP.

19. See, for example, Pohlmann, *Wilhelm von Gloeden*, photographs 25 and 26.

20. All quotes in Percy, *Lanterns*, 337–40. Here, Percy was also drawing from a long-standing trope in Western travel narratives. Such books, Matthew Frye Jacobson has pointed out, contained "the obligatory scene in which the western traveler dazzled

the 'natives' with some—often thoroughly mundane—display of technological know-how. The literature is rife with caricatured natives of various climes gaping in awe of clocks, compasses, magnets, or photographic equipment." See Matthew Frye Jacobson, *Barbarian Virtues: The United States Encounters Foreign Peoples at Home and Abroad, 1876–1917* (New York: Hill and Wang, 2000), 54.

21. William Alexander Percy, "Lanterns on the Levee, Manuscript Volume 1," 30, WAPP. The revised version is Percy, *Lanterns*, 340–41.

22. All quotes in Percy, *Lanterns*, 340–41.

23. On what historians call "imperial spectacle," see Jackson Lears, *Rebirth of a Nation: The Making of Modern America, 1877–1920* (New York: Harper Collins, 2009), 287–91; Amy Kaplan, *The Anarchy of Empire in the Making of U.S. Culture* (Cambridge, Mass.: Harvard University Press, 2002), esp. chap. 3; John Kasson, *Houdini, Tarzan, and the Perfect Man: The White Male Body and the Challenge of Modernity in America* (New York: Hill and Wang, 2002); and Jacobson, *Barbarian Virtues*.

24. Herbert S. Gorman, "A Crop of Spring Verse," *The Bookman* (June 1924): 468–69. See also "Something Worth Singing about in Enzio's Kingdom," *Boston Transcript*, April 30, 1924; *Sewanee Review*, January 1925, 106; and "Poetry," *New York Evening Post*, March 8, 1924; all clippings in WAPP.

25. William Alexander Percy to Anne K. Stokes, October 21, 1924, quoted in Spalding, "William Alexander Percy," 42.

26. WAPD, November 6, 1910, WAPP; Percy, *Lanterns*, 131.

27. William Alexander Percy to Francis Harmon, February 4, 1926, WAPP. In addition to serving on committees in Greenville, Percy was also attentive to its young people. He wrote to the Brooklyn YMCA about a young man from Greenville who moved to New York and had no money or friends; he paid for a six-month membership for him and asked that they look after him. See William Alexander Percy to Brooklyn YMCA, October 21, 1926, WAPP. Of New York's YMCAs, George Chauncey writes: "The YMCAs in New York and elsewhere had developed a reputation among gay men as centers of sex and social life"; George Chauncey, *Gay New York: Gender, Urban Culture, and the Making of the Gay Male World, 1890–1940* (New York: Basic Books, 1994), 155. On the YMCA and queer relationships, see Gustav Wrathall, *Take the Young Stranger by the Hand: Same-Sex Relationships and the YMCA* (Chicago: University of Chicago Press, 1998).

28. George Parmly Day to William Alexander Percy, March 14, 1925, WAPP.

29. William Alexander Percy to Mary Leitch, April 29, 1929, WAPP.

30. William Alexander Percy to Countee Cullen, April 20, 1925, WAPP; William Alexander Percy to Lindley Williams Hubbell, April 20, 1925, WAPP.

31. Lindley Williams Hubbell to William Alexander Percy, April 27, 1925, WAPP.

32. Lindley Williams Hubbell, *Dark Pavilion* (New Haven: Yale University Press, 1927), dedication page.

33. Significantly, Lindley Hubbell's biography follows a very similar trajectory with regard to nurturing students. He worked at the New York Public Library from 1925 to

1946 and then taught literature at a Connecticut high school until 1953, when a small inheritance from a cousin allowed him to move to Japan. He became a Japanese citizen in 1960 (and changed his legal name to Hayashi Shuseki) and never left the country. When he died in 1994, a group of friends, admirers, and readers published a book of reflections on Hubbell that expressed their admiration for him as a poet, teacher, and friend. Their writings depict a man who was unmarried, intensely private, and devoted to poetry. Their admiration is much like what others wrote about Percy, such as this remark from a former student in Japan: "In his daily life he could barely boil water on a gas range, but once he started to talk, he could discuss anything—religion, philosophy, literature, music, art. Anyone who went to see him—a friend, a former student, or someone taken to be introduced to him—would be so enchanted listening to him as to forget the passage of time." Another man wrote of falling in love with Hubbell, whose attractiveness was both physical and intellectual. "Didactic but seldom sententious, he offered observations which, when unwrapped, disclosed insight, awareness, discernment. He was interested only in the best," he wrote. See David Burleigh and Hiroaki Sato, eds., *Autumn Stone in the Woods: A Tribute to Lindley Williams Hubbell* (Middletown Springs, Vt.: P.S., A Press, 1997), 49 and 4. See also James Kirkup, "Obituary: Lindley Williams Hubbell," *The Independent*, October 17, 1994, http://www.independent.co.uk/news/uk/obituary-lindley-williams-hubbell-1443429.html (October 13, 2010).

34. Percy and Hubbell did correspond and see one another regularly until Percy's death. In one chapter of his autobiography, Percy published an hour-by-hour record of what he did during the day, and at one point he noted that he dashed off a letter "to Lindley about his arthritis," which suggests they kept in touch quite regularly. See Percy, *Lanterns*, 323. In addition, Percy mentions visiting Hubbell in New York in a 1940 letter to Charlotte Gailor. "I found Lindley on the edge of a breakdown and shipped him to Puerto Rico," he wrote. "I'm getting right fed up with neurotics." See William Alexander Percy to Charlotte Gailor, "Election Day 1940," CGP.

Though Percy and Hubbell's correspondence is not in Percy's papers, this does not mean it (and other evidence like it) does not exist somewhere. Martin Duberman's commentary on the subject is worth repeating: "Other corroborating records may still survive, and are only waiting to be retrieved. After all, to date we have accumulated only a tiny collection of historical materials that record the existence of *heterosexual* behavior in the past. . . . I myself believe that additional source material, possibly a great deal of it, relating to the history of homosexuality has survived and awaits recovery from well-guarded vaults." See Martin Duberman, "'Writhing Bedfellows' in Antebellum South Carolina: Historical Interpretation and the Politics of Evidence," in *Carryin' On in the Lesbian and Gay South*, ed. John Howard (New York: New York University Press, 1997), 23–24.

35. William Alexander Percy to Mary Edgar Comstock, April 21, 1925, WAPP.

36. Charles Fingerman to William Alexander Percy, March 6, 1930, WAPP. Percy sent this note to the editor at Yale and attached a note to the bottom: "This had better be

kept a dead secret from those trustful people (including myself) who believe in the possibility of permanent world peace." See William Alexander Percy to L. P. Soule, March 15, 1930, WAPP.

37. William Alexander Percy to Edmond Kowalewski, May 18, 1926, WAPP.

38. William Alexander Percy to L. P. Soule, May 19, 1926, WAPP.

39. Edmond Kowalewski to William Alexander Percy, June 20, 1926, WAPP.

40. William Alexander Percy to L. P. Soule, October 1, 1926, WAPP.

41. William Alexander Percy to Edmond Kowalewski, October 1, 1926, WAPP.

42. Edmond Kowalewski to William Alexander Percy, October 12, 1926, WAPP.

43. Edmond Kowalewski to William Alexander Percy, n.d., WAPP.

44. Edmond Kowalewski, *Deaf Walls* (Philadelphia: The Symphonist Press, 1933). See also Rev. Walter M. Zebrowski, "Philadelphia Born Polish-American Poet," *Polish American Studies* 20, no. 2 (July-December 1963): 75–80, which is a retrospective appraisal of Kowalewski's volume.

45. William Alexander Percy to Sarah Kilpatrick, June 2, 1932, quoted in Spalding, "William Alexander Percy," 109.

46. William Alexander Percy to Camille Percy, February 3, 1925, WAPP.

47. On the purchase of Brinkwood, see WAPAF. Janet Dana Longcope to William Alexander Percy, April 11, 1925, WAPP. In addition to her awareness that Percy was "living with a dean," some of Percy and Longcope's correspondence in the mid-1920s suggests they spoke somewhat openly about sex. For example, she wrote to him after his New York visit, apparently referencing a discussion they had had.

> Ten years ago I was bitter against my family for not telling me about life and sex and instincts but the longer I am a parent, the more difficult it seems to me to explain and I don't think the Victorians kept silence so much through principle as through puzzle. I wonder whether I shall end by being any more articulate than my mother. Our attitude today seems rather that of the child who pulls out the works to see what makes the clock tell time. Do you suppose, after we've made ourselves thoroughly familiar with the workings that we'll again take pleasure in the watch as an instrument?

See Janet Dana Longcope to William Alexander Percy, February 18, 1925, WAPP. In 1927 she wrote to him: "I'd like to talk to you first hand—about things as well as thoughts—and men's books, and the things that grow in fields and woods, and the feelings they rouse in the human heart, and what about sex, and sin, and love, and whether it all leads up to death, as the one perfect and undesiring state." See Janet Dana Longcope to William Alexander Percy, July 31, 1927, WAPP. Descendants of Janet Dana Longcope claim to have two suitcases full of letters from Will Percy to Janet Longcope but have not donated them to an archive—or let me look at them—because they feel the letters are "too private."

48. For a discussion of the queer culture in Florence, see David Leavitt, *Florence, A*

Delicate Case (New York, Bloomsbury, 2002), chap. 3; and Stanley Weintraub, *Reggie: A Portrait of Reginald Turner* (New York: George Braziller, 1965), chaps. 10 and 11.

49. Quotes from Richard Aldington, *Pinorman: Personal Recollections of Norman Douglas, Pino Orioli, and Charles Prentice* (London: William Heinemann, 1954), 25, 83–84. For more on Douglas's life, see Norman Douglas, *Looking Back: An Autobiographical Excursion* (London: Chatto and Windus, 1934); and Ralph D. Lindeman, *Norman Douglas* (New York: Twayne Publishers, 1965), esp. 11–92.

50. William Alexander Percy to L. P. Soule, October 1, 1926, WAPP.

51. William Alexander Percy to Norman Douglas, May 29, 1936, Norman Douglas Collection, series II, box 18, Beinecke Rare Book and Manuscript Library, Yale University, New Haven, Conn.

52. Florence Tamagne, *History of Homosexuality in Europe, 1919–1939* (New York: Algora Publishing, 2006), 142. On Orioli, see Aldington, *Pinorman*.

53. On Turner, see Weintraub, *Reggie*.

54. William Alexander Percy to Harrison Smith, April 12, 1929, WAPP. Percy wrote: "Obviously the corrections come from Regie [*sic*] and Pino rather than from Douglas and he writes bitterly that they fought over it as if they were deciding the partition of Poland. The most important thing is to change their names and I suggest the name of Carey for Regie [*sic*] and Berto for Pino."

55. Aldington, *Pinorman*, 6–7.

56. Norman Douglas, *Birds and Beasts of the Greek Anthology* (New York: J. Cape and H. Smith, 1929), ix–xi. Douglas also briefly mentions Percy in Norman Douglas, *Late Harvest* (London: L. Drummond, 1946), 26.

57. For more on homoerotic writing in this era, see, for example, Paul Fussell, *The Great War and Modern Memory* (New York: Oxford University Press, 1975), 270–306; Timothy D'Arch Smith, *Love in Earnest: Some Notes on the Lives and Writings of English "Uranian" Poets from 1889 to 1930* (London: Routledge & K. Paul, 1970); Mader, "The Greek Mirror"; and Robert Aldrich, *The Seduction of the Mediterranean: Writing, Art, and Homosexual Fantasy* (New York: Routledge, 1993).

58. Douglas, *Birds and Beasts*, xi.

59. Ibid., xi–xii.

60. The reviewer for the *New York Times* seemed to notice this sensuality as well as the indirect way Percy described it. He wrote, "The foreword, written by William Alexander Percy, will alone justify the book to all readers of 'South Wind.' It is a brief account of an encounter with Norman Douglas in a Florentine restaurant, plus some subsequent conversations that characterize the man with effective obliqueness while explaining how the book came to be written." See "A Menagerie from the Greek Anthology," *New York Times Book Review*, August 31, 1930; clipping in Norman Douglas Papers, Beinecke Rare Book and Manuscript Library, Yale University, New Haven, Conn.

61. Billy Francis, "An Interview with William Alexander Percy," *The Pica* (Greenville, Miss.), April 29, 1931; clipping in WAPP.

62. William Alexander Percy to L. P. Soule, October 1, 1926, WAPP.

63. William Alexander Percy to L. P. Soule, November 11, 1926, WAPP.

Chapter 12

1. William Alexander Percy to Witter Bynner, "Tuesday," n.d., Witter Bynner Papers, Houghton Library, Harvard University, Cambridge, Mass. Ellipses in original. The other letter from Percy to Bynner is cited in chapter 7 of this book. On Witter Bynner, see James Kraft, *Who Is Witter Bynner? A Biography* (Albuquerque: University of New Mexico Press, 1995); Richard Wilbur, ed., *Selected Poems of Witter Bynner*, with a biographical introduction by James Kraft (New York: Farrar, Straus and Giroux, 1977); James Kraft, ed., *Selected Letters of Witter Bynner*, (New York: Farrar, Straus and Giroux, 1981); Witter Bynner, *Journey with Genius: Recollections and Reflections Concerning the D. H. Lawrences* (New York: Octagon Books, 1974); and Brenda Maddox, *D. H. Lawrence: The Story of a Marriage* (New York: W. W. Norton & Company, 1994), 313–19. Bynner graduated from Harvard in 1902 and subsequently worked at *McClure's* magazine, where Percy published his first poem in 1908, so it is possible they met during these years.

2. William Alexander Percy, *Lanterns on the Levee: Recollections of a Planter's Son* (New York: Alfred A. Knopf, 1941), 247.

3. William Alexander Percy, *The Collected Poems of William Alexander Percy* (New York: Alfred A. Knopf, 1943), 349.

4. Henry Waring Ball Diary, March 6 to April 21, 1927, MDAH.

5. Percy, *Lanterns*, 251; Bertram Wyatt-Brown, *The House of Percy: Honor, Melancholy, and Imagination in a Southern Family* (New York: Oxford University Press, 1994), 239–40. The best sources on the 1927 flood are John Barry, *Rising Tide: The Great Mississippi River Flood of 1927 and How It Changed America* (New York: Touchstone, 1997); Lewis Baker, *The Percys of Mississippi: Politics and Literature in the New South* (Baton Rouge: Louisiana State University Press, 1983), chap. 8; and Pete Daniel, *Deep'n As It Come: The 1927 Mississippi River Flood* (New York: Oxford University Press, 1977). The Percy Papers contain almost no extant records pertaining to the flood.

6. Daniel, *Deep'n As It Come*, 5. For an excellent ecological history of the Mississippi Delta, see Mikko Saikku, *This Delta, This Land: An Environmental History of the Yazoo-Mississippi Floodplain* (Athens: University of Georgia Press, 2005).

7. LeRoy Percy to Ellery Sedgwick, April 27, 1922, WAPP.

8. Quoted in Barry, *Rising Tide*, 315; Neil R. McMillen, *Dark Journey: Black Mississippians in the Age of Jim Crow* (Urbana: University of Illinois Press, 1989), 147–49.

9. Percy, *Lanterns*, 252.

10. Ibid., 256; Barry, *Rising Tide*, 308.

11. Percy, *Lanterns*, 258.

12. Ibid., 257; Barry, *Rising Tide*, 308.

13. Percy, *Lanterns*, 257–58.

14. Quoted in Barry, *Rising Tide*, 319–20.

15. Wyatt-Brown, *House of Percy*, 244. The most thorough account of levee conditions, based primarily on oral histories with people who were there, is in Barry, *Rising Tide*, 303–35.

16. Quoted in Wyatt-Brown, *House of Percy*, 243.

17. Percy, *Lanterns*, 253.

18. Quoted in Barry, *Rising Tide*, 325.

19. Percy, *Lanterns*, 265–66.

20. Ibid., 267–68.

21. Ibid., 258–59, 267.

22. Daniel, *Deep'n As It Come*, 10.

23. Barry, *Rising Tide*, 407.

24. Ibid., 297 and 420.

25. Ibid., 296.

26. Ibid., 335.

27. Ibid., 420.

28. Ibid., 335.

29. William Alexander Percy to Charlotte Gailor, October 13, 1927, CGP.

30. William Alexander Percy to Camille Percy, September 13, 1927, WAPP; Janet Dana Longcope to William Alexander Percy, September 22, 1927, WAPP.

31. William Alexander Percy to Charlotte Gailor, October 13, 1927, CGP. On Percy and his friends' affectionate and campy manner toward one another, see the oblique note written to Percy while he was in Hawaii on the way home from Japan. Sketched out on the back of an envelope are two poems, possibly written by Huger Jervey, possibly by someone else. The first reads:

Ohio—
The sunshine is gorgeous, the ocean is blue
The pineapples delishoos, but we miss you.
Some poetess, eh what!!
Mother

And the second poem, on the other end of the envelope, reads:

If I were only a toad fish
A-surviving in a tank
Then maybe that young Mr. Percy
Would give me a look, by Hank!
M.E.S.
Here's to bigger and better obis!
Banzai! Kimona!
Yours truly,
M.E.S.

See envelope of Janet Dana Longcope to William Alexander Percy addressed to "Royal Hawaiian Hotel," October 29, 1927, WAPP.

32. William Alexander Percy to Col. F. W. Galbraith, April 4, 1921, WAPP. On American attitudes toward Japanese people, see Roger Daniels, *Coming to America: A History of Immigration and Ethnicity in American Life*, 2nd ed. (New York: Harper Perennial, 2002), esp. chap. 9; and Henry Yu, "Mixing Bodies and Cultures: The Meaning of America's Fascination with Sex between 'Orientals' and 'Whites,'" in *Sex, Love, Race: Crossing Boundaries in North American History*, ed. Martha Hodes (New York and London: New York University Press, 1999), 444–63.

33. William Alexander Percy to Charlotte Gailor, October 13, 1927, CGP.

34. E. Holliday to William Alexander Percy, December 14, 1927, WAPP; Janet Dana Longcope to William Alexander Percy, December 4, 1927, WAPP.

35. This letter from Percy to Longcope is not extant, but Longcope indicates this information in her reply. See Janet Dana Longcope to William Alexander Percy, January 8, 1928, WAPP.

36. Percy went to New York in February of 1921, 1922, 1925, 1926, 1927, 1928, and 1930. See Janet Dana Longcope to William Alexander Percy, February 12, 1921; Janet Dana Longcope to William Alexander Percy, December 13, 1921; William Alexander Percy to Camille Percy, February 3, 1925; Janet Dana Longcope to William Alexander Percy, February 18, 1926; William Alexander Percy to L. P. Soule, January 19, 1927; Janet Dana Longcope to William Alexander Percy, January 8, 1928; Janet Dana Longcope to William Alexander Percy, December 18, 1929; and Janet Dana Longcope to William Alexander Percy, n.d., "Sunday," 1930; all in WAPP.

37. Quoted in George Chauncey, *Gay New York: Gender, Urban Culture, and the Making of the Gay Male World, 1890–1940* (New York: Basic Books, 1994), 257. On the Hamilton Lodge Ball, see ibid., 257–64 and 332–34. On Gay life in Harlem in the 1920s, see also Eric Garber, "A Spectacle in Color: The Lesbian and Gay Subculture of Jazz Age Harlem," in *Hidden from History: Reclaiming the Gay and Lesbian Past*, ed. Martin Duberman, Martha Vicinus, and George Chauncey Jr. (New York: New American Library, 1989), 318–31.

38. Chauncey, *Gay New York*, 130.

39. Cynthia Sanborn Diary, May 22, 1929, in author's possession. The author would like to thank Pamela Tyler for pointing out this source.

40. Chad Heap, *Slumming: Sexual and Racial Encounters in American Nightlife, 1885–1940* (Chicago and London: University of Chicago Press, 2009), 194; see also David Levering Lewis, *When Harlem Was in Vogue* (New York: Vintage Books, 1981).

41. Barry, *Rising Tide*, 420–21 and 479; William Armstrong Percy, "William Alexander Percy: His Homosexuality and Why It Matters," in *Carryin' On in the Lesbian and Gay South*, ed. John Howard (New York: New York University Press, 1997), 80–82. Four of Barry's six interviewees remained anonymous.

42. Percy, *Lanterns*, 296 and 287. On homosexuality and race in this period, see especially Siobhan B. Somerville, *Queering the Color Line: Race and the Invention of*

Homosexuality in American Culture (Durham, N.C.: Duke University Press, 1999). See also Roderick A. Ferguson, *Aberrations in Black: Toward a Queer of Color Critique* (Minneapolis, Minn.: University of Minnesota Press, 2003).

43. Percy, "William Alexander Percy," 80 and 82. On interracial sex in the South, see especially Martha Hodes, *White Women, Black Men: Illicit Sex in the Nineteenth-Century South* (New Haven: Yale University Press, 1999); and Annette Gordon-Reed, *The Hemingses of Monticello: An American Family* (New York: W. W. Norton & Company, 2008).

44. Barry, *Rising Tide*, 420–21.

45. At the risk of stating the obvious: evidence of sexual activity typically only lasts a few hours. Furthermore, the "burden of proof" for homosex has always been higher than for heterosexual acts; historians often assume historical subjects were heterosexual until proven otherwise. In this particular case, though, the provenance of these oral histories are also problematic. *Rising Tide* is a sensationalized, dramatic narrative in which homosexuality serves as a spectacle. The book is unevenly footnoted, contains made-up dialogue, and often uses evidence out of context. None of the interviews were transcribed. Likewise, William Armstrong Percy's interview with Millie Commodore is not extant. Furthermore, these oral histories provided thirdhand accounts of rumors that circulated in Greenville some seventy years earlier. The only responsible interpretation is to allow that interracial relationships were a possibility. On *Rising Tide*'s lack of footnotes, see, for example, 299–304; for made-up dialogue, see 332; for evidence out of context, see 296.

46. Percy, *Collected Poems*, 19.

47. Wyatt-Brown, *House of Percy*, 254; Janet Dana Longcope to William Alexander Percy, October 3, 1928, WAPP.

48. Janet Dana Longcope to William Alexander Percy, January 8, March 17, April 11, and October 3, 1928; all in WAPP. It was likely during this trip out west that Percy met the poets Carl Sandburg and Vachel Lindsay, who visited him in Greenville during the 1930s.

49. Percy, *Lanterns*, 270; Wyatt-Brown, *House of Percy*, 258.

Chapter 13

1. Jay Tolson, *Pilgrim in the Ruins: A Life of Walker Percy* (New York: Simon and Schuster, 1992), 396. On LeRoy Pratt Percy, see ibid., 41–45; Bertram Wyatt-Brown, *The House of Percy: Honor, Melancholy, and Imagination in a Southern Family* (New York: Oxford University Press, 1994), 250–55; and Lewis Baker, *The Percys of Mississippi: Politics and Literature in the New South* (Baton Rouge: Louisiana State University Press, 1983), 147–49.

2. Quoted in Lewis A. Lawson and Victor A. Kramer, eds., *More Conversations with Walker Percy* (Jackson: University Press of Mississippi, 1993), 24.

3. Tolson, *Pilgrim in the Ruins*, 26.

4. William Alexander Percy, *Lanterns on the Levee: Recollections of a Planter's Son* (New York: Alfred A. Knopf, 1941), 310.

5. Tolson, *Pilgrim in the Ruins*, 32–36. Walker Percy later opened his novel *The Second Coming* with a scene set on a country club golf course—a setting he always used to create ironic distance from "the South" as a reified, authentic place. See Walker Percy, *The Second Coming* (New York: Farrar, Straus and Giroux, 1980).

6. Quoted in Tolson, *Pilgrim in the Ruins*, 42.

7. John Jones Interview with Phinizy Percy, MDAH.

8. Ibid.; Walker Percy, introduction to William Alexander Percy, *Lanterns on the Levee: Recollections of a Planter's Son* (Baton Rouge: Louisiana State University Press, 1973 [repr.]), viii.

9. The 2010 amount is from the U.S. government CPI inflation calculator, http://data.bls.gov/cgi-bin/cpicalc.pl (October 26, 2010). For Percy's account balance, see "William Alexander Percy Ledger," 102, WAPP.

10. John Jones Interview with Phinizy Percy, MDAH.

11. Ibid.; Tolson, *Pilgrim in the Ruins*, 82; Patrick Samway, *Walker Percy: A Life* (New York: Farrar, Straus and Giroux, 1997), 39; Walker Percy, "Uncle Will's House," in *Signposts in a Strange Land*, ed. and with an introduction by Patrick Samway (New York: Farrar, Straus and Giroux, 1991), 66. Foote quoted in William C. Carter, ed., *Conversations with Shelby Foote* (Jackson: University Press of Mississippi, 1989), 207.

12. Quoted in Lewis A. Lawson and Victor A. Kramer, eds., *Conversations with Walker Percy* (Jackson: University Press of Mississippi, 1985), 262.

13. Ibid., 11.

14. Arnold Rampersad, *The Life of Langston Hughes*, vol. 1, *1902–1941, I, Too, Sing America* (New York and Oxford: Oxford University Press, 1986), 231–32. Walker Percy had a different memory of this episode: "My Uncle, being the idealist and liberal that he was, introduced [Hughes] at a meeting by saying, 'Now here's a man who's black and an activist who has risen above the issues of race and ideologies involved in being a black activist and who's now become a poet.' Whereupon Langston Hughes got up and read the most ideologically aggressive poetry you can imagine." Quoted in Lawson and Kramer, *Conversations with Walker Percy*, 261.

15. Lawson and Kramer, *Conversations with Walker Percy*, 262; Carter, *Conversations with Shelby Foote*, 166.

16. John Jones Interview with Phinizy Percy, MDAH.

17. On Faulkner, see Ben Wasson, *Count No 'Count: Flashbacks to Faulkner* (Jackson: University Press of Mississippi, 1983), 61–63; on Sandburg, see Mary Stewart Interview with LeRoy Percy, July 26, 1994, Greenville, Miss., in author's possession; on Sullivan, see Walker Percy, "Uncle Will's House," 65; on Lindsay, see Baker, *The Percys of Mississippi*, 162.

18. John Jones Interview with Phinizy Percy, MDAH.

19. William Alexander Percy to Mark Clifton, March 7, 1930, WAPP.

20. Lawson and Kramer, *Conversations with Walker Percy*, 258.

21. Lawson and Kramer, *More Conversations with Walker Percy*, 24.

22. Quotes in Carter, *Conversations with Shelby Foote*, 159.

23. Bertram Wyatt-Brown, *House of Percy*, 273.

24. Quoted in Samway, *Walker Percy*, 43.

25. Quoted in Tolson, *Pilgrim in the Ruins*, 90.

26. Lawson and Kramer, *Conversations with Walker Percy*, 255.

27. Accounts of this episode can be found in Tolson, *Pilgrim in the Ruins*, 98–100; Wyatt-Brown, *House of Percy*, 273–75; Baker, *Percys of Mississippi*, 152; and Samway, *Walker Percy*, 54–57.

28. Quotes in Tolson, *Pilgrim in the Ruins*, 99.

29. Samway, *Walker Percy*, 59.

30. Tolson, *Pilgrim in the Ruins*, 100.

31. John Jones Interview with Phinizy Percy, MDAH.

32. Wyatt-Brown, *House of Percy*, 275.

33. Samway, *Walker Percy*, 58–59.

34. Walker Percy, introduction to William Alexander Percy, *Lanterns*, ix, xi, and xviii.

35. Percy, *Lanterns*, 315–16.

36. Ibid., 321; and Walker Percy, introduction to William Alexander Percy, *Lanterns*, xi.

37. Janet Dana Longcope to William Alexander Percy, "Sunday," 1930, WAPP.

38. Quoted in Samway, *Walker Percy*, 43.

39. Quoted in ibid., 51.

40. Poem in Tolson, *Pilgrim in the Ruins*, 94; quote in Baker, *The Percys of Mississippi*, 177.

41. Carter, *Conversations with Shelby Foote*, 72, 41, 156–59.

42. Walker Percy, introduction to William Alexander Percy, *Lanterns*, x–xi.

43. Quoted in Baker, *The Percys of Mississippi*, 164.

44. William Alexander Percy to Walker Percy, May 4, 1938, quoted in Billups P. Spalding, "William Alexander Percy: His Philosophy of Life as Reflected in His Poetry" (M.A. thesis, University of Georgia, 1957), 108. See also David L. Cohn, *God Shakes Creation* (New York: Harper & Brothers, 1935); David L. Cohn, *Where I Was Born and Raised* (Boston: Houghton Mifflin Company, 1948); David L. Cohn, *The Mississippi Delta and the World: The Memoirs of David L. Cohn*, ed. James C. Cobb (Baton Rouge: Louisiana State University Press, 1995).

45. Josephine Haxton Interview with Leon Zachary Koury, September 4, 1978, William Alexander Percy Library, Greenville, Miss. On Leon Koury, see also Patti Carr Black, *Art in Mississippi, 1720–1980* (Jackson: University Press of Mississippi, 1998), 201–3. See also Amy Evans Interview with Clarke Reed, Greenville, Miss., July 25, 2005. Reed said of Koury:

Leon Koury. You heard—heard about him? He was a protégé of Will Percy's and—and a sculptor—not bad, not bad, and he—and he—that was his family grocery store or something back in the early part of the—early to mid—late to mid-century. And he had made a joint out of it called Orbit Lounge, see. [Laughs.] And I think it was kind of—it scared the—the heck out of Doe's; you know, there was an unruly crowd over there and—and he—at that time unusual—gay crowd; you know, Leon was a homosexual and he didn't—but it—it was kind of out of place, kind of odd looking stuff around. I went—went in there several times. It didn't last long—the Orbit Lounge.

Full transcript available at http://www.southernfoodways.com/documentary/oh/does_eat_place/clarke_reed.shtml (October 26, 2010). Will Percy also mentioned Leon Koury in *Lanterns on the Levee*: "Leon has no right to have so much sense with so few years and no experience: he's just a genius." See Percy, *Lanterns*, 324.

46. Josephine Haxton Interview with Leon Zachary Koury, September 4, 1978, William Alexander Percy Library, Greenville, Miss. Emphasis in original.

47. Hank Burdine, "The Coffee House Blues of Leon Koury," *Delta Magazine*, September/October 2008, 174.

48. Leon Koury to Roy A. Bee, reprinted as "The Spark and the Flame," *Delta Review Magazine*, July/August 1965, 46–47. The author would like to thank Bill Beckwith for pointing out this source. In 1961 Koury opened a bar at 426 Nelson Street in Greenville that he called the Orbit Lounge, of which he said: "I wanted it to be the kind of place where creative people could come together, talk, socialize, listen to good music and exchange ideas." Though the bar did not last long, it suggests the kind of open-minded artistic community that existed in Greenville at midcentury. Quotes in Burdine, "The Coffee House Blues of Leon Koury," 174–75.

49. Telephone interview with Robert Marcius, March 30, 2011, in author's possession; Burdine, "The Coffee House Blues of Leon Koury," 174–75; Cassandra Langer, "Allen Frame: Photographer of Secret Desire," *The Gay and Lesbian Review*, September-October 2009, 30.

Robert Marcius described it as common knowledge in Greenville that Koury was gay; most people knew, he said, but they accommodated Koury because he was well liked, an excellent artist, and a private person. Marcius also recounted that Koury told him Percy was gay, but that Koury and Percy never had a sexual relationship. Likewise, Marcius described Koury as a mentor, friend, and advisor to him and his friends, not a sexual companion. "He was kind of like my therapist," Marcius said. "I could call him at four o'clock in the morning. He just loved to help people. He just wanted to help people become better human beings." It is important to understand the ways Percy (and Koury, it seems) saw art, creativity, and sexuality as intertwined. Art was, as Percy said, connected to the sex instinct; art was also, as Diotima said in the *Symposium*, a kind of reproduction, always an erotically charged act. To mentor younger artists was erotic but not necessarily sexual. This concept was significant to Percy, who enjoyed sex with other men but for whom queer relationships were not merely about sex. This may seem obvious to some, but in Percy's day—and to some extent, in the present—it was difficult for many Mississippians to disconnect homosexuality from the sex act. To "be gay" and to be morally serious and have a range of queer relationships, some of which were not sexual, was/is seen by some as incongruous and confusing.

50. Shelby Foote to Walker Percy, January 19, 1970, in Jay Tolson, ed., *The Correspondence of Shelby Foote and Walker Percy* (New York: W. W. Norton, 1997), 141.

51. Madel Jacobs, "Interview with William Alexander Percy," *Ephemera: A Student Literary Publication of the Mississippi State College for Women*, February 1939; clipping in WAPAF.

52. William Alexander Percy to Charlotte Gailor, March 23, 1936, CGP. It is unclear to whom Percy is referring in this instance. There is no other record of a "Bob" in Percy's records from the 1930s except in *Lanterns on the Levee*, in which Percy includes this entry from his diary: "6:30 P.M.—Bob and Sammy arrive, unannounced, from New Orleans." See Percy, *Lanterns*, 325. One of Percy's obituaries records that one of the pallbearers at his funeral was an "R. R. Horton of New Orleans," which perhaps refers to the same man. See "South Mourns William A. Percy," *Delta Democrat-Times*, January 22, 1942; clipping in WAPP.

53. Walker Percy to Shelby Foote, September 3, 1980, in Tolson, *Correspondence*, 265. Walker Percy was quoting Will Percy in this letter.

54. Ibid.

Chapter 14

1. William Alexander Percy to Charlotte Gailor, May 27, 1936, CGP; William Alexander Percy to Norman Douglas, May 29, 1936, Norman Douglas Papers, Beinecke Rare Book and Manuscript Library, Yale University, New Haven, Conn. On Western writers and the South Seas, see especially Michael Sturma, *South Sea Maidens: Western Fantasy and Sexual Politics in the South Pacific* (Westport, Conn.: Greenwood Press, 2002). On Somerset Maugham, see Jeffrey Meyers, *Somerset Maugham: A Life* (New York: Alfred A. Knopf, 2004), 117–21. On Margaret Mead, see Mead, *Coming of Age in Samoa: A Psychological Study of Primitive Youth for Western Civilization* (New York: Harper, 2001 [repr.]); and Mary Catherine Bateson, *With a Daughter's Eye: A Memoir of Margaret Mead and Gregory Bateson* (New York: W. Morrow, 1984). On Ruth Benedict, see Benedict, *Patterns of Culture* (New York: Mariner Books, 2006 [repr.]); and Margaret M. Caffrey, *Ruth Benedict: Stranger in This Land* (Austin, Tex.: University of Texas Press, 1989). And on the relationship between Margaret Mead and Ruth Benedict that deeply informed their work, see Hilary Lapsley, *Margaret Mead and Ruth Benedict: The Kinship of Women* (Amherst: University of Massachusetts Press, 1999); and Lois Banner, *Intertwined Lives: Margaret Mead, Ruth Benedict, and Their Circle* (New York: Alfred A. Knopf, 2003).

2. Margaret Mead, *Letters from the Field, 1925–1975* (New York: HarperCollins, 2001),

26–27. On the history of Samoa, see Mansel G. Blackford, *Pathways to the Present: U.S. Development and Its Consequences in the Pacific* (Honolulu: University of Hawai‘i Press, 2007); and Malama Meleisea, *The Making of Modern Samoa: Traditional Authority and Colonial Administration in the History of Western Samoa* (Suva: Institute of Pacific Studies of the University of the South Pacific, 1987).

3. Mead, *Letters from the Field*, 31.

4. Almost as soon as *Coming of Age in Samoa* appeared, it unleashed a storm of criticism and debate, which continues to this day. Mead's most vocal and persistent critic was Derek Freeman, as seen in Freeman, *Margaret Mead and Samoa: The Making and Unmaking of an Anthropological Myth* (Cambridge, Mass.: Harvard University Press, 1983); and Freeman, *The Fateful Hoaxing of Margaret Mead: A Historical Analysis of Her Samoan Research* (Boulder, Colo.: Westview Press, 1999). See also Dolores Janiewski and Lois W. Banner, eds., *Reading Benedict/Reading Mead: Feminism, Race, and Imperial Visions* (Baltimore: Johns Hopkins University Press, 2005).

5. A great deal has been written about Percy's racial views. For writing that condemns Percy's racism, see James W. Silver, *Running Scared: Silver in Mississippi* (Jackson: University Press of Mississippi, 1984), 217–29; and Florence Murray, "Racial Poison Is Advised Reading for Local Pupils," *The People's Voice* (New York, N.Y.), January 12, 1946; "*Lanterns on the Levee*, by William Alexander Percy," *Boston Transcript*, March 29, 1941; and Charles Curtis Munz, "Mr. Percy's Culture," *The Nation*, May 31, 1941, 644; all clippings in AKP. For insightful reflections on Percy's paternalism, see John O. Hodges, "William Alexander Percy's *Lanterns*: A Reply from a Mississippi Sharecropper's Son," *Southern Quarterly* 43 (Fall 2005): 28–49; and McKay Jenkins, *The South in Black and White: Race, Sex, and Literature in the 1940s* (Chapel Hill: University of North Carolina Press, 1999), 75–108. For praise of Percy's treatment of blacks, see Hodding Carter, *Lower Mississippi* (New York: Farrar & Rinehart, 1942), 403; and Lewis Baker, *The Percys of Mississippi: Politics and Literature in the New South* (Baton Rouge: Louisiana State University Press, 1983), 163.

6. William Alexander Percy to Charlotte Gailor, August 10, 1940, CGP.

7. William Alexander Percy, "The White Plague," manuscript in WAPP.

8. Mead, *Coming of Age in Samoa*, 137 and 69.

9. Ibid., 202.

10. Ibid., 139.

11. Ibid., 153–54.

12. Margaret Mead, *Sex and Temperament in Three Primitive Societies* (New York: William Morrow & Co., 1935), 322.

13. Percy, "The White Plague."

14. Ibid.

15. Ibid.

16. Ibid.

17. Percy uses this phrase in *Lanterns on the Levee: Recollections of a Planter's Son* (New York: Alfred A. Knopf, 1941), 228.

18. Percy, "The White Plague." For an example of the kinds of racial science prevailing in Percy's day, see, for example, Charles Benedict Davenport, *Heredity in Relation to Eugenics* (New York: Henry Holt and Company, 1911), which was a bestseller. For more recent scholarship on eugenics and racial science, see Daniel Kevles, *In the Name of Eugenics: Genetics and the Uses of Human Heredity* (Berkeley: University of California Press, 1985); Kenneth Ludmerer, *Genetics and American Society: A Historical Appraisal* (Baltimore: Johns Hopkins University Press, 1972); and Paul Lawrence Farber, *Mixing Races: From Scientific Racism to Modern Evolutionary Ideas* (Baltimore: Johns Hopkins University Press, 2010).

19. Percy, "The White Plague."

20. Ibid.

21. Ibid.

22. Ibid.

23. Percy, *Lanterns on the Levee*, 20.

24. Ibid., 23.

25. Ibid., 299 and 22.

26. Ibid., 299–300.

27. Ibid., 309.

28. Ibid.

29. Hodding Carter, *Where Main Street Meets the River* (New York: Rinehart & Company, Inc., 1952), 67–68.

30. John Jones Interview with LeRoy P. Percy, December 14, 1979, MDAH.

31. The primary literature on sharecropping in the 1930s is immense; the following listing includes several of the most important texts. For sociologists' work on sharecropping, see Charles S. Johnson, Edwin R. Embree, and W. W. Alexander, *The Collapse of Cotton Tenancy* (Chapel Hill: University of North Carolina Press, 1935); Rupert B. Vance, *Human Geography of the South* (Chapel Hill: University of North Carolina Press, 1932); William C. Holley, Ellen Winston, and T. J. Woofter Jr., *The Plantation South, 1934–1937* (Washington, D.C.: Works Progress Administration Research Monograph 22, 1940; repr. 1971); Arthur F. Raper, *Preface to Peasantry: A Tale of Two Black Belt Counties* (Chapel Hill: University of North Carolina Press, 1936); Arthur F. Raper and Ira De A. Reid, *Sharecroppers All* (Chapel Hill: University of North Carolina Press, 1941); and Charles S. Johnson, *Shadow of the Plantation* (Chicago: University of Chicago Press, 1934). Two primary socialist tracts against sharecropping are Norman Thomas, *The Plight of the Share-Cropper* (New York: League for Industrial Democracy, 1934) and Howard Kester, *Revolt among the Sharecroppers* (New York: Covici, Friede, 1936; repr. 1997). For work done on sharecropping by artists, see Richard Wright, *12 Million Black Voices: A Folk History of the Negro in the United States* (New York: Viking Press, 1941); Erskine Caldwell and Margaret Bourke-White, *You Have Seen Their Faces* (New York: Modern Age Books, 1937); Erskine Caldwell, *Tobacco Road* (New York: Grosset & Dunlap, 1932); and James Agee and Walker Evans, *Let Us Now Praise Famous Men* (Boston: Houghton Mifflin, 1941).

32. On this transition, see especially Bruce J. Schulman, *From Cotton Belt to Sunbelt: Federal Policy, Economic Development, and the Transformation of the South, 1938–1980* (New York: Oxford University Press, 1991); Jack Temple Kirby, *Rural Worlds Lost: The American South, 1920–1960* (Baton Rouge: Louisiana State University Press, 1986); and Pete Daniel, *Breaking the Land: The Transformation of Cotton, Tobacco, and Rice Cultures since 1880* (Urbana: University of Illinois Press, 1987).

33. For sociological and anthropological work on Mississippi in the 1930s, see especially John Dollard, *Caste and Class in a Southern Town* (New Haven: Yale University Press, 1937); and Hortense Powdermaker, *After Freedom: A Cultural Study in the Deep South* (New York: Viking Press, 1939; repr. 1993).

34. H. L. Mencken and Charles Angoff, "The Worst American State," *American Mercury* 24 (September-November 1931).

35. Ibid., 5, 10, 13, 180, 183, 178.

36. Ibid., 9, 11, 6. Literacy rates and teacher salaries can be a misleading statistic for Mississippi, as there was a vast disparity in education for whites and blacks. In Mississippi in 1930, white illiteracy was about 3 percent, while black illiteracy was close to 25 percent. See Roger D. Tate Jr., "Easing the Burden: The Era of Depression and New Deal in Mississippi" (Ph.D. diss., University of Tennessee, 1978), 9–11. Salaries for teachers was accordingly unequal for white and black schools. One study of the Mississippi Delta found that the average teacher salary for the 1935–36 school year was $103.90 a month for whites and $39.18 a month for blacks; the average cost per white child for the session was $84.59, while the average cost per black pupil was $6.74. See *Mississippi Education Journal* 13, no. 6 (March 1937): 111.

37. Mencken and Angoff, "The Worst American State," 371.

38. Rupert B. Vance, *Human Geography of the South* (Chapel Hill: University of North Carolina Press, 1932), 266 and 270.

39. In 1930 there were 80,072 farms in the Mississippi Delta, and 77,845 (or 97 percent) were devoted to cotton monoculture. Charles Felder Reynolds, "The Economic and Social Structure of the Yazoo-Mississippi Delta" (Ph.D. diss., University of Virginia, 1947), 58 and 30.

40. Ibid., 63.

41. Holley, Winston, and Woofter, *The Plantation South, 1934–1937*, 36.

42. Quoted in Paul Good, *The American Serfs* (New York: G. P. Putnam's Sons, 1968), 11.

43. A curious companion to the antisharecropping social thought of the 1930s was a resurgence of agrarianism. Led by the Southern Agrarians, a group of intellectuals and writers loosely associated with Vanderbilt University in the late 1920s and early 1930s, this antimodern mode of thought rejected the urban/industrial transformation as crass and dehumanizing and called for a revitalization of agrarian life. See Twelve Southerners, *I'll Take My Stand: The South and the Agrarian Tradition* (New York: Harper & Brothers, 1930; repr. 1977); Maurice Kains, *Five Acres and Independence* (New York:

Greenberg, 1935); Ralph Borsodi, *This Ugly Civilization* (New York: Simon and Schuster, 1929); and Borsodi, *Flight from the City* (New York: Harper & Brothers, 1933).

44. Throughout 1936, Raymond McClinton lived on Percy's plantation as part of his research for his thesis director, University of North Carolina sociologist Rupert Vance. Vance was a sociologist and founder of the "Chapel Hill School," or the "Regionalists," of the 1930s. This group was, among other things, dedicated to studying and improving the living conditions of southern sharecroppers. The Regionalists, with their progressive attitudes toward race and industry, came into sharp disagreement with the Nashville Agrarians. See Daniel J. Singal, *The War Within: From Victorian to Modernist Thought in the South, 1919–1945* (Chapel Hill: University of North Carolina Press, 1982), esp. part 2. For McClinton's study, see Raymond McClinton, "A Social-Economic Analysis of a Mississippi Delta Plantation" (M.A. thesis, University of North Carolina, 1938).

45. McClinton, "A Social-Economic Analysis," 8 (acreage), 9 (shares), 23–24 (managers), 16–17 (Percy), 9 (store and railroad).

46. Ibid., 11 (tenant families), 86 (total tenant population), 89 (non–family member population), 86–87 (female heads), 91 (child population).

47. Ibid., 28 (coupon books), 30 ("supervision charge"), 29 (average total credit per year), 39–44 (gross and cash incomes), 69 (quote about latest styles), 85 (automobiles). For cotton price in 1936, see U.S. Department of Agriculture, *Agricultural Statistics, 1941* (Washington, D.C.: Government Printing Office, 1941), 117. For black attitudes toward labor and cash, see Neil R. McMillan, *Dark Journey: Black Mississippians in the Age of Jim Crow* (Urbana: University of Illinois Press, 1989), esp. chaps. 4 and 5.

48. McClinton, "A Social-Economic Analysis," 62 (quote about cut screens), 71 (malaria and pellagra).

49. Ibid., 80 (gardens), 105 (Saturday night parties and quote), 76 (reading material), 78 (tobacco use), 104 (Christmas party). On the northern black press, and the *Chicago Defender* in particular, see especially Davarian L. Baldwin, *Chicago's New Negroes: Modernity, the Great Migration, and Black Urban Life* (Chapel Hill: University of North Carolina Press, 2007); and Adam Green, *Selling the Race: Culture, Community, and Black Chicago, 1940–1955* (Chicago: University of Chicago Press, 2006).

50. This story is recounted in Percy, *Lanterns*, 290–91.

51. Ibid., 292, 306, 309.

52. McClinton, "A Social-Economic Analysis," 17 (distrust of Percy quote), 20 ("landowner" quote).

Chapter 15

1. William Alexander Percy to Charlotte Gailor, n.d., March 1937, CGP.

2. William Alexander Percy, draft manuscript of *Lanterns on the Levee*, WAPP.

3. William Alexander Percy, *Lanterns on the Levee: Recollections of a Planter's Son* (New York: Alfred A. Knopf, 1941), foreword.

4. Harold Strauss to Alfred A. Knopf, March 16, 1939, AKP.

5. Harold Strauss to Alfred A. Knopf, n.d., AKP. On the history of popular media portrayals of the South during the 1930s and 1940s, see especially Jack Temple Kirby, *Media-Made Dixie: The South in the American Imagination*, rev. ed. (Athens: University of Georgia Press, 2004); and Edward D. C. Campbell Jr., *The Celluloid South: Hollywood and the Southern Myth* (Knoxville, Tenn.: University of Tennessee Press, 1981).

6. William Alexander Percy to Charlotte Gailor, September 19, 1940, and "Election Day 1940"; both in CGP.

7. William Alexander Percy to Charlotte Gailor, January 29, 1940, CGP.

8. Harold Strauss to William Alexander Percy, August 16, 1939, CGP.

9. Harold Strauss to Alfred A. Knopf, n.d., AKP.

10. Harold Strauss to Alfred A. Knopf, March 1, 1940, AKP.

11. Harold Strauss to Alfred A. Knopf, July 24, 1940, AKP.

12. William Alexander Percy to Charlotte Gailor, "Election Day 1940," CGP.

13. Ibid.

14. William Alexander Percy to Wells Lewis, April 11, 1941, AKP.

15. William Alexander Percy to Charlotte Gailor, January 27, 1941, and March 4, 1941; both in CGP.

16. *New York Times*, May 18, 1941; clipping in AKP.

17. Walker Percy, introduction to William Alexander Percy, *Lanterns on the Levee: Recollections of a Planter's Son* (Baton Rouge: Louisiana State University Press, 1973), xii.

18. Percy, *Lanterns*, 11.

19. Ibid., foreword and 348.

20. Ibid., 334.

21. Ibid., 333.

22. Ibid., 334.

23. Ibid.

24. Ibid, 336–37. We have already looked at two of these vignettes earlier; they recount Percy's encounter with a goatherd in Greece and his picnic with Huger Jervey and two Turkish men, during which they watched a nude swimmer. See chapter 11.

25. Ibid., 332–36.

26. All quotes in ibid., 342.

27. All quotes in ibid., 345–47.

28. Ibid., 348.

29. Alfred A. Knopf to William Alexander Percy, April 21, 1941, and December 24, 1941; both in AKP.

30. William Alexander Percy to Alfred A. Knopf, April 14, 1941, AKP.

31. William Alexander Percy to Alfred A. Knopf, March 25, 1941, AKP.

32. *Boston Traveler*, April 25, 1941, AKP.

33. *United Press Red Letter*, April 17, 1941; *Grand Rapids Herald*, March 16, 1941; both in AKP.

34. *Topeka Daily State Journal*, April 15, 1941, AKP.

35. *Stamford Advocate* (Connecticut), April 2, 1941, AKP.

36. *Knoxville News-Sentinel*, March 9, 1941; *Nashville Banner*, March 12, 1941; both in AKP.

37. *Dallas Morning Herald*, n.d., AKP.

38. *Richmond Times-Dispatch*, March 16, 1941, AKP.

39. William Alexander Percy to Harold Strauss, March 24, 1941, AKP.

40. William Alexander Percy to Alfred A. Knopf, April 24, 1941; May 19, 1941; and September 17, 1941; all in AKP.

41. *Jackson Daily News*, n.d.; see also *Delta Democrat-Times*, March 11, 1941; both in AKP.

42. *Journal of Negro Education*, Winter 1945, 69, AKP.

43. Charles Curtis Munz, "Mr. Percy's Culture," *The Nation*, May 31, 1941, 644–45, AKP.

44. William Alexander Percy to Alfred A. Knopf, June 5, 1941, and June 16, 1941; both in AKP.

45. William Alexander Percy to Wells Lewis, April 11, 1941, AKP.

46. William Alexander Percy to Charlotte Gailor, April 22, 1941, AKP.

47. David L. Cohn, *The Mississippi Delta and the World: The Memoirs of David L. Cohn*, ed. James C. Cobb (Baton Rouge: Louisiana State University Press, 1995), 179; Lewis Baker, *The Percys of Mississippi: Politics and Literature in the New South* (Baton Rouge: Louisiana State University Press, 1983), 172.

48. William Alexander Percy to Charlotte Gailor, March 4, 1941, CGP.

49. William Alexander Percy to Charlotte Gailor, March 16, 1940, and March 4, 1938; both in CGP.

50. William Alexander Percy to Charlotte Gailor, February 4, 1941, CGP.

51. William Alexander Percy to Charlotte Gailor, "Thursday," CGP; Lewis A. Lawson and Victor A. Kramer, eds., *Conversations with Walker Percy* (Jackson: University Press of Mississippi, 1985), 263–64.

52. William Alexander Percy to Charlotte Gailor, "Thursday," CGP.

53. William Alexander Percy to Charlotte Gailor, January 3, 1942, CGP.

54. John Jones Interview with LeRoy Percy, Dec. 13–14, 1979, MDAH.

55. Ibid.

56. "South Mourns William A. Percy," *Delta Democrat-Times*, January 22, 1942; clipping in WAPP. John Jones Interview with Phinizy Percy, April 17, 1980, MDAH.

57. "South Mourns William A. Percy." "For Will," *Delta Democrat-Times*, January 22, 1942; clipping in WAPP. For other obituaries, most of which draw from the information provided in the AP wire, see "William A. Percy, Author, Lawyer, Taken by Death," *New Orleans Times-Picayune*, January 22, 1942; "William Percy Dies; Southern Author was 56," *New York Herald-Tribune*, January 22, 1942; "William A. Percy," *Memphis Commercial Appeal*, January 22, 1942; "Wm. A. Percy, Mississippi Writer, Dies," *Atlanta Journal*, January 22, 1942; "William A. Percy, Writer, Lawyer Dies," *Birmingham News*, January 22, 1942; "Will Percy, Poet and Author, Dies," *Nashville Tennessean*, January 22, 1942;

"Noted Dixie Poet, Author Passes Away," *Asheville Times*, January 22, 1942; "56-Year-Old Southern Author Dies at Home," *Mobile Register*, January 22, 1942; "This Morning," *Birmingham Age*, January 23, 1942; "Dis an' Dat," *Delta Democrat-Times*, January 25, 1942; "Friends Learn of Death of Mississippi Author," *Louisville Times*, January 27, 1942; all clippings in WAPP.

58. Ben Wasson to Arthur Chitty, February 6, 1960, WAPAF; John Jones Interview with LeRoy Percy; "Campaign to Save Percy Home," *Delta Democrat-Times*, May 7, 1969; "A Percy Memorial," *Delta Democrat-Times*, May 9, 1969; "Demolition Begins on Old Percy Home," *Delta Democrat-Times*, June 26, 1969; "The Time Has Come," *Delta Democrat-Times*, June 29, 1969.

Epilogue

1. John Jones Interview with Phinizy Percy, April 17, 1980, MDAH; Mary Stewart Interview with LeRoy Percy, July 26, 1994, Greenville, Miss., in author's possession. Stewart performed this interview as part of her dissertation research. See Mary Campbell Stewart, "William Alexander Percy: The Poet and His Delta Country" (Ph.D. diss., University of Maryland, 1995). The historian Lewis Baker has also indicated in conversation with the author that he was involved in the process by which the Percy estate removed papers before making a donation to the archives. Another thesis writer, Billups Phinizy Spalding, was refused access to certain parts of Percy's papers before the estate donated the papers to the archive. Spalding included several of Percy's letters and unpublished poems in an appendix to Billups P. Spalding, "William Alexander Percy: His Philosophy of Life as Reflected in His Poetry" (M.A. thesis, University of Georgia, 1957). In the appendix, he writes: "The two poems which I am including below were found by the present writer as he was searching through file cabinets at Percy's Trail Lake Plantation. The poems were contained in a manila envelope with the words 'Clippings for 1924' written on the outside. Also in the envelope I found two vignettes. One, 'Death in the Rain,' is included in this appendix. I was not granted permission to include the second story." Quoted in Spalding, "William Alexander Percy," 229.

2. In addition to the evidence in Greenville, there is likely more in Massachusetts. In a conversation with the author, the family of Janet Dana Longcope indicated they had "two suitcases full" of letters from Will Percy to Janet Dana Longcope, but the family feels they are "too private" to donate to an archive.

3. Essays that have influenced my thinking on the relationship between archives and sexuality include John D. Wrathall, "Provenance as Text: Reading the Silences around Sexuality in Manuscript Collections," *Journal of American History* 79, no. 1 (June 1992): 165–78; Martin Duberman, "'Writhing Bedfellows' in Antebellum South Carolina: Historical Interpretation and the Politics of Evidence," in *Carryin' On in the Lesbian and Gay South*, ed. John Howard (New York: New York University Press, 1997), 15–33; Margaret Rose Gladney, "Personalizing the Political, Politicizing the Personal: Reflections on Editing the Letters of Lillian Smith," in *Carryin' On in the Lesbian and Gay*

South, ed. Howard, 93–103; John D'Emilio, "Reading the Silences in a Gay Life: The Case of Bayard Rustin," in *The Seductions of Biography*, ed. Mary Rhiel and David Suchoff (New York: Routledge, 1996), 59–68; and Estelle B. Freedman, "'The Burning of Letters Continues': Elusive Identities and the Historical Construction of Sexuality," *Journal of Women's History* 9, no. 4 (Winter 1998): 181–200.

4. Phinizy Percy quoted in John Jones Interview with Phinizy Percy; Walker Percy quoted in his introduction to William Alexander Percy, *Lanterns on the Levee: Recollections of a Planter's Son* (Baton Rouge: Louisiana State University Press, 1973), xviii.

5. From these nine men, there are precisely four letters in Percy's papers, each mostly informational. See Huger Jervey to William Alexander Percy, January 12, 1920; Sinkler Manning to Carrie Stern, August 14, 1914; Lindley Williams Hubbell to William Alexander Percy, April 27, 1925; and Gerstle Mack to LeRoy Percy, July 3, 1924; all in WAPP. In 1980 Walker Percy wrote to Shelby Foote: "I've been reading a batch of letters written by Uncle Will to Gerstle Mack, over 100 letters spanning 1918 (right after war) to 1941, a few months before his death"; see Jay Tolson, ed., *The Correspondence of Shelby Foote and Walker Percy* (New York: W. W. Norton, 1997), 265. All efforts by this author to find these letters have been unsuccessful.

6. George Chauncey, *Gay New York: Gender, Urban Culture, and the Making of the Gay Male World, 1890–1940* (New York: Basic Books, 1994).

7. Richard King, *A Southern Renaissance: The Cultural Awakening of the American South, 1930–1955* (New York: Oxford University Press, 1980), 97.

8. John Howard, *Men Like That: A Southern Queer History* (Chicago: University of Chicago Press, 1999), 184, and see also chaps. 1 and 4; Donna Jo Smith, "Queering the South: Constructions of Southern/Queer Identity," in *Carryin' On in the Lesbian and Gay South*, ed. John Howard (New York: New York University Press, 1997), 381.

9. John Barry, *Rising Tide: The Great Mississippi Flood of 1927 and How It Changed America* (New York: Touchstone, 1997), 297; Bertram Wyatt-Brown, *The House of Percy: Honor, Melancholy, and Imagination in a Southern Family* (New York: Oxford University Press, 1994), 205.

10. William Alexander Percy to Mrs. Archie Barkle, March 21, 1930; quoted in Spalding, "William Alexander Percy," 109.

11. William Alexander Percy to John Seymour Erwin, n.d., 1940; quoted in Bertram Wyatt-Brown, "In and Out of the Closet: Twentieth-Century Southern White Male Authors and Cultural Alienation," unpublished manuscript in author's possession. The author would like to thank Bertram Wyatt-Brown for pointing out this source.

INDEX

passim; awarded *Croix de Guerre* and *Medaille du Roi Albert*, 158; as editor of Yale Series of Younger Poets, 201–5, 208–9; as mentor to younger artists, 201–5, 236–41; as leader during flood of 1927, 211–19; as adoptive father, 226–42 passim; family memory of WP, 275–76. *See also* Archives and evidence, silences in

—*Enzio's Kingdom and Other Poems*, 190–96, 200–201; reception of, 200, 203, 205

—gender and sexuality, perspectives on: 5–6, 10–13, 18, 36–41, 90, 95–97, 114, 141–42, 149, 174–76, 190–96, 200–201, 207–8, 210–11, 266; sexual awakening, 53–58; "Greek bisexuality," 62–63; interracial sex, 221–23; in Samoa, 243–51

—*In April Once*, 161, 164–78 passim, 191; reception of, 171–74, 176–78

—individual poems and sketches by: "An Epistle from Corinth," 53–54, 63, 177; "Sappho in Levkas," 54–57, 137, 169, 191, 194, 223; "A Canticle," 63; "After Hearing Music," 85; "Fifth Autumn," 95–97; "To C.P.," 96–97; "Longing," 119–20, 121, 137; "Arcady Lost," 123–24, 137; "The Happy Isles," 124; "A Sea-Bird," 124–25; "Ecstasy," 125; "For Music," 125; "Soaring," 125; "Song," 125; "In New York," 139–43; "Poppy Fields," 149; "Mr. W. H. to the Poet," 167–68, 173, 202; "In April Once," 168–70, 191, 194; "Riolama," 170; "Night off Gallipoli," 170–71; "Enzio's Kingdom," 190–95; "His Peace," 195; "Safe Secrets," 195–96; "Three April Nocturnes," 210–11; "The White Plague," 245–51

—*Lanterns on the Levee*, 8, 30, 38, 67, 71, 95, 121, 130, 166, 198, 222, 245, 251–53, 259–60, 274, 282, 283; writing of, 261–70; reception of, 270–72

—race, perspectives on: 8–9, 81, 93–94, 118, 179–81, 199–200, 214, 216–17, 229–30, 252–53; and childhood nursemaid, Nain, 30–32; and childhood playmates, 32–34; in Egypt, 70; and slavery, 146–47; and African American soldiers in World War I, 152–55; in Japan, 219–20; in Samoa, 243–51; and southern history, 248–51; and sharecropping, 253–60

—*Sappho in Levkas and Other Poems*, 121, 123–25, 126, 130, 135, 145, 173, 191; reception of, 135–37

—spirituality and ethics, perspectives on: 11, 39, 48, 66–67, 114, 134, 137, 269–70, 282–83; loss of faith in Christianity, 52–54, 69; critique of Christian sexual ethics, 53–54, 62–64, 190–96, 244–46; Apostle Paul, 53–54, 63, 177; ethics of sexual freedom, 53–57, 190–96; the occult, 70–71; advice to adopted sons, 234–36

—travels of: Paris (1904–5), 60–65; Mediterranean (1904–5), 65–71; Egypt (1905), 69–70; Germany and Switzerland (1907), 86–88; Europe (1908), 90; Europe (1909), 99; Greece (1911), 119; Europe (1914), 127–28; Utah and Wyoming (1915), 135; New York (1916), 137–43; Belgium (1916–17), 145–47; France (World War I, 1917–19), 149–160; Jackson Hole, Wyo. (1920), 163; Capri (1922), 189–90, 194–95; Mediterranean (1924), 196–200; New York (1925), 205; Italy (1926), 205–8; Japan (1927), 219–20; New York (1928), 221–22; New Mexico (1928), 224; New York (1929–30), 225; Europe (1930), 228; Jackson Hole, Wyo. (1932), 234; Washington, D.C. (1932), 234; Samoa (1936), 243–48; Sewanee (1937), 261–63; Grand Canyon (1940), 264; New York (1940), 265; Baltimore (1941), 274; Charleston (1941), 274; New York and Massachusetts (1941), 274; Sewanee (1941), 274

—youth and education of: at Harvard, 1–2, 74–91 passim; childhood, 30–41 passim, 301 (n. 2); personal tutors, 36–41; at Sewanee, 42–58 passim

Percy, William Alexander ("The Gray Eagle," WP's grandfather), 18–25, 182, 212, 227

Percy, William Armstrong (WP's uncle), 20, 25–26

Percy, William Armstrong (historian), 222

Phaedrus, 46

Picasso, Pablo, 60

Pierce, James Mill, 79–80, 165

Pius X (pope), 67–69, 70

Plato, 45–46

Turner, Nat, 16
Turner, Reginald, 173, 206–8
Twelfth Night (Shakespeare), 112

Ulrichs, Karl Heinrich, 45
Uncle Tom's Cabin (Stowe), 77
University of Mississippi, 163
University of the South (Sewanee, Tenn.), 26,
    42–58 passim; and Hellenism, 43–48; WP
    teaches at 98–99, 161–62; dismisses Percy,
    162–63
University of Virginia, 26, 74, 107

Vance, Rupert, 256
Van Dresser, Will, 25
Vardaman, James K., 99–119 passim, 181, 251
Vaughan, Malcolm, 173–74, 202
Verdun, Battle of, 144, 145
Vesey, Denmark, 16

"W.H.G.," 114–15, 132
Washington, Booker T., 185
Washington County Historical Society, 3–5,
    13
Watts, Sarah, 78

White League, The, 22
White Line, The, 22
Whitman, Walt, 79, 80
Wilde, Oscar, 12, 44, 45, 47, 110–11, 165, 168,
    173, 206
Williams, John Sharp, 103, 117
Williams, William Carlos, 136, 201
Willson, Augustus E., 90
Winckelmann, Johann, 66
Winthrop Hall (Harvard), 75, 76
Wister, Owen, 79
World War I, 128–29, 133–35, 138, 144–60
    passim, 243–44
Worthington, Samuel, 3–5, 16
Wright, Richard, 178
Wyatt-Brown, Bertram, 12, 117, 119, 282
Wynn, Billy, 155

Yacovone, Donald, 25
Yale Series of Younger Poets, 201–5, 208–9,
    231–32
Yale University Press, 126, 167, 201
You Never Can Tell (Shaw), 84

Zangwill, Israel, 114